SONS
OF CAIN

ALSO BY PETER VRONSKY

Serial Killers
Female Serial Killers

SONS
OF CAIN

A History of Serial Killers
from the Stone Age
to the Present

PETER VRONSKY

BERKLEY
New York

BERKLEY
An imprint of Penguin Random House LLC
375 Hudson Street, New York, New York 10014

Library of Congress Cataloging-in-Publication Data

Names: Vronsky, Peter, author.
Title: Sons of Cain: a history of serial killers from the stone age
to the present/Peter Vronsky.
Description: New York : Berkley, [2018]
Identifiers: LCCN 2017046780 | ISBN 9780425276976 |
ISBN 9780698176140 (e-book)
Subjects: LCSH: Serial murderers—History.
Classification: LCC HV6505.V76 2018 | DDC 364.152/3209—dc23
LC record available at https://lccn.loc.gov/2017046780

First Edition: August 2018

Printed in the United States of America
5th Printing

Cover images: *Lycaon Transformed into a Wolf from Metamorphoses by Ovid*, 1589,
Hendrick Goltzius, Wikimedia Commons; *Vlad Țepeș, the Impaler, Prince of Wallachia*,
Wikimedia Commons; *England, Whitby, fan in costume in archway on 100th anniversary
of publication of Bram Stoker's novel* Dracula, 1997, Dod Miller/Photonica World/Getty Images;
H. H. Holmes, Wikimedia Commons; *Jack the Ripper Letter* © PA Images/Alamy Stock; Marie
Becker, 1905, Wikimedia Commons; *Myra Hindley*, 1966 © Keystone Pictures USA/Alamy Stock
Photo; *Serial Killer Andrei Chikatilo*, Terry Smith/Contributor/The LIFE Images Collection/
Getty Images; *David Berkowitz* © Everett Collection Historical/Alamy Stock Photo;
Jeffrey Lionel Dahmer © PA Images/Alamy Stock Photo
Cover design by Emily Osborne
Book design by Kelly Lipovich

In memory of Dave Walker, murdered at the Gate of Death in Angkor Wat, Cambodia, February 14, 2014.

———————————

"I want a Tibetan sky funeral with flagellants beating themselves to the song."

CONTENTS

ILLUSTRATIONS

www.sonsofcainserialkillers.com

I

On the Origin
of the Species:
The Evolution of
Serial Killers

ONE

Serial Killers: A Brief Introduction to the Species

In the beginning was the Word.

—JOHN, 1:1

When I encountered my first serial killer in 1979, I did not know there was such a thing. The term "serial killer" did not exist except in the close-knit world of FBI behaviorists and homicide investigators who in the 1970s were dealing with a sudden surge of unsolved murders, across different jurisdictions, that appeared to be linked to single unknown perpetrators. Ted Bundy, who killed at least thirty-six college-aged women across six states, would emerge from that era as the prototypical postmodern serial killer. But in the movies, in true crime and fiction literature, in the news media, in popular culture, even in forensic psychiatry, there was no agreed-upon term for what Ted Bundy was, or for what I encountered, the way we have "the word" for it today: serial killer.

My brief chance encounter with one—the first of my three random encounters with different serial killers before they were identified and captured—occurred on a December Sunday morning in New York. I was stranded in the city over a weekend and needed to find an inexpensive place to stay until Monday. I decided to try a hotel on the far west end of 42nd Street on the farthest fringe of the Times Square district.

Unlike the tourist- and family-friendly version today, in the 1970s the neighborhood around Times Square and 42nd Street (nicknamed

"Forty-Deuce" or "the Deuce") was very nasty, a teeming souk of hard-core porn "adult" bookstores, peep shows, grind house movie theaters, knife stores, massage parlors, strip joints, live sex acts, souvenir shops, hot dogs and hand jobs, street drugs, junkie bars, flophouse welfare hotels and prostitutes of every age, shape and gender. It was New York's neon-lit Whitechapel, with its own Ripper too, as I was about to find out.

There were forty thousand prostitutes working the streets and store-front parlors of New York in 1979,[1] so many that the NYPD at one point had to put up barricades along the sidewalks of Eighth Avenue to keep the girls and their pimps from spilling over into the road and blocking traffic.

Unless you were briskly on your way to or from the Port Authority Bus Terminal, you were on the Deuce for one of four reasons: to buy, sell, be sold or be hunted if you were stupid or careless enough. There were 2,092 murders in New York in 1979 and 2,228 in the year after that. In 1990, murders would climb to a record high of 2,605.[2] It was dangerous. On the single block of 42nd Street between Seventh and Eighth Avenues, an average 2,250 crimes were being reported annually, more than on any other block in New York, and 30 to 40 percent of the offenses were serious Part I felonies (homicide, forcible rape, robbery).[3]

As I approached the hotel that Sunday morning at daybreak, I thought I had a pretty good idea as to what I might be getting into. I had been to New York many times before on movie and documentary projects and shot all sorts of edgy things. Sometimes I'd stayed in one of the fleabag hotels around Times Square but this was the first time I had ever wandered off the map as far as Tenth Avenue, into the adjoining neighborhood that since the 1880s had been called Hell's Kitchen. Today it's bursting with foodie fad restaurants and hip little bars and the neighborhood has been renamed a more upscale and condo-friendly Clinton. But in the 1970s it was definitely still Hell's Kitchen. Between 1968 and 1986 the Westies, an Irish gang, killed between sixty and one hundred victims there, carving their corpses into pieces in the tenement house bathtubs where today all the cozy, cute little restaurants are.

I wasn't sure I wanted to stay the night there, but it was conveniently close to the film lab I needed to go to the next morning before catching my plane home, and it was cheap. So before committing myself by checking into this medium-sized five-story hotel, I decided to take a walk around the hallways and stairways, scout it out and see for myself just how bad it was and who or what might be lurking in the corridors.

As I waited in the small lobby for the elevator, it seemed to be stopped forever on an upper floor. It was annoying. I was young and impatient. When the elevator finally came down and the doors slid open, I took an extra-hard look at the jerkoff who had kept me waiting for what seemed like ages, although probably it wasn't longer than a minute.

He looked like . . . well, like anybody. Ordinary. Just another white guy in his early thirties. The only odd thing about him was that despite the cold he had a sheen of feverish perspiration on his forehead. As he got off the elevator he walked into me as if I was not there—walked through me—bonking me on the knee and shin with a soft-sided bag that felt as if it had bowling balls in it: rounded, hard and heavy. He didn't say anything, apologize or even give me a glance back. He looked so ordinary that if I had been asked to describe him for a police composite sketch, I could not have. But as he'd annoyed me, I did give him enough of a look to later recognize him if I saw him again, even if I couldn't describe him from scratch. My last glimpse of him was from inside the elevator as the door closed on me. His back was turned to me and he was strolling calmly toward the door to the street with his bag dangling at his side.

It was an entirely random encounter with a monster who had brutally bound, gagged, raped, tortured and killed two street prostitutes in his room upstairs, sawed off their heads and hands and stuffed the severed body parts in a bag. As I was approaching the lobby of the hotel, he laid their headless torsos in the pools of thickening blood on the mattress, soaked them in lighter fluid and set it all on fire. He then left with his bag of body parts and calmly took the elevator down as I was impatiently waiting and fuming in the lobby below.

Of course, I did not know any of that at the time.

MONSTRUM

He had come to my attention in the first place only because he had annoyed me. I would not have noticed him otherwise. I surmise today—as a profiler might—that he was holding the elevator door at his floor until he was satisfied that the fire was spreading. He would have obsessively craved that kind of complete control over his crime scene that serial killers seek in their futile attempts to be fulfilled by what they do. It's *all about* control for them. That is intrinsic to serial killers.

Taking an elevator down was a reckless act, especially after setting a fire, as it meant he would have to go by the front desk to exit. That kind of recklessness is also intrinsic to serial killers. *I* would have taken the stairs, but then I am not a serial killer.

In the end, that brazenness would lead to his arrest. Six months later, in May 1980, he returned to a New Jersey motel where less than three weeks earlier he had tortured and murdered another prostitute and jammed her handcuffed, battered and mutilated corpse under a bed to be found by a housekeeper the next morning. None of the motel staff noticed or remembered him. That is how *forgettable* he was. It was only when motel employees, already spooked by the previous murder, heard a woman screaming in his room that police were called.

That was how thirty-three-year-old Richard Francis Cottingham, aka "the Times Square Torso Ripper," was apprehended and identified. His victim, Leslie Ann O'Dell, an eighteen-year-old prostitute, was rescued and survived to testify at his trial.

Richard Cottingham, who upon his arrest told police, "I have problems with women," had been raised in a stable, upper-middle-class, strict Catholic family in New Jersey. Mom was a housewife while Dad was an insurance company executive in Manhattan. Their son "Richie" was a high school track star and appeared to be well-behaved. After graduating, Richard became gainfully employed as a computer console operator at the offices of Blue Cross Insurance in midtown Manhattan. Like his father, he would commute to work from his home in New Jersey, where he lived with his wife and three children. But he had a whole other secret life too. He had two mistresses, both nurses, who did not know about each other, and a string of casual girlfriends, favorite escorts and random pickups, and once in a while, whenever he got the urge for it, he would torture, rape and kill one of them. He killed at least three of the women he had been acquainted with. He preferred, however, random victims he would pick up on the streets or in bars. Working a shift from four p.m. to midnight, Cottingham committed his savagely sadistic murders between dates with his mistresses, his hours at Blue Cross and his commute home to his family in Lodi, New Jersey.

Cottingham was eventually convicted of five murders, and recently (in 2010) he suddenly pleaded guilty to a sixth murder, committed forty-three years ago. He is suspected in at least an additional thirty to fifty unsolved murders in New York and New Jersey between 1967 and 1980. (See Richard Cottingham crime scene photos and other illustrations for *Sons of Cain* on www.sonsofcainserialkillers.com.)

After literally bumping into him in the lobby that morning, I rode upstairs and smelled the smoldering fire and caught a glimpse of smoky mist and tiny cinders swirling in the corridor just as the fire alarms began to sound. The hotel was evacuated before I saw any heavy, dense smoke or flames, and I exited by a stairwell into an indoor parking garage and out onto 42nd Street just as the fire department was pulling up out front. I did not hang around in the cold to watch, and I walked away in a "New York minute" to stay somewhere else, without learning what had taken place.

The next morning, when I arrived at the film lab, I glanced at the newspapers strewn around the reception room. The headlines screamed about fire and headless torsos. While I realized that the hotel fire was where I had been the previous morning, I did not immediately connect the guy on the elevator to any of it. I did not have the familiarity we all do today with the phenomenon of serial killers and what they do, to form an immediate connection in my mind between the jerkoff with the bag of "bowling balls" and the murders upstairs. Nobody thought that way back then. It was only much later, after Cottingham had been arrested and I first saw his picture in the papers, that it all suddenly fell into place. It was the jerkoff who had kept me waiting! I immediately recognized him. Only then did the "bowling balls" suddenly take on a different meaning.

One of the two headless victims in the hotel room, estimated by the medical examiner to be in her teenage years, was never identified and remains a Jane Doe to this day. But police were able to identify the second victim a month after the murder. She had worn leather high-heeled Philippe Marco sandals, an exclusive brand, which police were able to trace to a store in Paramus, leading them to believe that the victim lived in New Jersey. Police then focused on reports of missing women in New Jersey from around the date of the murder and eventually linked spinal X-rays and a caesarean scar on the torso to hospital records belonging to twenty-two-year-old Deedeh Goodarzi, an upscale escort living in Trenton. In 1978, she had given birth by caesarean section to a baby girl, whom she immediately gave up to the state of New Jersey for adoption, nineteen months before her murder.

After Deedeh was identified, her mug shots from prostitution arrests were widely published. She was indeed upscale, elegant and tastefully dressed in her arrest photos, with sultry dark looks, full lips, long black hair and beautiful almond-shaped eyes. When Deedeh failed to return home, there were people in New Jersey who cared enough about her to quickly report her missing to police, which helped investigators to zero in on her hospital records.

She was reported in the media to have been born in Kuwait, raised by her grandparents there and brought to the United States at the age of fourteen by her father, who had immigrated here earlier. She lived a troubled life in Long Island and New York City. She dropped out of high school and ran away from home around the age of sixteen. Deedeh ended up working as a marginally upscale "call girl" escort in New York, Florida, Nevada and California before settling in Trenton, New Jersey.

Her sad story, her face and eyes would haunt me for decades afterward. At twenty-two she was only a year younger than I was when she was murdered. I marveled at how long a road Deedeh must have traveled to *her* encounter with a serial killer, just mere hours before my own road led me to *my* encounter with the same killer.

I wondered what happened to her head, with which I had been bumped, with those beautiful eyes and that flowing dark hair. What did Cottingham do with it? As hard as police searched in the vicinity of the hotel for the missing heads, even sending down divers off the rotting piers on the nearby Hudson River, they never found them. Cottingham had taken the heads with him to some final secret place.

Over the decades since, I occasionally wondered what happened to the baby girl Deedeh had given up for adoption, like a tiny soul in an escape capsule, desperately launched to safety from the chaos of her mother's unhappy life, nineteen months before her savage murder, the only trace of herself she left behind. I wondered if the girl had survived the maw of a state adoption system, what trajectory she had been thrown on, where she had landed and whether she would ever know anything of her birth mother's identity and fate. I imagined her drifting through life like crash debris left floating in the wake of chaos and murder.

Back then, I still did not have the term "serial killer" to comfort me with its neat descriptors of what it was I had bumped into in that hotel lobby. The murder appeared to me as supernaturally monstrous as stories in the *Tales from the Crypt* comic books I had read as a kid. I might as well have encountered Dracula, the Werewolf, Frankenstein's monster or some other movie ghoul.

In a world where serial killers had not yet been definitively named, categorized and described, I was left with a sensation of having encountered a monster, in the ancient sense of the original Latin word, "*monstrum*": "an omen or warning of the will of the gods."[4]

That encounter would forever shape how I would later write about serial killers. In futile attempts to somehow humanize serial killers or "secularize" their monstrous attributes, much of the current literature on serial killers disavows the monster construct. But I found myself starting from the opposite pole. I experienced a *monstrum*, one not so much bearing omens of the will of the gods, but of us, of ourselves, of our society. I came to see them as monstrous, misshapen reflections in a distorted mirror to human civilization.

My brief personal close encounter with a monster inspired my pursuit to understand the phenomenon of serial murder and its social and forensic history. Where and how did these monsters first appear? Where did they come from, and why was there such a dramatic increase in their numbers in the last decades of the twentieth century, to the point that I randomly crossed paths with one of them, and then, later, another, and then a *third*? Were there just so many of them from the 1970s through to the 1990s that I would randomly encounter three different serial killers—in New York, Moscow and Toronto—all by chance and all before they had been identified as serial killers? For a long time, I thought these three encounters were freakishly unusual, but as we shall see, they were not actually all *that* unusual.

The only thing that distinguishes me from you, or others who have unknowingly and randomly brushed by serial killers, is that in my case I later became aware of who *my* serial killers had been. Most people never find out, fortunately.

Although Cottingham never attained the level of fame that other serial killers did, he fascinated many insiders in the field of serial homicide. The renowned profiler Dr. Robert Keppel, who dealt with super serial killers like Ted Bundy and Gary Ridgway, the "Green River Killer," considers Cottingham the Mount Everest of sadistic serial killers. Keppel wrote, "Years after Cottingham had been put away, as I tried to figure out what could drive the sexually sadistic serial killer subtype, I kept asking myself what it was that ultimately intrigued me about the Cottingham cases. Partly it was the level of sadistic torture that Cottingham acted out on his victims. He didn't kill them and desecrate their bodies; he forced them to experience pain and humiliation before he killed them. Then he desecrated their bodies."[5]

What strikes me most about my brief encounter with this serial killer was how entirely normal and forgettable he was. Cottingham did not look "evil" or monstrous. There was nothing menacing about him. He did not have fangs, red eyes, foul steaming breath or yellowed claws. He was not screwy looking or twitchy. He wasn't babbling crazily or splattered in blood (even though he had just sawn off the heads of two victims), nor did he have a Hannibal Lecter aristocratic charm and bearing. At worst, he looked a little stoned and blank eyed, which I guess is what satiated bloodlust looks like.

He was so ordinary that by the time I got off the elevator on his floor I had already forgotten him, and I did not think of him again until I saw his picture in a newspaper.

After Cottingham was caught, I sought to better understand what he was. The first true-crime book about serial murder that I read was *The Stranger Beside Me*, Ann Rule's seminal 1980 account of the iconic serial killer Ted Bundy, but the term "serial killer" did not appear in the pages of her definitive book when I read it.

Before the 1980s, movies had been made, articles and books had been written, about serial killers like Jack the Ripper, H. H. Holmes, Albert Fish, Ed Gein, the Boston Strangler, the Son of Sam, John Wayne Gacy, and the Hillside Strangler(s), but except for cops among themselves occasionally, nobody called any of them "serial killers" or, more importantly, classified them as a specific and unique species of murderer. Each one was a self-contained case.

Canadian social anthropologist Elliott Leyton's 1986 book, *Hunting Humans: The Rise of the Modern Multiple Murderer* (first published in the US as *Compulsive Killers: The Story of Modern Multiple Murder*), was probably the first popular book to comprehensively describe the phenomenon of serial killers and their social history. While the term "serial killer" appears in the pages of his book, it was still not a term familiar enough to the public for the publisher to use in the book title.[6]

The pendulum of writing about serial killers swings between monstrosity and psychology, between mythology and history, between the monstrous-supernatural and the forensic-scientific. Serial killers, I finally realized, are what we decide they are, and that definition constantly changes with history and society. But for centuries before the 1980s, we had no idea of what they were or how to describe them, other than as "monsters."

COINING THE TERM "SERIAL KILLER"

Before we could recognize what serial killing was, we needed a term for it. Throughout most of its modern history, serial killing had been given a host of different labels, like "stranger-on-stranger murder," "recreational killing," "pattern murder," "thrill killing," "multicide," "psycho murder," "sequential homicide," "compulsive murder," "multiple murder," "motiveless killing," "lust murder," "spree killing" and, confusingly, "mass murder," which today we define as a single rampage of multiple murders. Nobody agreed on a single term for serial killing or what defined it, nor did anybody assemble all those different multiple-killer profiles and their characteristics into named constellations or categories.

Today "serial killer" is as generic and as familiar a term as "Kleenex,"

"Scotch tape" or, ominously, "dumpster." But thirty-five years ago, our perception of serial killers was reminiscent of the first scenes of a zombie movie, the ones where everybody is running around at the early stage of a zombie apocalypse, trying to figure out what is overrunning civilization. Is it an epidemic disease? A weaponized toxin? A genetic mutation? A pathological rabid cannibal rage? Is it an alien virus? Is it something supernatural? And why is this zombie plague spreading?

By 1979, when I had my first encounter, we were already well into what would later be called the "serial killer epidemic," and it was only going to get worse, with an unprecedented surge of serial murder in the United States and around the world, but we still had not named what this thing was. Having read *The Stranger Beside Me*, I understood that Cottingham was something like Ted Bundy, something like Jack the Ripper, something like the Boston Strangler, something like John Wayne Gacy, something like all the recently reported "multiple pattern thrill killers" from the 1960s and 1970s like Edmund Kemper, Jerry Brudos, Juan Corona, the Hillside Strangler(s), Dean Corll, the Son of Sam, and the unidentified Zodiac Killer. Yet there seemed to be more differences between each killer than similarities. Some targeted only female prostitutes, some only gay men, some only children, some only college-aged women. Some mutilated their victims; some did not. Some killed only with their hands, others with rope, or stockings, or knives, or guns. Some were stationary, killing in one specific place; others were migratory, traveling thousands of miles in their search for victims. Some left bodies by the side of the road, while others kept them buried in secret backwoods "cemeteries" of their own. They all did the same thing in essence—they killed multiple victims—but each one seemed to do it in his own particular way or pattern. Thus the early use of the term "pattern killers" to describe them.

The popular notion of serial killers came from movies like *Psycho*, *Frenzy*, *Dirty Harry*, *10 Rillington Place*, *Eyes of Laura Mars*, *Deranged*, *Maniac* and *Terror Train*, many of which were inspired by actual cases. Serial killers were largely perceived as simply madmen, or inexplicable monsters like the supernaturally invincible Jason of the *Friday the 13th* movies or Michael Myers from *Halloween*. In fact, the first *Halloween* and *Friday the 13th* movies came out, respectively, in 1978 and 1980, before the term "serial killer" was introduced into the mainstream.

There was no single word that everybody agreed named what these predatory monsters were or how they functioned. And without "the Word" we had no idea of "the Thing." While law enforcement had an awareness of the growing phenomenon, the rest of us in the general public and the media were blind to it.

It was only in May 1981 that the serial-killer and serial-murder constructs first began appearing in the mass media. Regarding Wayne Williams, suspected in the murders of thirty-one children in Atlanta between 1979 and 1981, the *New York Times* wrote:

> The incident underscored the belief of many law-enforcement officials and forensic scientists in Atlanta that only some of the killings are the result of a "serial" or "pattern" murderer.... [7]

If the *New York Times* is America's national "paper of record," then Wayne Williams is our first "serial killer of record." There is no single story as to who coined the term "serial killer," and it is entirely plausible that several people independently proposed the term. According to the late true-crime author Ann Rule, California detective Pierce Brooks first coined it.[8] True-crime author Michael Newton points out that the term is used by author John Brophy in his 1966 book *The Meaning of Murder*.[9] Author Harold Schechter and criminal-deviance scholar Lee Mellor discovered that Ernst August Ferdinand Gennat, the chief of the Berlin police, used the term "*serienmörder*" (serial murder) in the 1930s to describe the crimes of Peter Kürten.[10]

The earliest English-language use of the term "serial killings" I've found in print was by the biblical scholar, historian and concentration-camp survivor Robert Eisler, in his annotations to a lecture he gave on sadism and anthropology to the Royal Society of Medicine in London in 1948. The lecture was published posthumously in 1951 as a heavily foot-noted book entitled *Man into Wolf: An Anthropological Interpretation of Sadism, Masochism, and Lycanthropy*. In describing innate infantile sadism, Eisler wrote:

The serial killings in the "Punch and Judy" plays for children are so enjoyable because the puppets are of wood and the beaten skulls sound so wooden and insensitive. Nevertheless this enjoyment is certainly the harmless "abreaction" of the cruel urges of infancy.[11]*

While perhaps various people proposed it, I personally believe the most plausible coiner of the term "serial killer" as we are familiar with it today is FBI agent and behavior-sciences profiler Robert K. Ressler. In his memoirs, Ressler writes that he felt the popular term for serial murder, "stranger killings," was inappropriate because not all victims of serial killers were strangers. Ressler was lecturing at a police academy in England in 1974 when he heard the description of some crimes as occurring in "a series"—a series of rapes, arsons, burglaries or murders.

Ressler said that the description reminded him of the movie industry term for short episodic films shown on Saturday afternoons during the 1930s and 1940s: "serial adventures." Audiences were lured back to movie theaters week after week by the inconclusive ending of each episode—the so-called cliff-hanger. Instead of providing a satisfying conclusion, these endings increased the tension in the audience. Likewise, Ressler felt, after every murder serial killers experience a "cliff-hanging" tension and a desire to commit a more perfect murder than before, one that is closer to their fantasy. Rather than being satisfied when they murder, serial killers are compelled to repeat their killing in a cycle, a pattern of serial-movie-like "cliff-hanger" murders. "Serial killing," Ressler argued, was a very appropriate term for the compulsive multiple homicides that he believed he was dealing with.[12]

---

*Even earlier, possibly, the words "Whitechapel serial killer" apparently are used in a newspaper article in the November 9, 1888, edition of the *London Daily Post*'s coverage of Jack the Ripper. The words appear in a stock house montage of Victorian-era newspaper clippings, the authenticity of which I was not able to confirm before this book went to press. See the end of the first paragraph in the second column of the newspaper in the image: http://www.alamy.com/stock-photo-the-londonpost-november-9th-1888-clippings -of-the-fifthand-final-52938673.html. Thanks to Bettye McKee for pointing this item out to me.

CATEGORIZING SERIAL KILLERS

As Ressler was struggling with what to call them, he, his colleague John E. Douglas at the FBI's Behavioral Sciences Unit (BSU) (today called Behavioral Analysis Unit [BAU]) and forensic nurse Ann W. Burgess were interviewing twenty-nine incarcerated sexual serial killers and seven solo sexual murderers, asking them about their childhoods, their fantasies and what *they* thought they were doing. Conducted in the late 1970s and early 1980s, these interviews would later spawn the FBI's controversial profiling system of *organized/disorganized/mixed* classifications of serial killers:

- *Organized* serial killers carefully plan their crimes, patiently stalk their victims, often use charm and guile to abduct them or gain control over them, come prepared with weapons and restraints and attempt to clean up the crime scene to destroy forensic evidence. They tend to encounter and abduct their victims at one location, kill them at another and dispose of their bodies at yet a third location, making it very difficult for investigators to piece together a timeline. They are smart, social, physically attractive, married or in relationships, gainfully employed, dress well, have neat apartments, drive well-maintained and clean cars, etc.;

- *Disorganized* serial killers do not plan their murders, and they often act on a whim, spontaneously using sudden brute force (blitz) to abduct and subdue their victims. They lack the social skills to charm their victims and are often loners or drifters and are unemployed. They use improvised weapons found at the scene to kill their victims, often abandon the victims' bodies where they first encountered and killed them and leave behind messy crime scenes with lots of evidence. They live in messy apartments, are often physically repulsive and drive decrepit, poorly maintained cars, etc.

Unfortunately for the FBI system, very few serial killers fall neatly into one or the other category. Most serial killers exhibit a mix of characteristics from both categories, and thus the FBI introduced a third category, *mixed*, a rather meaningless combination of the first two categories.

Despite the flaws in the *organized/disorganized/mixed* system, it was a breakthrough, the first attempt to classify individual serial killers into categories or species with specific characteristics in a way that aided investigators in the field. The focus of the FBI research was not so much to unravel the mystery of a serial killer's psychology but to understand how the nature of a crime scene could contribute to identifying the perpetrator, or in FBI-speak, the "unsub"—unknown subject. As John Douglas famously stated, "If you want to understand the artist, look at his work."

The results of these interviews with incarcerated offenders were published in a 1988 textbook, *Sexual Homicide: Patterns and Motives*, one of the first scientific-academic book-length studies focused almost entirely on sexual serial killers, their fantasies, childhoods, characteristics and behaviors, and a rudimentary guide to profiling them.[13] Its three authors, Ressler, Douglas and Burgess, are among the American pioneers in serial-offender profiling and crime-scene psychological analysis, along with earlier pioneers like Walter C. Langer, who profiled Adolf Hitler for US intelligence in the 1940s; LAPD psychiatrist Dr. J. Paul de River in the 1940s; New York psychiatrist James Brussel, who famously profiled serial bomber George Metesky in the 1950s and the Boston Strangler in the 1960s; and later, LAPD homicide detective Pierce Brooks, FBI agents Howard Teten and Roy Hazelwood, Michigan forensic psychologist Richard Walter and Washington State attorney general's investigator Robert Keppel.

With the publication of *Sexual Homicide* in 1988, we now had a fuller understanding of the term "serial killer" and a much more specific, albeit rudimentary, road map to what it entailed. Three years later the film adaptation of Thomas Harris's novel *The Silence of the Lambs* widely popularized the serial killer and FBI profiler as high-concept adversaries.

THE SERIAL KILLER SURGE IN THE 1970s–1980s

If you are over the age of fifty, as I am, you will remember a more innocent world without the specter of serial killers, a world that at first
appeared safe and innocent but transformed into a place overrun by
zombielike serial-killing human monsters.

Father Knows Best and *Leave It to Beaver* were more than just clichéd
TV shows from the late 1950s and early 1960s; there was a palpably real
naïveté in that era, especially if you were a kid. In those days few imagined a world where the dad in *Leave It to Beaver* might be burying bodies in the basement or sodomizing the Beaver while Mom might be
posing in explicit classified ads to lure victims to their home, or that big
brother Wally might be torturing the family cat while masturbating to
men's adventure magazines or peeping through the neighbor's window
with a knife in hand.

In the innocent 1950s, milk came in clear glass bottles delivered to
the door by milkmen in pristine white uniforms, not sold in waxed paper cartons printed with the faces of missing children. People really did
leave their doors unlocked and windows thrown open in the 1950s and
early 1960s.

But *everything* changed by the end of the 1960s. The virulence of the
rising rate of serial killing in that epoch is astounding.

- According to the Radford University/FGCU (Florida Gulf Coast
  University) Serial Killer Database, out of 2,236 serial killers on
  record in the United States between 1900 and 2000, 82 percent
  (1,840) made their appearance between 1970 and 2000;[14]

- Another study of 431 serial-killer cases in the United States between 1800 and 2004 found that 65 percent (234 cases) occurred
  between 1970 and 2004;[15]

- In the twenty-five-year period of 1970 to 1995, there was a tenfold
  increase in active serial killers compared to the 169 years between 1800 and 1969.[16]

This last thirty-year surge in serial killers exponentially outpaced the growth of the general population in the United States. It felt so much like a plague by the 1980s that the Centers for Disease Control (CDC) in Atlanta began to look into the phenomenon of serial murder and Congress held hearings on the issue.[17] (See chapter thirteen for more on the "serial-killer epidemic.")

Just consider the frequency of the term "serial killer" in the *New York Times*. In the decade after its first use, in 1981, the term "serial killer" appeared 253 times in the paper; in the 10 years after that, in the 1990s, it appeared 2,514 times.[18]

By the 1990s, serial killing had become a major source of obsessive entertainment, not only for the few killers perpetrating it, but for millions of consumers watching it in the movies and on TV and reading about it. There were serial-killer trading cards, calendars and fan clubs and collectors of serial-killer "murderabilia." By the 1990s, serial killers were entrenched in American popular culture, taking their place with dinosaurs, cowboys, baseball and zombies.

CLOSE ENCOUNTERS OF THE THIRD KIND WITH SERIAL KILLERS

Seven years after my brief encounter with Cottingham in New York, I went to work for CNN. In its early Ted Turner start-up days, CNN had hired many of its staff and technicians from the newsrooms of local television stations in Atlanta, where Turner Broadcasting was based. Almost everybody I worked with had a story to tell of their close encounters with the Atlanta serial killer Wayne Williams, who had sought work as a freelance cameraman for local TV news. Hearing these stories, I felt less lonely in my brief encounter with Cottingham in 1979.

Then in October 1990 I randomly encountered my *second* serial killer.

While shooting a documentary in Moscow in a tent city full of protestors, I was approached for an interview by the notorious serial killer Andrei Chikatilo, aka "the Red Ripper" or "Citizen X." This was a few weeks before he returned to his hometown in the Ukraine to kill his

fifty-third victim and was arrested. For years he had been killing, mutilating and sometimes cannibalizing women, teenagers and small children of both sexes, and when he was caught his fifty-three victims
propelled him to the top of the list of the most prolific serial killers of all
time. (Currently he stands at number six.[19])

Unlike my awkward, wordless encounter with the more obscure
Cottingham eleven years earlier, this encounter involved a conversation
lasting several minutes (I speak Russian) in which Chikatilo attempted
to persuade me to film an interview with him. It was not murder that
Chikatilo wanted to talk about but some absurd story about how organized criminals in his hometown were building public toilets near his
apartment house and how he had come to Moscow to personally lodge
a complaint with the Russian president Mikhail Gorbachev.

I thought his story was dumb (especially compared with the griev-
ances of other Russians in that tent city), and not wanting to waste any
of our precious videotape to record him, I turned him away. (In 1990,
broadcast-camera videotape was very expensive and difficult to find in
Russia.) As with Cottingham, I found out only much later whom I'd encountered, my second monster in the wild. My random encounters with
two serial killers, *my two serial killers*, were looking like weird math.
Serial killers are rare. And while anything can happen *once*, like a lightning strike, to randomly encounter serial killers *twice* was odd. But at
the same time, it made me think there might be others I have encountered without realizing it; maybe there were *three—or even more—*and
this notion eventually inspired me to write my first book about them, in
2004.

And indeed, by virtue of the FBI redefinition of serial killing in 2005
from at least three victims to two victims, I realized that I had actually
encountered *three* serial killers in my life. I met my third in the early
1980s as he was about to become a serial killer, between his first and
second murders.

I was working undercover within the Ku Klux Klan on a documentary shoot. Gary "Mick" MacFarlane was a security officer for the local
den of the KKK and had already murdered one victim. At trial he had
been found not guilty by reason of insanity. He sat out a stretch in a
psychiatric facility and was released a few years later after psychiatrists

determined him cured. MacFarlane found a job as a security company dog handler and joined the KKK. A few years after I met him, I read in the papers that he had murdered a second victim. In the 1980s, that did not make him a serial killer, but once the FBI downgraded the definition of a serial killer from three to two victims, he retroactively became *my* third serial killer. I thought, how crazy is that, to have encountered three serial killers without having sought them out?

I should not have been all *that* impressed by my multiple "close encounters" with serial killers. By the time I met the first of *my* serial killers in 1979, a US president's wife had met *her* serial killer, when John Wayne Gacy as the director of Chicago's annual Polish Constitution Day Parade hosted President Jimmy Carter's wife, Rosalynn, in May 1978. The White House released an official photo of the first lady posing with Gacy.[20] Six months later, to the embarrassment of the White House, police would find twenty-six corpses rotting in the crawl space of Gacy's home and several more buried elsewhere.

At about the same time, Jimmy Carter's vice president, Walter Mondale, was meeting *his* serial killer, the teenaged Jeffrey Dahmer, who arranged a spontaneous visit for himself and some classmates with the vice president as a prank during a high school trip to Washington, D.C. (having failed in his attempt to secure a visit with President Carter).[21]

And in 1977 the governor of California Jerry Brown was not only encountering *his* serial killer but was dancing with and hugging her. Dorothea Puente, the "Death House Landlady" who buried some of her nine elderly victims in the rose garden of her Sacramento, California, boardinghouse, bought tables at political fund-raising events, at one of which she met and danced with the governor.[22]

If there were serial killers visiting television newsrooms, escorting first ladies, touring the White House and dancing with governors, then my own little encounters were beginning to look pretty lame. Everybody seemed to be running into serial killers.

Rodney Alcala, who would be convicted for the murders of seven women and suspected in as many as 130 murders, is alleged to have taken filmmaking lessons in 1970 from Roman Polanski, who the previous year just barely missed an encounter of his own with Charlie Manson's cult killers (arguably a species of serial killers) when they killed his pregnant wife, Sharon Tate.[23] (Actor Steve McQueen and author Jerzy Kosinski were also invited to the house on the night of the murders but did not go.)

Serial killers were even making appearances on TV. The same Rodney Alcala appeared as a contestant on *The Dating Game* in 1978 (and won), while serial killer Edward Wayne Edwards, who murdered at least five victims, appeared on two game shows, *To Tell the Truth* and *What's My Line?*, even though he was a convicted felon.[24] (More recently, the British necrophile serial killer Stephen Port, the "Grindr Killer," appeared on *Celebrity MasterChef UK*, making meatballs, while at the time he was killing and then raping at least four male victims.)[25]

By now serial killers were even randomly crossing paths with other serial killers. The Chicago satanic-cult serial killer Robin Gecht, later linked to the gang rape/mutilation/cannibal murders of seventeen female victims, was employed as a laborer by John Gacy, neither aware of the other's serial killing.

Adolph James "Jimmy" Rode, aka Cesar Barone, claimed he was personally "tutored" by Ted Bundy when he was briefly jailed with him in Florida. Barone was assigned work distributing food trays and would later tell people that Bundy had whispered to him how easy it is to kill women and hide the evidence.[26] Barone later raped and murdered four women.

And then there was the ultimate! A case of one serial killer murdering another serial killer, when Wayne Henley shot Dean Corll (the "Candy Man") in 1973, after the two of them had together tortured, raped and murdered twenty-eight male teenagers in Houston, Texas. Corll threatened to make Henley his twenty-ninth victim; Henley struck first and *Dexter*ed Corll.

It really did seem like a zombie plague with serial killers now infectiously biting out new serial killers and even turning on one another.

By the 1990s, everybody was familiar with the term "serial killer" and many people had encountered one for themselves, however randomly or briefly. Along with Polanski, other celebrities reportedly encountered serial killers. Sean Penn, serving sixty days in Los Angeles County Jail for reckless driving in 1987, exchanged notes with Richard Ramirez, "the Nightstalker."[27] Blondie lead singer Debbie Harry was up by Ted Bundy in the early 1970s while hitchhiking and fled _____ when she became suspicious of his behavior.[28] Some celebrities even fell victim to serial killers. In 1978 Larry Flynt, the flamboyant publisher of *Hustler* magazine, was shot and paralyzed for life by Joseph Paul Franklin, a "missionary" species of serial killer, who had killed at least eight victims and perhaps as many as twenty-two, acting on racial hate and an obsession with interracial couples. (Flynt's magazine had depicted interracial sex.) The Italian fashion designer Gianni Versace was murdered on the front steps of his home in Miami Beach by spree serial killer Andrew Cunanan in 1997. In 2001, actor Ashton Kutcher discovered the body of his girlfriend, murdered by alleged serial killer "the Hollywood Ripper," who is awaiting trial for three murders committed between 1993 and 2005 and is suspected in another seven.[29] Air force colonel and serial killer Russell Williams piloted the Canadian equivalent of Air Force One, and flew not just the prime minister but other dignitaries, including Queen Elizabeth—all while videotaping the rape-murders of two women, including an air force corporal under his command, and perpetrating hundreds of fetish burglaries of women's underwear.[30]

Since *Serial Killers: The Method and Madness of Monsters* was published, I have received dozens of letters in which people recount stories of serial killers they were picked up by while hitchhiking, or knew in school or at work, lived next door to, et cetera. Most of the stories are plausible and often check out against timelines and locations. If they were lucky, people's encounters were harmless. A few even had positive stories to tell, including one from an ex–Marine scout sniper who had a sexual encounter with gay serial killer Randy Kraft, the "Scorecard Killer" or "Freeway Killer," in California. Kraft was convicted of drugging, sodomizing and murdering sixteen young men, some of them Marines, and suspected in sixty-seven other murders. In his letter to me the ex-Marine claimed that Kraft had given him direction in life and had "saved" him. In 2013 he published his story, writing, "He made me feel special in the most irresistible way. For one impossibly beautiful California afternoon, I was very much in love with him. And I've never had another man, before or since, affect me that way."[31]

In a way it makes sense. We all routinely encounter dozens of people a day, and so do serial killers. Serial killers do not kill most of the people they encounter. So there are thousands of people who knowingly or unknowingly had personal encounters with these monsters. Only for the unlucky few it goes bad.

That number of the unlucky, however, grew dramatically in the 1970s and 1980s as corpses began piling up in abandoned lots, in bushes and woods, in secret cemeteries, by roadside ditches, in dumpsters, in culverts, floating in rivers and swamps, buried in gardens and basements or wrapped in plastic bags and stacked in attics or recorded on videotape or Polaroid photos squirreled away as death trophies. I began to wonder how many serial killers an average person might have stood in line behind at a McDonald's, sat next to on a bus, parked a car near at a shopping mall or just passed by randomly on the street.

Even one of my readers turned out to be a notorious serial killer. Dennis Rader, the "BTK Killer," had my first book in his possession along with a book by a colleague, forensic psychology professor and author Katherine Ramsland, when he was identified and arrested.[32] Pondering this "professional endorsement" shivers me out to this day.

By the 1990s, even if one hadn't personally encountered any serial killers, everybody agreed on what they were: white males who killed for sexual reasons in at least three separate events with cooling-off periods in between. But by the 2010s, everything had changed. A profiler could no longer count on an "unsub" being a white male. Studies were showing that 50 to 60 percent of serial killers were now African-Americans[33]— except they rarely became front-page news. Offenders tend to kill within their own race, and serial killers often target prostitutes and marginalized victims, exactly the type of victim that garners less interest and attention in the media. The murder of eleven impoverished minority women by Anthony Sowell, "the Cleveland Strangler," in 2007 and 2008 made the news only because he kept their bodies in his house despite complaints from neighbors about the smell of decaying flesh. Lonnie Franklin Jr., "the Grim Sleeper," is suspected in hundreds of murders of marginalized women in California that went mostly overlooked and unreported for three decades, until he was finally convicted in 2016 for eleven serial killings. Lorenzo Gilyard, "the Kansas City Strangler," was linked to the murders of thirteen women and convicted in six of the murders. Most of his victims had cloth or paper towels stuffed into their mouths, were raped and strangled and were missing their shoes. Despite the high body counts, the names of these African-American serial killers are less prominent than those of white serial killers like Ted Bundy or John Wayne Gacy.

By the 2000s almost one in every six serial killers was a woman, 53 percent of whom killed at least one child or female victim, and since the 1980s, slightly more female serial killers preferred strangers as victims, challenging the "black widow" stereotype who kills her husbands or lovers only.[34] Known as the "quiet killers," women are often not even recognized as serial killers. Genene Jones, for example, a Texas nurse suspected in the murders of sixty infants in her care, was prosecuted for the murders of only two infants and received a sentence that made her eligible for release in 2017. In a desperate bid to prevent her mandatory release in May 2017, authorities charged her for additional murders going back to 1977–1982. Female serial killers are also known to team up with male serial-killing lovers, like Karla Homolka in Canada, who partnered with her husband, Paul Bernardo, in the rape-murders of three teenage girls, including her younger sister; and Charlene Adell (Williams) Gallego, who partnered with her husband, Gerald, in the rape-torture murders of ten victims. Interestingly, after their arrests and testimony against their husbands, both women received relatively light sentences; they now live in freedom. (I describe all three cases in detail in *Female Serial Killers: How and Why Women Become Monsters* [2007]. See also *Paul Bernardo and Karla Homolka: The Ken and Barbie Killers* [2016] for an account of Karla Homolka's postprison life.)

No sooner did we think we knew what serial killers were than we had to rethink it all.

REDEFINING SERIAL KILLERS

There have been many proposed definitions of serial killing, including:

- When someone murders at least three persons in more than a thirty-day period (R. Holmes and S. Holmes);[35]

- At least two fantasy-driven compulsive murders committed at different times and at different locations where there is no relationship between the perpetrator and victim and no material gain, with victims having characteristics in common (Steven A. Egger);[36]

- When an individual, acting alone or with another, commits two or more separate homicides over a period of time, with breaks between each murder event (Vernon Geberth);[37]

- Premeditated murder of three or more victims committed over time, in separate incidents, in a civilian context, with the murder activity being chosen by the offender (B. T. Keeney and K. Heide);[38]

- When someone commits at least ten homicides over time. The homicides are violent and brutal, but they are also ritualistic— they take on their own meaning for the serial murderer (Helen Morrison);[39]

- When someone murders two or more victims, with an emotional cooling-off period between the homicides (Deborah Schurman-Kauflin).[40]

Before 2005, the traditional definition of serial killing was the one the FBI first introduced in the 1980s: three victims on separate occasions with a "cooling-off" period in between. It is still often wrongly cited as the current definition. The FBI eventually realized the "three victims" definition presented all sorts of statistical and conceptual problems. It excluded murderers who have an obvious, identifiable serial-killer psychopathology but are apprehended after their first or second murder, before they can commit the requisite third. It did not account for serial offenders against whom only two convictions were made, thus excluding on a technicality some notorious historic serial killers, like Albert Fish, Ed Gein, Albert DeSalvo and Wayne Williams, who were all convicted for only one or two homicides, notwithstanding persuasive suspicions of many more victims. Most accounts of serial-killer convictions typically include an additional number of "suspected in" murders. Once a serial killer is convicted in one jurisdiction, often other jurisdictions do not bother taking the costly effort to extradite him and put him on trial.

Experts also argued over whether serial killers are defined by the compulsive sexual-fantasy components inherent in their crimes. We debated whether the perpetrators were always male. Were the victims always strangers, and if so, should hit men, gangbangers, genocidal war criminals and terrorists be considered serial killers, since they are killing strangers in separate incidents interspersed by cooling-off periods? Or does a serial killer need to choose his or her own victim, and what constitutes choice? Is serial killing a secondary symptom of behavioral disorders such as psychopathy or sociopathy, or is it an addictive paraphilia (sexual perversion) of its own called erotophonophilia? (More on paraphilias and erotophonophilia below.) Many of these debates are still ongoing in conferences and in the pages of forensic academic literature.

During a conference of experts in 2005 at the San Antonio Serial Murder Symposium sponsored by the FBI's National Center for the Analysis of Violent Crime (NCAVC) Behavioral Analysis Unit (BAU), the FBI finally proposed a new definition of serial murder as "the unlawful killing of two or more victims by the same offender(s) in separate events" *for any reason*, including "anger, thrill, financial gain, and attention seeking."[41]

In other words, women, genocidal killers, contract and gangland killers, missionary-type serial killers like those who might target abortion doctors or interracial couples, and even terrorists are included under the FBI's new broad umbrella defining what constitutes a serial killer today: anybody who kills two or more people in distinctly separate incidents.

Most experts today agree on this definition of serial killing as the murder of *two or more* victims for *any motive* on *separate occasions* with a *cooling-off period* in between.[42] There are, however, still ongoing debates as to what exactly constitutes a cooling-off period and its minimum length.[43] Consider, for example, Andrew Cunanan, who murdered Gianni Versace after killing four victims over several weeks; Paul John Knowles, who killed eighteen victims in a four-month spree in 1974; Christopher Wilder, who killed eight women in a six-week cross-country spree in 1984; or the Washington Beltway snipers, who killed seventeen victims over a period of weeks. None of these serial killers returned to their everyday lives in a cooling-off period; they remained on the road in their "killing state" for weeks or even months. Are they a species of "spree serial killers"? Or is their crime a single incident stretched over a longer period?

The new definition would seem to open the book on past killers, to include profit killers, health-care killers, Munchausen-syndrome-by-proxy killers, black widows, war criminals, genocidal murderers, terrorists and contract killers, all of whom we find often have behavioral psychopathologies and disorders similar to those of "traditional" sexual serial killers, and cooling-off periods between their killings. We are going to have statistically more serial killers from the past than we thought, and a lot more coming at us in the future, under the new definition. It skews and confuses the statistical picture.

For simplicity's sake, in this book we will not dwell on the several categories of serial killers that lie outside the classic conception of the sexual-fantasy-driven killers, like for example:

- *comfort-hedonist serial killers*, who kill purely for material gain, a fee or profit, like the traditional female serial-killing "black widows" or organized-crime hit men or drug-cartel *sicarios*;

- *thrill-hedonist serial killers*, who seek amusement or publicity, or to reassert their "life force" or sense of power and control;

- *missionary serial killers*, who kill for revenge, or for racist, cult or religious or ideological motives, a category we can put genocidal war criminals and terrorists into, as well as murders of abortion doctors, of interracial couples, of immigrants, of homeless people, and even some categories of serial killers who target prostitutes to "cleanse" society of them and serial-killing custodial "death angels of mercy," like nurses and caregivers to the terminally ill, elderly or infants who "put them out of their misery";

- *visionary serial killers*, who are insane in the legal sense of the term, suffering from delusions or hallucinatory visions brought on by mental illness and who are unaware of their actions (a very rare category);

- *Munchausen-syndrome-by-proxy serial killers*, who seek sympathy and attention when people around them die. They are frequently but not always female, and include mothers and babysitters who kill children in their care, and nurses (including male nurses) who kill their patients to appear more heroic and attract attention from their peers, patients and family.

Although all these categories fit the current definition of a serial killer, they are not what we popularly imagine a serial killer to be: a man who kills to realize a sexual fantasy. These other typologies are less frequent than the "average" sexual serial killer and involve different psychopathologies. While subscribing to the two-victims-or-more-in-separate-incidents-for-any-reason definition, in this book, I mostly focus on the history of "traditional," fantasy-driven sexual serial killers, mostly male (although occasionally these types of sexual serial killers have had female accomplices).

THE NEW WORD: SERIAL EROTOPHONOPHILIA

While the FBI's organized/disorganized typology is useful from an investigative perspective, it is not helpful in the clinical-forensic-psychiatric field in understanding *why* sexual serial killers do what they do. Current forensic literature sometimes uses a rape-profile typology that classifies serial killers in terms of the following four motives:

- *power reassurance* (low-self-esteem "gentleman" serial killer): the offender seeks from the victim reassurance of his own virility and prowess as a lover in a delusion that he is pleasing his victim. The rape is planned, but the murder is not, and occurs when a victim's behavior shatters the fantasy of enjoying the rape and the perpetrator either coldly kills the victim in embarrassment or kills in a sudden rage of disappointment;

- *power assertive* (entitlement serial killer): the assertion of masculine power over a female or male victim, in which a rape is planned but the murder again is not, and occurs when the offender loses control over the extent of violence and force necessary to bring the victim under control;

- *anger retaliatory* (revenge-displaced anger serial killer): both the rape and the murder are planned. The murder often involves "overkill"— violence beyond what is necessary to kill the victim, who is usually female. The primary motive driving the killer is his need to avenge, get even with or retaliate against a female who somehow offended him, or her substitute. The rage is often inspired by a female with power over the offender in the past or present—his mother, wife, girlfriend, teacher or work supervisor;

- *anger excitation* (sadistic serial killer): both the rape and the murder are planned. The primary motive is a sadistic need to inflict pain and terror on the male or female victim for the sexual gratification of the perpetrator. The crime is characterized by prolonged torture and mutilation of the victim, generally before death but sometimes after. The murder itself is a lower priority for the offender, who focuses on the process leading up to it.

Some experts use a resurrected archaic term—"lust murder" or "hedonist lust murder" or, in academic-speak, "erotophonophilia"—to distinguish these offenders from all the many types of nonsexual serial killers.

The term "erotophonophilia" (lust murder) is derived from the name for the Greek god of love, Eros, and the word "*phonia*" (bloodshed or murder). It is defined as "murdering sadistically and brutally, including the mutilation of body parts, especially the genitalia,"[44] or "cruelty, torture, or other acts sexual in nature that ultimately culminate in the death of the victim and includes those acts of homicide commonly referred to as sexual sadism . . . This more broadly inclusive definition of sexualized torture includes conscious, unconscious, live, or dead victims."[45]

Because of its matrix of predominantly male psychopathological dysfunctions, this definition of serial erotophonophilia almost entirely excludes female serial killers from the classification, except in those relatively rare cases where women act willingly as accomplices of sadistic male erotophonophiliacs (the "Bonnie and Clyde syndrome," or hybristophilia).

Most of us can grasp the psychology of killing for profit or revenge, or for ideological motives, or because of delusions brought on by mental illness. It is altogether more difficult to wrap our minds around serial killing that includes acts of rape, torture, mutilation, cannibalism or necrophilia (sex with a corpse)—often perpetrated by what appear to be sane and functioning members of society, like the friendly neighbor with three kids, or the reliable coworker, or the guy at your front door delivering your packages.

A NEW HISTORY OF THE WORLD OF MONSTERS

This book offers a new, updated macrohistory of sexual serial killing and its investigation, expanding on the modern history I described in *Serial Killers: The Method and Madness of Monsters*, which began roughly from the age of Jack the Ripper, in the 1880s. This book starts at the beginning, with the Stone Age a million years ago, and Jack the Ripper comes only in the middle. This is a new history of the world of monsters from then until now.

Since my first book came out in 2004, an enormous amount of new research into the psychopathology and biochemistry of serial killers has been completed. Many of the emerging new theories on why there are serial killers are plausible and compelling, but at the same time contradictory and inevitably inconclusive. The mass of new research has revealed to us just how little we understand about serial homicide and how much more work there is left to do before we fully comprehend how these monsters are spawned.

I am not a profiler, forensic psychiatrist or clinician, but an investigative historian. My objective here is not to produce a comparative analysis of the many dozens of serial-killer theories, but to stand at a distance and attempt to understand serial killing from a historian's linear-narrative perspective and try to frame serial killing in a long-term historical-social-anthropological context. Entirely new fields and discoveries in anthropology have emerged over the last twenty years, giving us surprising insights into the nature of humans and our behavior, including our penchant for serial killing, both as spectator and as perpetrator. I seek to understand how serial killing fits into the arc of human history going back to the prehistoric era, which I have come to strongly believe holds the key to understanding serial-killer behavior in its essence and not just serial killers as a category of criminal themselves.

Every case of serial murder has its time and its place, a history and a geography, leading to that fateful instant when a serial killer and a victim intersect on an independently but synchronously chosen ground. The murder unfolds on a trajectory through time and space, history and geography, but one circumscribed by a hidden matrix of dark fantasies and bizarre sexual addictions, developed in some cases as early as the age of five. These fantasies and behaviors do not arise out of thin air but develop in a dense cultural, historical and social ecology, a cultural dialog of rage and madness that is fluid and changing and often defined by its time and place; a process that can be described as *Diabolus in Cultura*. (See chapter fourteen.)

Because the nature of serial killing is determined by historical, mythical and cultural parameters, including religious and moral precepts, the focus of this book is primarily on serial killers in Western society. In other civilizations and cultures, serial killing can take different forms. For example, South African police today contend with so-called *sangomas muti*, ritual serial killers who harvest children's body parts for magical medicinal practices, while police in Mexico (arguably a mix of Indigenous and Western cultures) face a phenomenon of narco-gang-cult ritual murders, and Shanghai, China, has seen serial murders of underclass migrant laborers.[46] The historical-economic-social dynamics of serial killing outside the world of Western Christendom is still waiting to be researched and explored.

TWO

Genesis: The Stone Age Reptilian Zombie Serial-Killer Triune Brain

Animal prius est homine.
[The animal is prior to man.]
—ANICIUS BOETHIUS, *ARITHMETICA*, 1.1.

Life is a never-ceasing duel between the animal instinct and morality.
—RICHARD KRAFFT-EBING, *PSYCHOPATHIA SEXUALIS*

I am convinced that our popular-culture obsession with zombies today is inspired by the surge of serial killers over the last fifty years, in the same way as in the past our shared myths about monsters, vampires, werewolves, ghouls and ogres were really all about unidentified human predators in the form of lust killers, cannibal murderers and necrophiles that have always been part of the fabric of humanity. In fact, two of the most enduring monsters in human imagination—the *preservative*, calculating, quasi-necrophilic vampire and the *destructive*, frenzied, cannibalistic werewolf—roughly correspond to the FBI's serial-killer typology of the calculating, coldly neat *organized* serial killer (Dracula) and the messy, impulsive, *disorganized* serial killer (the Wolf Man).

Having slowly shuffled up on us through the 1950s and 1960s, serial killers were overrunning us in what seemed like zombie herds by the 1970s and 1980s. And some of those serial killers were akin to sexualized horror-comic-book zombies, with bared teeth and drooling mouths, driven by unexplained, primordial, reptilian impulses to attack, bite, rape, kill, rape again, mutilate, dismember, harvest or eat body parts of their victims in ritual and instinctual-like frenzies. They were drinking blood (Richard Chase); trying to reanimate the corpses of their victims with electric current (Jerry Brudos) or injections of car-battery acid to the brain with turkey basters (Jeffrey Dahmer); harvesting human body parts for sex (Ed Gein, Jerry Brudos, Edmund Kemper, Douglas Clark); lipsticking satanic pentagrams on victims' bodies and scooping out their eyeballs (Richard Ramirez); keeping decaying corpses in chemical drums stored in their bedrooms, in the fridge to eat (Jeffrey Dahmer) or in garbage bags in their parents' attic and basement ("Dead raccoons," Kendall "Stinky" Francois told his parents when they complained about the smell coming from eight bodies hidden in their house); burying bodies under their suburban bungalow crawl spaces (twenty-six buried by John Wayne Gacy), in their rose garden (seven by Dorothea Puente), in a fruit orchard (twenty-five by Juan Corona) or under their boat shed (seventeen by Dean Corll); dumping them on Hollywood hillsides (ten by Kenneth Bianchi and Angelo Buono); collected in forested or bushy boneyards where they could be revisited for necrophilic sex (Ted Bundy, Arthur Shawcross, Gary Ridgway); and posing them, dismembered, mutilated or decapitated, in weird tableaus at crime scenes to greet arriving first responders (Richard Cottingham, Rodney Alcala and Danny Rolling). It seemed like the stuff of Hollywood slasher horror movies, but those fictional killers had nothing on these real-life monsters.

WHAT MAKES A SERIAL KILLER: THE CURRENT THEORIES

Current theories about how the psychopathology of the serial killer is shaped in his early childhood include such causes as a lack of infantile bonding and neglect; or its opposite, stifling maternal overprotectiveness; or formative childhood trauma, or sexual or physical abuse, or rejection; abandonment; loneliness; lack of familial stability; or personality disorders like psychopathy, sociopathy, borderline personality disorder, antisocial disorder, or dissociative identity disorder, dissociative amnesia or dissociative fugue states; or physical injuries to the head; or exposure to violent media or to true detective magazines or pornography or biblical passages; or religious ecstasy; or substance abuse; or genetic propensity; or by Asperger's syndrome or autism spectrum disorder; or some organic brain disorder or chromosome abnormality or abnormal blood or urine chemistry, allergy or a combination of all of the above.[1] In other words, we know very little—next to nothing—about why there are serial killers.

All the factors we've discovered in convicted serial killers, in their biochemistry, their childhood histories, injuries and traumas and in their psychopathology, we can also find in the backgrounds of many non–serial killers, some even ostensibly productive members of society with no criminal record. The X factor that makes a serial killer has not been conclusively identified, certainly not by the standards that define modern scientific, medical and psychiatric clinical practice.

One thing we do agree upon is that serial killers are made in childhood, approximately twenty years *before* they start killing (at the average age of twenty-eight).[2]

One other thing we know for sure about serial killers is that most of them are not insane in the legal sense of the word. They know exactly what they are doing—the illegal nature of their acts as well as the consequences—and take extraordinary measures to conceal their crimes. Some serial killers are highly self-aware and curious about the sick compulsions that drive them. They research forensic psychiatric literature to understand themselves, but in the end, they have little empathy for their victims, and no remorse. As serial killer Richard Cottingham recently explained, he was very aware of his impulses, but "my inability to 'want' to control these impulses is what made me who I am."[3]

Many serial killers (but not all) can be diagnosed as psychopaths on Robert Hare's standard test *Psychopathy Checklist Revised* (*PCL-R*), but that fails to definitively explain their behavior, because we have not figured out what exactly psychopathy is either, or why some psychopaths become serial killers while others become successful corporate CEOs or congressmen.

It is estimated that one in every 83 Americans[4] and one in 166 Britons[5] is a diagnosable psychopath. That gives us some 3.8 million psychopaths in the current United States population alone. That would be a lot of serial killers! Most of us have at least once either dated a psychopath or worked with one—or are psychopaths ourselves—but only a rare few psychopaths become serial killers.

My approach here will be to go beyond social, psychological and biochemical theories to take an *evolutionary* view of human serial-killing behavior to explain its origins. Whether we interpret it in the language of psychology, sociology, criminology or biochemistry, I propose that the unifying underlying impulse driving serial killers is defined by natural evolutionary prerogatives; serial killers are what Mother Nature intended *all of us* to be in the wild before civilization.

THE FOUR "F"S OF EVOLUTIONARY SURVIVAL AND THE TRIUNE BRAIN

If you set aside the supernatural qualities of zombies—the idea that the dead can be undead—fictional zombie and real serial-killer behavior originates physiologically and biogenetically from the same anatomical place: a small knot at the base of the brain called the *basal ganglia* (or *basal nuclei*), also known as the *R-complex* or the "reptilian brain."

Like an archeological site, our brains consist of temporal layers, three separate brains from different eras of our evolutionary past, stacked and wired together in parallel loops, each layer more ancient and primitive than the next. The resulting whole is called the triune brain.[6]

The reptilian R-complex is the oldest and most primitive part of our brain. Found in animals from lizards and birds to cats and dogs to apes and humans, the primordial R-complex drives a set of instinctual self- and species-preserving behaviors: running away, killing, eating and reproducing, or more crudely put, the "four Fs" of evolutionary survival: Fleeing, Fighting, Feeding and Fucking. If any one of these instincts malfunctions in a species, the species will eventually become extinct.

Until relatively recently in evolution, humans were driven to perform these functions instinctually, in the same way other animals do.

Yale University neuroscientist Paul D. MacLean described the functioning of the R-complex as a "primitive interplay of oral, aggressive and sexual behavior."[7]

Since no species can survive without the functioning of these instincts, they are very deeply hardwired into the core of our brain, our psychology, our mind and personality—into our "soul," if you like—driving us like a coiled spring to be constantly choosing between fleeing in fear, fighting and killing in rage, biting and eating in hunger, and mating and reproducing in lust.

And for the longest time humans did nothing else: we did not draw on cave walls, sing songs, tell stories, build shelters, domesticate animals or plant food. We just spent all our waking time running away from danger or killing it, gathering food or killing it and eating it, and having sex anytime the strongest males among us demanded it. Life was horribly simple.

When food was scarce in the Stone Age, we sometimes combined what we killed in fear and anger with what we killed for food, and sometimes even with what we had sex with; in times of distress, combat, conquest or famine, our species easily slipped into a mindless, instinctual cocktail of sexualized aggression, cannibalism and necrophilia.

Today our still-functioning R-complex reptilian brain interacts with a second, newer, more evolved *paleomammalian complex*, or *limbic system*, a part of the brain that hosts a variety of emotions, long-term memories and sensory and motor functions. It is the part of our brain that sees, hears, tastes, smells and recognizes things, and recalls associated emotional states and motivational behaviors.

This newer limbic system is wired down to our more primitive R-complex and sends it sensory and emotional signals that trigger in the reptilian cells of a healthy human brain the appropriate "four F" survival response to the situation—"appropriate" being the operative term.

What actually makes humans different from other animals is the level of evolution of a third layer of our brain, the more recent *neomammalian complex*, or *neocortex*. It is present in mammals but not in other animals. In humans it is highly developed and overrides and moderates the interface between the R-complex and the limbic system. Our ultrahigh intellectual abilities, like language, logic, reasoning, the artistic and creative impulse, abstract thinking, rationalization, imagination and fantasy, are all rooted in the neocortex.

The highly complex neocortex frames our impulses and actions in philosophical-spiritual, cultural, linguistic, expressive and psychological contexts; it is why we have a concept of good and evil, which is non-existent in the animal world, and why, when we behave like animals, we can become serial killers. (Although it can be argued that animals rarely kill for recreation in the way some humans do.)

Until about forty thousand years ago, prehistoric humans, like other animals, were motivated mostly by pure fear, aggression, and feeding and mating instincts, without much imagination or philosophy or self-awareness or remorse or any of the "neuroses" that the "human animal" is endowed with today. The very recent capacity of the human neocortex to reason, deduce, abstract, moralize, project, imagine and fantasize creates a layer of conceptual, rational (or sick, irrational) modulators of limbic-system functions—our impulses, desires and memories—and determines how they might be interpreted or neurotransmitted to the reptilian brain.

Our three brain layers are constantly inputting and outputting, triggering reptilian instincts while also analyzing and controlling them through the conceptual capacity of the neocortex.

Not all neuroscientists agree on the concept of the triune brain,[8] but for those who do, it is obvious that a lot can go wrong when you have three cerebral systems working with one another, each more archaic than the last. One short circuit, and the whole thing can go spinning homicidally out of control, with the primitive, reptilian brain doing what it has no business doing: taking control of the limbic system.

As Johns Hopkins University psychologist Dr. John Money wrote,

The limbic region of the brain is responsible . . . for predation and attack in defense of both the self and the species. In the disease of sexual sadism, the brain becomes pathologically activated to transmit messages of attack simultaneously with messages of sexual arousal and mating behavior.[9]

Another psychologist sums it up more simply:

> The predatory serial killer is literally a limbically kindled "engine of destruction." He won't stop and he doesn't want to because nothing in life could possibly replace the thrill of dominating and destroying....[10]

FROM REPTILIAN RAPIST CANNIBALS TO CIVILIZED CITIZEN SERIAL KILLERS: THE BIG HISTORY OF HUMANS

Big History is a relatively new formal field of history that considers humans from the perspective of the natural history of the earth, its biosphere and even the evolution of our universe. It strips down human behavior, including serial killing, to its essential biological and anthropological models. Big History integrates the history of humans into the overall history of everything. Let's remove serial killing from its context of social, legal and psychological norms, and look at it as part of the history of nature on the planet.

To grasp the scale of human life on earth it can be helpful to think of years as dollars. For example, the universe is 13.8 billion years old, planet Earth is 4.5 billion years old, dinosaurs lived and vanished between 230 and 65 million years ago and cavemen appeared around three million years ago, but written human history goes back only about 5,500 years (to 3500 BC) before it fades into the dark of mythology and prehistoric times. Compare the buying power of 13.8 billion dollars with that of 5,500 dollars and you get some sense of the scale of human civilization versus the age of the universe and our planet. Human civilization isn't petty cash, but it's not an impressive sum either.

Hominids, or apelike mammals, emerged about fifteen to twenty-five million years ago, and the humanlike subspecies *Homo habilis* (tool-making man) and *Homo erectus* (upright-walking man) emerged as distinct species about three million years ago, followed by the more advanced Neanderthal (*Homo neanderthalensis*) species.

We *Homo sapiens*—modern "thinking man"—emerged on the African continent relatively recently, perhaps as early as 1.8 million years ago or as late as 200 thousand years ago. About 60 to 100 thousand years ago *Homo sapiens* invaded Europe and Asia and began to war with the Neanderthal species, which was dominant there. As both Neanderthal and *Homo sapiens* were skilled at making edged weapons from stone, this was artificially armed war, unlike the conflicts between other animals.

This total-war death clash between Neanderthals and *Homo sapiens* ended about thirty to forty thousand years ago with the victorious *Homo sapiens* the only humanoid species left standing on earth. I guess that is the good news. The bad news, according to many anthropologists, biologists, Big Historians and other scientists, is that we serially killed, raped and ate our way to the top of the food chain in an evolutionary process just like that of any other predatory species.[11] Just as Mother Nature intended. The only difference is that we did it with stone weapons against a prey armed with the same.[12] What does this reveal to us about serial killers today?

THE OLDEST COLD CASE: THE SERIAL KILLING OF THE NEANDERTHALS

Just as serial-homicide studies are beginning to lose sight of a continually moving horizon in their attempts to determine why there are serial killers, anthropological sciences likewise are in a state of upheaval today. Every year there are new anthropological and archeological discoveries, with skeletal remains submitted to constantly improving techniques of DNA, and genome analysis and carbon testing of artifacts, continuously changing our understanding of the chronology of the development of human life on planet Earth and what it means to be a human, let alone a human serial killer.

Like cold-case crime scenes but hundreds of thousands, even millions, of years old, newly discovered prehistoric caves, campsites, villages, graves, dump sites and even prehistoric latrines with fossilized feces are revealing more and more about the diet, behavior, intelligence and psychopathology of early humans.

Entirely new branches of science have emerged, like *paleogenomics*, which reconstructs our prehistoric past through DNA analysis of fossilized human remains. Paleogenomics led to a startling discovery in the mid-2000s that some humans today have up to 4 percent Neanderthal DNA in their own genome.[13] This suggests that *Homo sapiens* interbred with Neanderthals.[14] Most likely, that took place through genocidal conquest and rape, because that's what we humans routinely did and still do when we go to war.[15] While nominally punishable in the modern era under national criminal and military codes of the countries whose soldiers are perpetrating the offenses, their enforcement and prosecution in wartime are sporadic. Rape historically was such a ubiquitous and ordinary behavior of male humans at war that it was not explicitly outlawed in international conventions governing the laws and customs of war until 1996, and only in 2008 did the United Nations finally declare wartime rape as a category of "war crimes, crimes against humanity or a constitutive act with respect to genocide."[16]

It's been argued by some scholars and critics that the biblical account of Cain's murder of his brother, Abel, in the book of Genesis is an allegory of the genocide of the Neanderthals echoing from our primordial evolutionary memories which still rattle around in our collective subconsciousness like fragments of long-forgotten nightmares—a form of prehistoric collective trauma. During the Stone Age when the two hominid species clashed, the Neanderthals were mostly nomadic herdsmen like Abel, while the *Homo sapiens* were on the brink of emerging as settled farmers like Cain. In that context, all humans might be the sons of Cain, carrying his homicidal "mark," and especially so, the serial killers among us.[17]

Forty thousand years ago, humans emerged victorious over Neanderthals, but the price of that victory was that for a span of thousands of years we had to systematically destroy everybody and anybody who was not like us. Our brains had to be hardwired to sustain that kind of constant homicidal aggression toward "others" through countless generations. Rather than temporarily condition ourselves for war or train to become warriors for a few months or even a few years, as we do today, in the Stone Age we had to kill and kill constantly, for tens of thousands of years, as a way of life, until we emerged as an unchallenged (serial-killing) species.

NECROPHOBIA AND DEVIANT "VAMPIRE GRAVES"

What happened to the aggressive, serial-killing *Homo sapiens* personality over the last forty thousand years that today makes us universally condemn serial killing as aberrant? Having risen to the top through unbridled conquest, humans as a killer species now had to be inhibited from turning on *one another* with those deadly stone tools. In fact, one of the theories as to why Neanderthals were defeated despite being physically larger and more powerful than *Homo sapiens*, and equally adept at making spears and stone-edged weapons, is that Neanderthals had no inhibitions against killing and eating one another.[18] They helped us *Homo sapiens* to kill them off.

Why did *Homo sapiens* not slaughter and eat themselves into extinction even though we were capable of systematic cannibalism in times of famine just as the Neanderthals were?[19] What was that one thing that nature (or God, if you prefer) endowed the human species with that the Neanderthals and other extinct hominid species lacked?

Primitive humans developed a *neurosis*, an irrational or imaginary fear, one not caused by an actual threat: *necrophobia*—a fear of the dead.*

According to Big Historian and psychologist Akop Nazaretyan:

> The Georgian philosopher Mamardashvili [1990] wrote that the human species began when one individual mourned the death of another. Unfortunately, empirical data from archeology and ethnography force us to reformulate this elegant aphorism. The reformulated version does not sound that romantic: *the (proto-)humans began with the fear of the dead*[20] [emphasis in the original].

---

*The argument that necrophobia is a rational impulse necessary to protect humans from contracting diseases from corpses is undermined by the presence of a powerful olfactory response in humans to the smell of decaying flesh.

Necrophobia apparently begins to emerge in humans around the time that we were killing off the last of the Neanderthals, in the late stages of the Middle Paleolithic Age (Middle Stone Age) about thirty thousand to forty thousand years ago.

We know about necrophobia from the archeological evidence from prehistoric *deviant burial* sites (defined as burials that do not conform to previous norms of burial), sometimes described in popular media as "vampire graves," which incorporated unique features that were intended to keep the dead from rising, presumably to exact vengeance on the living.[21]

Archeologists have cataloged numerous prehistoric (and ancient-modern) deviant burial sites around the world indicating "evidence for practices, which indicate fear of the dead (*necrophobia*). These practices usually include methods for the restriction of the dead in the grave by weighing down the body with large rocks, decapitation or the use of nails, wedges and rivets."[22]

There are such burial sites everywhere in the world, from the Zhoukoudian ("Peking Man") site in China, where the positions of the tibias of two Paleolithic skeletons indicate that their legs had been tied after death[23]; to Khirokitia, Cyprus, where heavy millstones were placed on the head or torso[24] of Neolithic bodies from 4500 BC; to bound Egyptian mummies; to the Australian aboriginals' piercing of the neck of the dead with a spear to fix it to a hollow wood coffin and the Tasmanians' tying of the body's hands and legs and the placement of a heavy stone over it; to the beheading of corpses in Italy[25]; pinning the dead under a heavy stone in the Mediterranean and Balkan regions[26]; and the ancient Spanish practice of nailing the corpse to the wood of the coffin.[27] Observers in the nineteenth century had already concluded that the tradition of cemetery headstones was a popularization of eons of the necrophobic immobilization of the dead under heavy stones or mill wheels.[28] (While there are some academics who claim that Neanderthals also practiced ritual burials, their findings to date are inconclusive and represent a minority.)[29]

When we look at serial killers today, we immediately recognize that a necrophobic instinct that the majority of us have is lacking in them. Serial killers fearlessly "make" corpses, interact with them, handle and dismember them, transport them and worse: some serial killers manifest an impulse on the extreme opposite pole to necrophobia, a fetishistic sexual desire for the dead—*necrophilia*. Sometimes accompanying serial murder, rape and cannibalism, necrophilia can also include erotic cannibalism, drinking of blood (*vampirism*) and other bodily fluids or the harvesting of body parts as totems or trophies to be eaten.

The term "necrophilia" is derived from the Greek "*nekros*" ("dead") and "*philia*" ("love for"). It was coined relatively recently, in the 1850s, to describe a French serial necrophile, François Bertrand, the "Vampire of Montparnasse" (see chapter seven). The exact frequency of necrophilia in serial-murder cases is somewhat controversial. On the high end, the *Sexual Homicide* study by the FBI in the 1980s concluded that "a sexual act" was committed *after* a victim's death in 42 percent of 92 victims they studied.[30] Among the low-end estimates, statistics in 2014 from the FBI's Behavioral Analysis Unit indicate that "postmortem sexual activity" was present in 11.2 percent of the 480 cases of sexual serial murder involving 92 male offenders in the study.[31]

If forty thousand years ago we were routinely killing and raping our Neanderthal enemies as a way of life, and if we were sometimes feeding on them too, then using their corpses in acts of necrophilia to satisfy an instinctual sexual urge prior to eating them was not something remote from primitive evolutionary hedonistic feasting-fornicating homicidal behavior of early humans. And yes, necrophilia, as we have recently discovered, is not exclusively a human behavioral trait. Mallard ducks have been observed engaging in homosexual necrophilic sex, evidence that there is some sort of deep-seated natural biological impulse at work in necrophilia (and homosexuality), not just human psychology.[32]

If we approach necrophilia from its opposite pole of necrophobia, the fear of the dead and its evolutionary function as argued by Big Historians, we might scratch at the roots of what this sexual attraction for the dead in serial killers might entail on a macro level of human evolutionary behavior and why we feel so powerful a revulsion to it today. Even Sigmund Freud, who had no problems venturing into bizarre psychological concepts such as penis envy, anal-expulsive personality development and the Oedipus complex, said he could not deal with necrophilic acts or lust murder because he found them a "kind of horror" too "far removed from the normal."[33]

Serial killers don't develop out of nowhere a desire to kill, rape, mutilate, cannibalize or have sex with the dead; they find it in themselves as an array of deeply embedded primitive instincts which humans are all endowed with at birth but are *supposed to be* taught in childhood by healthy familial upbringing and positive societal norms to suppress. Serial killers are not actually made; those of us who aren't serial killers were *unmade* as such when we were children, through good parenting, stable family environments and the sheer luck of not being exposed to some random source of trauma. (Which explains why it comes as no surprise that serial killers often report familial breakdown and trauma in their childhood histories.)

Some Big Historians argue that our unique necrophobia explains why all previous species of hominids became extinct while our *Homo sapiens* species did not. Necrophobia was the result of an evolutionary transformation of a subset of survival instincts, necrophilia, into a neurosis, necrophobia, that transformed quasi-animal-like *Homo sapiens* into that civilized "thinking herds of crazies" we are today, as one Big Historian has described humanity.[34] *Not* to have a capacity to kill, eat and rape would have been "abnormal, sick and crazy" in the Stone Age. The basic survival and evolution of early hominids depended on the dominance and procreation of the most naturally physically fit and virile. There was no place for the weak, the impotent, the ill, the disabled or the aged, for those unable to defend themselves, hunt or breed. Hominids at best abandoned the weak of their own species, and at worst raped, killed and ate them, without the slightest stirrings of empathy or remorse. Essentially, we hominids were a psychopathic serial-killer-rapist-cannibal species because that is precisely how we needed to be to survive in the cruel world of natural selection. Mother Nature is a cruel psychopath herself, with no empathy for her progeny.

THE TECHNO-HUMANITARIAN BALANCE HYPOTHESIS

Our development of necrophobia some forty thousand years ago as we finished murdering Neanderthal people was how Mother Nature corrected herself after endowing hominids with the deadly gift of tool-making.

Hominids began fashioning stone tools perhaps as early as two or three million years ago.[35] Our earliest tools, called Oldowan tools, were made from pieces of flint, the edges of which were shaped by flaking to a remarkable razor sharpness.* They became highly lethal handheld weapons that enhanced hominids' killing capacity beyond their natural strength.

As the Nobel Prize–winning zoologist and ethologist Konrad Lorenz described in his magisterial book *On Aggression*, the more powerful a species' natural killing ability, the more pronounced is its instinctual inhibition against aggression within that species.[36] Naturally equipped predatory killing machines such as lions, tigers, sharks and eagles relatively rarely kill members of their own species, but rats and doves are highly aggressive toward their own; "peaceful" doves peck one another's eyes out and rats cannibalize one another. As hominids were not fitted with powerful jaws, thick pelts or deadly claws and fangs, their natural inhibition against intraspecies violence was correspondingly very low. Prehistoric hominids wantonly killed one another like rats, with little consequence to their species.

But when hominids created stone weapons, evolution went off the tracks; it was the beginning of an arms race. *Homo sapiens* were not the only species of hominids that made stone weapons; our rival Neanderthals did too, and even more archaic species prior to them, perhaps as long as three million years ago according to recent discoveries.[37]

It can be argued that one of the reasons these various prehistoric species of hominids became extinct was that, with naturally low inhibitions on intraspecies violence, they led an unbridled life of not only killing rival species, but serially murdering one another with their "unnatural" stone weapons until there were only two species left standing: Neanderthals and *Homo sapiens*. Neanderthals were not only equally capable of toolmaking, but were also physically stronger than *Homo sa-*

---

*Some animals manifest the rudimentary use of twigs, branches and rocks as "found" building material and primitive tools, an ability they might have developed recently, over the last two million years, but they do not fashion and shape tools.

piens and had larger brains. So why didn't they wipe us out rather than the other way around? Because somewhere in the mid- to late Paleolithic Age, about forty thousand to one hundred thousand years ago, the newest of the breed, we, the *Homo sapiens* species, began developing that irrational fear that our dead could rise and take vengeance on the living—necrophobia. We became afraid to kill one another.

This kind of "demobilization" and gradual suppression of our unbridled killing instincts through necrophobia fits into the *technohumanitarian balance hypothesis*, which argues that as humans develop more powerful and destructive weapons they simultaneously develop more sophisticated means of inhibiting their use. Just as the development of machine guns and chemical and nuclear weapons was accompanied by international conventions on WMD nonproliferation, the concept of war crimes, and the founding of the United Nations, necrophobia was a primitive natural arms-limitation program as a response to the increased use of stone weapons.[38]

This gave *Homo sapiens* the winning advantage over Neanderthals in our genocidal war with them, as Neanderthals not only fought us but continued to slaughter one another at the same time. It also prevented us from slaughtering ourselves into extinction once we were victorious over all the other hominid species.[39]

With the rise of deviant burials, we also find increasing archeological traces of human remains of those who died at a later age, in ill health, suggesting that along with necrophobia came compassion, empathy, deeper familial and tribal ties and organized care for the aged and the sick despite their inability to contribute to the species as hunters or breeders. People began to survive into later age because they were taken care of by those stronger than themselves. Both the fear of the dead and compassion (empathy) for the weak and aged required a degree of societal organization and intellect. The fit went to hunt while the unfit stayed home and began ritually painting their collective fantasies and desires on cave walls: the birth of the intelligentsia and leisure. The oldest known traces of cave drawings, located in Spain, go back to about forty thousand years ago, about the time we had successfully killed off the Neanderthal people and begun manifesting fear of the dead.[40]

Necrophobia and cave art were two signs of the emergence of civilization and the shift of the hominid species from mere "psychopathic"-animal-survival state to empathetic evolutionary progress: the triumph of the human and its superior intellect. It's these things that define us as human. We are the only animals with funerary and mourning rituals and the only animals to export our memories from our brains to shared media, beginning with cave drawings and progressing to the Internet.

And indeed, despite occasional historical peaks of warfare, statistically, *Homo sapiens* has become progressively less violent with time. While it seems like our wars have become more deadly, in statistical reality, per capita deaths in warfare have declined. Studies of Pacific-region Stone Age aboriginal tribal warfare reveal that it was far more deadly per capita to its communities than the megakilling of World War II ever was (with the exception of the race war waged in Eastern Europe from 1939 to 1945 by Nazi Germans against Jews and Slavic peoples).[41]

No matter what we read in newspapers or see in the media, statistically speaking, in advanced societies, civilian murder rates have declined over the centuries, albeit with ebbs and flows. For example, the homicide rate in idyllic colonial America in the 1700s was 30 murders per 100 thousand people, but in the worst decade of the modern era, the 1990s, the homicide rate in the US was 10 to 11 murders per 100 thousand people on average.[42] In the current dramatic rise of murder in Chicago, one of the worst in the United States, the murder rate between 2005 and 2015 ranged between 17.3 and 18.8 per 100 thousand, still only roughly half of what it was in colonial America.[43] Only at its craziest recent worst, in 2016, has Chicago approached a murder rate comparable to that of colonial America.[44]

THE SERIAL KILLER CIVILIZED

It was only around fifteen thousand years ago that our species finally began settling down by developing agriculture and domesticating animals, abandoning our animal-like life of hunting and gathering. We began assembling together in organized societies around our farms and in villages and, later, cities—civilizations. Fifteen thousand years is not a lot of time in which to undo the cerebral wiring of at least two hundred thousand years of dog-eat-dog, four-Fs serial-killer behavior. As a species, we were serial killers for a lot longer than it has been socially unacceptable to kill and eat whomever we want to whenever we feel like it.

Those old, deeply embedded reptilian survival instincts continue to rage, spark and fire but now are supposed to be held in check by our higher limbic system and neocortex. When we get angry enough to kill, most of us don't. Our civilized neocortex has been conditioned to put the brakes on those limbic impulses through societal proscriptions and parental rearing.

But while our emerging civilization demanded that we "behave ourselves," our reptilian brains were not that quick to respond and transform. Humans today are basically a refurbished model, not a newly manufactured species suited to the modern world our advanced intellects have engineered.

Serial killing, rape, cannibalism and necrophilia as modern psychiatric disorders in civilized humans represent an evolutionary turning inside out—a lycanthropic *versipellis*, or reversion to what we once were. Primitive vital evolutionary instinctual imperatives with the dawn of civilization become paradoxically entropic, destructive and ultimately criminal.

If we distill aggression, serial killing, rape, sadism, cannibalism and necrophilia to their historical evolutionary and anthropological imperatives, then today a serial-killing cannibalistic impulse is like the appendix, now obsolete and vestigial. Its destructive character can be compared to, for example, our evolutionary fat-storage metabolism—necessary for survival in the wild when food was scarce, but causing obesity in modern advanced societies (especially in North America) where there is unrestricted access to copious amounts of cheap, processed, sugar- and salt-saturated junk food produced to sell rather than nourish. Our advanced cerebral neocortex knows and understands this, but our reptilian and limbic systems compel us to eat shit just the same, because we can, whether we are really hungry or not.

We snack as compulsively as serial killers kill.

We can describe serial killing with scientific terms like "psychopathy" and "erotophonophilia," which reveal *how* humans come to kill, but they do not explain *why*.

I suspect we are too frightened of the answer to look into the face of why: because nature, in the past, for very good reasons, equipped us with a capacity for serial killing. That's why.

In conclusion, we might all perhaps be born as serial killers, but most of us are raised and socialized out of it. Serial killers are not made; they are unmade. We are, after all, born uncivilized—wetting ourselves, putting everything into our mouths, screaming when we want attention, wantonly hitting other children and snatching their toys—but most of us are very quickly taught to be otherwise. In fact, it has been argued that serial killers are precisely infantile in their temperaments and sexual compulsions, "emotionally immature" and childishly narcissistic to an extreme level.[45] Those children who remain undersocialized for the various clinical reasons psychologists put forth, from trauma and abuse to psychopathy and biochemical factors, essentially remain in the "natural" evolutionary crisis-survival state in which they were born, and mature into serial-killing humans, as nature without civilization intends them to be.

Simply put, serial killers today are what *we all were* forty thousand years ago. To quote the inimitable Pogo, "We have met the enemy and he is us." It's a quote I could sadly repeat at the end of each chapter in this book like a death rattle of a mantra. Just as there is a little bit of Neanderthal DNA in some of us, there is primitive serial-killer DNA too.

THREE

Psychopathia Sexualis: The Psychology of the Lust Serial Killer in Civilized Society

Enough of this kind of horror.

—DR. SIGMUND FREUD, *THE SEXUAL LIFE OF HUMAN BEINGS*, 1905[1]

Love exists above the belt, lust below.

—DR. JOHN WILLIAM MONEY, *LOVEMAPS*, 1986

Once we became civilized and developed language, we began using it to describe ourselves, including the serial-killing parts of us. The earliest surviving written records, Sumerian clay tablets and Chinese oracle bone inscriptions, date to about 3500 BC. For most of the last 5,500 years, humans viewed serial killers as supernatural monsters, for example werewolves or vampires. As for "ordinary" human murderers who killed for greed, anger, vengeance or jealousy, these tended to be looked upon from a religious perspective as evil or even possessed by the devil. The notion that a human would kill repeatedly, pathologically, was rarely touched upon.

With the dawn of the age of reason, we began to recast the nature of human behavior in secular form. Serial lust killing, cannibalism and necrophilia became linked to primitive core evolutionary instincts, misplaced aggression, reproductive impulses and hunger, expressed in the human animal as twisted fantasies, or what we came to call perversions.

A version of this primitive-atavistic behavioral model, which I introduced in the previous chapter, was in fact one of the first theories of modern criminology, advanced by the famed forensic psychiatrist Cesare Lombroso (1835–1909), known as the father of criminology.

Lombroso's criminal-behavior theory was rooted in the anthropological, evolutionary and biological spectrum rather than the psychological. Influenced by Darwinism, Lombroso argued that all crime was a kind of evolutionary failure. Serial killers (and other violent criminals), he argued, were atavists, throwbacks to a prehistoric primitive state. Criminals were primitive or subhuman types, characterized by physical features reminiscent of those of apes, lower primates, and early man, preserved, Lombroso said, in "modern savages."

Lombroso's failure and eventual downfall (and where his argument differs from mine) were because of his insistence that these atavistic features were hereditary and were reflected in a criminal's physical appearance. When it turned out that many murderers and rapists did not have primitive, apelike features, Lombroso's Italian school of criminology yielded to the French school led by Dr. Alexandre Lacassagne (1843–1924), a pioneer in forensic sociology and criminal psychology, who argued that criminals are not naturally born but *made* through social and psychological circumstances. (More on Lacassagne in chapter eleven.)

So, are we all born potential killers, and raised and socialized to inhibit our natural killing capacity, or are we born pacific creatures among whom a few are desocialized or driven by trauma and mental disorders into becoming serial murderers?

PSYCHOPATHIA SEXUALIS: THE PARAPHILIC CATALOG

A milestone in our modern understanding of the psychopathology behind sexual serial murder came in 1886, two years before the Jack the Ripper murders, when Austrian psychiatrist Richard Krafft-Ebing (1840–1902) published *Psychopathia Sexualis: Eine Klinisch-Forensische Studie (Sexual Psychopathy: A Clinical-Forensic Study)*. In this book he cataloged and categorized a wide range of sexual crimes and disorders reported by psychiatrists (or alienists, as they were called in the nine-teenth century).

Krafft-Ebing labeled the fusion of reproductive sexual impulses (lust) and homicidal aggression *paraesthesia** (from the Greek *para*, meaning "unusual," and *aesthesia*, meaning "sensation"), which he de-fined as a "perverse emotional coloring of sexual ideas."[2] In addition to paraesthesia (the fusion of contradictory impulses), other sexual dis-orders were rooted in *hyperaesthesia* (exaggerated sexual impulses) or *anaesthesia* (an absence of sexual instincts).

Serial killing can be driven by a variety of different disorders result-ing from paraesthesia or hyperaesthesia. Today we call these disorders *paraphilias* (literally, "unusual loves"), or more commonly sexual devia-tions or perversions. One of the most well-known is sexual pleasure in causing pain, for which Krafft-Ebing coined the term "sadism," inspired by the French libertine Marquis de Sade (1740–1814), author of the sexu-ally violent novel *The One Hundred Twenty Days of Sodom*.

Found almost exclusively in males, a paraphilia is an obsession for a very particular and statistically unusual type of sex, without which the person cannot otherwise be aroused. Paraphilias include specific fantasy scenarios, an erotic fixation on a particular nongenital part of the anatomy (partialism), the sexualization of inanimate objects such as shoes (fetishes) and a substitution of another act for the sex-ual one.

We are not talking about a guy buying his girlfriend sexy lingerie or dressing in leather or latex on the weekend, but of a constant, daily, obsessive addiction for a period of six months or more, to the exclusion of being sexually aroused in any other way.[3] A person may have several different paraphilias at the same time, and paraphilias can change and mutate, but one paraphilia usually dominates until a different one takes hold.

There are dozens of different paraphilias, some of which are benign if engaged in with a consensual partner, such as:

---

*In modern medicine the term "paraesthesia" refers to a tingling type of numbness, not a perversion.

- *abasiophilia* (a preference for a disabled partner);

- *acrotomophilia* (a preference for amputees);

- *agalmatophilia* (*pygmalianism*, a desire for sex with dolls, mannequins or statues);

- *agonophilia* (a preference for a partner *pretending* to struggle);

- *altocalciphilia* (a fetish for high-heeled shoes);

- *coprophilia* (arousal from feces or from being defecated upon by or defecating on a willing partner);

- *formicophilia* (arousal from being crawled upon by ants or other insects);

- *gerontophilia* (a preference for a partner from an older generation);

- *hyphephilia* (arousal at the touch of certain things, such as feathers or hair, or a particular textile, such as leather);

- *klismaphilia* (sexual arousal from receiving or giving enemas);

- *maschalagnia* (a partialism for armpits);

- *masochism* (arousal from being dominated, restrained or hurt);

- *mixoscopia* (a desire to watch others having sex, with their consent);

- *nasophilia* (a partialism for noses);

- *oculophilia* (a partialism for eyes);

- *plushophilia* (a fetish for stuffed toy figures);

- *raptophilia* (*simulated* rape with a *consenting* partner);

- *trichophilia* (a fetish for hair).

Other paraphilias are more blatantly transgressive, dangerous and often criminal because their very premise is coercive or destructive:

- *amokoscisia* (a desire to slash or mutilate females);

- *anthropophagolagnia* (rape accompanied by cannibalism);

- *anthropophagy* (cannibalism);

- *biastophilia* (rape/sex with a nonconsenting partner);

- *colobosis* (mutilation of male genitalia);

- *erotophonophilia* ("lust murder" accompanied by mutilation of the victim before or after death);

- *exhibitionism* (exposing oneself to unwilling strangers);

- *flagellationism* (sexual satisfaction from whipping or beating a person);

- *frotteurism* (rubbing against unwilling subjects);

- *hybristophilia* (a desire in a female to partner with a male serial killer, one of the few female paraphilias);

- *mazoperosis* (mutilation of female breasts);

- *necrophagia* (cannibalism of corpse flesh in advanced stages of decomposition);

- *necrophilia* (sex with a corpse);

- *necrosadism* (mutilation of corpses);

- *pederasty* (anal sex with male children);

- pedophilia (sex with prepubescent children);

- *perogynia* (mutilation of female genitalia);

- *piquerism* (or *picquerism*) (sexual gratification through the use of a knife or other sharp object as a substitute for a penis to penetrate, stab or slash a victim);

- *sadism* (sexual arousal from dominating, humiliating or causing pain to an unwilling subject);

- *scopophilia* (voyeurism; watching others undress or have sex without their consent).

While Krafft-Ebing can be considered a pioneer in recognizing the pattern and nature of paraphilias, his vision of what constituted "normal" sexuality was firmly of its time. For Krafft-Ebing *any* sexuality "that does not correspond with the purpose of nature—i.e., propagation— must be regarded as perverse."[4] But despite his heteronormative value judgments, Krafft-Ebing did successfully identify a psychological process and catalog its various manifestations.

A paraphilia emerging in childhood, he discovered, is usually the axle around which serial killing will rotate in adulthood.

RAISING CAIN: MAKING CHILDREN INTO SERIAL KILLERS

We generally believe male serial killers are "made" at a very early age, sometimes as young as four or five, when a child is experiencing a mess of instinctual sexual impulses (which he does not understand as "sexual") and simultaneously experiences some kind of traumatic event with which the sexual impulse is fused.[5] (Female serial killers also develop in childhood; however, the psychosexual component is less central to their development. There are far fewer instances of female paraphilics, and dysfunctional female child and adolescent fantasies are more focused on revenge, self-esteem, control and aggression, rather than on the sublimation of trauma and rejection into sexual violence. That's why female serial killers tend not to abduct, torture, mutilate or rape their victims unless partnered with a male serial killer.)

An obstacle to understanding this early process of "fusing" is that child sexuality under normal circumstances is a taboo subject; it is ethically and technically difficult to study in a "normal" clinical context. Childhood sexuality usually falls within the purview of clinicians when the child is dysfunctional or a victim of abuse, but the average sexual behavior and development of "normal" children mostly occurs outside

an event horizon visible to clinical observation. But some general observations can be noted: sonograms show that male fetuses experience
erections in the womb. (There is no way of determining corresponding
vasocongestion in the genitals of female fetuses.) Male infants have
erections, and children of both sexes engage instinctually with the plea-
surable sensations resulting from touching themselves and sometimes
one another.[6] This sexual instinct, at its primary subconscious childhood stage, can be shaped, hammered, guided, misguided, distorted,
traumatized, abused, misused, exploited, shamed and punished by an
array of human, cultural, religious, media, environmental and circumstantial factors.

It is a perilous world for children, and their sexual instincts can be attacked or distorted or "vandalized" by intentional or unintentional inter-
actions with other people, both their peers and adults. This "vandalism"
of the sexual instinct can sometimes come from television, a video game,
the Internet or the pages of a magazine, or in its worst and most damaging
form, from predatory sexual abuse. Most children grow up routinely
dodging psychosexual dangers, but as adults we somehow tend to forget
(or supress in our own memories) the daily sexual perils of childhood.

Any one of these minor or major disruptions of the sexual instinct
can trigger the evolution of a paraphilic state. Of the killers in the FBI
sexual homicide interview study, those reporting childhood sexual
abuse (43 percent) began to fantasize about rape at an average age of 11.6
years.[7] And trauma is not necessarily what *we as adults* might perceive
as traumatic—although often it is—but what *the child* perceives at the
time as traumatic, from parental divorce, verbal abuse or spanking, or
unintentionally glimpsing pornographic images all the way to being
beaten or raped or witnessing such acts. The degree of every trauma and
its damage is personal to the individual exposed to it.

Jerry Brudos, "Lust Killer" or "Shoe-Fetish Killer"—Oregon, 1969

One of the more dramatically simple and vivid examples of childhood
paraphilic paraesthesia in a serial killer can be found in the case of Jerry
Brudos, who murdered four women, dressed their corpses in attire he had

a fetish for, photographed them and had postmortem sex with them. He cut off and kept the foot of one of his victims in a freezer and used it to model his collection of high-heeled shoes, which he had accumulated through burglaries and by knocking women down in the street and fleeing with their shoes. He dressed another victim in his favorite heels and attempted to reanimate her with currents of electricity, causing her corpse to kick off the shoes in spasmodic convulsions that aroused him.

Brudos recalled that when he was five he found a beautiful pair of shoes in a garbage dump and brought them home. Playing on the floor, he would have observed up close his mother or other women wearing these kinds of shoes and in some way this proximity to female power excited him, although he would not have understood this at the time. In playful innocence and curiosity, and perhaps even lust, little Jerry put on the shoes to show his mother his mastery over the objects of his desire. But his mother freaked out at the sight of her son tottering about in high heels in a state of naïve pleasure. Shrieking, she admonished him for being wicked, and made a big show of burning the shoes and shaming Jerry.

A minor trauma in the scheme of things, but from that moment on, high-heeled shoes were shamefully sexualized and Brudos became saddled with a secret fetish, an infantile instinctual lust fused with loathing, anger, humiliation and submission to his mother's controlling punishment. For the rest of his life, Brudos was left trying to reconcile the living female foot with her inanimate high-heeled-shoe substitute.[8] His journey to murder and necrophilia began with his early need to mediate the sacred-sexual animate with the profane-sexual inanimate, something only death can bridge.

By itself, the high-heeled-shoes episode did not make Brudos a serial killer. He had many other issues typical of serial-killer childhoods, including a dysfunctional family and constant rejection and abuse by his mother. He also suffered the abandonment by other female figures typical of serial-killer childhoods. Unwanted by his mother, little Jerry became attached to a neighbor who treated him kindly; he fantasized that she was his real mother and found comfort in her presence, but the woman died of diabetes. He also developed a close friendship, which he described later in very sweet and tender terms, with a girl of his own age, who died of tuberculosis. These losses and a sense of abandonment deeply marked Brudos's psychology.

In first grade he was caught stealing his teacher's shoes from her desk drawer and humiliated in front of his classmates. His mother's disdain for him and other females' abandonment of him now fueled rage toward women in general, a need to control them, force them to stay with him. Come under his will.

As he progressed into puberty, his sexual development expanded his foot fetish and shoe fetish to other parts of the female figure that shamed him to anger or abandoned him to despair. Brudos branched out to stealing lingerie, tight skirts and clingy sweaters.

At the age of seventeen, Jerry Brudos crossed the danger line. He was arrested after he involved an unwilling human victim in his fetish fantasies. He forced a neighborhood girl to pose and perform sexual acts while he photographed her and beat another girl with his fists when she refused to do the same. Brudos was shunted into counseling, and allowed to graduate high school. He did not immediately reoffend, and he found gainful employment at a radio station. When he was in his twenties, he married and fathered two children and seemed to settle down. He appeared to be healed. Saved. Redeemed.

His wife later testified that Brudos was a gentle and considerate lover with her but that he insisted she dress in lacy underwear and high-heeled shoes before he could become aroused. She was happy to play along, but after the birth of their first child, his once-compliant wife found herself too busy and too fatigued for playful sex; she began refusing to "dress up" to satisfy his paraphilias. Brudos was catapulted back into his fantasy world of infantile hurt and rejection, abandoned and humiliated by yet another significant woman in his life.

In the basement and garage of their home he constructed off-limits "man caves," where he kept a growing collection of lingerie and high-heeled shoes. Sometimes he dressed up in them, posing in front of a mirror or taking photos as he compulsively masturbated to fantasies of possessing scantily clad females in high heels (as did serial killers Dennis Rader and Russell Williams).

All that remained for his paraphilia to go homicidal was some kind of trigger.

Two things happened shortly before Brudos began killing. At the radio station he was severely injured and lost consciousness in an electrocution accident that nearly killed him. Those who knew him observed that "Jerry was never quite the same after that." Whether it was the final cause of or trigger for his killing we will never know for sure. But Jerry took a heavy electric shock to the head, no question about that.

Shortly after the accident, his second child was due to be born. Brudos had planned to attend the birth in the delivery room, to hold his wife's hand and wipe her brow, but at the last minute, he was rebuffed by his wife. Once again, he felt rejected or abandoned by a significant female. Shortly after that, the killing began.

Now twenty-nine years old, close to the average age of twenty-eight when serial killers begin to kill, Brudos began abducting females and taking them to his garage and basement, murdering them and storing their corpses in the household freezer to take out and thaw to use as dress-up sex dolls before harvesting some of their body parts and dumping the rest of their remains into rivers, while his wife and children lived and played upstairs. Brudos amputated the breast of one victim and severed the foot of another victim,

A harmless fetish for high heels became deadly when a socially inept Brudos felt compelled to kill in order to harvest a foot for his collection of shoes. In this way, an ostensibly harmless fetish, like the calm eye of a storm, can center in its repression a hurricane force of swirling homicidal paraphilic compulsions.

DESTIGMATIZING "HAPPY" PARAPHILICS TODAY

The stigmatization of paraphilias that Brudos experienced growing up in the 1940s and 1950s is a frustrating notion because in the West today, so many paraphilias have become acceptable practices to be playfully enjoyed by consenting couples. Recently many paraphilias have been formally delisted as disorders requiring treatment in the fifth edition of the *Diagnostic and Statistical Manual of Mental Disorders* (*DSM-5*).

In the *DSM-5*, a paraphilia is not considered a disorder needing intervention if it causes no "distress or impairment" to the individual and if there is no coercion, harm or risk of harm to others. The *DSM-5* concludes, "A paraphilia is a necessary but not a sufficient condition for having a paraphilic disorder, and a paraphilia by itself does not necessarily justify or require clinical intervention."[9] This is the current psychiatric view of the wide new open ranges of consensual human sexuality in the context of "normal" versus "abnormal" (or in the language of the *DSM*, the *normophilic*).

In its treatment of all paraphilias, psychiatry has progressed toward the recognition of gender and sexual nonconformity by delisting from classes of disorders all distress-free, "happy" paraphilics. This reevaluation of what constitutes "abnormal" sexuality began with the delisting of homosexuality as a mental disorder from the second edition of the *DSM* in 1973.[10]

Had Jerry Brudos been reassured that his foot fetish and shoe fetish were nothing to be ashamed of—no big deal—he might not have been compelled to shamefully and secretively pursue it to the death of his objects of desire.

In summary, paraphilias can be socially constructed in childhood by the disruption of the relationship between the reptilian brain and the limbic region, caused by environmental-circumstantial cultural experiences rather than disruptions of the "natural" state of sexuality, which today we no longer securely define simply and exclusively as being for the mere purpose of reproduction.[11]

One question is, what if high-heeled shoes did not exist? Would Jerry Brudos have become a serial killer?

When we take a historical look at serial murder in later chapters, we will see how some homicidal paraphilias indeed change over time along with changing social, cultural, technological, fashion and decorative psychosexual norms.

"VANDALIZED LOVEMAPS": FROM LOVE TO LUST, FROM CHILD TO PARAPHILIC SERIAL KILLER

John William Money (1921–2006), a professor of medical psychology and pediatrics at Johns Hopkins University, proposed the "vandalized lovemap" theory of paraphilias. He focused on the clash between love and lust in Western Christian culture, between the male perceptions of the female as either "Madonna or whore" in a social and cultural construct shaped by archaic theology. Money defined a "lovemap" as the way a person navigates the dichotomy between lust and love. He wrote:

> The definitive characteristic of the sexosophy of Christendom is the doctrine of the split between saintly love and sinful lust. This doctrine is all-pervasive. It penetrates all the institutions of contemporary Christendom . . . The cleft between saintly love and sinful lust is omnipresent in the sexuoerotic heritage of our culture. Love is undefiled and saintly. Lust is defiling and sinful. Love exists above the belt, lust below. Love is lyrical. Lust is lewd. Love is heralded in public. Lust is hidden in private. Love displayed is championed, but championships for lust are condemned. Love is candid, and speaks its name. Lust is clandestine and euphemizes its name. In some degree or other, the cleavage between love and lust gets programed into the design of the lovemaps of all developing boys and girls.[12]

It explains the good husband/father/boyfriend serial killer—who is capable of sustaining a lyrical, saintly love for his wife and children while he harbors a defiling and sinful, murderous lust toward other women—like Richard Cottingham, who separated his love for his wife and two mistresses from his sadistic lust for the women he abducted, tortured, raped and murdered; or Dennis Rader, the BTK Killer, who raised a family and was a Lutheran church elder all while he stalked and killed women; or Gary Ridgway, the Green River Killer, a gainfully employed and reliable truck painter raising a family while having necrophilic sex with at least forty-nine female murder victims.

John Money described paraphilias as emerging in the form of "tragedy or trauma turned into triumph." The trauma is the defacement of a child's conventional, heterosexual—"normophilic"—lovemap by abuse or neglect or rejection or humiliation or one of the many other traumatic things that can occur in childhood; the triumph is the rescue of lust from the sexual-psychological wreckage left by the trauma and the

assignment of that lust to a new, redesigned paraphilic lovemap or fetish. Money argued:

> The new map gives lust a second chance, but at a price. The price is
> that the new map dissociates the saint from lust, and the sinner
> from love. The Madonna and whore are forever sundered, and like-
> wise the provider and the profligate. Lust belongs only to the whore
> and the profligate, love to the Madonna and the provider. The Ma-
> donna and the provider are, like Dr. Jekyll, dissociated from the
> whore and the profligate, their equivalents, respectively, of Mr.
> Hyde.[13]

In the "triumph of survival" model, Money compares paraphilic sexual addicts to people who become addicted to the danger of extreme
sports, or marathon runners who thrive on transcending their pain and
exhaustion to feed on the euphoria that the body generates to buffer the
pain.

This "survival" model complements the very popular "trauma control" model of serial-killer psychopathology. Many argue that serial
killing is not so much about sex and lust as about an extreme need for
power and control by the serial killer to compensate for their loss of
control in childhood when they were subjected to trauma or abuse.

Like Krafft-Ebing and Lombroso, John Money has fallen out of
favor; his controversial beliefs included an insistence that gender identification is learned and not innate and that pedophilia can be of a
benign, affectional type.[14]

Even though there are legions of forensic psychiatrists, psychologists, neuroscientists, physicians, profilers, criminologists and sociologists studying the question of why and how the powerful sexual
reproductive instinct is merged with the aggressive killing or feeding
instinct, we still have not entirely figured it out. While we have some
sense of the paraesthesia process, its root causes remain an elusive
mystery.

In general, there is a consensus that early-childhood traumas can
trigger an abnormal fusion of the sexual-reproductive impulse with an
ostensibly unrelated emotion or impulse—resulting in a variety of para-

philias.[15] The cause could be behavioral, or it could be environmental, or it could be genetic, or psychological, or biochemical, or a combination of all; we just don't know yet or understand how serial killers are spawned.

(For a more extensive overview of the nuances of serial-killer psychopathology, I refer the reader to my first book, *Serial Killers: The Method and Madness of Monsters*, and to the excellent sources listed at the end of this book.)

The problem with all these theories and scenarios is that millions of people have the same childhood traumas, family disorders or head injuries that serial killers do, and many even have the same dark fantasies, but only an extremely rare few act on them to become predatory serial murderers.

The final X factor that "completes" a serial killer remains elusive, and as long as it does, we should not be too hasty in discounting good, old-fashioned biblical Evil (see *Ockham's razor* in chapter ten).

FROM FANTASY TO REALITY: THE CYCLE OF ACTING OUT COMPULSIVE SERIAL-KILLING FANTASIES

While paraphilias give a conceptual structure to a serial killer's fantasies—a "signature," in profiling terminology—these fantasies on their own do not make a serial killer. Many people have transgressive fantasies without acting them out or becoming obsessed by them. In surveys of healthy college-aged males with no criminal convictions, 62 percent admitted to fantasies about having sex with a female child and 33 percent admitted they would rape a woman "if nobody would ever know and there wouldn't be any consequences."[16]

Many men are turned on by a woman wearing high heels, but they do not even imagine killing her and cutting her foot off the way Jerry Brudos did. Loving couples can engage in various degrees of "rough sex" (groping, nibbling, "love biting," scratching, hair pulling, etc.)—as Shakespeare put it, "a lover's pinch, which hurts, and is desired" (*Antony and Cleopatra*, act 5, scene 2). This kind of aggressive consensual sexual play may tap into primordial animalistic mating urges, but to actually harm one's partner is not part of it.

What makes a serial killer different is his willingness to take these aggressive urges off the playful-fantasy map and put them on the road to reality, to *literally* act them out, even if doing so injures or kills the unwilling subjects of the fantasy.

The "trauma control" model of serial homicide argues that the child not only develops paraphilias in a fusing process, but, to survive the trauma, withdraws emotionally in an attempt to control it. The child forms an emotional scar by developing what we refer to as psychopathy— a defensive emotional flatness that protects the victim from the psychological pain of trauma but results in an absence of limbic-system emotion across the board, especially a lack of empathy for others or a sense of conscience or feelings of guilt, responsibility or remorse. Psychopathy combined with fantasies of revenge and need for control, which become sexualized with puberty, can produce a raging adult serial killer.

There are some who believe that psychopathy can begin as early as infancy when a baby is not physically bonded with his mother. For example, serial killer David Berkowitz (the "Son of Sam," as he referred to himself in a letter to police) was adopted as an infant and raised by apparently loving, nurturing parents, yet he possessed an inexplicable rage that drove him as a child to kill his adoptive mother's canary.

Given up by his birth mother in a prearranged adoption, the hours-old child was torn from his first grasp of her, perhaps forcing the skittish little infant David to angrily scuttle off into the dark emotional safety of psychopathy, never finding his way out again. Fuse blown, wires melted, an irreparable microbreak in the baby's neural pathways.

Twenty-three years later, after finding his birth mother and feeling rejected by her again, Berkowitz went on a serial rampage, shooting women and happy couples on dates while sending taunting letters to the press.

The problem with the trauma-control model is that while some serial killers score highly on psychopathy tests, only a tiny minority of psychopaths become serial killers. Many psychopaths end up as successful and productive business executives, Silicon Valley entrepreneurs,

Wall Street fund managers, real-estate developers, attorneys, performing artists, Hollywood agents, television evangelists or politicians—people with careers in which a lack of empathy and concern for the feelings of others is a plus rather than a detriment. Some use their destructive hypertalents to destroy their rivals and collect salary bonuses and praise for doing so. Others crash and burn, destroying their lives and the lives of those around them with their lies, irresponsible risk-taking, double-life secrets and crimes and misdemeanors, but without murdering anybody.

The FBI sexual homicide study concluded that psychopathy is only one of many factors in the making of a serial killer. The most common characteristics of serial killers' childhoods are trauma and family instability. In adolescence, a range of sexual paraphilias combine with trauma-induced psychopathy or with one of its variants, such as sociopathy, antisocial personality disorder, and other behavioral syndromes. (The simplest explanation I've heard for the difference between psychopathy and sociopathy is that a sociopath is defined by what *he does*, a psychopath by what *he is*.) It's a diagnostic issue: a difference in opinion on the nature of the same thing between factions of psychiatrists.

Sexual abuse is not the only type of trauma experienced by serial killers as children; family dysfunction that results in feelings of abandonment is frequently reported too. It causes them to withdraw into a fantasy world in which they seek control and revenge. Often their post-traumatic psychopathy or distancing leads them to behave in a way that triggers further rejection or bullying by their peers, fueling a deepening sense of abandonment, loneliness and isolation, and retreat into violent and vengeful fantasies in which the child finds comfort and control. For a serial killer it is *all about* control.

All this is occurring at the same time as the child is developing his sexuality. While most children develop "normal" relationships with understood boundaries, the lonely "serial killer" child is excluded from this kind of interaction and becomes withdrawn and isolated in his own private fantasy world.

In that dark universe of developing hormonal sexual impulses the adolescent begins psychologically "self-medicating" with compulsive masturbation to arousing and comforting primitive, aggressive revenge and control fantasies, a powerful conditioning process often involving angry sensual interaction with increasingly fetishized dolls, erotic imagery, or fetish items—especially items of female attire, which symbolize those who wear them: the punishing and rejecting subjects of the gestating serial killer's infantile desires and angers. These objects or substitutes are often mutilated or destroyed in a child's rage, which continues to pulse and grow in the adolescent until it matures in the adult offender when that rage and destruction can dangerously shift from the inanimate fetish item to the animate female figure draped in it.

As children, serial killers sometimes subject themselves to sexualized ritual abuse before they shift the rituals to others in adulthood. Harvey Glatman, the "Glamor Girl Slayer," tied his female victims in elaborate "detective magazine" bondage poses, photographed them and then raped and strangled them. (See chapter fourteen for more on Glatman.) When he was three years old his mother discovered him tying his penis to a string attached to a bureau drawer. When he was an adolescent, his parents found him in a bathtub practicing autoerotic asphyxiation with his penis and neck tied to the faucets. When he was fourteen his parents took him to a psychiatrist after discovering rope burns around his neck. Some of the killers in the FBI sexual homicide study reported that by the age of six they had obsessions for high-heeled shoes, female underwear and rope, which as adults they incorporated into their serial-killing rituals.

Gradually as adolescents they will begin "test driving" their fantasies out in the real world. Before he began killing, Ted Bundy used to disable women's cars with no concrete motive other than to see what the victims would do. Doing so satisfied in Bundy a need to bring under control the subjects of his desire. Ed Kemper mutilated his sister's dolls before graduating to voyeurism. One day his sister teased him that he liked his schoolteacher and wanted to kiss her. Ed replied, "If I kissed her I'd have to kill her first."

Sometimes young offenders act out their fantasies by committing lesser crimes, such as setting fires or committing acts of animal cruelty (cats are most frequently targeted) or voyeurism, or through thefts of female garments or break-ins where they simply stand over a sleeping victim observing them without acting further, an act of control over the sleeping subject. Having tested their limits of excitement, they escalate; for example, they break in to stand over a sleeping victim, this time with a knife in hand. When Ted Bundy was three years old, his fifteen-year-old aunt once awoke to find little Ted slipping three butcher knives under her bedcovers.[17] Eventually the offender is no longer satisfied with the control they exert over an unaware sleeping victim and increase the level of control by plunging that knife into them and making them dead. Many of Bundy's victims were attacked and mutilated in their beds as they slept. Taking possession of a corpse—necrophilia—is the ultimate level of control. While Ted Bundy also abducted some of his victims, the actual abduction was instrumental to his "collection" of a victim he could make into a corpse to later enjoy under his control in secret remote locations where he would keep clusters of victims. (Just like the Green River Killer.) Other serial killers might thrive on the actual abduction as a means of control. Profilers will often start breaking down in that way whether a serial killer's specific actions are instrumental (MO—*modus operandi* or method of operation) or purely pathological ("signature"). (See chapter ten for more on "signature.")

So-called "facilitators" like alcohol, drugs and pornography are also used to enhance fantasy scripting and lower the inhibitions on acting fantasies out. The drug of choice for serial killers is alcohol; one recent study of sexual killers found that 64 percent were drinking at the time of their offense.[18] Other substances reported by serial killers are amphetamines, cocaine, hallucinogenics and cannabis.

Finally, there is often a trigger or "last straw" event: a firing from work, a marriage collapse, a breakup, the birth of a child, an accident, even an unintended murder (such as when a sleeping victim unexpectedly wakes up). Often the identification of a serial killer begins with a survey of stressful-event triggers in the suspect's history plotted on a timeline of homicides.

Every serial killer has a first murder, when he becomes a onetime killer, not yet transformed into a serial killer. Some bungle it on the first try and are apprehended before they can kill again, leaving behind only a serial killer's pathological "signature," but not the requisite number of victims; some of them after serving a long sentence for their first murder or even two murders are then paroled and begin killing again.

For example, serial killer Peter Woodcock (David Michael Krueger) murdered three children as a teenager and was confined to a psychiatric facility for thirty-four years until he was deemed sufficiently healed to be allowed a day pass to go to a pizzeria in town. He immediately killed and mutilated his fourth victim, a fellow inmate, on the grounds of the facility, and then went for the pizza, after which he turned himself in to the police.[19] Arthur Shawcross murdered two children in 1972, served a fourteen-year sentence and, within two years of his release, began a series of twelve necrophile murders.

Some serial killers are so troubled by their first murder that they resist committing another murder for years before a fantasy or some new trigger finally unleashes them into their serial killing spree (Jeffrey Dahmer or Richard Cottingham, for example). Others become addicted from their very first kill.

As symptoms of psychopathy seem to fade along with testosterone levels in middle age, unapprehended successful serial killers begin to kill less frequently and even stop altogether in their forties and fifties. Like Gary Ridgway or Dennis Rader, offenders can accumulate huge numbers of victims before going into retirement or semiretirement, only to be identified years later by new investigative techniques applied to decades-old evidence.

GOING SERIAL: CHASING THE "DRAGON'S TAIL" OF THE SECOND-KILL ADDICTION

The second murder is the transformational one that differentiates the "ordinary" onetime murderer from the serial killer. Ian Brady, who murdered five children in the 1960s, described his second murder as "the psychic abolition of redemption," and explained that "the second killing will hold all the same disadvantages, distracting elements of the first, but to a lesser degree. This allows a more objective assimilation of the experience. It also fosters an expanding sense of omnipotence, a wide-angle view of the metaphysical chessboard. In many cases, the element of elevated aestheticism in the second murder will exert a more formative impression than the first and probably of any in the future. It not only represents the rite of confirmation, a revelational leap of lack of faith in humanity, but also the onset of addiction to hedonistic nihilism."[20]

Paraphilias function simultaneously in the imagination as fantasies and in the reality of attempts to realize those fantasies. The attempt to express the paraphilia as perfectly as it is fantasized is highly addictive, especially when the addiction is conditioned by years of masturbatory orgasmic response. The average male serial killer begins killing around the age of twenty-eight, which means that it may take more than twenty years for deeply harbored and escalating childhood fantasies to develop into actual acts of killing.[21]

When murder, rape or mutilation is acted out, the perpetrator is frequently overwhelmed and depressed to find that this newly tasted reality is nowhere near as satisfying and comforting as the long-held fantasy had been. Thus he can become addicted to "improving" and perfecting reality to the standard of the fantasy, while at the same time feeling despondent over his inability to return to the pleasure and comfort of the fantasy before he had tasted the reality.

Over time a serial killer will attempt to develop skills and techniques to gain more control over the victim to ensure that he or she "performs" exactly like the victims in his fantasy script. For some serial killers, reducing victims to inanimate objects by killing them—"evicting them from their bodies" and "making dolls," as Edmund Kemper described his murders—is often the easiest way to gain that control. The offender might also escalate his brutality to compensate for losing the satisfaction derived from his previous fantasies.

Despite this, the serial killer can *never* achieve a reality as perfect as his fantasy. (That's why it's called "fantasy," stupid!) The perpetrator is now perennially chasing the dragon's tail of his sexual fantasy, never able to catch it. Serial killing is an addiction.

Some serial killers with no fantasy world left to retreat into, or imagination to create a new one, become sloppy and berserk and are apprehended by the police—like Ted Bundy in his final frenzied murders in Florida, or Richard Cottingham as described above, or Kenneth Bianchi, one of the Hillside Stranglers. Some serial killers just stop killing and retreat into a new parallel matrix of fantasies that might not involve murder (Albert DeSalvo, the "Boston Strangler," for example), while others vanish into the prison system for other dysfunctional offenses, commit suicide or just surrender and confess to the police, the way Ed Kemper did after killing his mother.

Some serial killers become dormant and, if DNA technology or some other break doesn't help cold-case detectives catch up to them, might never be identified. Others, of course, die before being caught. Some of the most famous unidentified serial killers are Jack the Ripper (London, 1888), the Cleveland Torso Killer (1930s) and the Zodiac Killer (California, late 1960s).

II

Serial Killer Chronicles:
The Early Forensic
History of Monsters

FOUR

The Dawn of the Less-Dead: Serial Killers and Modernity

That which surprises you so much is the daily habit of that beast; for this he lives, for this he loses sleep, for this he burns the midnight oil.

—SENECA ON CALIGULA

I thought I was doing you guys a favor . . .

—SERIAL KILLER GARY RIDGWAY, THE "GREEN RIVER KILLER," TO POLICE

Psychology alone does not explain the existence of serial killers. Many premodern serial-killing cases were circumstantial "crimes of necessity" perpetrated by so-called "comfort-hedonist" serial killers: bandits, robbers, pirates or cannibals whose primary motive was survival or material gain in an era when life was cheap and institutional law enforcement virtually nonexistent. Among the comfort-hedonist killers were notorious female poisoners who killed for personal gain, power or revenge, or at the behest of paying clients.

Closer to our current understanding of sexual-fantasy-driven serial killing, there were also cases of gratuitous, sadistic murders perpetrated by powerful tyrants and aristocrats for their personal amusement. Unlike those college-aged males who fantasized about rape "if they could get away with it," despots and tyrants *could* get away with it. Early historical serial killings that featured elements of a sexual-sadistic pathology were frequently perpetrated by individuals who had the wealth, power and leisure time to fantasize about and indulge in serial murder for pleasure and recreation. (One of the early terms used for serial killers was "recreational killers.")

For a very long time, it was a popular notion that "ordinary" male sexual serial killers did not exist until the last two centuries. Jack the Ripper stands in our imagination as the first "modern" sexual serial killer, and there are several theories to explain him, notably the urbanization and industrialization that began in the Western world around the 1750s.

SERIAL KILLING AND LEISURE

One theory about the rise of sexual serial killers goes like this: From prehistory until Western civilization became industrialized and modern, most human beings were too busy desperately seeking safety, food and shelter to think about their sexual needs and fantasies. People fantasized mostly about surviving the night. The daily priority of most humans was finding something to eat and a warm, safe place to spend the night where they wouldn't be robbed and killed.

Few had time for a "hobby" like sexual serial killing; everyone was too busy struggling not to die.

However, a rare few despots and aristocrats had the affluence and leisure time to indulge desires beyond survival, like political power, imperial expansion, sexual variety and erotica, and the patronage of artists.

For example, there are historical accounts of Roman emperors who killed for no reason other than hedonistic pleasure, like Caligula (12–41 AD) and Nero (37–68 AD); sadistic rulers like Ivan the Terrible (1530–84); and mad warlords like Vlad Drăcul, "the Impaler" (1428?–77?), who inspired Bram Stoker's *Dracula*.

Gilles de Rais, "Bluebeard" (1405–40), one of the richest men in France and Joan of Arc's battlefield companion, was accused of torturing, raping and murdering hundreds of children. Elizabeth Báthory (1560–1614), the Hungarian "Blood Countess," was accused of murdering peasant girls and bathing in their blood in the belief that doing so would restore her youthful appearance.

While they were aristocrats, what differentiates them from other sadistic tyrants is that neither Gilles de Rais nor Elizabeth Báthory had *formal* power over life and death the way Caligula might have had over his victims. Their murders were "private" criminal acts, illegal even by the feudal law under which they ruled and exercised their powers. Unlike Caligula and other imperial despots, de Rais and Báthory were arrested, put on trial, convicted and sentenced for their crimes despite their aristocratic rank (although there are good arguments made by some historians that they were both framed for reasons of power politics).[1]

These despots who were reported to revel in "hands-on" killing had the leisure time to indulge in it. They did not kill for political motives, for example, to acquire or retain power. Their killing had no practical purpose but was compulsive and committed for personal satisfaction. Many serial killers today seek exactly that kind of power over life and death that murderous tyrants had in the past. Power and control, not sexual lust, often drive serial killers, even if they express their power and control through sexual means.

THE ANCIENT ARISTOCRAT SERIAL KILLERS: BLOODLUST AND POWER

Characterizing demented despots as serial killers is not simply an exercise in hindsight. They were recognized as human monsters in their own time and condemned by their contemporaries and peers. Today we often shrug off serial killings by ancient warlords, tyrants and despots as acts of primitive power politics and assume their behavior was accepted as such in their time. Historical records show, however, that these murderers were perceived by observers in *their own times* as unusual or pathologically aberrant.

Accounts of King Herod's biblical-era murder of his wife Mariamne include accusations that he kept her corpse for seven years, during which he performed acts of necrophilia.[2] Talmudic references to "the doing of Herod" are linked to *The Last Gate*, a second-century volume in the Babylonian Talmud, which reports that Herod "preserved her body in honey for seven years. Some say that he had intercourse with

her, others that he did not. According to those who say that he had intercourse with her, his reason for embalming her was to gratify his desires."[3]

Caligula (12–41 AD)

The Roman Empire, with its crucifixions and gladiatorial "games,"
seems barbaric in many ways, but even in this society where gratuitous
killing was a popular public amusement, "private" serial killing was
condemned. Take the case of Roman emperor Gaius Caesar, "Caligula"
(12–41 AD).

Caligula was suspected of impregnating his own sister Drusilla and
then disemboweling her to prevent the birth of a child who would rival
his own divinity. But by many accounts, Caligula also tortured and
murdered dozens of victims merely for the fun of it.

The Roman statesman, philosopher and author Seneca the Younger
(4 BC–65 AD) in his essay *On Anger* (*De Ira*) described Caligula's wanton killings and condemned his obsessive impatience to torture and his
propensity (or "signature," in modern serial-killing profiling terms) for
gagging his victims as he watched them die. Seneca wrote:

Only recently Gaius Caesar slashed with the scourge and tortured . . .
both Roman senators and knights, all in one day, and not to extract
information but for amusement. He was so impatient of postponing
his pleasure—a pleasure so great that his cruelty demanded it without delay—that he decapitated some of his victims by lamplight, as
he was strolling with some ladies and senators on the terrace of his
mother's gardens . . . What was ever so unheard of as an execution
by night? Though robberies are generally concealed by darkness, the
more public punishments are, the more they offer as an admonition
and warning. But here also I shall hear the answer, "That which surprises you so much is the daily habit of that beast; for this he lives,
for this he loses sleep, for this he burns the midnight oil." But surely
you will find no other man who has commanded that the mouths of
all those who were to be executed by his orders should be gagged by
inserting a sponge, in order that they might not even have the power

to utter a cry. What doomed man was ever before deprived of the breath with which to moan? . . . If no sponges were to be found, he ordered the garments of the poor wretches to be torn up, and their mouths to be stuffed with the strips. What cruelty is this?[4]

Imagine: Caligula's cruelty (he *gagged* his victims and killed them *at night!*) was shocking in a society where serial killing was institutionalized as a spectator sport staged for thousands in huge arenas. Men being tortured to death or thrown to wild animals or forced to kill one another with exotic weapons in gladiatorial games while prostitutes plied their trade beneath the stands to customers sexually aroused by the spectacle of death and bloodletting—that's entertainment. But gagging and killing people at night? Sick! To paraphrase a line from *Apocalypse Now,* accusing Caligula of cruelty in Imperial Rome was like handing out speeding tickets at the Indy 500.

Like the cliché that Eskimos have many different words for snow, the Romans really did have a vocabulary for different states and degrees of violence and cruelty. Seneca categorized violence and torture with a functional purpose, such as crucifixion or public executions in arenas, as *crudelitas*, and considered it to be rational; it had a constructive objective, such as to prevent rebellion or to punish criminals. (The word "cruelty" has its origin in the Latin "*crudos,*" meaning "bloody" or "raw," or "unfeeling.") But gratuitous violence without profit or purpose (*compendium*), killing for its own sake, was called *feritas* ("wildness," "animal ferocity"). This violence was attributed to an irrational *ira* (anger or rage) and Seneca argued that unlimited power and luxurious affluence was an *excītum* (excitation) of *ira.**

The audience appeal of public killings concerned some observers at the time. An intoxicating excitement induced by viewing bloodshed was called *cruenta volupatate inebriabatur* ("voluptuous inebriation on cruelty").[5] Athenagoras, in *Embassy* 35, states that "seeing a man killed in the arena is much like killing him." Seneca wrote, "Throwing a man to

---

*Two thousand years later, one of the profiling systems for serial killers and rapists uses the term "anger excitation" to describe the most vicious category of perpetrators, those motivated by unbridled sadistic fantasies and impulses.

the lions is like tearing him apart with your own teeth."[6] Lactantius in *Divine Institutes* (6.20.9–14) defines the death-game spectator as a *particeps*—"participant."

It was not just the actual violence and cruelty of the "games" that concerned our ancient ancestors. They were as concerned as we are today about *simulated* violence and death in entertainment, in theater. The ancients had not yet coined a term for what we today call sadism, but back in 350 BC, the Greek philosopher Plato recorded this dialog with his former teacher Socrates, about the pleasure audiences derive from seeing people suffer in theatrical plays: "Must I remind you . . . of the pleasures mixed with pains, which we find in mournings and longings? How people enjoy weeping at tragedies? And are you aware of the condition of the soul in theater, how there also we have a mixture of pain and pleasure?"[7]

Almost exactly six hundred years later, Saint Augustine had the same concerns about joyful responses to suffering portrayed in theatrical drama. "Stage plays also captivated me, with their sights full of the images of my own miseries: fuel for my own fire. Now, why does a man like to be made sad by viewing doleful and tragic scenes, which he himself could not by any means endure? Yet, as a spectator, he wishes to experience from them a sense of grief, and in this very sense of grief his pleasure consists. What is this but wretched madness?"[8]

PREMODERN SERIAL KILLING: THE ROUTINE LIFE OF TRAUMA

According to the "leisure" theory of serial killing, ordinary people in the premodern world did not have the leisure to percolate their childhood traumas into a serial killer's rage and need for revenge and control; ordinary people didn't even have childhoods back then; children were perceived as "small adults."

Not only was there no time to brood but no social concept of "child abuse"; sexual violence, abandonment and other traumas that we today associate with the serial-killer psychology were simply facts of daily life. Everyone saw animals slaughtered for food and tortured for amusement, witches and heretics were publicly burned at the stake, criminals were tortured and executed in the public square, exposure to sex was unavoidable in communal living quarters and incest must have been ubiquitous, considering we developed deep religious proscriptions against it (along with those to rape, cannibalism, necrophilia and murder). Children routinely lost their parents to disease or violence and were themselves so often subjected to violence and rape that victims did not necessarily feel different from everybody else in the way traumatized children today might feel alienated.

SERIAL KILLING: PRINT MEDIA, INDUSTRIAL URBANIZATION AND THE "ADMINISTRATIVE STATE"

Another reason that medieval children didn't grow up to be serial killers more frequently might be that people lived predominantly in small villages and hamlets where everybody knew one another and traveling strangers were feared, suspected and closely watched. It would have been difficult to commit multiple murders without calling attention to oneself.

Or perhaps *we just don't know how many serial killers there really were*. As I and others have argued, it was so difficult to conceive of such monstrous human beings that the most gruesome crimes were attributed to monsters: werewolves, vampires or witches. We'll look at this further in chapter five.

Then we have the emergence of newspapers and the rise of literacy in the nineteenth century. These resulted in an increase in *the reporting* of human serial predators. So perhaps it wasn't that there were more serial killers but that they were made more known by the new media, which were consumed by an increasingly literate public.

At the same time newspapers were spreading reports of crime, a new modern policing system was being implemented. The first modern police force in the Western world was the London Metropolitan Police, formed in 1829. (While European cities like Paris and Berlin had "police departments," these were royal or federal paramilitary gendarmeries concerned with public order and defense of the monarch or the republic against rebellion and revolution, not crime-fighting police forces in the modern sense.) Thus, the apparent rise of serial killers in the nineteenth century, per this theory, had to do with the rise of modern state-sponsored crime-fighting institutions that had not previously existed and media reporting on them. In other words, there were not more serial killers per se, but more police to discover and apprehend them, and more newspapers to report their apprehensions.

The other part of this modernity argument is that with industrialization, the anonymity in huge new cities bursting with masses of impoverished people not only cloaked the identity of the serial killer but provided him with a large and anonymous victim pool of destitute strangers about whom nobody cared. It was one thing to kill a peasant child in an agrarian village where the entire community, kin and clan would raise an alarm: the hue and cry. It was an entirely different matter to target a resident of the teeming slums of industrial-era London, Paris, New York or Chicago, where nobody would notice or care about the victim.

With the emergence and rise of the middle classes with industrialization, there was an accompanying attitude held by them that they were surrounded by "dangerous classes"—the urban poor, unskilled industrial laborers, servant girls, gin-plague alcoholics, prostitutes, orphans, beggars, unwed mothers, vagrants and homeless.

Desperate and marginalized people were feared and loathed by the growing middle and upper classes, which is what led to the formation of police forces; they were to protect the affluent from the lower classes, not to protect the lower classes.

Jack the Ripper victimized the same kind of person despised by the property-owning middle class of his time, and which many serial killers prefer to this day: marginalized street prostitutes.

THE DAWN OF THE LESS-DEAD: "MIMETIC COMPULSION"

That classist fear and loathing of Jack the Ripper's time remains to this day, according to criminologist Steven Egger. It is not that there are more serial killers but that there are more available victims whose worth is discounted and devalued by society. Egger maintains that there is a climate today—a serial-killing ecology or culture—in which certain categories of murder victims are considered "less-dead" than others, such as prostitutes, homeless transients, drug addicts, the mentally ill, runaway youths, senior citizens, minorities, Indigenous women and the inner-city poor; these victims are all perceived by society as less-dead than, say, a white college girl from a middle-class suburb or an innocent fair-haired child. Sometimes the disappearance of these victims is not even reported. Criminologists will label them the "missing missing"[9] (see chapter thirteen).

Egger writes:

> The victims of serial killers, viewed when alive as a devalued strata of humanity, become "less-dead" (since for many they were less-alive before their death and now they become the "never-were") and their demise becomes the elimination of sores or blemishes cleansed by those who dare to wash away these undesirable elements.[10]

We popularly regard serial killers as disconnected outcasts, as those who reject societal norms, but more often the opposite is true. In killing prostitutes, Jack the Ripper was targeting the people that Victorian society chose for its most vehement disdain and scorn. As Angus McLaren observed in his study of Victorian-era serial killer Dr. Thomas Neill Cream, who murdered at least five less-dead victims (prostitutes and women coming to him seeking abortions), Cream's murders "were determined largely by the society that produced them."

The serial killer, according to McLaren, rather than being an outcast, is "likely best understood not so much as an 'outlaw' as an 'oversocialized' individual who saw himself simply carrying out sentences that society at large leveled."[11] Social critic Mark Seltzer suggests that serial killers today are fed and nurtured by a "wound culture," "the public fascination with torn and open bodies and opened persons, a collective gathering around shock, trauma, and the wound," to which serial killers respond with their own homicidal contributions in a process that Seltzer calls "mimetic compulsion."[12]

Or, as the late Robert Kennedy once put it more simply, "Every society gets the kind of criminal it deserves."[13]

As Gary Ridgway, the Green River Killer of forty-eight prostitutes, said to police after his arrest, "I thought I was doing you guys a favor, killing, killing the prostitutes. Here you guys can't control them, but I can. You can't hurt anybody. You can't; you can arrest them and put cuffs on them, might be a little bit rough on them a little bit. But you can't stop the problem. I was doing you a favor that you couldn't, you guys couldn't do."

News media is probably the single worst contributor to the "less-dead" syndrome. In the mid-1990s, the trial of William Lester Suff, who murdered thirteen women in the Lake Elsinore region of California, went virtually unreported. Suff killed drug-addicted street prostitutes and left their bodies behind strip-mall garbage dumpsters, posed so as to call attention to their drug habits. But Suff went on trial in the middle of the O. J. Simpson case. What are thirteen dead crack whores compared to two upscale victims in tennis-white Brentwood slaughtered at the hands of a celebrity? And how about Joel Rifkin, who murdered as many as seventeen prostitutes in the New York and Long Island area? The media abandoned his story to cover Colin Ferguson's massacre of six "respectably employed" suburban commuters. Joel Rifkin's trial, in which he was convicted of nine murders, wrapped up in relative obscurity despite the number of victims. We might not even know his name if an episode of *Seinfeld* had not made it a butt of jokes.[14] For the media covering serial murder, it is not the number of victims that counts anymore, but their celebrity status or credit rating—the trade-off these days is one upscale SUV in the driveway for every ten dead hookers in a dumpster.

Politicians too care less about the less-dead. When some twenty-five Indigenous women went missing in Vancouver, Canada, in the late 1990s, their families begged that the Police Board offer the same 100-thousand-dollar reward it had offered the previous month for information about a series of residential garage break-ins on the city's affluent west side. The mayor scoffed at the families' petition, saying, "Some of these girls have been missing for a year. All of a sudden . . . it becomes a major event." He wasn't financing a location service for hookers, he told the families.[15]

The Vancouver Police Department responded that they "would consider supporting 'mini-rewards' of $1,000 to the women themselves if they make their whereabouts known to police."[16] The police position was that "the women were capriciously hiding in an attempt to taunt the police and the women could be lured out by a $1,000 'reward.'"[17]

The fragmentary remains of some of the missing women were eventually found among the forty-nine victims whom Robert Pickton was later charged with killing and dismembering on his pig farm. When he was arrested in 2002, he said he was disappointed not to have made it an even fifty.

SERIAL-KILLER MODERN MOBILITY AND URBANIZATION

For some time, there was a theory that the surging rate of serial murder in the United States in the post–World War II years had to do with the unique ubiquity of the American automobile, which increased the mobility of serial killers, freeing them to roam across jurisdictions to kill with anonymous impunity. The FBI's Highway Serial Killings Initiative, launched in 2009 to investigate more than five hundred unsolved homicides linked to interstate freeways, appeared to confirm this sense of the US highway system "circulating" serial killers like bad blood in the body of the American nation. But despite the number of unsolved homicides along the highways, the stereotypical image of the highly mobile "drifter" serial killer is a myth. The reality is scarier: 74 percent of serial killers stay close to home, killing in the comfort of their own state.[18] They are more likely to be your neighbor than a drifter.

Essayist and environmentalist Ginger Strand challenged the theory that the interstate highway system increased the number of serial killers by giving them easy mobility and anonymity.[19] Strand argues that the freeways, especially because of the way they were built in the 1950s and 1960s through lower-income neighborhoods, have indeed contributed to rising serial murder—not by mobilizing killers, but by increasing the less-dead victim pool. The freeways' construction destroyed inner-city communities and scattered people into soulless and degrading public-housing ghettos. Strand writes, "In its first decade [1956–1966], the interstate highway program destroyed some 330,000 urban housing units across the nation, the majority of them occupied by minorities and the poor. After that the pace picked up. No one knows the exact number, but estimates are that the highway program displaced around a million Americans."[20] This had dual consequences; the displacement of poor and minority communities created a pool of less-dead victims, while the chaos and degradation destabilized families and spawned serial killers.

Strand recounts how a thriving and prosperous Bronx was destroyed in the 1950s when vibrant low-income neighborhoods were razed to make way for the Cross Bronx Expressway and its dispossessed residents were packed into high-rise public-housing ghetto complexes. In Atlanta too, the vital and prosperous Auburn Avenue neighborhood known as Sweet Auburn, pronounced by *Forbes* magazine in the 1950s "the richest negro street in the world," was ripped apart by an elevated interstate freeway in 1966. Vibrant African-American-owned neighborhood businesses, cultural institutions, churches and family homes were destroyed, forcing low-income residents into bleak, anonymous, high-density public-housing complexes.[21]

The expropriation and destruction of Sweet Auburn to connect Interstate 20 would give serial killer Wayne Williams his vast victim pool of vulnerable children a decade later. Strand writes, "I-20 would play a key role in Atlantans' understanding of why, in the late seventies, their children began to disappear."[22]

The destruction of families and communities wrought by the building of highways through the hearts of poor and minority communities in New York, Miami, New Orleans, Detroit, Chicago, Nashville, Boston, Atlanta, Los Angeles and other cities, along with the crack cocaine epidemic of the 1990s, took its toll and is still taking it. Devastated, broken and degraded families produce serial killers.

The several-decades-long process of destroying inner-city minority communities and families has produced a viral new pool of both serial killers and victims. While in the past serial killers were thought to be predominantly white males, today Eric Hickey's survey shows that from 2004 to 2011, 57 percent of all serial killers were African-Americans; while the Radford/FGCU Serial Killer Database indicates that in the 2010s, almost 60 percent of serial killers are African-Americans[23] (this even though African-Americans make up only 13.2 percent of the American population).[24]

It is true that the overall murder rate has dropped significantly since the 1990s, but I wouldn't feel too optimistic. Between the job losses and financial stresses on family life caused by the global recession of 2008 and the unceasing horror and death of the War on Terror that our young sons and daughters are called upon to wage before returning home to raise families, we should not anticipate any long-term reduction in serial killing as this current generation of children mature toward that average age of twenty-eight when serial killers first kill.

FIVE

Lupina Insania:
Criminalizing Werewolves
and Little Red Riding Hood
as Victim, 1450–1650

They are aware of the pleasure they experience when as
wolves . . .

—JEAN BODIN, *DEMONOMANIA OF WITCHES* (1580)

Species non mutatur. (The species never changes.)

—CLAUDE PRIEUR, *DIALOG ON LYCANTHROPY* (1596)

Even before industrialization, serial killing was not the exclusive pre-
rogative of affluent aristocrats as once thought; in fact, there were plenty
of ordinary shopkeeper, artisan, peasant and vagrant serial killers too.
And despite the urbanization theory, we will see that serial-killer cases
occurred in both urban and rural settings.

A thousand years before Jack the Ripper, the Anglo-Saxon epic
poem *Beowulf* featured a serial killer as its antagonist, according to
Brian Meehan's essay "Son of Cain or Son of Sam? The Monster as Serial
Killer in *Beowulf*." Meehan argues that the *sceadugenga* ("shadow
walker," "dark walker," "moor stalker," "night goer") named Grendel in
Beowulf is a serial killer who is targeting vulnerable warriors passed out
from too much drinking.

Like trusting coeds, like prostitutes who enter strangers' cars, these warriors have a weakness, a vulnerability the murderer exploits. Every night they drink themselves insatiable and when Grendel comes they lie as passive before him as any dozing victim of Richard Ramirez or young male handcuffed by Wayne Gacy. Further, Grendel murders for the sake of murder . . . When he murders, he enjoys inflicting humiliation and pain, violating the human body by gutting and eating it; like Jeffrey Dahmer and his brother-in-fiction Hannibal Lecter . . . Like Albert DeSalvo, he has a bizarre reverence for the people he kills and the places where he kills them.[1]

Nonetheless, recognizable serial killers are sparse in the historical record until about the mid-1400s. It was during the Renaissance that serial killers began appearing in judicial records, at an annual apprehension rate almost comparable to the per capita rate of serial killers in the modern United States. As many as 300 serial killers were put on trial in Europe in the 200 years between 1450 and 1650.[2] (For comparison, in the United States there were 431 serial killers in the 204 years between 1800 and 2004 according to Eric Hickey's data.)[3] Except they were not called serial killers back then. The serial killers were arrested, charged and tried as werewolves or lycanthropes, at the time a newly introduced ecclesiastical crime punishable by death.

To understand better some of the sociohistorical dynamics of how we came to define serial killers in modern times and the mystery of their surging appearance during the so-called serial-killer epidemic in the 1970s and '80s, along with the rise of the FBI's Behavioral Sciences Unit, ViCAP and a type of serial-killer-apprehension "industry," we can take a closer look at the rise of the "serial werewolf epidemic" and the related witch-hunting "industry" from 1450 to 1650, which in some ways foreshadowed the recent serial-killer epidemic.

THE WEREWOLF OR LYCANTHROPE

"Lycanthrope" comes from the Greek "lykánthropos" (lykos, "wolf"; and anthrōpos, "man"). "Wer" is an old Anglo-Saxon word for "man" (from the Latin "*vir*," or "male" [see: "virile"]); thus "werewolf" in English. The earliest recorded use of the term "werewolf" in the Anglo-Saxon world goes back to the year 1000 AD as a synonym for the Devil in the *Ecclesiastical Ordinances* of King Cnut.[4]

The notion that animals can become evil or be possessed by evil spirits or the Devil, and that humans can in turn be possessed by those evil animal spirits once bitten by them, or transform or shape-shift into savage animal-monster predators willingly through rituals, pacts with the Devil or magic devices, or unwillingly by a curse or magic spell, is common to many cultures around the world throughout history.[5] In ancient Greece werewolves were known as *veykolakas* ("wolf skinned"), and in ancient Rome the term was "*versipellis*," meaning "turned skin." Later in France werewolves become known as *loup garou*, in Italy *lupo mannaro*, in Portugal *lob omen*, in Spain *hombre lobo*, in Germany *werewolf*; in Russia *volkolak* ("wolf-skinned one"), in Poland *wilkołak* and in the Balkins *vukodlak*; and in Arabic *qutrub* ("cucubuth"). In regions where there were no wolves other predatory animals were substituted: weretigers in India; wereleopards, werelions, werehyenas and werejackals in Africa; werefoxes in China and Japan.[6] Werewolf beliefs are described among the Navajo as late as the 1940s.[7]

The history of the belief in werewolves and their link to acts of rape, mutilation, murder, and cannibalism is a long and circular one, going back to the Greek myths of Lycaon, the king of Arcadia, who was changed into a wandering wolf as punishment for secretly attempting to feed sacrificial human flesh to the god Zeus. Greek myths tell the story of the inhabitants of Parnassus who were led by a pack of howling wolves to a mountaintop where they established a new city, Lycorea. According to the myth, the Parnassians practiced "Lycaon's Abomination," a ritual in which a child is sacrificed and its intestines made into a stew eaten by shepherds, one of whom would then turn into a werewolf condemned to wander for eight years, regaining his humanity only if he refrained from eating human flesh.[8] (Contrary to popular myth, the term "lycanthrope" is not derived from mythical king Lycaon, but from "*lykos*," the similarity in names apparently a confusing coincidence.)[9]

In his 1948 book on the nature of sadism, *Man into Wolf: An Anthropological Interpretation of Sadism, Masochism and Lycanthropy* (in which is found one of the earlier uses in English print of the term "serial killings"), Robert Eisler argued that the ancient werewolf myths, along with the phenomena of sadism and cannibal lust serial killing, are primordial memorial artifacts in our triune brains lingering on from the transformation of humans from their original vegetarian state to a carnivorous one as well, occurring perhaps as late as the last ice age, which fully receded only about 15 to 22 thousand years ago.[10]

It's an interesting theory. There is certainly a persuasive range of evidence today that, physiologically, humans are not naturally equipped to hunt and eat meat, since we lack actual canine teeth (we only call them that) and have clawless hands, more suitable for picking fruit or vegetation than for taking down, killing and tearing into wild game. Humans have long intestines unlike the typically short intestines of carnivores, which quickly expel "rotting meat" from their digestive tracts.[11] All this suggests that we are not naturally omnivorous meat eaters, and according to Eisler, that screws up our psyches today. We saw in chapter two how in times of famine and crisis, primitive vegetarian hominids from *Homo erectus* and *Homo neanderthalensis* to *Homo sapiens* turned to hunting and eating meat and even resorted to cannibalism if necessary (we did not develop agriculture until about ten to fifteen thousand years ago).

Eisler argued that before the last ice age receded, humans in cold climates with insufficient vegetation and berries to gather and eat became predatory carnivores, clothing themselves in animal skins for warmth and sometimes cannibalizing one another when animal prey became scarce. Eventually these fur-clad human predators migrated south to temperate regions like furry monsters—werewolves or turn-skinned *versipellises*—where they encountered gentle, still-vegetarian humans and attacked, raped, killed and sometimes ate them. These furry killers were not exclusively males either. Eisler writes of the erotic draw of the "Venus in Fur" theme in Western art and literature as representing

> . . . the nude bloodstained maenad or "raving woman" in her bear, lynx or fox-pelt, coursing with her furiously excited male partners in the pack of the Wild Hunter through the primeval forests, vying with them in bloodlust when they came "in at the death" and finally assuaging in a wild embrace their common, mad excitement after

the omophagic orgy, feasting on the live, raw and bloody meat of the quarry.[12]

Eisler ventured that sadism in humans is an artifact of the survival-hunting impulse and compares it to cats that sometimes toy with and maul a captured bird or mouse without necessarily eating it. Indeed, the FBI's sponsored study *Sexual Homicide: Patterns and Motives* confirms that some sadistic serial killers were triggered and aroused to attack and kill mindlessly like predatory animals by the sight of their victims attempting to flee.[13] For example, serial killer Robert Christian Hansen, the "Butcher Baker" who murdered between seventeen and twenty-one women in Alaska from 1972 to 1983, would fly his female victims in his small plane out to his remote hunting cabin as "guests," then force the women to run naked through the wilderness as he sadistically hunted them down. It was all about the pleasure of the hunt, rather than of the kill.

The fur-clad-animal werewolf myth was imprinted in our collective unconscious, along with an incipient penchant for pursuing, overcoming, killing, raping and cannibalizing human prey. This sadistic impulse in humans today is like an obscure error in a line of DNA code in our primitive brain that becomes "buggy" in civilized societies and triggers in some the emergence of a viral serial killer (as with obesity as described in chapter two).

The Ancients on Werewolves

We assume that our ancestors were ignorant, believing that the world was flat and that witches float when thrown into water and that possession by the Devil and demons or transformation into wolves explained acts of what appeared to be motiveless murder. And perhaps illiterate peasants generally believed those things. But the educated elites among our ancestors were not all *that* dumb. As early as 500 BC, a thousand years before Columbus, the Greek mathematician Pythagoras was arguing that the earth is spherical, not flat.[14] And likewise, many ancient thinkers and academics were sensibly arguing that werewolves, vampires and other monsters were figments of our imagination, delusions or symptomatic of diseases or organic disorders.

In the early part of the first thousand years of Christianity in the Western world, theologians rejected and condemned what they saw as ancient pagan werewolf beliefs. In his *De Anima* (*On the Soul*), one of the early Christian church fathers, Tertullian (Quintus Tertullianus c. 155–220 AD), argued that it was impossible for the human soul to pass into animals and that people might "behave like an animal" but not actually transform into one. Saint Ambrose (339–97 AD) insisted that the idea of lycanthropy was nonsense and a product of "invented stories."[15]

According to early Christian theology, only God has the kind of transformative power to make man into a beast. The Devil, at best, could only deceive humans into believing that they had been transformed into witches, werewolves or other monstrous creatures. In the fifth century, Saint Augustine explained in his *City of God*:

> The demons can accomplish nothing by their natural power . . . except what God may permit . . . And indeed the demons, if they really do such things as these on which this discussion turns, do not create real substances, but only change the appearance of things created by the true God so as to make them seem to be what they are not.[16]

By 787 AD Emperor Charlemagne decreed that a belief in witches was a stupid superstition and that the burning of accused witches was a pagan custom and he outlawed it. To burn a witch was a crime akin to murder.[17] By the year 1000 AD the Christian canon law books, the *Canon Episcopi* (*Capitulum Episcopi*) declared the belief in werewolves, witches and sorcerers and other supernatural monsters not only nonsense, but unchristian as well, a heresy punishable by ten days of penance on bread and water.[18] The *Canon Episcopi* went on to specifically condemn as heretics (infidels) anyone believing in the literal existence of werewolves, witches, demons or monsters:

> Whoever therefore believes that anything can be made, or that any creature can be changed to better or to worse or be transformed into another species or similitude, except by the Creator himself who made everything and through whom all things were made, is beyond doubt an infidel.[19]

In the Christian theology of the Middle Ages, other than to deceive and trick people, the Devil could do nothing without God's permission. The alleged power of Satan had become so degraded by 1400 that he was no longer regarded with horror and revulsion but had become instead the familiar curly-tailed red cartoon figure, a trickster at his worst.[20]

Authorities were still executing people for performing sorcery or witchcraft, both women and men, but not as supernatural, superpowered beings themselves, like broomstick-flying witches, a subtle but important distinction. The crime was known as *maleficium*—causing harm by the use of occult means—and was thought to be perpetrated by mortal men and women, akin to using poison today. The word itself literally meant "mischief" or "wrongdoing" and appears in Anglo-American legal language today as "malfeasance"—a willful act intended to do harm. In other words, one could perform witchcraft and be punished for it without being a supernatural witch. Witchcraft was perceived as a criminal act performed by ordinary human beings.[21]

When it came to werewolves, it was not just priests, monks and theologians who declared lycanthropy nonsense; Byzantine physicians one after another from the fifth to the seventh centuries argued that a belief in lycanthropy was itself a diagnosable delusional mental disorder, a form of melancholy or a disease. Paul of Aegina (620–90 AD), for example, wrote in his *On Medicine*:

> Those suffering from lycanthropy go out during the night imitating wolves in all things, and lingering about tombs until morning. You may recognize these persons by these marks; they are pale, their vision feeble, their eyes dry, tongue very dry and the flow of the saliva stopped; but they are thirsty, and their legs have incurable ulcerations from frequent falls. Such are the symptoms of the disease. You must know that lycanthropy is a species of melancholy.[22]

The terms "clinical lycanthropy"; *lycomania*; *lupine insania*; *mania lupine*; "wolf man syndrome" or *insania zooanthropica* to this day refer to a rare psychiatric disorder in which a subject believes himself or herself to have been transformed into a wolf or another savage animal. Clinical lycanthropy is differentiated from lycanthropy, which is defined as an occult belief in the supernatural transformation or shape-shifting of humans into wolves or other animals. (Although "*lycos*" specifies "wolf," the term "lycanthropy" is generally applied to the metamorphosis of humans into any animal. Such general metamorphosis can be more accurately called zoanthropy or reverse intermetamorphosis.)

There was a period in the nineteenth and early twentieth centuries when it was believed that clinical lycanthropy was waning, as very few people believed in werewolves anymore, but the resurgent prevalence of werewolves in modern literature and film fueled a corresponding recent resurgence of cases of clinical lycanthropy, which is associated symptomatically with a class of schizophrenic psychosis disorders, or with delusional misidentification of the "self."[23] (In some medical literature, the use of the street drug MDMA—XTC or ecstasy—has been linked to a resurgence of clinical lycanthropy.)[24]

Werewolves had been so rationalized and medicalized by the year 1000 that they became subject to a medieval type of "heroin chic" romanticism in literature, in which they were frequently portrayed as attractive, lonely, suffering, victimized, self-sacrificing, chivalrous heroes in fictional and mythological tales emerging during the Grail romance era. The "chivalrous werewolf" narratives often feature a noble knight or prince who transforms into a werewolf to protect the subject of his romantic love, but while he is a werewolf she betrays him by stealing his transformative device—either a potion, a ring, a belt or his clothes—trapping him forever in his lovelorn werewolf state.[25]

People in the West during the Middle Ages were well on the way to accomplishing a harmoniously rational vision of a godly world without Satan and monsters in it, and as the Renaissance—the "rebirth" of knowledge, culture and humanism—began to dawn in the fourteenth century, one would have expected that the newly "reborn" Church and society would now reach even greater heights of knowledge and harmony. We even invented a printing press to spread liberating knowledge to the people! Unfortunately, history never does what we expect it to. The Renaissance brought knowledge and great art but also paranoia, death, disorder, continental warfare, the Great Witch Hunt and our first recorded serial-killer epidemic in the form of a surge of werewolf cases.

UNITY IN CRISIS AND THE CRIMINALIZATION
OF THE WEREWOLF

The transformation of the "chivalrous werewolf" into a serial-killing monster occurred as part of the so-called Great Witch Hunt of 1450 to 1650, when thousands of women were systematically tortured, raped and killed in witchcraft prosecutions, which it is not an exaggeration to characterize as a Church- and state-sponsored campaign of serial murder (see chapter six).

Witch hunts, whether for witches and werewolves or for Jews, Jacobites, republican antimonarchists, anarchists, communists, gays, illegal immigrants, Islamist terrorist sleepers or even serial killers, frequently occur in societies where elites become divided and insecure.

Witch hunts are directed at unifying elites to homogeneously lead the masses under the guise of an urgent and immense threat that discounts a previous plurality of free thought and liberty: for example, the post-9/11 notion that we now need to sacrifice some of our deeply held beliefs in individual liberty and privacy in the name of collective security against terrorism. It is not reaching too far to compare our current fear of terrorists with our past fear of witches. For example, the chance of an American being killed by a terrorist is an extraordinarily unlikely 1 in 20 million, compared to being killed in a car accident (1 in 19 thousand), drowning in their own bathtub (1 in 800 thousand), or being struck by lightning (1 in 1.5 million), yet society is in an acute state of anxiety over the terrorist "threat."[26] It's not about logic but perception. Witch hunts tend to publicly focus on threats that cannot be easily explained or demonstrated, as a substitute for or diversion from what might actually be dividing the elites at the time.

What was dividing the educated European elites in the 1400s? Religion and the unity of the all-powerful Church in Rome. In Western Europe, there was only one Church that could make or unmake kings: the Catholic Church. You did not become king unless the Papacy blessed your reign. As a kingmaker, the Church faced numerous secular power challenges to its primacy from alternative antipopes to outright new Christian movements that would eventually culminate with the birth of a rival Protestant Church in 1517.

Elites became divided over which faction of Christianity they would adhere to and support and seek sanctification of their thrones from. With the introduction of Gutenberg's printing press in the 1450s, a phenomenon comparable to the introduction of the Internet in the 1990s, suddenly all these divisive religious issues and debates went viral among the literate elites. The elites who were showered in a mass of "alternative" facts and evidence needed to be quickly reined in and unified behind the Church in Rome against an internal threat perhaps greater than the issue of its own corruption: the division of the Church.

The Church now called upon the elites to unify behind it in a great war—a Christian *jihad* or internal crusade—a war that the Church claimed it had always been fighting against the Devil and the Devil's foot soldiers: hidden sleeper cells of heretics, witches, sorcerers, demons, vampires and werewolves, all working in partnership with the Devil.[27] Suddenly the Devil, who was just a funny little trickster, was now given all these new powers, a kind of satanic Osama bin Laden masterminding witchcraft, the occult and the making of monsters.

In a Patriot Act–like papal bull (decree) issued on December 5, 1484, the pope called upon ecclesiastical and civil authorities everywhere to forget their differences and cooperate with contractor Church inquisitors and demonologists in their war on witches, monsters and heresy, guided by the Dominican inquisitor Heinrich Kramer, who would issue a notoriously misogynist manual for witch-hunting called *Malleus Maleficarum* (*The Witches' Hammer*).

Full of theological errors and contradictions, the book explained the chaos of religious dissent by blaming it on the Devil's "terrorists": witches and werewolves. Printed in fourteen editions between 1486 and 1520, the *Malleus Maleficarum* in some parts of Europe would become a handbook for inquisitors, prosecutors and judges.[28]

The *Malleus Maleficarum* claimed that, along with witches, werewolves literally existed through pacts with the Devil, who Kramer maintained had greater powers granted to him by God than the Church previously was willing to admit. Disagreeing with the general wisdom of the time, Kramer argued that human beings could never be certain about reality; any phenomenon could be different from what it appeared to be and could be a demonic illusion. In contrast to previous thought, which denied the reality of demons, Kramer denied the reality of reality.[29] A lot of people were going to die for this now.

Kramer double-talked his way around the proscriptions the Church imposed against beliefs in lycanthropy and argued that either werewolves were real wolves possessed by demons or they were humans who were bewitched by the Devil to believe they had the prowess and ferocity of werewolves:

> Thus, as to the question of whether they are true wolves or demons in forms that appear this way, one says that they are true wolves but are possessed or impelled by demons in two different ways. One way is without the working of sorcerers . . . These things happen through an illusion on the part of demons when God is punishing some nation on account of its sins. The other way is also an illusion on the part of sorcerers. For instance . . . a story about a certain man who thought that he was turned into a wolf at specific times when he was lurking in caves. He entered these caves at a specific time and while he remained fixed there, he imagined that he became a wolf and went around devouring children. Since in reality it was merely a demon possessing a wolf that was doing this, he falsely thought while dreaming that he himself was going around. He remained deranged in this way until he was found lying in the forest hallucinating.[30]

Some civil authorities were hostile to this new faction of church demonologists, and dragged their feet on prosecuting those charged with being witches or werewolves. Had not the *Canon Episcopi* declared the belief in creatures like witches and werewolves heresy? Kramer wrote that perhaps it was a heresy instead to obstinately deny the existence of witches and werewolves.[31]

Since the witch-hunting craze was a result of a schism in the Catholic Church, one would have hoped that the schismatic Protestants would have rejected it. But both Catholics and Protestants turned to witch-hunting as a means of cultivating unity, adding each other's religion to the list of capital offenses as they embarked on the Thirty Years' War (1618–48), in which Catholics and Protestants slaughtered each other, leaving behind at least eight million dead.

I don't want to suggest that Heinrich Kramer's kooky procedural manual *Malleus Maleficarum* defining witches in 1486 was anything like John Douglas, Robert Ressler and Ann Burgess's *Sexual Homicide: Patterns and Motives* defining serial killers in 1988, but it was in a way. While *Malleus Maleficarum* was lunatic raving and *Sexual Homicide* was a scholarly study (albeit statistically problematic with only thirty-six murderers as subjects), both works functioned as "manuals" to explain preexisting pandemic aberrant social phenomena that had not been systematically categorized or incorporated into any forensic system until their publication. In the same way that *Sexual Homicide* became a procedural manual for profiling serial killers, *Malleus Maleficarum* became a procedural manual for profiling witches and werewolves. The difference of course being that while *Sexual Homicide* described a phenomenon that actually existed—serial killers—*Malleus Maleficarum* described a fantasy phenomenon that did not exist—witches and werewolves. But historically the two books functioned in similar ways.

THE SERIAL LYCANTHROPE TRIALS

Both real wolves and fantasy werewolves for centuries had been blamed whenever a child or a woman was found mutilated or cannibalized, but they were rarely systematically investigated, policed or prosecuted. Frequently these cases occurred on the outskirts of villages, the victims either traveling to a market or tending sheep or working in the field on the edge of forests, but out of sight of the village proper. There were no police to investigate these deaths and no forensic sciences to discern the nature of the wounds and deaths. Each community or local feudal authority dealt with such cases in its own way.

The Church in the 1450s stepped into this patchwork of jurisdictions and declared that contrary to previous thought, monsters like witches and werewolves not only existed but were an ecclesiastical crime, and that civil authorities were now obligated to enforce and punish it on behalf of the Church's inquisitorial courts. Werewolves and witches became legally an existing phenomenon, profiled and criminalized by the *Malleus Maleficarum* as a Devil's instrument and pursued, investigated, judged and punished by a combination of ecclesiastical and secular authorities.

We know today that nonrabid wolves rarely attack people, and it is easy for us to imagine in the past a migratory serial killer pouncing on victims at random and mutilating them in a bloodlust, perhaps even in a psychotic state, imagining that he is a werewolf. These delusional (or "visionary") psychotic-schizophrenic serial killers suffering from an organic mental disease exist, like Richard Chase, the "Vampire of Sacramento," who murdered and grotesquely mutilated five people from 1977 to 1978, and Herbert Mullin, the "Die Song Killer," who killed and mutilated thirteen people in Santa Cruz from 1972 to 1973 in the belief that his "sacrifices" would prevent earthquakes.

Two things happened in the 1400s. Werewolves, witches and other monsters were defined and criminalized by *Malleus Maleficarum*, and a bureaucracy and "industry" to investigate, pursue, arrest, punish and exterminate those monsters arose: a type of "police." Simultaneously we begin to see werewolves appear before the court system now mandated to prosecute this new menace to Christendom. Increasingly the accusations will now begin to appear in historical court records.

These trials of werewolves that today we easily recognize as very mortal serial killers began to occur during the 1450–1650 witchcraft prosecutions. I believe that these serial killers existed earlier, but that either they rarely reached a formal trial, the trial records did not survive, or, especially in the pre–printing press era, the popular accounts of their cases were not mass-produced and distributed. Accounts of medieval serial killers might still be sitting somewhere, waiting to be discovered among rare handwritten manuscripts in some monastery. Until the printing press, very selective historical records were kept.

Also, prior to *Malleus Maleficarum* serial killers would not have been formally prosecuted as werewolves, since it was a heresy to believe in werewolves. Until the witch hunt began, there was no systematic, proactive policing mechanism in the European world. There were no police departments or prosecutorial agencies in the way there would be a systemic and organized inquisitorial witch-hunting investigative machinery pursuing heretic suspects, collecting evidence and bringing the accused before ecclesiastical courts. Courts of justice and proactive law enforcement in the premodern world concerned itself mostly with crimes against the king and his landholding aristocracy, against public order, against encroachments on the rights and property of the elite landowners and failure to remit taxes.

Crimes like murder or rape among peasants, which did not challenge authority, disturb public order or disrupt property interests and taxation, were handled in the community in which they occurred, often through vigilante justice or vendetta or blood-money settlements, outside a formal court system—or at best by the local feudal lord's arbitrary authority. Prior to the 1450s, serial killers if identified and captured were probably lynched or pitchforked to death by the community without much judicial procedure.

But with the rise of the witch hunt we see a spate of serial-killer trials suddenly appear in the historical record, including those of the infamous aristocrats Gilles de Rais in 1440 and Elizabeth Báthory in 1611, both of their trials initiated with accusations of witchcraft and black magic and only secondarily associated with charges of multiple murder.[32] But it wasn't just aristocrats who were brought before the courts. There was a significant number of commoners charged with these "recreational" crimes as well.

Compared with the witch trials described in the next chapter, werewolf trials were rarer, but the defendants are very recognizable today as typical serial killers. There were at least 300 werewolf trials in western Europe between 1450 and 1650 (compared with 40 thousand to 100 thousand witch trials) and although not all the trial records survived, among some of the ones that did the accused have a remarkably familiar modern pathology. Here, for example, to start with, is a relatively well-known case (among historians who study serial killers) of a werewolf in Germany in 1589 that could easily describe a modern-day serial killer like John Wayne Gacy.

Peter Stubbe, "Werewolf of Bedburg"—Germany, 1589

Peter Stubbe (or Peeter Stübbe, Peter Stumpf, Peter Stump) in Bedburg, Germany, perpetrated eighteen serial murders, raping, killing, mutilating and cannibalizing his victims, all in the same community where he lived. Arrested in 1589, Stubbe was accused of making a deal with the Devil to acquire powers to transform himself into a werewolf to satisfy his obsession for fame and celebrity and his depraved sexual lusts.

The trial was reported in an early example of popular true-crime literature, a pamphlet printed in 1590 and translated into English and widely distributed throughout Europe at the time.[33]

> [Peter Stubbe] . . . from his youth was greatly inclined to evil and the practicing of wicked arts even from twelve years of age till twenty . . . gave both soul and body to the Devil forever, for small carnal pleasures in this life, that he might be famous and spoken of on earth.

Stubbe appeared to be a functioning member of the community:

> He would go through the streets in comely habit, and very civilly, as one well known to all the inhabitants thereabout, and often times he was saluted by those whose friends and children he had butchered, though not suspected for the same . . .
>   Within the span of a few years, he had murdered thirteen young children, and two goodly young women pregnant with child, tearing the children out of their wombs, in most bloody and savage ways, and after ate their hearts panting hot and raw, which he accounted dainty morsels and best agreeing to his appetite.

Stubbe, it was reported, had even raped and impregnated his daughter and then murdered and cannibalized her child.

As every successful true-crime narrative calls for a motive, Stubbe's murders are attributed to a pact with the Devil, in which he was given a magic belt (or girdle) that when worn would transform him into a werewolf in whose guise he could enjoy his bloodlust.

Conveniently as he was escaping the scene of his latest murder with hunters closely behind him in pursuit, Stubbe . . .

> . . . slipped his girdle from about him, whereby the shape of a wolf clean avoided, and he appeared presently in his true shape and likeness, having in his hand a staff as one walking toward the city. But

the hunters, whose eyes were steadfastly bent upon the beast, and seeing him in the same place metamorphosed contrary to their expectation, it wrought a wonderful amazement to their minds; and, had it not been that they knew the man so soon as they saw him, they had surely taken the same to have been some Devil in a man's likeness; but for as much as they knew him to be an ancient dweller in the town, they came unto him, and talking with him, they brought him by communication home to his own house, and finding him to be the man indeed, and no delusion or fantastical notion, they had him brought before the magistrates to be examined.

The pamphlet concludes that Stubbe was condemned on October 18, 1589 . . .

. . . judged first to have his body laid on a wheel, and with red hot burning pincers in ten different places to have the flesh pulled off from the bones, after that, his legs and arms to be broken with a wooden ax or hatchet, afterward to have his head struck from his body, then to have his carcass burned to ashes.

This pamphlet is probably the earliest unambiguous historical account of an "ordinary" serial killer in the sense that we have of serial killers today. Stubbe is living as a prominent and respectable citizen in the community he is secretly victimizing, just like serial killer John Wayne Gacy, who was a successful contractor and "good neighbor" who had the honor to host the first lady Rosalynn Carter on her visit to Chicago. Typical of serial killers, Stubbe is reported as "inclined to evil" from the age of twelve to twenty.

Pierre Bourgot and Michel Verdung—France, 1521

A less certain account is of Pierre Bourgot and Michel Verdung, the Werewolves of Poligny, who were executed in 1521. They were supposedly a pair of serial-killer werewolves who, thanks to a pact with the Devil, transformed into homicidal creatures. The two of them killed a random woman (or child, in other accounts) gathering peas in her garden, murdered and ate a four-year-old girl, killed another girl and drank her blood and ate parts of her neck, and killed a fourth girl, aged eight or nine. Bourgot confessed that he "had broken her neck with his teeth because she had once refused his request for alms; and as soon as he had done the awful deed, he begged then and there for alms in honor of God."[34]

Gilles Garnier—France, 1574

Gilles Garnier was convicted for multiple murders committed while he was allegedly a werewolf in France in 1574. The case report reads:

> The said Garnier on the day of Saint Michael, being in the form of a werewolf took a young girl ten or twelve years old near the woods of Serre, in the vineyard of Chastenoy a quarter of a league from Dole, and there he killed and butchered her, as much with his hands in the semblance of paws as with his teeth, and ate the flesh of her thighs and arms, and had carried some to his wife. And for having taken another girl, and killed her to eat her, if he hadn't been prevented by three people, as he has confessed. And fifteen days later, for having strangled a young child ten years old in the vineyard of Gredisans, and eaten the flesh of his thighs, legs, and belly. And since then for having killed, while in the form of a man, and not that of a wolf, another boy twelve to thirteen years old, in the woods of the village of Perouse, with the intention of eating him, if he hadn't been prevented from doing so, as he confessed without being forced or coerced. He was condemned to be burned alive, and the sentence was carried out.[35]

"Werewolf or Demon Tailor of Chalon"—France, 1598

A case of an unnamed urban, community-functioning "werewolf" similar to Peter Stubbe was reported in 1598 in Chalon, France. The trial records of the sixteenth-century Jeffrey Dahmer–like serial killer have not survived, allegedly destroyed by authorities because of its obscene content. The name of the defendant was destroyed along with the court records in a process of *Damnatio memoriae* ("condemnation of memory"), but fragmentary surviving sources describe the offender as a tailor who lured children into his shop, where he raped them, slit their throats and then "powdered and dressed" their corpses and ate them.

When his shop was raided, authorities discovered a barrel containing the partial remains of numerous victims, reminiscent of the chemical barrel of body parts found in Jeffrey Dahmer's apartment in 1991. Whether the unnamed tailor himself claimed to be a werewolf is unclear, but he was nicknamed the "Werewolf of Chalon" or "Demon Tailor of Chalon."[36]

Jean Grenier—France, 1603

The 1603 case of Jean Grenier, a thirteen-year-old boy accused of serial killing as a werewolf in Coutras, near Bordeaux in southwestern France, is one of the better-documented cases and a seminal case in Europe's "lycanthrope epidemic" and early-modern forensics.

According to his own testimony, Jean either ran away from home or was run off by his father after he began a nocturnal life as a werewolf. Grenier testified that his stepmother had witnessed him "vomit up from his throat the feet of dogs and the hands of little children."[37] Horrified by what she saw, she refused to return home until his father drove him away.

Homeless, the boy roamed in the vicinity, begging, and frequently approached young girls tending sheep in the fields. He caught the attention of local authorities after a group of girls reported a disturbing encounter with him. The account of the case states:

> The appearance of the lad was strange. His hair was of a yellowy red and densely matted, falling over his shoulders and completely covering his narrow brow. His tiny pale-gray eyes twinkled with a look of hideous savagery and cunning, from deep sunken hollows. His complexion was of a dark olive color; the teeth were strong and white, and the canine teeth protruded over the lower lip when the mouth was closed. The boy's hands were large and powerful, the nails black and pointed like [a] bird's talons. He was poorly clothed, and seemed to be in the most abject poverty. The few garments he

had on him were in tatters, and through the holes the emaciation of his limbs was clearly visible.[38]

The girls stated that the boy made advances toward them, declaring that he would marry the prettiest among them, and then he said to them:

Every Monday, Friday, and Sunday, and for about an hour at dusk every other day, I am a wolf, a werewolf. I have killed dogs and drunk their blood; but little girls taste better, their flesh is tender and sweet, their blood rich and warm. I have eaten many a maiden, as I have been on my raids together with my nine companions. I am a werewolf! If the sun were to set I would soon fall on one of you and make a meal of you!

The girls fled in terror, and their account of the strange encounter piqued the interest of authorities, as over a period of months an infant and several girls in the region had been found viciously murdered, mutilated and partly cannibalized. The boy was eventually identified by another girl, thirteen-year-old Marguerite Poirier, who had been complaining to her parents that the beggar boy had been scaring her with his stories of being a werewolf while she was tending to sheep.

Jean had often stated to her that he had sold himself to the devil, and that he had acquired the power of roaming the country after dusk, and sometimes in broad day, in the form of a wolf. He had told her that he had killed and eaten many dogs, but that he found their flesh less appetizing than the flesh of little girls, which he regarded as an ultimate delicacy. He had told her that this had been tasted by him not unfrequently, but he had specified only two instances: in one he had eaten as much as he could, and had thrown the leftovers to a wolf, which had come up during the meal. In the other instance he had bitten to death another little girl, had slurped up her blood, and, being in a ravenous condition at the time, had consumed every portion of her, except the arms and shoulders.

Marguerite's parents at first dismissed the complaints of their daughter as childish flights of imagination. (In a similar case of parental skepticism, Ed Gein, *Psycho* necrophile serial killer, occasionally babysat children for neighbors. The children, while playing in his house, saw shrunken human heads, skull cups and suits made of mummified female skin and reported this to their parents, who laughed off the stories.) One day little Marguerite came home early in a distraught state and recounted that, with her shepherd's staff, she had beaten off the boy after he transformed into a strange animal that attacked her. She described it "as resembling a wolf, but as being shorter and stouter; its hair was red, its tail stumpy, and the head smaller than that of a genuine wolf." The vagrant boy Jean Grenier was taken into custody and questioned, and quickly confessed to the attack, stating, "The charge of Marguerite Poirier is correct. My intention was to have killed and eaten her, but she beat me off with a stick. I have only killed one dog, a white one, and I did not drink its blood."

When pressed, Grenier confessed that he had once entered an unguarded house in a small village, the name of which he did not remember, and had found an infant asleep in its cradle. As no one was around to stop him, he snatched the baby out of its cradle, dragged it behind the garden, killed it and ate as much of it as satisfied his hunger. He claimed that he shared the remains with a wolf. He also confessed to murdering a girl as she was tending sheep in the parish of Saint Antoine de Pizon. She was wearing a black dress, he remembered, but he did not know her name. He said he tore her to death with his nails and teeth, and then ate her. Six weeks before his capture he had fallen upon another child, near a stone bridge in the same parish, but was prevented from killing her by a passerby.

There was earnest and extensive investigation into Grenier's confessions. They were not accepted at face value. The authorities assembled witnesses, recorded testimony and carefully reviewed the details of the confessions to ascertain their veracity. The mutilation and murder of the girl wearing the black dress was confirmed and Jean was escorted to the scenes of the crimes by the court, which meticulously reviewed his firsthand familiarity with the victims and the circumstances of their deaths. The possibility that Grenier had been delusional was extensively explored by the court.[39]

In his testimony before the court, the boy claimed that when he was ten or eleven years old he had encountered a mysterious black figure he knew only as the "Master of the Forest," who "signed him with his fingernail" and gave him a wolfskin and an ointment that when rubbed on his body gave him the physical prowess and appetite of a wolf.

To the court of that time this was an admission that Grenier had made a pact with the Devil; it was an open-and-shut case of witchcraft, a capital crime. In June 1603, the court sentenced the boy to be put to death by hanging and then to be burned in the public square. But the case did not end there.

The Grenier Appeal and Werewolf Forensics: "They Are Aware of the Pleasure They Experience When as Wolves."

Much had changed by the 1600s since the early werewolf trials of the 1400s and 1500s. We often assume that the principle of the insanity defense is a modern phenomenon emerging from the famous 1843 case in Britain of Daniel McNaughton, who was charged with murdering a man whom McNaughton in his delusionary state mistook for the prime minister, whom he believed was conspiring against him. In a precedent-setting judgment, McNaughton was acquitted by "reason of insanity" and confined for the remainder of his life in an insane asylum, where he died twenty-two years later.

Even today the principles of legal insanity in Anglo-American jurisprudence are known as the McNaughton rules (sometimes spelled M'Naghten), which state that an incapacity to discern the difference between right and wrong or to perceive or understand the consequences of one's actions mitigates the criminal culpability of a perpetrator. But the principles of insanity pleas go back much earlier.

In continental Europe, where Roman law was practiced until the eighteenth century, when it was supplanted by the Napoleonic code (as opposed to common law in Britain, where the McNaughton case was tried), there was a similar principle. In addition to the evidence against a defendant, his or her legal and mental culpability were routinely assessed without a special plea, as it was in the Grenier case. If insanity could be proved, such that criminal acts were committed while the accused was not in possession of full mental capabilities, the defendant could be acquitted or their sentence reduced. However, the defense had the burden of explicitly proving that the defendant was not faking insanity. Physicians were increasingly called as expert witnesses to testify about werewolf defendants' insanity pleas.[40]

In 1603 there was such an appeal to the provincial parliament at Bordeaux for clemency for Jean Grenier. Some interesting forensic arguments were put forth in favor of the boy never actually having transformed into a wolf: one of his victims had her dress slipped off intact, rather than torn away as by a wild animal. For the court, this was significant forensic evidence:

> It is remarkable that he said that it was he who lowered her dress, because he did not rip it. This is something that we observed, to show that while real wolves tear with their claws, werewolves tear with their teeth, and just like men they know how to remove the dresses of the girls they want to eat without ripping them . . . But what shows this miserable boy to be completely trained by the Devil, and won over and conquered according to the desire and intention of the Evil Spirit, is the cruelty he confessed to having committed while wearing the wolf's skin, namely, eating children. He confessed that he had taken them by the throat, just like a wolf does. The Devil had instructed him, for he had undressed them without tearing their clothing, a particular habit characteristic of the werewolf. He confessed that he has a taste for it; the Devil awakened this desire in him.

The court essentially ruled that werewolves are not people literally transformed into wolves but people possessed by the Devil to *behave as if* they were transformed into werewolves. It was the best explanation we had for serial killers back then.

Similar to later debates on whether serial killers are legally insane— that is, whether they are aware that their acts are wrong—the lower court, in originally sentencing Grenier to death, was guided by the legal doctrine on werewolves advanced by French judge Jean Bodin in his 1580 work *Demonomania of Witches*. In it, he argued that while the Devil can transform a man into a werewolf, as a werewolf the man retains his human understanding.

In other words, like our serial-killing psychopath, a werewolf, even if literally transformed by the Devil into a monster, is nevertheless aware of his wrongdoing. If so, a werewolf was not legally insane (unable to discern the wrongfulness of his acts) and was therefore culpable for his crimes. Instead of psychiatry's notion of psychopathy, however, the conceptual framework was theological demonology. Bodin argued:

> The essential form of man—his understanding—does not change at all, but only his body changes [in the condition of lycanthropy] . . . Men are sometimes transformed into beasts but they retain their human understanding and intelligence . . . They are aware of the pleasure they experience when as wolves . . .

The appeals court also reviewed the possibility that Jean Grenier suffered from the disease of clinical lycanthropy as the ancients had diagnosed it. *That* would have been an effective insanity defense. According to the appeal verdict,

> Nothing has been neglected in this affair in order to clarify the truth of this crime, for this young werewolf was visited by two physicians, who agree that this young boy is of a black and melancholic humor. Still, he is not afflicted with the illness that is called *lycanthropy*, so that we do not have a case of an imaginary metamorphosis.

Nonetheless, Grenier's death sentence was commuted on September 6, 1603, in a remarkably modern sensitivity and compassion for his youth, circumstances and mental state. The trial record states:

> The court, in the end, takes note of the age and the imbecility of this young boy, who is so stupid and so mentally impaired, that children of seven or eight normally show more reasoning than he does. This boy is so malnourished and so undersized that one would not think

him ten years old. . . . Here is a young boy abandoned and driven out by his father, who had a stepmother for a mother, who roamed the fields, without a guide and without anyone in the world to look after him, begging for his food, who had no instruction whatsoever in the fear of God, whose nature was corrupted by evil seduction, daily necessities, and despair, all conditions that the Evil Spirit exploited. The court does not want to contribute further to the misery of this young boy, whom the Devil had armed against other children. The court rules after due consideration of all matters, including the inconsistencies of his testimony and other aspects of the trial, to save his soul for God rather than judge it to be lost. Moreover, according to the report of the good monks who began to instruct and encourage him, he is already showing that he abhorred and detested his crimes, as witnessed by his tears and his repentance.

The court dismissed and dismisses the appeals and, for the verdict resulting from the trial, condemned and condemns Jean Grenier to be locked up for the remainder of his life in one of the city's monasteries. He is to serve this monastery for the rest of his life. He is prohibited from ever leaving there under the penalty of hanging or strangling.

Seven years later, like an FBI agent from the Behavioral Sciences Unit interviewing an incarcerated serial killer, the werewolf-and-witchcraft advocate Pierre de Lancre, a judge and King Henri IV's special counselor, visited Jean Grenier in the monastery to interview him. Lancre reported:

I found that he was a young man of twenty or twenty-one, of medium height, rather small for his age, with wild-looking eyes that were sunken and black, and completely distraught. His eyes gave the impression that he was ashamed of his misfortune, which he seemed to understand somewhat; he did not dare look anyone straight in the eye. He seemed a bit dazed, not that he did not understand what he heard or failed to do promptly what the good fathers asked of him. Rather he was hardly devout, and he did not seem to understand easily even simple things that only seemed commonsensical.

He had very long and bright teeth that were wider than normal, protruding somewhat and rotten and half black from being used to lash out at animals and people. His fingernails were also quite long and some were completely black from the base to the tip, even that of the thumb of the left hand, which the Devil prevented him from trimming. With regard to those that were so black, one could say that they were half worn down and more broken than the others, and less normal, because he used them more than he used those on his feet. This clearly shows that he was indeed a werewolf, and that he used his hands both for running and for grabbing children and dogs by the throat.

He cleverly confessed to me that he had been a werewolf and that while in this condition he had roamed the fields following the commands of the Lord of the Forest. This he confessed freely to everyone and denied it to no one, believing that he would avoid all criticism and disgrace for this situation by saying that he was no longer a werewolf . . .

We observed that he greatly despised his father, believing that he was responsible for the bad training he received. He believed, moreover, that he was a werewolf, for he had declared that he would use the same wolf's skin as he did. This is why, when he came to some understanding of his affliction, he hated him for it when I made him see it so strongly. He confessed to me also, in a straightforward manner, that he still wanted to eat the flesh of little children, and that he found the flesh of little girls particularly delicious. I asked him if he would eat it if he had not been prohibited from doing so, and he answered me frankly that yes he would, and more that of girls than that of boys because they are more tender.[41]

DEFENDING SERIAL LYCANTHROPES

Not all the literate elites and scientists testifying before the courts in the cases of werewolves and witches believed in the existence of these kinds of supernatural phenomena. The forensic debate on werewolves, when they reached the courts as the Grenier appeal did, were focused on two questions:

- First, did certain humans literally transform into werewolves and were these people possessed by the Devil?

- Second, were these people deluded (perhaps by the Devil) into believing that they had become werewolves?

In other words, the same old question: did werewolves (and witches) exist, or did these people have delusions, in what we would today describe as a psychopathology, mental illness, or behavioral disorder?

These were urgent questions argued at the time. The debate on werewolves between witch-hunting demonologists and physicians during the Renaissance era would foreshadow the debates between theologians and forensic psychiatrists (alienists) in the nineteenth century on what they termed *homicidal mania* or *monomania*, and even the debates ongoing today between profilers and criminologists, sociologists and psychologists, on the fundamental psychopathology of serial killers, necrophiliacs and cannibals and what they represent in medical and psychiatric terms.

In 1596, Claude Prieur, a Franciscan monk, heretically denied the existence of werewolves in his *Dialog on Lycanthropy, or Transformation of men into wolves, commonly called werewolves, and if such a thing can be done*. In it he argued:

I have not heard that he left his human form, but rather that men could be found that were so cruel that they merited being called brutal beasts rather than reasonable creatures, in order to delight in all ungodliness . . . We have so many examples of them that it seems impossible to me to say the contrary, that is, of men who, turning and changing themselves into a foreign form, devour the people that they meet, even other beasts, and especially young children. And as for me, I do not say that they are monsters, but truly men, and by nature of the same species as you and me . . . I will concede to you that there might be found people acting so much against nature that they attack human bodies, dead or alive, in order to devour and eat them, especially small children, and that they might have the appearance of wolves, of which I can confirm for you some very recent examples, as we have heard recently by reliable letters from Paris dated the twentieth of August, on which day two little children had been eaten by the ones about which you have heard spoken, & about which as one says there are seventeen of them in the same place, and as many in the other neighboring towns: But I will never agree (as the Church fathers also will not do) that such people take on another form, in order to hide by this means their human form, for we have already proved the contrary through those doctors. . . . in few words, remember this sentence of the philosopher; *Species non mutatur*, the species never changes.[42]

The copious amount of material published on this question suggests that this issue of "men transformed into beasts" must have arisen frequently. Reading these sixteenth-century case notes is a frustrating experience because one begins to realize that people back then not only *should have* known better, but *did* know better. Of course werewolves did not really exist; but if not, what are they?

These questions were asked and appear to us as modern as questions about serial killers today: Were werewolves sick and insane? Were they suffering from a disease with an organic cause? This is a question that proponents of the biochemical explanation for serial killers debate today, suggesting that genetic traits; blood or urine chemistry; chromosome structure; levels of testosterone, serotonin, dopamine, norepinephrine, gamma-aminobutyric acid (GABA) or hormones; abnormal neurological physiology; or behavioral disorders like Asperger's syndrome, an autism-spectrum disorder, could be the key to explaining serial-killer behavior. These types of questions were not only theoretically debated, but put before the courts during some of those werewolf trials, with expert witnesses called in to testify.

From the mid-1500s, physicians (albeit of a premodern humoral medicine) began to participate through academic publications and in courtroom testimony in the debate surrounding the Devil, witchcraft and werewolves, which had previously been the realm of demonologists, theologians, lawyers and judges. The debate concerned not only insanity and melancholia as alternative explanations for alleged cases of witchcraft and werewolves, but also the possibility of the Devil or witchcraft causing illnesses in the body and the criteria for distinguishing between insanity of a biochemical (humoral) origin and a demonic possession. The early stirring of forensic-scientific thought in the mid-1500s came hand in hand with the Renaissance-era rebirth of the Devil, witches and werewolves.

Jacques Roulet Werewolf Appeal, 1598

In 1598, thirty-five-year-old Jacques Roulet (Rollet) was caught literally red-handed after murdering, mutilating and cannibalizing a fifteen-year-old boy near Angers, France. During his trial Roulet confessed to murdering and cannibalizing a series of children and adults, claiming that he used an ointment to transform into a werewolf. (The use of an ointment by lycanthropes is a common theme in trial records.) In his 1599 account of the case, Jean Beauvoys de Chauvincourt argued that Roulet's claims of being a werewolf were a ploy to advance an insanity defense. Beauvoys de Chauvincourt contemptuously wrote:

> Seeing that he could not deny that which he had confessed, embracing a simulated madness as the means of his salvation, admitted having eaten iron carts, windmills, lawyers, prosecutors and sergeants, meats that because of their great hardness, and because they were not well seasoned, he had not been able to digest very well . . . The judges of Angers for these confessions sentenced him to death, without taking into consideration the diabolical cunning in which Satan his master had instructed him, that is, to counterfeit madness . . .[43]

Amazingly, Roulet's insanity plea on appeal was accepted by the French parliament, which upon reviewing the case commuted his death sentence to a two-year confinement in an insane asylum at the Hospital Saint-Germaine. Like a television pundit today editorializing on a light sentence handed down by a judge, Beauvoys de Chauvincourt wrote:

I believe that said Lords of the Court interpreting all things in a good way, as they have custom to do, considering the rustic nature of the man, his inconsistencies, his manner of living, his attitude, his actions, and in short his entire behavior, have only sentenced him for two years to said place, in order that, during this time, they might more easily be able to go over with a fine-tooth comb and in minute detail his condition and his morals. For if, following the daily observation that they will make of his actions, they notice so much as a little bit of his wickedness, he has not escaped and is only pulling on his choke collar and soon they will have tightened it.

CLINICAL *LYCANTHROPIA–LYCOMANIA* *LUPINA INSANIA*

We see in werewolf trial records that the courts were acutely aware of the possibility of some organic disorder, described as *lycanthropia* or *lycomania*. The English scholar Reginald Scot attacked as superstition the notion of supernatural transformations of humans into werewolves as described by the *Malleus Maleficarum* and proposed by Bodin. Published in 1584, Scot's book *The Discoverie of Witchcraft Wherein the Lewde Dealings of Witches and Witch Mongers is Notablie Detected* ridiculed witch-hunters and the notion of human transformation.[44] Scot simply stated, "*Lycanthropia* is a disease, and not a transformation . . . A disease proceeding partly from melancholy whereby maniacs suppose themselves to be wolves, or such ravenous beasts. For *Lycanthropia* is of [what] the ancient physicians called *Lupina melancholia* or *Lupina insania*."

This issue of lycanthropy as a clinical disease is a compelling one, especially if we explore the link between whatever it was that those werewolf cannibals were and today's proponents of biochemical explanations for serial-killer behavior. Even today, clinical lycanthropy baffles us and psychiatrists question whether ancient lycanthropy as described by Byzantine and Greek physicians for nearly two thousand years was the same mental malady manifested during the lycanthrope epidemic.

A thousand years of medical descriptions of clinical lycanthropy, or *lycomania*, are very consistent not only with werewolf reports but with descriptions of vampires as well. The sufferer wanders at night and avoids daylight; there is a lack of saliva, accompanied with crusted foaming at the mouth, dry red eyes, clawlike fingernails, discoloration of skin, abnormal hair growth, sores on the lower legs, disfigurement of the feet and hands, grotesquely distorted facial features and bizarre disordered behavior. Recent medical literature on historical lycanthropy has identified the disease of *congenital porphyria* as having features with the kind of behavioral and physical symptoms reported in the defendants accused of being werewolves.[45] The most consistent picture is that of a man, but occasionally of a woman or child, who wanders about at night. He may come from a family that produced a werewolf previously; thus, lycanthropy was held to be familial. The werewolf's skin is pale and has a yellowish or greenish tint and numerous excoriations. The mouth is red, the eyes are unsteady and the exposed parts are hairy.

Congenital porphyria, which in its advanced stages produces extensive facial lesions and mutilation of the hands, is a rare recessive-gene disease in which there is an inability to convert porphobilinogen to porphyrin in the bone marrow. Among its characteristics that are of particular interest in relation to werewolf symptomology is severe photosensitivity accompanied by a vesicular erythema that is particularly noticeable in summer or in mountainous regions. There is a tendency for the skin lesions to ulcerate and infect cartilage and bone, destroying structures such as the nose, ears, eyelids and fingers. Hypertrichosis and pigmentation may develop on the photosensitive areas and teeth may turn red or reddish-brown. Nervous manifestations are most common in the acute intermittent variety but may occur in the other types, *porphyria cutanea tarda* and the "mixed" type of *hepatic porphyria*.

A Google search for medical photographs of current patients suffering from porphyria reveals images of people with movie-werewolf-like features: furry faces; snarling, disfigured mouths with jaggedly broken teeth; hairy bodies covered in sores and lesions; disfigured, clawlike fingers and feet.[46] The images of current porphyria patients very much match the physical descriptions that witnesses gave of the boy werewolf Grenier.

Furthermore, the use of psychotropic concoctions to treat the disorder or ergot poisoning common in the era resulting in hallucinations or erratic behavior is also hinted at by the frequent references in the trials to the use of ointments and potions by werewolves, echoing recent reports of links between a resurgence of clinical lycanthropy and the use of the street drug ecstasy.[47]

Werewolves victimized a broad category of people, from both male and female children to adolescents and young maidens. Gradually, however, in the culture of "private" serial victimization, the immoral promiscuous female, especially the prostitute, becomes increasingly the serial werewolf's preferred category of victim, deserving of the savagely cruel punishment the werewolf dispenses.

LITTLE "LESS-DEAD" RED RIDING HOOD: THE EMERGENCE OF THE PROSTITUTE AS PREFERRED VICTIM

We see in the folklore of the Werewolf era the promiscuous woman or prostitute emerge as a preferred "less-dead" victim for the werewolf serial killer to stalk and target, the kind of victim who to this day remains a preferred target of serial killers. The strange story of Little Red Riding Hood and her encounter with a wolf emerges in oral tradition throughout Europe precisely during the 1450–1650 werewolf epidemic. While we are all familiar with the "G-rated" Brothers Grimm and Walt Disney versions of the tale, there are some thirty different variants from its original telling, with some passages that are lewd, troubling and confounding, describing not just wolves, but explicitly werewolves, cannibalism, sex and prostitution.

The first printed version of "Little Red Riding Hood" was written by Charles Perrault and appeared in his 1697 book *Tales of My Mother Goose*, which contained such other stories as "Cinderella," "Puss in Boots," "Bluebeard" and "The Sleeping Beauty." We often characterize Perrault's fairy tales as children's stories, but really they were folktales. Perrault's stories sometimes echoed dark historical themes and events.[48] His story "Bluebeard" was inspired by the serial killer Gilles de Rais with Perrault's version substituting wives for the children that de Rais had actually killed, while "The Sleeping Beauty" has long been cited for its necrophilic theme.[49]

In Perrault's version of "Little Red Riding Hood," she explicitly strips naked beneath the wolf's gaze before getting into bed under the covers with him to be eaten. There is no happy ending and no last-minute rescue by hunters in that version. It's a vile and dark horror story.[50]

In the earlier French oral tale "The Grandmother," on which Perrault based his written story, the wolf is described as a *bzou*, a French term for "werewolf" ("*loup-bzou*," "*loup-brou* or "*loup-garou*," depending on the French dialect of the region). The *bzou* encounters the girl on the way to her grandmother's house and asks her which path she intends to take: "The path of needles or the path of pins?" Little Red Riding Hood chooses the path of needles. This strange passage is mostly ignored by analysts or dismissed as nonsense, but Richard Chase Jr. and David Teasley point out that medieval prostitutes were known to identify themselves by a cluster of lace needles at their shoulder.[51]

The *bzou* takes the other path and arrives at the grandmother's house and kills her before the girl gets there. After cutting up the grandmother's corpse into edible morsels and draining her blood into a wine bottle, the creature disguises itself as the grandmother and awaits the arrival of the girl, whom he then tricks into cannibalizing her grandmother in a perversion of the Christian communion, in which Christ's flesh and blood are offered as bread and wine. In the original story, a cat comments, "For shame! The slut is eating her grandmother's flesh and drinking her grandmother's blood."[52]

In some versions of "Little Red Riding Hood," she is fully aware that her grandmother has been substituted by the wolf. When he invites her to join him in bed, she first performs an elaborate striptease for the wolf, removing each item of her clothing—her bodice, her dress, her petticoat, her shoes and her stockings—meticulously described in the story, item by item, with a fetishistic precision as she strips naked before the hungry, panting wolf and tosses the items one by one into the fire. Then she gets into bed with the wolf, and after the ritual exploratory foreplay—"Oh, Grandmother, what big arms you have . . . what big eyes . . . what big teeth . . ."—she is ravished, murdered, and eaten by the wolf.

In other versions Little Red Riding Hood, standing naked before the bed after her striptease, tells the wolf she needs to relieve herself before joining him under the bedcovers. The *bzou* invites her to "do it" in the bed. The girl counters that she needs to defecate. The *bzou* does not relent and he invites her to defecate in the bed. The girl insists that she wants to do it outside, and the wolf ties a string to her and allows her to go out. Out of the wolf's sight, Little Red Riding Hood ties the string to a tree branch and escapes. In other versions she is rescued by a passing hunter.

We are all familiar from childhood with the sanitized kiddie version of "Little Red Riding Hood," but not with the depraved, paraphilic, cannibalistic version that was being told by people at the time of its origin: a brutal time, a time of fear and loathing, torture, rape and murder, heresy and witchcraft, and bloodsucking vampires and fierce cannibal werewolves lurking at the door. Our vistas of the past are fragmentary and obscured. It's like gazing out into the past across an arctic sea of moving icebergs without seeing the menacing mass of ice below the surface. Monsters like Peter Stubbe or Jack the Ripper occasionally clamber out on the surface for us to glimpse the horror, but most of it lurks all around us, out of view in the dark, below the surface. In the past as today, occasional episodes of serial-killer werewolves horrified us with their monstrousness, and I am not the only historian to suggest that the subjects of these sporadically reported cases of werewolves and cannibal killers are the precursors of our modern serial killers.[53] And the question, of course, is, why are there not *more* cases from that era, and why, considering the echoes of the "less-dead" labeling of prostitutes in stories like "Little Red Riding Hood," are there no recorded cases where prostitutes are primarily targeted in the way Jack the Ripper or even the Green River Killer or dozens of other modern serial killers targeted prostitutes?

One answer to that might be that while prostitution itself was frowned upon or tolerated as a "necessary evil," and despite proscriptions against "fornication," and "deviant" practices like oral or anal sex, by the Church, sexuality in general in the distant past was more open and accepted and much less repressed than it was to become in the nineteenth century.[54] There was less anxiety about sexuality; there were fewer "hang-ups." Moreover, female sexuality was defined by the notion of women as property, belonging first to their father and then after marriage to their husband. Female propriety was more of an issue to the property-owning upper classes than to the impoverished masses, by whom an unmarried daughter might be regarded as a burden rather than a family asset (as in many Third World societies today). Until relatively recently, rape was perceived first as an offense against a father's or husband's honor and property interests, and only second as a crime against the victimized woman.

Rape and serial homicide today are intrinsically tied to a cultural psychopathology of anger and hate of woman bred in some men from childhood. In childhood males find themselves at the mercy of their mothers, and growing up is a process of negotiating degrees of independence from the maternal female figure, gradually turning toward the female sexual figure. But women as mothers are not infallibly perfect, and many mad things can go wrong in that alchemy of raising a boy child, threatening a male's self-esteem, leaving behind deeply seated frustrations, resentments, traumas and angers and a sense of lack of control in the face of female sexual power. Historically male-dominated society is marked by the male aspiration to somehow tame and control that daunting female sexual power. Lest they find themselves once again infantilized by the power of "Mother" (as serial killers sometimes say, instead of "my mother"). Religious and moral proscriptions on female sexuality divide women into "good," obedient and virtuous wives, mothers, sisters and daughters and "bad," uncontrollable harlots who refuse to surrender their sexual power to the authority and possession of one male. The ultimate offender is the prostitute, who commercializes the one precious thing that virtuous women offer only to one "best man," their lover or husband. This madonna/whore dichotomy between "saintly love" and "profane lust," described by John Money in his theory of paraphilias, is seated not only in religious thinking but in social and political discourse, law and popular culture to this day.

While lycanthrope serial killers pathologically murdered and mutilated women and children criminally in private, in the next chapter I look at the public realm, where the Church and state will sanction a judicial mass serial rape, torture and killing of women in the name of the suppression of witchcraft.

SIX

Malleus Maleficarum:
The Great Witch Hunt as a
Serial-Killing-Woman Hunt

> Signs of a diabolic pact were always to be found in the victims'
> genitals.
>
> —MAX DASHU, *REIGN OF THE DEMONOLOGISTS:*
> *THE DIABOLIST LOGIC OF TORTURE TRIALS*

Parallel to the werewolf epidemic, there was an even larger witch epidemic that triggered a sustained organized campaign of torturing, raping and killing women. It is not an exaggeration to characterize this pathological systemic serial killing of women as a form of Church- and state-sponsored serial murder.

In the previous chapter, I argued that witch hunts occur when a society finds itself divided and that they are a way of unifying the elites by creating the illusion of a threat more urgent than the actual one dividing the society. In 1484, the pope called upon ecclesiastical and civil authorities everywhere to cooperate with Church inquisitors and demonologists in their war on witches, werewolves, monsters and heretics. The Dominican inquisitor Heinrich Kramer published the notoriously misogynistic manual for witch-hunting *Malleus Maleficarum* (*The Witches' Hammer*), in which, for pathological reasons we can now only guess at, he proclaimed that women have a propensity to enter sexual pacts with Satan, transforming into dangerous, superpowered creatures capable of flight and black magic. He declared that witches were not mortals practicing magic, but supernatural monsters, cannibalizing children and gathering in secret cells (covens) for meetings (witches' sabbaths).

The Great Witch Hunt of this era is like one of those icebergs floating by us in the dark of history. What was on the surface a religious hunt for witches actually disguised something more sinister: institutionalized, systematic paraphilic sadistic sexual torture murders of tens of thousands of women.

As historian Angus McLaren observed, serial murders are "determined largely by the society that produced them," and a serial killer was "best understood not so much as an 'outlaw' as an 'oversocialized' individual who saw himself simply carrying out sentences that society at large leveled."[1] Criminologist Mark Seltzer argues that serial killers take their cues from society and respond with their own homicidal contributions in a process he calls mimetic compulsion.[2]

If we want to look at rape culture or serial-murder culture at its worst, we must recognize the Great Witch Hunt of 1450 to 1650 as a serial-killing epidemic.

THE REAL SERIAL-KILLING EPIDEMIC: WITCH-HUNTING OR WOMAN KILLING?

Historians are still baffled by the orgy of executions for witchcraft in Renaissance-era Europe, with its peak coming roughly between 1450 and 1650, a period known as the Great Witch Hunt or the Great Hunt. The witch hunt has been portrayed by feminist historians as a femicide or gynocide—a deliberate systematic murder of women by men. It has been alleged that as many as nine million women were tortured and put to death by witch-hunters in a pogrom or "female holocaust." Some argued that this was a conspiracy of patriarchal quack physicians against rival female midwife health knowledge, a claim now discounted as historians have discovered that midwives gleefully collaborated in the prosecution and torture of witches.[3]

This is not the place to go into detail about the witchcraft trials other than to say that recent scholarship confirms that women were predominantly targeted in most regions but that the total numbers executed are much lower than the "hundreds of thousands to millions of women killed" as alleged by some historians in the 1980s and 1990s. The latest studies indicate that from 40 thousand to 100 thousand people were tortured and executed, of whom approximately 75 percent were women.[4] Not quite millions, but an extraordinary number just the same. (Incidentally, a comparative 75.4 percent of serial-killer victims today are women according to the recent FBI studies.)[5]

Assuming the *lowest* figure of forty thousand executed witches, over a period of two hundred years, one woman was killed this way every few days throughout this period. The witch hunt was a woman-hunting industry, institutionalized in a partnership between the Church and the state with the collaboration of a motley crew of lay subcontractors, demonologists, academics, pundits, self-appointed witch-hunters, torture "experts," notaries, dungeon keepers, and so on. And these women were not just killed; they were first degraded, horrifically tortured and mutilated, and frequently raped. It was state- and Church-licensed sadistic serial murder. There is no other appropriate way of describing it. This really was a serial-killing gynocide, as many feminist historians have termed it.

THE "DIABOLIST LOGIC OF TORTURE TRIALS"

Women accused of witchcraft were forced to confess to having sex with the Devil according to perverse, pathologically twisted sexual scenarios composed by the Church inquisitors presiding over the interrogations. The process of questioning and extracting a confession from women accused of witchcraft as specified in the *Malleus Maleficarum* is straight out of a serial killer's fantasy playbook.

The demented Kramer instructs that upon being taken into custody suspected witches are to be stripped naked and all their hair shaved, and that they are then to be searched, especially in their "most secret places that cannot be named." Once bound and restrained by the inquisitor and his assistants, their bodies would be pricked with needles, scraped and probed with instruments for the supposed "Devil's mark." Long needles were driven into moles and birthmarks, which were said to be immune to bleeding and to pain in a witch. If the victim reacted with pain, however, it was assumed she was faking it; if she bled, it was the Devil's illusion or excess "witches' milk" accumulated while the witch was imprisoned and separated from her familiars, who normally suckled blood from her third "witches' nipple" (usually a mole).

Bizarre gynecological probes and torture implements were applied to female genitals. The "pear" was an iron, pear-shaped dildo with a screw mechanism that when turned opened like jagged flower petals. It was heated and inserted into the vagina, anus or mouth and slowly screwed open. Red-hot pincers were used to tear off flesh, and the "spider," a sharp, iron forklike clamp, was specially designed to tear away females' breasts. Burning feathers were placed to the armpits and groin, fingers immersed in boiling water or oil and alcohol poured on the head and set alight. Boiling water or boiling oil enemas and douches "cleansed" the suspected witch of her lies. The use of the rack was popular in France, where an accused witch was pulled apart with ratcheted pulleys until loud popping and cracking was heard from the tearing and snapping of cartilage, ligaments and bones. Whipping was common; red-hot iron rods were inserted into the vagina or anus or used to burn out eyes. The "witches' chair" was an iron chair that had beneath its toiletlike seat a furnace that would be heated to slowly roast the genitals of the victim restrained in it. The *turcos*, a viselike instrument with protruding spikes, was used to rip out fingernails and toenails. Thumbscrews crushed fingers and toes at the base until blood squirted out. *Cashielaws* were a system of measured wedges inserted between planks fitted from ankles to knees, then driven in with a heavy hammer to slowly crush and break the bones.

Waterboarding, so familiar in our own witch-hunting in the twenty-first century, back then involved a more brutal form where a long knotted cloth was forced down the throat along with great quantities of water, sometimes boiling, and then violently jerked out. Usually reserved until last was the infamous strappado, in which the woman was attached to a pulley by her hands, bound behind her back, then raised and dropped, dislocating the shoulders, hands and elbows. Weights between forty and one hundred pounds would be attached to her feet to increase the pain and dislocate the hips, feet and knees.[6]

Sadistic sexual fantasies and impulses were blatantly fulfilled in these brutal acts of torture. It was always naïve to believe that because the Church was behind this madness, its functionaries would not rape or inflict any kind of sexual abuse on the female prisoners. They were, after all, on a mission for God. Did not the *Malleus Maleficarum* explicitly instruct that suspected witches are to "be stripped by respectable women of good reputation," and that when questioning witches inquisitors "should not allow themselves to be touched by her physically, especially on the naked wrist"?[7]

Similarly, it was believed until recently that during the Holocaust (another example of a state-sponsored epidemic of serial killing), Nazi perpetrators, because of draconian eugenic race laws prohibiting sex with Jews, did not rape their female victims. Recent scholarship has put that myth to the death it deserves.[8] Hitler's strict Nuremberg Race Laws had about as much effect inhibiting the sadistic lusts of Nazi genocidal serial killers as *Malleus Maleficarum* had on the sadistic lusts of gynocidal serial witch-hunters and their minions: none.

It is no coincidence that contemporary BDSM (bondage, domination/discipline, submission/sadism, masochism) subculture of erotic role-playing features Medieval and Renaissance "dungeon play" as a prominent psychosexual theme, echoing two centuries of torture sessions perpetrated by the witch-hunters still imprinted on our sex fantasies like some sort of collective sexophonic cultural engram, another one of those buggy lines of code in the cultural DNA—one of those mimetic compulsions as a form of sociohistorical trauma manifesting as sadistic fantasy. Of course, unlike contemporary BDSM dungeon play there was nothing playfully consensual about what transpired in the witch-hunters' dungeons during the Great Hunt.

According to historian Mary Daly:

> It is clear that the witches were physically and mentally mutilated and dismembered by their persecutors. A witch was forced to relieve her torture by confessing that she acted out the sexual fantasies of her male judges as they described these to her. The judges achieved erotic gratification from her torture, from the sight of her being stripped and gang raped, from seeing her mangled body, from forc-

ing her to "admit" acting out *their* erotic fantasies, from her spiritual and physical slow death. These disturbing and sadistic men were creating the delusion of devils other than themselves—projecting their own evil intent onto these "devils" which were mirror images of themselves . . .

Daly points out:

More likely, the woman, during her stripping, would be raped by the torturer's assistants, as happened to Frau Peller, the wife of a court officer, in her trial at Rheinbach in 1631. She had, incidentally, been accused of witchcraft because her sister had refused to sleep with the witch judge, Franz Buirmann . . . So little regard was given this preliminary torture that many court records ignored it and simply stated, "The prisoner confessed without torture."[9]

Historian Anne L. Barstow writes:

Performed on women by men, legal torture permitted sadistic experimentation and gratuitous sexual advances. When executioner Jehan Minart of Camvrai prepared Aldegonde de Rue for the stake, he examined her interior parts, mouth, and "*parties honteuses*" ["shameful parts"]. To try to force a confession from Catherine Boyraisonne, a priest applied hot fat repeatedly to her eyes, armpits, the pit of her stomach, thighs, elbows, and "*dans da nature*"—in her vagina. She died in prison, no doubt from injuries. And while a female was imprisoned, she might be raped—the young Lorrainer, Catharina Latomia, not yet pubescent, was raped twice in her cell and nearly died from it: these attacks were blamed on the Devil . . . Witch-hunting *was* woman-hunting. Jailers, prickers, and executioners all could take sadistic pleasure with female prisoners.[10]

All those obscene gynecological instruments of torture—heated iron tongs, probes, scrapers, crushers, claws, pins and needles—were designed for pathologically crazed witch-hunters obsessed with the "evils" of female genitalia. In *Reign of the Demonologists: The Diabolist Logic of*

Torture Trials in Early Modern Europe historian Max Dashu (Maxine Hammond) writes:

> Genital "searches" had become a routine part of the investigation of witchcraft, justified as a matter of duty by men of faith. In private, within the jail and torture-chamber, the perpetrators could boast and laugh with each other about their "Discoverie of Witchcraft." Any physical marks or irregularities could be made to serve as a sign of pact with the devil, and if none were found, they could be produced through torture. Because of their "whoredom," captors felt they could do anything to accused women, with total impunity.
>
> The witch-hunters saw the natural anatomy of the vulva and vagina as deviant and therefore suspect. Signs of a diabolic pact were always to be found in the victims' genitals. The labia minora, especially, were interpreted as teats sucked by demonic familiars.[11]

It *literally* was gynocide, as feminist historians call it.

The reason that we might have only a few hundred serial-killer werewolves on the trial record in this period is probably because the "ordinary" organized sexual serial killers were gainfully employed in expressing their mimetic compulsions on thousands of available female victims in state- and Church-sponsored dungeons. The Great Hunt was as if all those surveyed college males who fantasize about raping a woman "if they could get away with it" now *could* get away with it. And more.

Some of the men were even earning a bounty from every "witch" they raped, tortured and put to death, like the notorious self-appointed English "Witch Finder General" Matthew Hopkins in the 1640s. When an average daily working wage was 6 pence, Hopkins was billing English villages anywhere from 6 to 25 pounds for "cleansing" them of witches.[12] Just in one day in Chelmsford in July 1645, Hopkins condemned 29 people to death for witchcraft. In some places, 40 to 50 people at a time were being put to death in mass executions. Hopkins went so overboard that eventually there was a parliamentary inquiry into his activities and he was forced out of business. (Myth claims he himself was accused as a witch and hanged, but apparently, he died peacefully in retirement.)[13]

In the same way ancient Rome was a circus of cruelty and death, the Renaissance was an Indy 500 for the serial rape, mutilation, torture and killing of women; for the settling of scores by jealous neighbors or rejected suitors; for property seizure; for killing competition and rivals; and for pursuing sadistic pleasures.

We may never know exactly how many women were murdered this way, but whether it was 40 thousand or 100 thousand or even the unlikely figure of 9 million, we know one thing: every single victim, male or female, who was tortured and put to death for witchcraft was an innocent victim. It was an epidemic of serial killing of women, incubated in a culture of judicial rape and torture sanctioned by Church and state. I see no better definition of it than as an example of a mass sexual-serial-killing mimetic compulsion.

THE DECLINE AND WANING OF SERIAL KILLERS, 1650–1800

The early serial-killer surge in the form of werewolves seems to fade from the historical record after 1650, along with a gradual decline in witch-hunting. If we accept the notion that the root of the paranoia was in the division of ruling elites, then it is interesting to note that the catastrophic, world-war-like Thirty Years' War between Catholics and Protestants that polarized European civilization came to an end with the Treaty of Westphalia in 1648 and precisely afterward, the witchcraft and werewolf trials began to decline.*

The treaty did not necessarily unify the elites, but it gave "immunity" to religious dissent by declaring that a prince could choose which

*The last woman known to have been put to death as a witch in Europe was Anna Goeldi, a servant in Switzerland in 1782 accused of communing with the Devil in poisoning the daughter of her employer. In 2008, a Swiss Protestant Church council reviewed her case and absolved her of witchcraft (226 years too late).

religion would be practiced in his territory without being threatened with invasion as a heretic by neighbors of a rival religion. With that notion of a prince's territorial sovereignty, the treaty created a new, modern state system, in which we currently live and which we describe today as the "Westphalian system." Elites would now be leading the masses to kill one another over issues other than religion: dynastic succession, colonial conquest and, later, political ideology. We had to wait until 9/11 for our civilization to be engulfed again in a religious world war.

Accounts of serial killers in the form of bandits and pirates, female poisoners and cannibal clans continue to appear in the record throughout the 1700s, but the common sexual serial killer vanishes into obscurity along with the witches and the werewolves until late in the nineteenth century.

Why there were few (if any) sexual-serial-killer cases during this period in Europe or North America is a question that needs further research, but I would hypothesize that it had everything to do with the decline of the witch-hunting "enforcement" industry that had swept up serial killers into their net as "werewolves." Once the witch-hunting ended, so did the prosecution of serial lycanthropes.

As for the serial-killer torturers employed by the Church and state, once their license to rape, torture, and kill was suspended, like modern-day war criminals, they retired home to take their places as loved grandfathers and upstanding pillars of their community who never raped and killed again, at least not without permission from Church and state.

With the Church no longer in the witch-hunt business, it's not surprising to find fewer serial murders on record between 1650 and 1800. There was no organized police system to take reports of crime perpetrated against commoners, who made up the majority of the populace and presumably victims. In that era if you were a victim of a crime, or a family member of a victim, it was up to you to investigate the crime, gather and present evidence before a magistrate or grand jury, get an indictment, and pay for an arrest warrant to be issued, then pay a sheriff or constable to arrest the suspect, rent a jail, and pay a jailer to hold your suspect until trial, and then at your own expense deliver the prisoner to court and present your case before a judge and jury. Only if you managed to get a guilty verdict would the state then intervene by punishing the convicted with an execution of the court sentence. It was DIY justice 99 percent of the way.

There were no police departments or prosecutors in the sense we have today, except for the policing and prosecution of offenses against the state, the Church, or the aristocracy and elite interests. "Police" focused on issues like tax evasion, poaching and squatting. Killers, serial or otherwise, were no doubt unceremoniously lynched by the family of the victim or by the community without referring the case to the judicial system.

Between 1650 and 1800, reports of serial killers seem to be restricted to cases of bandits, pirates, predatory highwaymen and female poisoners, all of whom had endangered public order and property, freedom of movement or commerce and industry. But "ordinary" sexual serial killers, who like today were targeting predominantly marginalized "less-dead" subjects like peasants, vagrants, prostitutes and the destitute, did not come to the attention of state policing as long as their crimes did not threaten the elites or public order.

It was only with industrialization, when a large middle class emerged and began to share urban space in close proximity to masses of the poor and marginalized, that state authority turned its attention to crime, including serial murder, among all segments of the population and responded by establishing a complex administrative system that began to police crimes against "ordinary" people. Its purpose was not to bring justice to the poor, but to prevent violence from spilling over from the lower class (referred to often back then as the "dangerous class") into the lives of the middle and upper classes. To this day, critics accuse law enforcement and public authority of putting a low priority on the murders of prostitutes, the impoverished or homeless and other marginalized, "less-dead" victims on the basis of their social class and/or their race, with the two often inseparable.

There is also the issue of the public *reporting* of incidents of serial killing if they occurred, and the survival of those records if they existed. The hand-printed pamphlets that reported on lycanthrope prosecutions were rare and scarce. Newsprint media and journalism began to flourish only in the early nineteenth century, with the rise of common literacy, efficient steam-powered mass-printing technology and the new availability of cheap paper on which to print news and distribute it at a cost affordable for the newly literate masses yearning to be entertained by news of blood and murder. (It's a common maxim in the news media to this day: "If it bleeds, it leads.")

The weekly "penny dreadful" true-crime newssheet made its appearance in the 1830s and at its low price ushered in a new public hunger for popular accounts of crime that had previously been restricted to tales told orally, staged in Greek or Elizabethan theater or printed in limited-edition pamphlets or books which only a few could afford. This was the beginning of mass media and the genre of true crime and punishment.

We probably had per capita as many serial killers during those centuries as we have today, but acting without any obvious motive, they were as difficult to detect and apprehend back then as they are today. Serial killers were locally hunted down and killed or lynched, or their killings were attributed to wolves or bears or to lingering beliefs in supernatural monsters.

If cases of serial murder did reach the court system, the documents and transcripts could have easily been lost to history after being destroyed in any one of the dozens of civil insurrections or military conflagrations that engulfed Europe for centuries (or even in routine archival housekeeping).

As the scientific age of reason—the Enlightenment—began to take hold of Western civilization in the 1700s, the supernatural serial-killing monster as defined by the Church was supplanted by the secular serial-killer deviant as defined by the emerging science of forensic psychiatry, in parallel with the growth of the judicial-policing branch of the modern bureaucratic administrative state. By the 1800s, the supernatural werewolf- and witch-hunters like de Lancre and Kramer would be entirely supplanted by secular psychiatrists and criminologists like Krafft-Ebing, Lombroso, and Lacassagne.

SEVEN

The Rippers Before Jack:
The Rise of Modern
Serial Killers
in Europe, 1800–1887

No man, however quickly he may pray, could get through his rosary, or say ten Hail Marys in the time it took me to cut open her breast and the rest of her body. I cut up this person as a butcher does a sheep . . .

—CONFESSION OF SERIAL KILLER ANDREAS BICHEL, 1808

It was even a pleasure only to smell female clothing. The feeling of pleasure while strangling them was much greater than that which I experienced while masturbating.

—CONFESSION OF SERIAL KILLER VINCENZO VERZENI, 1871

The broken promises of the Renaissance era were eclipsed by the Enlightenment of the 1700s, which was defined by philosophers like Voltaire and Rousseau, who inspired radical new ideas of natural human rights to equality, personal liberty, democracy, freedom of expression, freedom of scientific inquiry from Church "superstition" and the pursuit of happiness for all classes and races (depending upon colonial imperatives and the profit margins of the African slave trade).

Before the 1800s it had been primarily the Church which defined the nature of evil, vice, perversion and madness. By the mid-1800s it was increasingly defined by the "soul healers": psychiatrists ("*psych*," from the ancient Greek for "soul," and "*iatry*," "medical treatment"). In this process of secularization and criminalization of monsters, the authority of state prosecution along with the authority of psychiatry would take center stage as serial crimes began to be prosecuted in secular courts and increasingly reported in popular print media.

From 1650 to about 1815, Europe lurched through the Dynastic Wars, the French Revolution and then the Napoleonic Wars. When peace came to Europe after 1815, industrialization was well under way; feudal *subjects* had transformed into national *citizens* and moved from the countryside into the crowded cities, while fragmented local feudal rule was replaced by the centralized administrative state and its newly formed police and judicial bureaucracies.

In the wake of that transformation, serial killers began to reappear on the historical-event horizon, not as monsters, but as criminals caught in the net of this new system of law enforcement. From this point on, these monsters would start taking the familiar shape of the serial killer, even though we did not call them that.

Serial Necrophile François Bertrand, the "Vampire of Montparnasse," Paris, 1850

It was not a case of serial murder but this case of serial "vampirism," as necrophilia was called at the time, that became a watershed in the emergence of modern forensic psychiatry and its new role in policing and justice. The Bertrand case galvanized the world of criminology and gave future forensic psychiatry a language and a conceptual context that would later figure in the psychiatric assessments of sexual serial killers.

Between July 1848 and March 1849, cemeteries in Paris were plagued by fifteen nocturnal disinterments of both female and male corpses, the females subjected to gross mutilation and, allegedly, *necrophagia* (eating of decayed corpse flesh) and varied sexual acts. As we so often see with the victims of lust serial killers, the female corpses were cut open, or "ripped," longitudinally along the torso and abdomen and their intestines extracted. Sometimes the heart and liver had been removed as well, and it was alleged at his trial that the perpetrator bit and chewed on some of the moldy cadavers.[1]

In some cases the corpses' mouths were "split to the ear" in Joker-like "smiley" faces (like in the infamous Black Dahlia case of the 1940s in Los Angeles) and the thighs of the female victims were slashed or their limbs entirely dismembered.[2] In his account of the case, French cultural historian Michel Foucault stated that the perpetrator would "cut them up with his bayonet, pull out the intestines and organs, and then spread them around, hanging them from the crosses and Cypress branches in a huge garland . . . there was evidence that the corpses, which were all, moreover, in a very advanced state of decomposition, had been sexually violated."[3]

The press dubbed the perpetrator the "Vampire of Montparnasse." Eventually a French army sergeant, François Bertrand, was arrested. At his military court-martial, the gallery was filled with journalists, forensic practitioners, psychiatrists and other academics from around the world. The British medical journal *The Lancet* covered the trial, explaining to readers the paradoxical moniker "vampire" left over from the days of witches and werewolves:

> This disgusting case recalls at once that form of mental aberration which reigned so extensively about a century and a half ago in the north of Europe and known under the name of vampirism. It will be recollected that vampires were suffering under a sort of nocturnal delirium which was often extended to the waking hours during which they believed that certain dead persons were rising from their graves to come and draw their blood hence arose a desire for revenge and burial places were disgracefully desecrated. Bertrand's case seems the very reverse of this; for we here see, not the dead rising to torment the living, but a man disturbing the peace of cemeteries in the most horrible manner imaginable.[4]

After his arrest, Bertrand was examined by Dr. Charles-Jacob Marchal de Calvi, a physician and psychiatrist of great repute to this day.[5] In the age of Darwinian criminology soon to be formalized by Cesare

Lombroso, Marchal expected the "vampire" to be a low-class, brutish, simian, cavemanlike "born criminal." Instead he was surprised by Bertrand's delicate, "civilized" features and intelligence.

Marchal agreed to testify in Bertrand's defense, arguing that the accused suffered from an "irresistible compulsion," which in the terminology of the era was called *monomania*, defined as a singular, pathological preoccupation or obsession in an otherwise sound mind. The term "monomania" is comparable to today's descriptions of compulsive behavioral disorders, neuroses, paraphilias, psychopathy, sociopathy and other behavioral personality disorders that are not accompanied by delusions or hallucinations.[6]

Marchal argued that Bertrand's monomania was so irresistible an impulse that it temporarily diminished his capacity to discern right from wrong, the basic requirement for a formal insanity plea.[7] This was only six years after the precedent-setting insanity plea in the McNaughton case (see chapter five).

Dr. Marchal's argument that Bertrand's "irresistible impulse" was equivalent to legal insanity was a radical departure from the principles of the McNaughton rule, as it would be again in 1955 to 1984 when the same argument was revived by American attorneys in the defense of serial killers. American lawyers argued in what became known as the volition defense that their serial-killing clients were "unable to conform their conduct to the law" as a result of an "irresistible compulsion" which was equivalent to legal insanity.[8] A Reagan-era Congress passed the Insanity Defense Reform Act that restricted the volition defense after John Hinckley Jr. was successfully acquitted by reason of insanity for his "inability to resist" the impulse to try to assassinate Ronald Reagan while under the spell of his obsession with actress Jodie Foster and the character she played in *Taxi Driver.*[9]

The evidence against Bertrand, along with his confession, was iron-clad. At issue in the trial was not even whether he was suffering from a mental disorder—nobody disputed that—but the nature and form of his disorder. Immediately after the trial followed a torrent of forensic and psychiatric literature in which leading French psychiatrists argued whether Bertrand's disorder was "erotic" (sexual) or "destructive" (sadistic-homicidal) or both; and if both, then which was "dominant," the erotic or destructive, and did it amount to legal insanity?[10]

Sexual attraction to the dead, or *necrophilia*, has many clinical, legal and cultural dimensions. It runs the spectrum from harmless romantic fantasy to homicidal compulsion, from *Sleeping Beauty* and *Twilight* romantic pseudonecrophilia to Ed Gein, *Psycho*, serial-killing necrophilia.

The current forensic authority on necrophilia is Dr. Anil Aggrawal. He categorizes necrophilia into ten progressively more severe classes:

1. *necrophilic role-players*, who engage in sex with willing partners who "play dead";

2. *romantic necrophiles*, who cannot bear separation from their loved ones who passed away and might mummify or keep their corpses;

3. *necrophilic fantasizers*, who engage in sex in proximity with the dead, in a funeral parlor or a cemetery;

4. *tactile necrophiles*, who are excited by touching or fondling corpses;

5. *fetishistic necrophiles*, who harvest and collect body parts, sometimes wearing them as amulets or jewelry, including the collection of enemy body parts (ears, skulls) as totems by soldiers in war (see chapter fourteen on the collection of Japanese body parts by GIs in the Pacific during World War II);

6. *necromutilimaniacs*, who focus on mutilating and destroying corpses;

7. *opportunistic necrophiles*, who do not necessarily fantasize about engaging in sex with corpses, but do so just the same if the opportunity arises;

8. *regular necrophiles*, who may occasionally engage in sex with the living but prefer sex with the dead;

9. *homicidal necrophiles*, who will kill the living in order to have sex with their corpses;

10. *exclusive necrophiles*, who are able to perform sexually only with the dead.[11]

It is a paradox of forensic scientific objectivity to classify a homicidal necrophile who kills people in order to have sex with their corpses (stage nine) as being one stage *less* severe than one who can *only* perform sexually with those already dead (stage ten).

Lee Mellor classifies necrophiles in a different way. He charts them on a graph between four fluid intersecting poles mapping a point by how long the corpse has been dead (warm to cold poles) balanced against the degree to which the necrophile preserves or mutilates the corpse (preservative to destructive poles). It's a scale that is more fluid in the dichotomy between the "disorganized, destructive, warm werewolf" type and the "organized, preservative, cold vampire" type of necrophile serial killer.[12]

Not everybody agrees on the criminality of necrophilia. Psychology historian Dany Nobus, for example, challenges how necrophilia's "diagnostic confusion with necrosadism and lust murder continues to inform contemporary views on the subject . . . the spurious identification of necrophilia with necrosadism and lust murder often continues to pervade popular and scientific accounts alike."[13]

The term "necrophile" itself was coined by Belgian psychiatrist Joseph Guislain in 1850, during the psychiatric debate that followed the Bertrand trial. Nobus has traced the term's first appearance in print to Guislain's 1852 French-language textbook *Leçons Orales sur les Phrénopathies* ("*Lectures in Psychology*"), featuring transcripts of lectures he delivered two years earlier.[14]

Despite Marchal's best efforts, the court rejected his insanity plea and Bertrand was convicted of violating Article 360 of the French Criminal Code, "Violation of a Grave or Tomb," which was directed at preventing grave robbing for valuables and the theft of cadavers for sale to medical schools, a minor offense carrying a penalty of three months to one year in prison and/or a fine between 16 and 200 francs. He received the maximum punishment of one year in prison.[15]

Contrary to all the reports of his suicide in 1850, after serving out his sentence François Bertrand was not even dismissed from the French army. Upon his release he served briefly as a private in a light infantry battalion in Algeria, and then settled in the Normandy port city of Le Havre, where he had the lucrative post of quartermaster for the army. On May 21, 1851, he married Euphrosine Corscelie Delauney, a seamstress. They apparently had children and remained married until Bertrand's death (cause unknown) on February 25, 1878, at the age of fifty-four.[16] Bertrand is not known to have committed any further crimes.

Robert Krafft-Ebing, the forensic psychiatrist and author of *Psychopathia Sexualis*, who would later popularize Guislain's term "necrophilia," along with "sadism" and "masochism," was only nine years old at the time of the Bertrand case. But the psychiatric debate about fetishes, paraphilias such as necrophilia, and their relationship to compulsive serial behavior in the case of Bertrand had a tremendous impact on Krafft-Ebing's later work and on our understanding of what drives serial killers to perpetrate murders accompanied by rape, mutilation and sometimes necrophilia.[17] The statistical estimates of necrophilia in cases of serial murder range from a high of 42 percent of cases to a low of at least 11 percent (chapter two).

France's First Modern Serial Killer: "The Wolf" or "Killer of Servant Girls," 1861

On May 26, 1861, at about two p.m. in Lyon, France, the country's third-largest city, an unemployed domestic servant, Marie Pichon, was crossing the busy Guillotière Bridge over the Rhône River. Lyon was in the heart of France's industrial belt and its large middle class employed many domestic servants. Marie was on her way to a servants' employment agency in the hope of securing some desperately needed work. It was there on that bridge that she would encounter *her* serial killer and survive to tell the tale.

A man suddenly rushed up from behind her, catching her attention with a light pluck at her dress. He asked if she knew where a servants' employment agency was located. He appeared to be in his fifties with a long, dark beard, an aquiline nose and very prominent blue eyes. He was clad in a blue workman's shirt, big shoes, and a gray hat with a large brim. Had he raised his hat, Marie would have seen that his head was strangely shaped, large at the base of his neck but coming almost to a cone at the top, covered in long, thick hair. A prominent scar or tumorous growth of some sort was visible on his upper lip. Marie would later say that she immediately recognized him as a "country person" by his clothing and comportment. His manner, however, was self-possessed and polite and Marie kindly told him that she herself was on the way to an employment agency seeking work as a servant and he could accompany her to the office.

What a happy coincidence, he exclaimed delightedly. His employer in the nearby town of Montluel, about twelve miles from Lyon, had urgently sent him to the city to hire a house servant. According to Pichon's statement, he said to her:

> "I have exactly the thing to suit you, I am gardener at a chateau near Montluel, and my mistress has sent me to Lyons with positive orders to bring back a house-servant, cost what it may."
>
> He enumerated the advantages I should enjoy, and said that the work would be very light, and the wages two hundred and fifty francs, besides many Christmas-boxes. A married daughter of his mistress paid her frequent visits, and always left five francs on the mantelpiece for the maid. He added, that I should be expected to attend mass regularly.
>
> The appearance, language, and manner of the man gave me so strong an impression of good faith, that, without a minute's hesitation, I accepted his offer, and we accordingly left by the train, which arrived at Montluel about nightfall—half-past seven.[18]

As she left the train station in Montluel and followed the man through the dusk along a road leading out of the small town, Marie's night of horror was about to begin at the hands of France's first modern serial killer. Some thirty years before Jack the Ripper, this serial killer would be dubbed by the French press "the Wolf," in the long tradition of "werewolf serial killers."

THE BRAVE NEW WORLD LIKE NO OTHER BEFORE

Marie Pichon and her assailant lived in a world that had been radically and rapidly transformed since the age of Little Red Riding Hood, werewolves and witch-hunters. Industrialization transformed Western civilization at its core. For some twelve thousand years the primary occupation of human beings had been growing and selling food and processing natural resources: tilling the land, hewing the wood, looming the cotton by hand and turning the clay. Arable land was the most valuable commodity in the old world, a key to wealth and power. In the preindustrial world the majority of ordinary people lived in the countryside in communities in which they were often closely tied by kin and clan relationships. These communities policed themselves through compulsory vigilance committees or citizen "watch and wards" during the night or by other unofficial means including lynching and vigilante mobs.

Two things transformed this world in the most spectacular way: steam power and the telegraph. Thirty years earlier, Marie's trip from Lyon to Montluel twelve miles away would have taken several hours. Now the trip by train took her and her assailant less than an hour. Steam power not only manufactured things faster, but it also moved people and goods faster and printed information faster and in more copious amounts and distributed it faster too. It also moved serial killers and their victims greater distances, not only to each other but away from potential witnesses.

The other source of this transformative speed was the telegraph, or what Tom Standage, in his history of it, called "the Victorian Internet."[19] It is not an exaggeration to describe the introduction of the telegraph in 1845 as being like the arrival of the Internet. Beginning in 1845 we had the capability of moving information at near-Internet speed—at least, at the speed of an electric current down a copper wire, one message at a time, without, of course, the bandwidth of today's fiber-optic Internet.

The world began to accelerate. People not only received new information faster, but they could now act on it faster, sometimes almost in real time. In government, business, diplomacy and warfare, not only could information be conveyed faster, but the logistics of deploying resources, troops or munitions were accelerated by the telegraph and steam power. The public too was covered in this new telegraphic information net, as daily news was telegraphed to newspapers and printed overnight on steam-driven presses and available to readers by the next morning.

These changes also transformed how serial killers navigated the urbanized and newly networked world, in which smaller, intimate, rural "organic communities" were supplanted by much larger, anonymous, urbanized "organized societies" where one was no longer identified by *who* they were, but merely by *what* they were: a factory worker, businessman, shoemaker, teacher, student, policeman, prostitute, vagrant, victim or, yes, once we finally named them, serial killer.

Martin Dumollard: Profile of a Serial-Killing Village Creep

Martin Dumollard, the serial killer who approached Marie Pichon on the bridge in Lyon, had already murdered at least three women and perhaps six or more. Dumollard was what we would today classify as an "organized" serial killer, painstakingly stalking and luring his victims into his trap. He used his charm and the promise of lucrative employment to entice young women to accompany him from the busy city and its many witnesses to his lonely, wooded killing grounds in the countryside outside the small town of Montluel.

Dumollard was born on April 21, 1810, in the neighboring village of Tramoyes, to a Hungarian revolutionary refugee by the name of Peter Demola, who changed his name to the more French-sounding Dumollard. Demola was an affluent landowner but an active antimonarchist and was wanted back home for plotting to assassinate the emperor of Austria-Hungary. During the Napoleonic Wars, Austro-Hungarian forces invaded part of France, and the family fled to Italy. There, Martin's father was identified, arrested and sentenced to death. Four-year-old Martin apparently witnessed his father's horrific execution by *écartèlement*, or quartering. His legs and arms were tied to four horses which tore his limbs from his torso while he was still alive. Martin would never be the same after seeing that.

Martin and his now impoverished and widowed mother returned to Tramoyes, where he was put to work as a shepherd taking care of a local landowner's herd. Dumollard probably did not have much of a childhood, but if he did, his cone-shaped head and the tumorous growth on his lip probably did not endear him to other children. It must have been a lonely existence, just the kind of loneliness in which damaged children develop their cycle of homicidal fantasies.

In 1840, despite his deformities, Martin managed to woo and marry Marianne Martinet, who worked as a servant for the same landowner as he. Marianne must have been dysfunctional in her own ways, because the two of them embarked on married life by making off with some of their employer's sheep. Martin was quickly arrested for the theft and served a one-year prison sentence. He and his wife eventually settled in the nearby village of Dagneux, abutting the town of Montluel. In 1844 Martin was again convicted, for petty theft, and sentenced to thirteen months in prison. Other than that, Dumollard attracted little attention. When his name first came up as a suspect in the murders, the town's mayor had no idea who he was.

The Dumollards lived in a ramshackle house and stable by the road in Dagneux and were unfriendly, showing themselves only when peddling small secondhand articles and clothing at local markets. Martin Dumollard was ill-tempered and kept strange nocturnal habits. Villagers would later recall that when he arrived home in the late hours of the night he would shout out to his wife a secret password so loudly that all the neighbors knew it by heart. But he did not come into open conflict with anybody and he kept to himself, as did his wife.

The First Victim

On February 28, 1855, six years before Marie Pichon's encounter on the bridge in Lyon, hunters came across the nude body of a woman in a thicket at Pizay, near the village of Tramoyes, where Dumollard had been born and about six miles northwest of his current residence in

Montluel-Dagneux. The victim was covered in freshly dried blood and had been killed by six blows to the head. Her clothes were missing except for her handkerchief, a collar, a black lace cap and a pair of shoes found nearby. It was assumed that she had been sexually assaulted. The body was brought to the church in Tramoyes, where it was photographed in the hope the woman could be somehow identified.

She was thirty-six-year-old Marie Baday, a servant who had been last seen in Lyon three days earlier. She had told acquaintances that a man from the country had offered her a well-paying position as a domestic if she could take the job immediately. On the same day that Marie Baday left Lyon with the stranger, another servant girl in Lyon, Marie Cart, had received the same offer from a strange-looking man with a disfigured lip from the country, but she delayed in deciding whether to accept the offer.

On March 4, the man returned to Lyon offering Cart the same job. This time she turned him down, but introduced the polite emissary to a friend of hers, Olympe Alubert, who immediately accepted the generous offer. The two of them arrived at Tramoyes at dusk. The man led Alubert into the same woods at Pizay where Baday had been found several days earlier. Today the thickets at Pizay are known locally as the *Bois de la Morte*—the Forest of the Dead.[20]

It's unclear whether Olympe had heard about or read in the Lyon newspapers about a dead woman found in the woods recently, and if she had, whether she knew that those were the woods the man was leading her into, but something in the situation alerted her intuition. As they approached the woods, she inexplicably took fright and ran off, seeking shelter in the first house she could find. Olympe did not have much to report to the police other than the suspect's physical description, including the deformed lip. Being six miles away from the village where Dumollard resided, he might as well have been a thousand miles away. Despite advances in communications, telegraph wires did not reach into the smaller villages of the countryside and even if they did, there was no systematic communication protocol between various police departments.

On September 22, 1855, Josephte Charlety was lured from Lyon by the same man. During the trip to her supposed new place of employment she too began to feel uneasy by his questions about her life savings. Claiming to be too tired to continue that night, Charlety stopped at an inn, agreeing to meet the man the next morning to continue the journey. Instead she stood him up and survived.

On October 31, twenty-two-year-old Jeanne-Marie Bourgeois was lured in Lyon by a man matching the same description and, also on intuition, fled from him during her voyage. By now police had arrested a suspect in the killing of Baday and were ignoring reports from "hysterical" women about their encounters with the strange man. Bourgeois was called in to view the suspect and stated that it was not the same man. Eventually the suspect was released.

In November 1855, Victorine Perrin was lured from Lyon. As he led her down a road some people approached and Dumollard fled with her belongings. Again a report was filed with police, but in a different jurisdiction. Even though by now authorities in various jurisdictions had the same reports of a man with a disfigured lip, and even the public was aware of the description, people in Dumollard's town did not make the connection (or if they did, they hesitated to report their suspicions to the police).

After his arrest, police would retrace Dumollard's movements between 1855 and 1861. They learned that he trolled for his victims in Lyon so frequently that he was known at his favorite hotel, where he would stop overnight. Police collected reports of numerous young women seen in his company, including a young woman whom he claimed was his niece, who spent the night with him at the hotel. Her identity and her fate were never determined, but hotel staff called as witnesses at Dumollard's trial identified some of her belongings found in his possession.

Dumollard's method was almost always the same. He would take the train from his small town into Lyon and descend into the urban crowd, trolling the main thoroughfares for his ideal victim: a servant girl in desperate need of employment. (He would recognize unemployed domestics by their manner of dress, their youth and the fact that they were in the street during working hours.) His opening ploy would be to ask directions to a servants' employment agency, as he did with Pichon. If his victim was, as he hoped, an unemployed servant seeking work, he would lay out the bait.

On January 17, 1859, Dumollard lured unemployed servant Julie Fargeat into the countryside some twenty miles northwest of Montluel-Dagneux. When he attacked her in a wooded area her screams brought Simon Mallet, a local farmer, to her rescue. Dumollard fled with Fargeat's belongings. But when she reported the attack to police, she was charged with vagrancy for failing to produce her identity papers, which Dumollard had run off with. We must not forget that in continental Europe the primary function of police until recently was to suppress popular rebellion and keep order among the working classes. They were not there to "protect and serve" all citizens, as police are mandated today.

On April 29, 1860, Dumollard lured Louise Michel to the same area. She managed to escape him to find refuge in a farmhouse belonging to Claude Aymond. Dumollard in the meantime fled across a field where he encountered Simon Mallet, one of the farmers who the year before had come to the aid of Julie Fargeat. Aymond and Mallet together went to their local police magistrate to report the attacks but the magistrate dismissed the notion of a "swollen lip" linking the two cases to the same offender. The report was filed away and not circulated beyond the small jurisdiction.

This is a classic example of "linkage blindness," which remains to this day one of the greatest challenges to serial-murder investigations: an inability by a police agency to recognize links from multiple cases to a single perpetrator. It's been an issue in the currently unsolved Long Island Serial Killer (LISK) case. Dumollard was getting away with his serial attacks in the 1860s as easily as Ted Bundy got away with his in the 1970s when police failed to connect him with a series of multi-jurisdictional murders.

The Capture of the "French Wolf"

Dumollard so far had been both careful and lucky, but when he targeted Marie Pichon in May 1861 he carelessly brought her to the train station at Montluel, into the police jurisdiction where he lived. After arriving in the evening at the small railway station in Montluel, where he was seen by witnesses who recognized him, Dumollard proceeded to lead Marie

Pichon away on foot toward what he told her was her new place of employment.

Pichon would later recount to police what happened next:

Placing my trunk upon his shoulder he desired me to follow, saying we had now a walk of an hour and a half, but that, by taking cross paths, we should quickly reach our destination. I carried, in one hand, a little box: in the other, my basket and umbrella. We crossed the railway and walked for some distance along the parallel road, when the man turned suddenly to the left and led me down a steep descent, skirted on both sides by thick bushes. Presently he faced round, saying that my trunk fatigued him, that he would conceal it in a thicket and come back for it with a carriage on the morrow. We then abandoned the path altogether, crossed several fields, and came to some bushes, in which he hid the trunk, saying we should presently see the chateau. After this, we traversed other fields, twice crossing over places that looked like dried-up water-courses, and, finally, through very difficult ways, rather scrambling than walking, arrived at the summit of a little hill.

I must mention something that had attracted my attention. Throughout the walk my guide seemed remarkably attentive, constantly cautioning me to mind my steps, and assisting me carefully over every obstacle. Immediately after crossing the hill I spoke of, his movements began to give me uneasiness. In passing some vines he tried to pull up a large stake. It, however, resisted his efforts, and, as I was following close on his heels, he did not persevere. A little farther, he stooped down and seemed to be endeavoring to pick up one of the large stones that lay about. Though now seriously alarmed, I asked, with all the indifference I could command, what he was looking for? He made an unintelligible reply, and presently repeated the maneuver. Again I inquired what he was looking for,—Had he lost anything?

"Nothing, nothing," he replied; "it was only a plant I meant to pick for my garden." Other singular movements kept me in a state of feverish alarm. I observed that he several times lagged behind, and, whenever he did so, moved his hands about under his blouse as though in search of a weapon. I was frozen with terror. Run away I durst not, for I felt he would pursue me; but I constantly urged him to lead the way, assuring him I would follow.

In this way we reached the top of another small hill, on which stood a half-built cottage. There was a cabbage-garden, and a good wheel road. My very fear now gave me the necessary courage. I resolved to go no farther, and at once said, "I see you have led me wrong. I shall stop here." Hardly had the words left my mouth, when he turned sharply round, stretched his arms above my head, and let fall a cord with a running noose. We were at this moment almost in contact. Instinctively, I let fall everything I carried, and with both hands seized the man's two arms, pushing him from me with all my strength. This movement saved me. The cord, which was already round my head, only caught and pulled off my cap. I shrieked out, "My God! My God! I am lost!"

I was too much agitated to observe why the assassin did not repeat his attack. All I recollect is, that the cord was still in his hand. I caught up my box and umbrella, and flew down the hill. In crossing a little ditch, I fell and bruised myself severely, losing my umbrella. Fear, however, gave me strength. I heard the heavy steps of the murderer in pursuit, and was on my legs again in an instant, running for life. At that moment, the moon rose above the trees on my left, and I saw the glimmer of a white house on the plain. Toward this I flew, crossing the railway, and falling repeatedly in my headlong course. Soon I saw lights. It was Balan. I stopped at the first house. A man ran out, and I was saved.

This time when the incident and description of the assailant with his deformed lip were reported to the police, the news quickly made its way into the towns of Montluel and Dagneux. Dumollard "the Wolf" had struck too close to home. Within the day village gossips and informants brought to the police's attention the strange, unfriendly couple that resided in Dagneux and the husband with his eccentric nocturnal habits and the distinctive deformity on his lip.

Police descended upon Dumollard's house and found what we recognize today as a serial killer's typical stash of trophies: articles that obviously did not belong to Dumollard's peasant wife, Marianne. There were items of a style typically worn by servant girls, whose employers demanded an "upscale" look: tailored silken dresses, linen, pieces of lace, ribbons, gowns, handkerchiefs, shoes, cheap costume jewelry. Some bore traces of blood; others had been roughly washed and wrung out. Police inventoried an extraordinary 1,250 items. A gendarme commented, "The man must have a charnel somewhere."

Both Martin Dumollard and his wife, Marianne, were taken into custody, as it was obvious she was aware of the stash of property. Now witnesses in Montluel came forward to report that Dumollard had been seen back in December 1858 arriving at the train station in the company of another young woman. Her baggage had been checked at the station but had never been retrieved.

Dumollard's wife, Marianne, confessed that on the night her husband was seen with the missing woman at the station, he "came home very late, bringing a silver watch and some blood-stained clothes. He gave me the latter to wash, only saying, in his short way, 'I have killed a girl in Montmain woods, and I am going back to bury her.' He took his pickax and went out. The next day he wanted to claim the girl's luggage, but I dissuaded him from doing so."

The Investigation and Trial of the Dumollards

The Montmain woods were located just beyond the northern limit of Dagneux, and Dumollard's house. The Dumollards were now brought to the location. Marianne was unable to point out the burial site and Martin refused to say anything. Eventually the search party detected an anomaly in the ground and began to dig there. They uncovered the skeletal remains of a female with a severe skull fracture. She was never identified.

The next day, the search moved to a communal wood, slightly north. This time Martin was more cooperative. He claimed that he was in the employ of two mysterious men who paid him to lure women from Lyon and deliver them into their hands in the countryside. They would murder the women, he said, and as a reward give him the victims' belongings. He pointed out a site in the woods where police then uncovered a well-preserved body of a female lying on her back, her left hand on her chest and a clump of soil clutched in her other hand, which seemed to indicate that she had been buried alive and attempted to dig herself free but suffocated in the earth.

Dumollard stated that his two mysterious patrons had also killed Marie Baday, whose body had been found at Pizay back in 1855, and that they also on separate occasions threw the corpses of three women off a bridge into the Rhône River. His wife, he said, was aware of the murders and burials and would wash the blood from the clothing, which she either wore herself or sold at markets.

In the end, police linked Dumollard with three corpses, one of which was never successfully identified, and to the attempted murder of seven women, including Marie Pichon. After his statement that his employers threw three women into the Rhône River, he was also suspected in the deaths of several women pulled from the river in the early 1850s, but the cases were too old to be conclusively linked to him.

Husband and wife were both put on trial in January 1862.

Marianne took the stand and testified that on two occasions her husband had brought clothing belonging to girls he said he had killed. She stated that she noticed some were stained with blood but she did not mention it to him. She described their relationship as being on "indifferent terms," with him frequently staying away nights or returning home late. Typical of female accomplices of male serial killers, she claimed that she remained with him and did not report his crimes because she was afraid of him.

The prosecution displayed items believed to have been taken from victims. There were 70 handkerchiefs, 57 pairs of stockings, 28 scarves, 38 caps, 10 corsets, 9 gowns and a multitude of other miscellaneous items. Some of the items were apparently stained with blood. (A definitive test to distinguish bloodstains from similar stains like those caused by rust, paint, plant spores or chewing tobacco was developed that year by Dutch scientist J. Izaak Van Deen, but not in time to be available for use in the Dumollard case.) Witnesses in court identified some of the items belonging to family members murdered by Dumollard.

At one point the judge asked Dumollard, "Do you recollect this dress?"

"Oh, perfectly."

"And you, Marianne Dumollard?"

"Of course. I have worn it."

"Have you not also worn a cap with marks of blood?"

"Certainly not. I would have *washed* it," she replied.

Throughout his trial, Martin Dumollard appeared almost uninterested, calmly munching on sandwiches during breaks and insisting that his two mysterious partners had committed all the murders. Of Marie Pichon, Dumollard claimed that he was deliberately trying to scare her off to "save her" from his homicidal confederates, who were waiting for him to deliver her. He denied attempting to throw a cord around her neck and claimed that he only threw his arms around her neck to frighten her.

At the end of the four-day trial the jury returned a guilty verdict. Martin was sentenced to death while his wife was sentenced to twenty years of hard labor. A guillotine was set up in the public square in Montluel and after being allowed a last meal with his wife, Dumollard went calmly to his death, insisting to the end that it was his employers who had murdered all the victims. He was executed on March 8, 1862. His head was delivered to the medical faculty in Lyon, where, after being studied for phrenological anomalies, the skin was peeled off the skull, cured and remounted like a mannequin head; it can be viewed today in its glass cabinet in the Museum of Medical Sciences and Health in Rillieux la Pape.[21]

The Psychopathology of Dumollard: Simple Robbery or Paraphilic Sex Crimes?

The Dumollard case was extraordinary in its time, and it was covered by newspapers as far away as the United States and Australia. Although Dumollard had been nicknamed the "French Wolf" in some of the press reports, his murders were not characterized by the frenzied "werewolf" mutilation and evisceration of victims.

The nonchalant serial murder by robbers and bandits was still a familiar crime in that epoch, and Dumollard's collection of articles of female clothing and his wife's collaboration in disposing of some of the belongings suggested to many that Dumollard's primary motive was material gain, and that *if* any sexual assaults took place, they were secondary, opportunistic acts rather than a primary motivator. After all, he had already been convicted twice for theft, and it was impossible to be sure whether the victims had been raped.[22]

None of that means that Dumollard was *not* pathologically driven by sexual fantasies and impulses. His sexual fantasy might have been to stalk women and take control of them by stripping them naked. It is not uncommon for a sex offender to be unable to ejaculate or even achieve an erection during the commission of his crime. Often sexual offenders get satisfaction only after they leave the crime scene and retreat with souvenirs to the privacy and security of their homes. Once there, they relive what they have just done, compulsively masturbating, sometimes with items taken from the victims—trophies or "totems," sometimes even body parts—which act to bridge their fantasy to the reality of what they have perpetrated. (Today, photos or videos made by the serial killer of the victim often are used as masturbatory totems.)

Dumollard's obsessive targeting, his days-long stalking of victims like Marie Cart, to whom he would patiently return if he failed to lure them away on the first try, suggests a pathological focus and energy far exceeding the profit obtained by selling a servant girl's clothing and cheap jewelry. If his murders were strictly about material gain, there were many easier, less risky, less time- and energy-consuming means. Dumollard was clearly driven by the pathological pleasure derived from trolling for victims and taking control of them. The victims' belongings were trophies.

DUMOLLARD VERSUS ALBERT DeSALVO, THE "BOSTON STRANGLER"

Dumollard might even have had issues with his peasant-shepherd class, forced upon him by his father's execution, versus the servant girls' marginally higher status. His case has some echoes a hundred years later in the case of Albert DeSalvo, the "Boston Strangler," who raped and murdered thirteen women in the early 1960s. Canadian anthropologist and serial-murder expert Elliott Leyton pointed out that DeSalvo made numerous statements about his low status.[23] DeSalvo felt that he had "married up" in class—his wife, Irmgard, came from a respectable middle-class family, as did his mother, who "married down" with Albert's abusive, low-class father. Similarly, Dumollard's parents came from the landowning middle class in Austria-Hungary before being impoverished by his father's revolutionary activities and execution.

DeSalvo first came to police attention not as a serial killer but in the "Measuring Man" incidents, a series of nonviolent, almost comical sexual crimes. He would pose as a talent scout for a modeling agency and ask women for permission to measure them. While wrapping a measuring tape around their bust and hips, he would "accidentally" touch and fondle them. Many women did not even notice DeSalvo's touch; complaints started to be made to police by angry women only when they realized that no photographer was coming to shoot their pictures.

When he was arrested as the Measuring Man, DeSalvo told police:

> I been a poor boy all my life, I come from a bad home, you know all that, why should I kid you? Look, I don't know anything about modeling or cameras . . . I'm not educated and these girls was all college graduates, understand me? I made fools of them . . . I made them do what I wanted and accept me and listen to me.

Later, after he was charged in the rape-murders of twelve elderly women and one college student, DeSalvo commented on his previous Measuring Man crimes:

> Mostly, I got a big kick out of those girls around Harvard. I'm not good-looking, I'm not educated, but I was able to put something over on high-class people. I know that they look down on people who come from my background. They think they are better than me. They was all college kids and I never had anything in my life but I outsmarted them. I was supposed to feel that they was better than me because they was college people . . . when I told them they could be models that was like saying the same thing: you are better than

me, you are better than anybody, you can be a model . . . Anybody with any sense could've found out. They never asked me for proof.

They was times when I was doing that Measuring Man thing that I hated them girls for being so stupid and I wanted to do something to them . . . something that would make them think, even for a little while . . . that would let them know that I was as good as they was, maybe better and smarter.

Dumollard too may have gotten psychosexual pleasure from fooling and taking control of "uppity," well-dressed, urban servant girls who looked down their noses at a peasant with a deformed lip and pointy cone head.

THE SERVANT GIRL FETISH

Dumollard's "hang-up" dovetailed with society's new fear and mistrust of urban modernity and female mobility. As industrialization created inventory-based retail stores and accounting and clerical work that enriched the middle classes, young, single women began to leave their country homes seeking jobs other than that of a schoolteacher, which was the only socially acceptable profession for "decent" unmarried women. Young women took up residence in cities away from the supervision of their families. Some found work in factories, and eventually stores and offices, but most young, single women were employed as servants in affluent upper- and middle-class households in need of cheap domestic help.

The potential sexual behavior of young, independent women unsupervised in the big city became known as the "girl problem."[24] For ages, the only women who went about in public spaces unsupervised were destitute vagrants and prostitutes. Now young, unmarried women were everywhere to be seen in public. Boardinghouses for single workingwomen, where they were strictly chaperoned and monitored, became a common feature of nineteenth-century cities. In the way that airline hostesses and nurses until very recently were endowed with a mythical promiscuity, all young, single, independent workingwomen were regarded as "sexually suspect"—especially servant girls, who became the focus of nineteenth-century pornography such as *My Secret Life* by "Walter," so explicit that it couldn't be published in its entirety in the US until 1966 or in Britain until 1995.[25] (See chapter ten for more on the nature of pornography in the mid-Victorian era.)

Moreover, servant girls were required by most of their affluent employers to dress presentably, to be finely perfumed and adorned. The fetishistic dimensions of servant-girl clothing, from uniforms to ordinary upscale dresses, were enormously attractive to fetishist paraphilics. (The "sexy French maid" outfit is still popular in sex-store lingerie and costume sections and trotted out with fishnets for giggles at Halloween parties.) There were so many servant girls out there that Dumollard was trolling for them effortlessly on just one bridge in downtown Lyon. They were even easier to lure away than a prostitute; after all, what prostitute would leave with a country bumpkin like Dumollard to turn a trick twelve miles away in a dark forest? (Or, at least, without a substantial show of cash up front?) But a servant girl—she was the perfect Little Red Riding Hood, ready to follow what she thought was a fellow-servant emissary from a wealthy potential employer.

That servant girls had been relegated to "less-dead" status in European society was evident in the French press, especially in the conservative national newspaper *Le Figaro*, which published jokes related to the Dumollard case, most of them bad sexual puns on the French word for "maid," which is "*bonne*," the same as "good."[26]

While it is not inconceivable that Dumollard murdered his victims literally for the "clothes off their back"—for some in that epoch clothes were the only thing of value they had (even today murders are not uncommonly committed for merely an iPhone or a pair of Nikes)—the fetishistic totem as which the clothing of his less-dead victims seemed to operate for him, and his retention of the items in his house, suggests that Dumollard was indeed driven by a psychopathological fetishistic compulsion rather than by money.

Martin Dumollard was himself, as a peasant, relegated to the less-dead. When in 1862 the painter Jean-François Millet exhibited his famous depiction of a peasant in the field, *Man with a Hoe*, many assumed it was literally a portrait of Dumollard. In 1863 the French critic and essayist Paul de Saint-Victor, inspired by the Dumollard case, wrote of the painting, "Imagine a monster without a brow, dim-eyed and with an idiotic grin, planted in the middle of a field like a scarecrow. No traces of intelligence humanize this brute at rest. Has he just been working or murdering? Does he dig the land or hollow out the grave?"[27]

Andreas Bichel, the "Girl Slaughterer," Germany, 1808

While the Dumollard case in 1861 was something unique and completely new to France, it was not all that new to the territory of Europe. A very similar case of servant-girl-clothing-fetish killings had unfolded in Bavaria, Germany. Just like Dumollard, Andreas Bichel targeted servant girls, his motive ostensibly the theft of their clothes, and his wife was reported wearing and selling some of the victims' clothing. And just like Dumollard's, Bichel's murders were in their time perceived as primarily motivated by money, with sexual or fetishistic overtones as opportunistic and secondary.

Unlike the Dumollard case, however, the Bichel case was revisited several times during the century and reshaped and rethought until it went from being considered serial robbery to serial lust mutilation fetish murder; it is an excellent example of how we construct our concepts of what serial killers are by redefining what we once thought they were. We are told that the past cannot be changed, but any historian knows that the past is infinitely changeable. The more we research and learn about the past, the more the past changes for us.

Andreas Bichel, forty-eight years old when arrested, was a familiar figure in his small town of Regendorf. Like Dumollard (and many serial killers) he had a record of petty thefts—in his case, of vegetables from a neighbor's garden and an attempt to drive off some hay from his employer's barn. Otherwise, Bichel did not attract unfavorable attention. He married, and he maintained a small cottage. After he was fired for his attempt to steal hay, he and his wife ran a tailor shop and secondhand-clothing store. (Before the rise of industrial manufacturing, most ready-to-wear clothing and shoes sold in shops were secondhand.)

Bichel was perceived as a town character, a wheeler-dealer running all sorts of little businesses—from his tailor shop, and directed at female customers—including an employment agency for servant girls and a fortune-telling service that promised unmarried girls a glimpse of their future husbands (his "crystal ball" was an ordinary magnifying glass that he had propped up on a wooden board).

In October 1806, Barbara Reisinger, a young peasant girl, told her parents she had an appointment with Bichel in his tailor shop to discuss finding work as a servant. Bichel's wife was in the shop when Barbara arrived, but she had to leave shortly afterward for work in another village. When the wife returned home, the shop was soaked with water. Bichel told her he had spilled a bucket of water. Barbara Reisinger, in the meantime, failed to return home.

When her father came looking for his missing daughter, Bichel said he had found a position for her in nearby Nuremberg. A few weeks later he sent a message to the father stating that Barbara had married an ambassador and had asked Bichel to collect her finest clothing from her parents and forward it to her. When her parents did not comply, Bichel turned up at their home to chide them for not passing on the clothes. Apologetically, Barbara's mother packed her daughter's best dresses, and her father helped Bichel transport the clothing back to his shop. In a world without telegraph or telephone, and with a high rate of illiteracy, perhaps Barbara's simple peasant parents never thought it odd that their daughter had not even sent them a letter reporting her good fortune and marriage.

In any case, there were no "police" with whom to lodge a missing-person complaint. A family suspecting foul play had to collect their own evidence and present it before a magistrate and secure warrants, all at their own expense. It was beyond the comprehension and means of a typical peasant. When the father heard that Bichel had been seen selling his daughter's clothing, he confronted Bichel, who denied it and threatened him. And there it ended, until another missing girl's family was not as easily dismissed.

On February 15, 1808, Katherina Seidel told her sisters she was going to Bichel's shop to have her fortune told. Bichel, she said, had told her that for the magic glass to work, she needed to change her clothes three times during the fortune-telling session and to bring only her finest dresses. Katherina Seidel never returned from her appointment.

When her sisters went to the shop to inquire about Katherina, Bichel said she had left in the company of a male stranger. The sisters were aware of the rumors about Barbara Reisinger's disappearance, and in fact, several women since then had been approached by Bichel and invited to bring changes of clothes to fortune-telling sessions, but their intuition had warned them off. A few months later, one of the sisters saw in another shop a tailor sewing what she recognized as cloth from a dress belonging to Katherina. When she inquired about it, the tailor told her he was filling an order for Andreas Bichel.

The Seidel family was more affluent and better educated than the peasant Reisingers, and they lodged a formal complaint with the magistrate. On May 20, 1808, Bavarian gendarmes arrived at Bichel's shop armed with arrest and search warrants for both Andreas Bichel and his wife. When Bichel was arrested, police noticed that he was attempting to dispose of a handkerchief he had in his possession. Seized from him and shown to one of the sisters, it was immediately identified as Katherina's.

When questioned, Bichel claimed he bought the handkerchief at a market and that he had invited Katherina to the shop when a young man, whose identity he did not know, entered and asked him to introduce him to Katherina. He claimed that Katherina had gone off with the stranger and that he heard she was now living in another town and was seen dressed in "French clothes." When asked about the "magic glass" Bichel denied telling fortunes and stated that another man had conducted fortune-telling sessions in his shop the previous year.

A search of the shop revealed trunks of female clothing, some of which was identified by the two missing girls' families. It was ascertained that Bichel's wife had sold some of the clothing, but she denied knowing where it came from. A further investigation identified several girls who had been invited for "magic glass" sessions with their three best dresses but had at the last minute changed their minds. The police now had a good idea of what they were dealing with, but how to prove it without a body or even signs of blood?

One of the Bavarian gendarmes was accompanied by his dog, which he noticed kept sniffing and pawing near a shed at the back of Bichel's house. On May 22, police began digging around the shed. Under a pile of straw and litter in a corner, they unearthed what looked like human bones. When they dug deeper, they discovered the lower half of a human torso and legs wrapped in cotton rags. In another corner, they unearthed the upper part of a headless torso and a decayed severed head. These were later identified as the remains of the missing servant girl Barbara Reisinger. The second corpse was found nearby, also cut in half. The body was identified as that of Katherina Seidel by a pair of earrings still worn by the dead girl.

Physicians who examined the corpses were puzzled by evidence that both upper torsos had been split open longitudinally down the chest and thorax with a knife driven in with a hammer, like a chisel. The arms were still attached to the torsos, but the feet had been severed at the ankles. Reisinger's body was too decomposed for the doctors to determine a cause of death, but Katherina Seidel's corpse was in a better state and revealed minor head trauma and a stab wound to the neck among the other injuries. The physicians reported that there was no reason to suppose that Katherina . . .

. . . was dead or even mortally wounded before she was cut up. She might have been stunned by a blow on the head, but it could not have been mortal, neither was the stab in the neck sufficient to have produced death . . . her death was occasioned by cutting open and dividing her body.[28]

Confronted with this evidence back in the police barracks, Bichel now offered to tell "the truth." He first concocted a lame story of how Katherina had been murdered by strangers in his house; then, after demanding assurances that he would not be punished for it, he confessed that in the heat of an angry argument with her, he struck Katherina on the head with a log but had never intended to kill her. Bichel built one layer of falsehoods on top of the last. But when asked about the second corpse, Bichel obstinately denied any knowledge of it.

Had this happened two years earlier, Bichel would have been put to torture. But Bavaria had joined the Napoleonic Empire and introduced the enlightened laws and policies advanced by Napoleon, including the abolition of torture on July 7, 1806.

The technique adopted to replace torture was to take the suspect to the scene of the crime, and if possible to interrogate him in view of the corpse. Police believed this technique never failed, especially with child murderers. (It's a technique police were still using in 1957, when they took Ed Gein to see the body of his mutilated victim to persuade him to confess. It worked.)[29]

Bichel was immune to the approach; confronted with the sight of the two dismembered corpses, he continued to deny knowing anything about the second corpse. But two days later, Bichel relented and admitted to murdering Barbara Reisinger, declaring his wife's complete innocence. She was released, which is a hint perhaps as to why Bichel might have made the confession.

Bichel stated that Barbara Reisinger had come into his shop in September 1806 for the purpose of finding employment as a servant. While they were talking, he was "struck" by an impulse to murder her for the dress she was wearing.

He offered to give her a glimpse of her future husband through a "magic glass," which she accepted. Bichel put before her a board with an ordinary magnifying glass attached to it, and warned her not to touch it under any circumstances. He explained that to ensure she did not, in her excitement at seeing her future husband in the glass, reach out for it, he had to blindfold her and tie her hands behind her back before beginning the session. The naïve girl eagerly agreed. Bichel confessed that he then killed her with a knife stab to her throat and that she "instantly fell" with a single sigh. He was then suddenly overwhelmed by a desire to see her insides, and he cut her open from chest to sternum, exposing her internal organs. Afterward he chopped her body into pieces, to conceal it more easily, and buried the pieces at the shed. He strewed sand and ashes in the shop to absorb the massive pools of blood, and washed the mess away with water.

In the year after murdering Barbara, Bichel said, he attempted to lure other girls into his trap, but failed until he came upon Katherina Seidel.

On the day of the murder, I sent for Katherina, and when she arrived, I said to her, since we are quite alone, I will let you look in my magic mirror. But you must go home and fetch your best clothes, so that you may be able to shift yourself several times. When she had returned in her common working clothes, carrying her other things in her apron, I rolled a white napkin round a board, and brought a spyglass, both of which I laid upon the table, forbidding her to touch either that or the glass. I then tied her hands behind her with a bit of packing string, the same which I had before used for Barbara Reisinger, and bound a handkerchief over her eyes. I then stabbed her in the throat with a knife which I had in readiness. I had a desire to see how she was made inwardly, and for this purpose I took a wedge, which I placed upon her breast bone, and struck it with a cobbler's hammer. I thus opened her breast, and cut through the fleshy parts of her body with a knife. I began to cut her open as soon as ever I had stabbed her; and no man, however quickly he may pray, could get through his rosary, or say ten Hail Marys in the time it took me to cut open her breast and the rest of her body. I cut up this person as a butcher does a sheep, chopping the corpse with an ax into portions which would go into the pit which I had already dug for it on the hill. The whole time I was so eager that I trembled, and could have cut out a bit and eaten it. When Seidel had received the first stab, she screamed, struggled, and sighed six or seven times. As I cut her open immediately after stabbing her, it is very possible that she may still have been alive when I began cutting. I buried the fragments of the body, after having carefully locked the doors. I washed the bloody shift and gown belonging to Seidel twice, and hid them from my wife, as a cat tries to hide its young, carrying them about from one place to another. I put the other bloody things into the stove, and burned them.

My only reason for murdering Reisinger and Seidel was desire for their clothes. I must confess that I did not want them; but it was exactly as if someone stood at my elbow, saying, "Do this and buy corn," and whispered to me that I should thus get something without risk of discovery.[30]

In February 1809, Bichel was sentenced to death by being "broken on the wheel from the feet upward, without the previous mercy-stroke, and his body to be afterward exposed on the wheel." It was a cruel and barbaric sentence, and under the enlightened Napoleonic influence in Bavaria, it was commuted to a quick death by beheading—not as an act of mercy to Bichel but "out of regard to the moral dignity of the state, which ought not, as it were, to vie with a murderer in cruelty."[31]

"THE STRATEGY OF SERIALIZATION": TRANSFORMING BICHEL INTO A SERIAL-KILLING FETISH RIPPER

Andreas Bichel became known as the Bavarian *Mädchenschlächter*— "maiden slaughterer." In the Dumollard case, the psychiatric debate on his motive had focused on the question of whether it was sexual or material gain or both, while in the Bertrand case the debate was as to whether his motives were "erotic" or "destructive." But in the trial of Andreas Bichel fifty years earlier, those kinds of questions were not raised immediately.

The case of Bichel was first described in a book of unique forensic cases published in 1811 by Anselm Ritter von Feuerbach, a Bavarian judge.[32] Feuerbach describes Bichel as a weak and timid individual who secretly rages at those he feels offended him but is too cowardly to express himself. He is portrayed as subjecting himself to the social order because his "effeminate" character is too weak for him to act out openly against the society he secretly despises and feels wronged by; this is perhaps an early attempt to describe psychopathy. Feuerbach writes, "If these characteristics of cruelty, harshness, avarice, and timidity joined by the rudeness of the mind, the lack of education and formation, even a limited intelligence, which tends to stare stupidly at one point, then the character has achieved a state in which crimes such as the ones committed by Bichel are possible."

Focusing on Bichel's stubborn lying and determination to confess to no more than what was exposed of his crimes, Feuerbach argued that Bichel was an example of the *fallen man*, who succumbed to crime out of weakness. Feuerbach saw Bichel's cowardly timidity, combined with greed, as the cause of his criminality. His motive was material gain, while his timid psychopathology allowed him to pursue that objective through murder while maintaining a respectable civil identity (a mask of sanity) in front of his neighbors and the community. As for Bichel's pathological dissections of the victims' chest cavities, Feuerbach hardly mentions them, and he dismisses them as secondary opportunistic acts of no importance to the nature of the crime itself.[33]

After his conviction, Bichel was forgotten and faded from public memory. When the Dumollard case broke in 1861, the press drew no parallels with Bichel, despite the remarkably similar circumstances: multiple murders of servant girls, allegedly for their clothes.

Bichel suddenly reappeared on the record in 1886, two years before Jack the Ripper, in the pages of Richard Krafft-Ebing's *Psychopathia Sexualis*. Krafft-Ebing includes Bichel along with other case studies of sexual-lust murder, but rejects and abridges the conclusion of Feuerbach and the court, that greed was the motive for the murders. Historian Peter Becker recently accused Krafft-Ebing of falsely constructing the notion of a serial sexual psychopathology through what Becker calls "the strategy of serialization." Characterizing Krafft-Ebing, who was the Chair of Psychiatry at the University of Vienna, as an "author," Becker alleges bad scholarship and flawed science:

With abridged, serial quotations from different sources, authors such as Krafft-Ebing tried to overcome the problem of a complexity of motives that led to the killings. The monotonous repetition of descriptions of murder, lust, and hereditary taints was one of the solutions to this problem. This style of narrative gave the impression that these cases revealed a common driving force that was hidden only from the untrained gaze and exerted its influence at all times and at all places.[34]

Indeed, in Krafft-Ebing's book, the case of Bichel is offered as "the most horrible example, and one which most pointedly shows the connection between lust and a desire to kill . . . Lust potentiated as cruelty, murderous lust extending to anthropophagy [cannibalism]."[35]

Labeling the case in Latin—*puellas stupratas necavit et dissecuit* ("girls raped, killed and dissected [hewed]")—Krafft-Ebing offers no case details other than a single short paragraph quoting Bichel:

I opened her breast and with a knife cut through the fleshy parts of the body. Then I arranged the body as a butcher does beef, and hacked it with an ax into pieces of a size to fit the hole which I had dug up in the mountain for burying it. I may say that while opening the body I was so greedy that I trembled, and could have cut out a piece and eaten it.

In his confession, however, Bichel stated that his first murder was on a "sudden impulse" to kill Barbara Reisinger "for the dress she was wearing"—not to rob her of her dress, but literally *for the dress* she was wearing. It was as fetishistic a sex crime as were Dumollard's killings. Bichel would state, "My only reason for murdering Reisinger and Seidel was desire for their clothes." His various statements that his victims no longer needed their clothing because they now wore "French style" dresses are strangely elaborate and repetitive, revealing a preoccupation with female style and attire, suggesting, again, some sort of pathological obsession.

Numerous serial killers have been triggered by a victim's attire or kept collections of fetish clothing they forced abducted victims to wear. Obviously, these homicidal clothing fetishes are shaped not only by the fashion of the era, but by what the fashion is associated with, what meaning it is imbued with and how that meaning is imprinted and sexualized and portrayed in the cultural media available at the time. There is somewhere a doctoral thesis waiting to be written on the history and evolution of homicidal-fetish fashion wear.

For Krafft-Ebing, who was instrumental in identifying fetishes—the sexualization of inanimate objects—the pathological motives for Bichel's murders were crystal clear. The tying of the victim's hands behind her back, the blindfolding, the mutilation and dismemberment—these were "signature" serial murders. The dismemberment of the bodies was entirely unnecessary for concealment, since he buried them in his yard rather than transporting the body parts to distant locations. The dismemberment and burial weren't for concealment but for control and eventually possession of his victims beyond their deaths. The clothes that Bichel kept, just as in the case of Dumollard, became the fetishistic totems of that control and possession. That's why so many choice items of the victims' clothing in both cases were found among the killers' possessions and not sold, as they would have been if profit had been the motive.

The "Race of Bichels"

The Bichel case would raise its head during the Jack the Ripper murders in 1888. After his first "canonical" murder, that of Mary Ann Nichols on August 31, before he was nicknamed Jack the Ripper, the London newspaper the *Pall Mall Gazette* referred to a "race of Bichels" and to the sexual psychopathology of the murder.

A PRECEDENT FOR THE WHITECHAPEL MURDER

Owing to its exceptional atrocity and seeming purposelessness, it has been suggested that the Whitechapel murder must need be the work of a maniac. The utter poverty of the woman is against the supposition that the murderer's motive could be greed; jealousy is equally out of the question; there is nothing to show that she had enemies; and, even assuming a motive, no sane malefactor, after cutting his victim's throat, would deliberately mutilate her out of pure fiendishness.

A striking case of this sort, resembling in several of its features the Whitechapel murder, occurred some four score years ago in Bavaria. In 1806 there lived at the village of Regensdorf a day laborer of the name Andreas Bichel . . . His motive, as he alleged, was to appropriate the girls' clothing—of which, however, he admitted he had no need, and could only dispose of with great difficulty . . .

There is, unfortunately, no reason to believe that the race of the Bichels is extinct. It is probable that the miscreant who committed the Whitechapel murder has much in common with him. None but a densely stupid man, devoured by greed, would risk his neck for such insignificant plunder as he could obtain from a street-walker; none but a stealthy coward would steal on a woman unawares and cut her throat; and, finally, none but a creature with a lust for blood and devoid of all sense of pity would, after killing his victim, mutilate her body.[36]

There are no references in the *Pall Mall Gazette* article to Krafft-Ebing's 1886 *Psychopathia Sexualis* because the book would not be translated into English until 1892. But by 1888, on the eve of Jack the Ripper, in the days *before* the Whitechapel serial killer would become legendary as the archetypal modern serial killer, the notion of sexual-lust mutilation killing was familiar even for newspaper readers, with or without Krafft-Ebing.[37]

Dumollard and Bichel were hardly the only serial killers of the pre–Jack the Ripper era. They are only the tip of a large iceberg. Cases of pathological sex crimes, including serial murder, were cropping up everywhere on both sides of the Atlantic.

What follow, in chronological order, are outlines of the more prominent "forgotten" serial killers in the Western world *before* Jack the Ripper made his appearance.

Giorgio Orsolano, the "Hyena of San Giorgio" or "Cannibal Sausage Maker"—Italy 1835

Giorgio Orsolano was born in 1803 in the small town of San Giorgio Canavese, near Turin in northern Italy. After his father died he was given up by his mother to be raised and educated by his uncle, a priest. Apparently, the uncle was unable to manage the unruly Orsolano and returned him to his mother, who essentially allowed him to run wild. As a teenager, he committed several petty thefts, including stealing candles from a church.

In June 1823, he was arrested at the age of twenty for attempting to rape sixteen-year-old Teresa Pignocco, whom he ambushed while she was relieving herself in a forest. The victim's cries had brought her mother to the scene, forcing Orsolano to flee, but he was easily identified in the small town. (A more recent version of this case on Italian *Wikipedia*, citing the original court records, claims that Orsolano held Pignocco prisoner in her home for six days.[38]) On December 15, 1823, Orsalano was sentenced to eight years in prison for the attempted rape and several counts of theft. He proved to be a model prisoner and was apprenticed in the prison pharmacy.

After serving his full sentence, Orsalano was released on December 13, 1831, with a certificate of good conduct and returned to his small town, where he was employed in a pharmacy and then leased a store where he attempted to operate a delicatessen, which failed. During this time, he began dating his second cousin, Domenica Nigra, a twenty-four-year-old widow who owned a wineshop.[39] After his business failed, Orsolano moved into her premises and the couple added a tailor-and-textiles shop and sausage making to Domenica's wine store.

On June 24, 1832, approximately six months after his release from prison—Orsolano would have just turned thirty, close to the average age of twenty-eight when a serial killer first kills—nine-year-old Catherine Givogre disappeared from town. Search parties failed to find any trace of her.

On February 14, 1833, ten-year-old Catherine Scavarda vanished. Again, search parties could find no trace of the missing girl. Even though wolf attacks on humans are extremely rare, it was believed that wolves attacked and carried off both girls in a famine year. Despite his record, no suspicion fell on Giorgio Orsolano, who appeared to have settled down into the life of a respectable village shopkeeper. On July 7, 1833, a daughter, Margherita, was born to Orsolano and Domenica, and in April 1834 they married.

March 3, 1835, was the Tuesday market day in San Giorgio, and also the last day of the carnival leading up to Lent. The town was chaotic with celebrants, visitors and merchants. Fourteen-year-old Francesca Tonso came in from the nearby village of Montalenghe to sell eggs in the market square. She never returned home. Her parents went into town to search for their daughter. Perhaps Orsolano thought he and the girl would not have been noticed together in the carnival crowds that day, but witnesses very quickly recalled that he purchased eggs from the girl in the market and that she was last seen accompanying him to his store to be paid. But when the parents called on Orsolano's store, they were rudely rebuffed by him.

The distraught parents now filed a complaint with a magistrate, who questioned Orsolano. He claimed that the girl left after being paid and perhaps had been robbed on her way home, a plausible scenario. There was insufficient evidence to search Orsolano's premises. Orsolano in the meantime fled to his uncle's house, where he asked for funds and prepared to become a fugitive. The record is murky as to what exactly happened next, but it seems that suspicious citizens broke into Orsolano's store and searched it themselves, discovering a pair of clogs, a girl's cap and a scrap of cloth, which the parents identified as belonging to their missing daughter. A more thorough search of the store revealed a cabinet with fresh bloodstains and indications that an attempt had been made to wash them out. A wet sack was also found, and it was assumed that the body of the girl was transported in it.

In the village a cry broke out for the "werewolf" to be immediately lynched, and Orsolano was transported to a nearby police barracks for his own safety and to be questioned again. Orsolano vehemently denied murdering the girl and claimed that the fresh blood was from a goat he had slaughtered that day. One of the gendarmes questioning Orsolano played the "good cop" and plied the suspect with wine and brandy, suggesting that he confess and claim insanity. His tongue loosened by drink, Orsolano now confessed that he had lured the girl to the store, raped her and dismembered her, then carried her body parts in the sack out to a riverbank in the forest. Gendarmes located the body parts.

Orsolano confessed to luring the two other missing girls to his store, raping them, dismembering them and scattering their body parts in the forest for animals to consume. No trace of them was found. Orsolano was charged with the three rape-murders and stood trial with due haste on March 10, 1835, a week after the murder. He was sentenced to death by hanging, and a week later in the public square of San Giorgio Canavese his sentence was executed before a crowd of ten thousand people who came to see the "monster" put to death. Many were disappointed that instead of a savage werewolf giant they saw a diminutive (1.63 meters, or 5 feet, 4 inches), pale-skinned fellow who appeared courteous and calm.

After his execution, Orsolano's body was taken away by three surgeons from the University of Turin who autopsied the corpse in search of anomalies that might explain his behavior. Other than larger-than-average testicles, no anatomical abnormalities were observed. A plaster mold taken from his head and a pencil sketch of it are on display in the University of Turin's Luigi Rolando Museum of Human Anatomy.[40]

The wheels of justice in Piemonte moved fast—fourteen days from crime to trial to execution. But the fame, rumors and legends behind what is probably Italy's first modern serial killer took a little longer to mature in a world on the cusp between ancient myths and modern history. Rumors began to circulate that Orsolano confessed to eating parts of the girls he murdered. Eventually these rumors expanded to say he ground the girls' body parts into sausages, which he sold from his shop. Orsolano was nicknamed in local dialect as the "Jena (hyena) of San Giorgio" while the townspeople became known as the *mangiacristiani*—the "Christian eaters" or cannibals.

Orsolano became the subject of lore, a bogeyman story told to frighten children. According to the legend, Orsolano would lay out sausage treats and samples to lure children to his store and was caught when a customer found a child's fingertip in a salami. By the early twentieth century *The Hyena of San Giorgio* became a popular children's puppet-theater play in the Piemonte region; it was banned by Mussolini in the 1930s and revived as a theater play in the 1980s. Recently the case has been rediscovered in Italian media and popular culture as that of Italy's "first serial killer."[41]

Manuel Blanco Romasanta, "Werewolf of Allariz"—Spain, 1852

Manuel Blanco Romasanta murdered fourteen victims in the Galicia region of Spain. Romasanta was born in 1809 and was raised as a girl until the age of six.[42] That is a familiar theme in the childhoods of serial killers. For example, the mother of American serial killer Henry Lee Lucas sent him to the first day of school dressed as a girl, wearing a dress, with his long hair set in curls. Lucas would eventually kill his mother. Serial killer Ottis Toole, who would partner with Lucas in a murder spree, was also dressed as a girl by his mother. Carroll Edward "Eddie" Cole, who murdered fifteen victims, was dressed as a "Mamma's little girl," in frilly skirts and petticoats, and forced to serve drinks to his mother's guests. John Wayne Gacy was forced to wear his mother's underwear as a humiliating form of punishment. Numerous other serial killers, including Doil Lane, Charles Albright, and Charles Manson (if you accept him as a serial killer by proxy—a cult serial killer), are known to have been forcibly dressed as girls in their childhoods.[43]

Romasanta was apparently bullied in school and further humiliated as an adult when he grew to only four feet eleven in height. He eventually married and was employed as a tailor. (Reading these pre-twentieth-century cases, one is left with the impression that tailors were as prominent among serial killers as are long-distance truck drivers today.) Romasanta also freelanced as a guide and a trader (perhaps as a smuggler as well) through the bordering mountain ranges.

In 1844 Romasanta fled his home after being accused of killing a bailiff attempting to enforce a debt collection. Settling in a small village under a false name, he worked as a cord maker, cook and weaver making yarn. Working mostly with women, Romasanta was considered effeminate by the villagers. Romasanta continued to act as a mountain guide, and at some point he began murdering women and children he was guiding. He was seen selling small items belonging to the missing victims. Romasanta was arrested and charged in nine murders in September 1853, but confessed to thirteen (not including that of the bailiff). Victims' families accused him of being a *sacamantecas* ("fat extractor"), a traditional Spanish bogeyman that captures children in a sack and extracts their body fat for soap. (This is a common theme in nineteenth-century Spanish serial-killer cases.)

At trial he claimed that his uncle initiated him in lycanthropy, earning him the nickname "Werewolf of Allariz." The court immediately dismissed his claims of supernatural lycanthropy, but psychiatrists came forward suggesting that perhaps Romasanta was suffering from clinical lycanthropy. There was a familiar debate in the pioneering psychiatric community: was Romasanta mentally ill or faking clinical lycanthropy? Eventually the court concluded, "His inclination to vice is voluntary and not forced. The subject is not insane, dim-witted or monomaniacal, nor were these [conditions] achieved while incarcerated. On the contrary, he instead turns out to be a pervert, an accomplished criminal capable of anything, cool and collected and without goodness but [acts] with free will, freedom and knowledge."[44]

Romasanta was sentenced to die by garrote, but the queen of Spain commuted his sentence to life in prison. Romasanta apparently died in prison on December 14, 1863.[45]

Louis-Joseph Philippe, the "Terror of Paris"—France, 1866

On January 8, 1866, seventy-three-year-old Marcel Maloiseau came home to his apartment building late in the evening. As was his habit, he stopped at the second-floor apartment, intending to bid good night to Marie Bodeux, a prostitute he had befriended. (Ironically, her apartment was above a police station.) The door was ajar, and when Maloiseau stuck his head in, he saw by the flickering light of a candle a man standing before a mirror, adjusting his tie. Not wanting to disturb his friend's business, Maloiseau retreated into the hall to await the man's departure. When the man did not emerge, Maloiseau stepped back into the doorway, and the man now hastily exited, muttering a good night. Maloiseau found Marie Bodeux dead on the floor, soaked in blood, her throat so deeply cut that she was nearly decapitated. Maloiseau raised the alarm and police rushed into the apartment, but it was too late to catch up to the man.[46]

The scene was a familiar one to the Paris police. Over the past five years, eight women, mostly prostitutes, and two of their children had been murdered in the same way as Marie Bodeux: first strangled into unconsciousness, and then their throats cut to near decapitation. The killer would then wash up in a sink or basin and ransack the victim's apartment for valuables. It is unclear from the reports whether the victims were raped. The police even had a physical description of the killer from several witnesses, including a woman who escaped his attack. Some described him as an ordinary-looking man except for a distinctive tattoo that read "Born under an unlucky . . ." with a star beneath.[47]

Three days later, on January 11, Madame Midy, an artist, heard a knock on her door. When she opened it, she immediately recognized thirty-five-year-old Louis-Joseph Philippe, who had recently done some work in her apartment. Philippe was inquiring about a tool he claimed to have left in her apartment. When she told him she had found no tools, he drew from beneath his jacket a pillow case, asking if it belonged to her. Annoyed by Philippe's questions, Midy turned her back on him. That was when he suddenly pounced on her, threw the bag over her head and forced the cloth with the fingers of his one hand into her mouth while attempting to strangle her with his other hand.

Midy began to scream and struggle, bit him and managed to break free. Luckily for her a neighbor heard the commotion and came to the door. Philippe calmly brushed by the neighbor, saying, "Madame Midy has suddenly taken ill; I am going for the doctor; I don't think it is serious." He managed to get as far as the street before neighbors caught up to him and restrained him. A long knife was found in his possession and a police search of his apartment turned up several bloodstained items belonging to some of the victims, including Marie Bodeux.

Louis-Joseph Philippe had been born in 1831 in Velleminfroy, in eastern France near the Swiss border. He served in the French army but apparently was punished and dismissed for drunken misbehavior. After his discharge he made his way to Paris. Witnesses would later testify that Philippe was a good worker but had a drinking problem. A waitress in a wine bar testified that he said to her, "I am very fond of women, and I accommodate them in my own way. I first strangle them, then I cut their throats. Wait a bit and you will hear me talked about."[48]

Philippe began killing shortly after his arrival in Paris and is believed to have committed eleven murders between 1861 and 1866. His killings were all characterized by his first strangling the victims and then cutting their throats so deeply that they were almost decapitated, a method very similar to that of Jack the Ripper later. Although they suspected him in ten murders, police could find evidence linking him to only four murders: Julie Robert, a twenty-six-year-old prostitute; Flore Mage, thirty-two years, and her four-year-old son; and Marie-Victorine Bodeux. Philippe was sentenced to death on June 28, 1866, and guillotined in July.

Eusebius Pieydagnelle, "Blood Butcher"—France, 1870

In 1870, in Vignevieille, France, Eusebius Pieydagnelle, a twenty-four-year-old former butcher's apprentice and clerk, surrendered to authorities and confessed to killing six people. According to the evidence presented in court, Eusebius came from a "highly respectable family" and was well educated. He lived across the street from a butcher shop, and stated, "The smell of fresh blood, and appetizing meat, the bloody lumps—all this fascinated me and I began to envy the butcher's assistant, because he could work at the block, with rolled-up sleeves and bloody hands." Although his parents were opposed, Eusebius found employment with the butcher and was overjoyed at the opportunity to butcher animals all day long. He stated that he was obsessed with blood and would have an orgasm at the sight and smell of it.

His father eventually took Eusebius away from the butcher shop and apprenticed him to a notary. This threw Eusebius into a deep depression and he began killing. His first victim was a fifteen-year-old girl into whose bedroom he crept as she slept. He described the murder:

> As I looked at the lovely creature my first thought was that I should like to kiss her. I bent down . . . but I paused—a stolen kiss is no use. But I could not bring myself to wake her up. I looked at her lovely neck and at that moment the gleam of the kitchen knife that lay beside the girl struck my eyes. Something drew me irresistibly toward the knife.

He killed five or six more times, stating that he would orgasm whenever he stabbed his victims. His last victim, before he surrendered to police, was his former employer, the butcher.

Vincenzo Verzeni, the "Vampire of Bergamo"—Italy, 1871

In northern Italy, near Bergamo, in December 1870, a fourteen-year-old girl, Johanna Motta, set out to a neighboring village but failed to return.

She was discovered lying by a path in the fields, with her abdomen cut open and her torn-out intestines and genitals flung near the crime scene. She had been suffocated with dirt forced into her mouth and appeared to be strangled. Nearby, under a pile of straw, were found remnants of her clothing and a piece of flesh cut from her calf.

In August 1871, a twenty-eight-year-old woman, Elisabetta Pagnoncelli, was found by her husband in a field when she failed to return home. She had been strangled and her intestines were protruding through a deep wound in her abdomen. The next day, nineteen-year-old Maria Previtali reported that her cousin, twenty-two-year-old Vincenzo Verzeni, had dragged her out into a field of grain and attempted to strangle her. When he stood up to see if anyone was coming, she managed to talk him into letting her go. Verzeni was arrested and he confessed:

> I had an unspeakable delight in strangling women, experiencing during the act erections and real sexual pleasure. It was even a pleasure only to smell female clothing. The feeling of pleasure while strangling them was much greater than that which I experienced while masturbating. I took great delight in drinking Motta's blood. It also gave me the greatest pleasure to pull the hairpins out of the hair of my victims. I took the clothing and intestines, because of the pleasure it gave me to smell and touch them. At last my mother came to suspect me, because she noticed spots of semen on my shirt after each murder or attempt at one. I am not crazy, but in the moment of strangling my victims I saw nothing else. After the commission of the deeds I was satisfied and felt well. It never occurred to me to touch or look at the genitals and such things. It satisfied me to seize the women by the neck and suck their blood. To this very day I am ignorant of how a woman is formed. During the strangling and after it, I pressed myself on the entire body without thinking of one part more than another.[49]

Verzeni admitted that he experienced sexual pleasure whenever he choked a woman. Previously he had experienced orgasms while pressing his victims' throats without killing them, but in the case of the two murder victims his sexual satisfaction took so long that they died. He sucked the blood of his victims and tore a piece of flesh from Motta's calf to take home and roast, but hid it under a haystack for fear that his mother might suspect him. Verzeni stated that at age twelve he discovered that he derived sexual pleasure from wringing the necks of chickens. In the four years before the murders he attempted to strangle three other women, including his former nurse while she slept sick in bed.

In the 1800s an influential school of Italian criminology led by Cesare Lombroso held that physical features revealed innate criminal character; therefore, close attention was paid to Verzeni's physiognomy. The clinical assessment of Verzeni concluded:

> It seems probable that Verzeni had a bad ancestry—two uncles are cretins; a third, microcephalic, beardless and one testicle wanting, the other atrophic . . . Verzeni's family is bigoted and low-minded. He himself has ordinary intelligence; knows how to defend himself well; seeks to prove an *alibi* and cast suspicion on others. There is nothing in his past that points to mental disease, but his character is peculiar. He is silent and inclined to be solitary. In prison he is cynical. He masturbates, and makes every effort to gain sight of women.

The description of this nineteenth-century sexual serial killer is remarkably typical of the ones of today. Verzeni was of average intelligence and showed no signs of mental disease but was "peculiar and inclined to be solitary." Vincenzo Verzeni was sentenced to life imprisonment in 1872 and died in prison in 1918.

Carlino (Callisto) Grandi, the "Child Killer"—Italy, 1875

Carlino (Callisto) Grandi was a twenty-six-year-old wheelwright and wagon repairer in Val d'Arno Incisa, a small village near Florence. Grandi was born with congenital alopecia (hairlessness), a head too large in proportion to his body, oversized feet and hands and six toes on one of his feet. He was judged to have no more intelligence than a seven-year-old. He was the "village idiot" and a target of bullying and taunts all his life. Nonetheless, Grandi was self-supporting, repairing wagons and wheels in a shop in the center of the small town.

Village boys often came into his shop to taunt and bait him. Grandi apparently attempted to curry their favor, sometimes giving them little treats or wooden toys, but he failed to get the respect he desired. Over the next two years he murdered four village boys between the ages of four and nine, luring them one by one into his shop, where he had already dug graves in the soft earthen floor. He hit some over the head with a piece of heavy wagon wheel and strangled others into unconsciousness and buried them alive. There was no evidence that he sexually attacked them.

On August 29, 1875, he was caught red-handed attempting to murder a nine-year-old boy. The corpses of the four missing boys were unearthed from shallow graves the same day and Grandi was arrested.

Grandi confessed that he killed the children in revenge for the endless bullying he received over his various physical and mental disabilities. Italian forensic psychiatrists argued that he should be certified insane. The Italian media called for the formation of a national society for the prevention of cruelty toward the mentally and physically disabled, proclaiming that not only four-legged animals deserve dignity, but two-legged as well.[50]

During his trial Grandi was often incoherently grandiose and paranoid, claiming to be eighty years old, a painter and a telegrapher. While in prison, despite his apparent learning disabilities, he composed theatrical comedies and novels based on his own case. The court rejected claims of insanity, and Grandi was convicted of murder and sentenced to life imprisonment. Fortunately for him, Tuscany had abolished the death penalty in 1786. (The rest of Italy would follow in 1889. Except during the Fascist period under Mussolini, Italy has not had capital punishment since.) Italy's forensic psychiatrists protested the decision to convict Grandi as a criminal, and the nature of criminal insanity became the subject of a lively debate. L'ammazzabambini—"the Child-killer"—was released after serving twenty years and was immediately confined to a psychiatric facility, where he died in 1911.[51]

Juan Díaz de Garayo, *"El Sacamantecas"* (the "Fat Extractor")—Spain, 1879

Juan Díaz de Garayo committed six murders, mostly of prostitutes. Garayo was born on October 17, 1821, into a peasant family near Salvatierra in the Basque region of Spain. He worked as a farmhand, shepherd and coal miner, married a landholding widow in 1850 and had five children, two of whom died young, typical of that era. The marriage was apparently a happy one, but his wife died in 1863. Garayo's second marriage was less happy, as there were conflicts between his wife and his children. She died from smallpox in 1870 and Garayo apparently committed his first murder shortly after that.

On the afternoon of April 2, 1870, Garayo hired a prostitute in his town of Vitoria and took her outside the city gates where they had sex near a stream. The agreed price had been five Spanish *reals* but Garayo now offered the woman only three. When she protested, Garayo threw her to the ground and choked her until she lost consciousness. He then dragged her to the stream and submerged her face in water until she drowned. Garayo rolled the corpse on its back and stripped it nude, apparently contemplating and fondling the dead woman. Before leaving the scene, he covered her with her clothing. She was found the next morning by a servant picking flowers.

In 1871 Garayo married his third wife, an alcoholic with whom he would have an even more tempestuous relationship than with his previous wife. He would be married to her for five years.

On March 12, 1871, Garayo encountered a destitute woman begging on the street. He offered her five *reals* in exchange for sex. As she had not eaten that day, he advanced her one *real* to purchase some bread and a glass of wine, and she agreed to meet him later that day outside town. After they had sex, Garayo attempted to shortchange the woman (according to his own confession) and in the ensuing fracas he strangled her. The body was discovered the next day.

On August 21, 1872, Garayo turned from prostitutes to the next "less-dead" category of victim: a servant girl. On the road outside of town he encountered a thirteen-year-old girl headed into Vitoria on an errand. He seized her, carried her off the road into a ditch and strangled her until she lost consciousness. He then raped her and afterward strangled her to death. He left her body hidden in the ditch and returned to Vitoria by two o'clock that afternoon. The body was discovered the next day, but again there were no witnesses or any obvious suspects.

Eight days later Garayo hired a twenty-nine-year-old prostitute to meet him at dusk outside town. He instructed her to walk a distance ahead of him in order that witnesses would not see them together. When they arrived at the agreed-upon place and had sex Garayo again provoked his victim by underpaying her. When she argued he strangled her. He thought he had killed her but then she moved; so he plucked out her long, spikelike hairpin from her hair, straightened it out and drove it through her heart. Her body was found next to a stream. A passing soldier was held in custody until he was cleared, and after that no further suspects came to anyone's attention. There was now a townwide panic, with many women refusing to step outside alone day or night, but when no further murders took place, eventually things settled down. And of course, unlike in modern times, there was no police department or investigators trying to solve the murders.

In August 1873 Garayo attempted to strangle another prostitute but her screams brought people to the scene. Garayo fled before he could be identified.

In June 1874 he attempted to strangle a sickly beggar woman on the road outside of town; again her cries brought people to the scene and again Garayo fled. But the beggar woman identified him; she said Garayo was drunk and attacked her for no reason. But nobody bothered to file a complaint with the gendarmerie about an assault on a "less-dead" homeless beggar.

The attacks then inexplicably ceased for four years.

In 1876 Garayo's alcoholic wife suddenly died, from an undetermined cause. A month later he married his fourth and last wife, Juana Ibisate, an aged widow. After his arrest Garayo was questioned about his third wife's mysterious death but he insisted that he had not murdered her; he had no reason to lie, as he had confessed to the other murders.

On November 1, 1878, Garayo attacked a miller in her kitchen as she was cooking. He attempted to strangle her, but the muscular woman overpowered him instead and forced him to flee. She identified him and filed a complaint with the gendarmes. Garayo was sentenced to two months in prison. He was now fifty-seven years old . . . over-the-hill in the male serial-killer "career" curve.

On August 25, 1879, Garayo attacked a beggar woman on the road, but she beat him off and ran into Vitoria, screaming. Garayo asked his wife to negotiate a settlement with the woman and fled town to wait until things cooled off. The beggar woman accepted eighty *reals* not to file a complaint with the police.

On September 7, after receiving news that it was safe to return home, Garayo was on the road back to Vitoria when he encountered María Dolores Cortázar, a twenty-five-year-old servant girl headed in the same direction with a basket of food. He accompanied her along the way in conversation, passing a postal worker on his route. When he was sure that there was nobody to interrupt him he suddenly pushed the woman off the road, seized her scarf, tied it tightly around her neck and demanded sex. When she resisted, he threatened her with a knife, and when she continued to resist, he stabbed her several times in the chest and proceeded to rape her. Believing her still alive, he then fatally stabbed her in the stomach and abdomen. Garayo hid the girl's body and her basket, and instead of returning to Vitoria, he now ran off into the hills.

At this point Garayo was beginning to manifest that frenzied self-destructive escalation that some serial killers embark upon. Ted Bundy is probably the most dramatic example of a serial-killer meltdown. On trial in Colorado for coldly and calculatingly murdering numerous women, Bundy escaped and made his way across the country all the way to Florida, where he proceeded to run wild. In Tallahassee he slipped into the Chi Omega sorority house, full of sleeping girls, and in a span of fifteen frenzied minutes, Bundy killed, raped, bit, chewed, battered, strangled and mutilated two college girls and attacked two more, who barely survived their severe injuries. On his way out of town he attacked a fifth victim eight blocks away, severely injuring her. Fleeing from the national media and public heat of the "Chi Omega murders," Bundy then crazily drove a stolen vehicle to Lake City, where he snatched a twelve-year-old girl from her junior high school while she was on an errand for her teacher. He raped and murdered the girl and left her body in a pig shed thirty-five miles away. These alarming, rageful murders led to Bundy's quick apprehension a few days later. This kind of personality disintegration can occur when a serial killer either begins to take stock of his own madness or feels disillusioned and depressed that his murders are not living up to his fantasies. It's a form of serial-killer burnout, at which point some surrender, some commit suicide, some retire and never kill again, and some go into a frenzied kamikaze mode.

Like Bundy, Garayo was now flailing, hesitating to return to Vitoria from the hill country. He ended up sleeping under a bridge that night. In the morning he entered a town and purchased breakfast at an inn before heading back out into the countryside. On a nearby hilltop he encountered fifty-two-year-old farmer Manuela Audicana returning from a market with a basket of food. Garayo engaged her in conversation, telling her he was searching for a lost mare. When it suddenly began to rain, the two of them took shelter beneath a tree, whereupon Garayo propositioned the woman. When she attempted to flee, he overpowered her and strangled her with her own apron until she lost consciousness. He stripped off her clothes and attempted to rape her but found himself unable to complete the act. In a rage, he then stabbed the woman in the heart, slashed open her abdomen and extracted her intestines and her kidney. Afterward he wiped his hands on the victim's dress, threw her clothing over her corpse and ate the food in her basket. He slept under a bridge a second night. In the morning he cleaned himself up, tossed his weapon into the river and headed home to Vitoria. No sooner had he gotten home than news came that two slain women were found in the countryside that same morning. After changing his clothes, Garayo fled again.

This was too much for the authorities to ignore. The local magistrate now initiated an investigation, sending gendarmes out to search for witnesses and evidence. The postal worker provided a description of the man he saw with the victim, and police got wind of the attack on the beggar woman in August and quickly came to the conclusion that it had been perpetrated by the same man who had served two months for the attack on the miller. An arrest warrant was issued for Juan Díaz de Garayo, and two weeks later he was arrested. During twelve days of questioning, he first denied all the accusations, but police appealed to his religious piety, persuading him that a confession would bring divine forgiveness. Garayo eventually confessed to the murders and provided detailed descriptions of each of the six killings and four attempts. There does not seem to have been a trial, as he pleaded guilty in the murders. On November 11 he was sentenced to death for the last two murders.

Garayo appealed his sentence on the grounds of insanity. Psychiatrists for the defense argued that Garayo was an "imbecile" and had committed the crimes under the influence of a "partial madness" or "intermittent monomania, amidst long intervals of lucidity." Psychiatrists for the prosecution argued that Garayo was lucid and aware of what he was doing, and therefore legally sane. His appeal was refused and he was executed by garrote on May 11, 1881.

A popular story circulating before Garayo's arrest was that the murders were the work of a *sacamantecas* who killed women and children to make soap from their fat. Garayo said he himself had heard this, and that his disembowelment of the last victim was a calculated attempt to fan the rumor to throw suspicion off himself and the real motive for the murders, his sexual impulses. It's more likely that he simply couldn't stop himself from escalating his brutality.

Many serial killers in Spain were labeled *sacamantecas*, but it was Garayo who became *the sacamantecas*.

All these cases in France, Germany, Italy and Spain transpired before the 1888 Jack the Ripper murders, and some of the cases display the same signature and psychopathology. A similar pattern of pre–Jack the Ripper serial killings occurred in the United States, as we will now see.

EIGHT

Back in the USA: The Rise of the Modern American Serial Killer

The Western was really about serial killing all along.
—MARK SELTZER, *SERIAL KILLERS: DEATH AND LIFE IN AMERICA'S WOUND CULTURE*

The United States was not immune to serial murder in the eighteenth and nineteenth centuries. As in Europe, many of the known American serial killers prior to the Jack the Ripper era were pathological or profit-hedonist female serial poisoners—like Lydia Sherman, the "American Borgia" (10 victims: 1864–71); Sarah Jane Robinson, the "Poison Fiend" (8 victims: 1881–86); and Jane Toppan, "Jolly Jane" (31 victims: 1885–1901)—or outlaw profit killers preying on frontier settlers and travelers, like the Harpe Brothers in Tennessee in the 1790s or the Bloody Benders and their "murder inn" in Kansas, 1869–72.[1]

Life on the frontier was violent and often beyond the pale of civilization. Although in many ways American Western movies exaggerate and glorify the reality of "gunfighter" murderers, social critic Mark Seltzer was not exaggerating when he commented on our fascination with frontier violence, "Serial murder and its representations have by now largely replaced the Western as the most popular genre-fiction of the body and of bodily violence in our culture . . . the Western was really about serial killing all along."[2]

In literature on serial killers, the United States has often been perceived as the "natural habitat" of serial killers, especially during the

1970s and 1980s, with 76 percent of the world's serial killers.[3] Today, of all serial killers in the world between 1900 and 2010 cataloged in the Radford University/FGCU serial-killer study, the US's share has declined to 67 percent (2,743 out of 4,068), followed in order of magnitude by Britain, South Africa, Canada, Italy, Japan, Germany, Australia, Russia and India.

Who is considered the "first" American serial killer depends on the "flavor of the month" in literature, film and other popular media. At this writing, Herman Webster Mudgett, also known as Dr. Henry Howard Holmes or simply H. H. Holmes, is often called America's "first modern serial killer." A Google search for "first serial killer" returns his name, along with Jack the Ripper, as a top result.[4] Recently, film director Martin Scorsese announced he is making a film, with Leonardo DiCaprio as Holmes, based on the Erik Larson bestseller *The Devil in the White City: Murder, Magic, and Madness at the Fair That Changed America*.[5] Hollywood's publicity machine went into action to tout Holmes as "America's first serial killer" as a prelude to the upcoming movie and the History Channel has been broadcasting a "fantasy documentary" series *American Ripper*, which ridiculously claims H. H. Holmes as not only the first American serial killer, but possibly Jack the Ripper as well.

I will outline the Holmes case first, and then chronicle five earlier sexual serial killers in the United States. Most of the cases occurred *before* Jack the Ripper (1888), while a few, including Holmes, caught the attention of the authorities and the media shortly afterward. (Holmes was arrested in 1895, seven years after the Whitechapel murders, but he claimed he had killed for many years before that.)

Herman Webster Mudgett, or H. H. Holmes—Chicago–Philadelphia, 1895

A Chicago-based contemporary of Jack the Ripper, the renegade physician, bigamist and fraud artist was convicted in 1895 in Philadelphia of only one murder, of his employee and insurance-fraud coconspirator Benjamin F. Pitezel; but the evidence is persuasive that Holmes took custody of three of Pitezel's children and later murdered them as well.[6] Beyond those four murders, the Holmes story is very tenuous.

After his conviction, Holmes published a confession to a total of twenty-seven murders—of men, women and children—for a variety of motives, including selling their bodies as anatomical medical specimens, insurance fraud, mortgage and loan fraud, property theft, inconvenient mistresses, jealousy and perhaps even pathological motives (he was a notorious womanizer).

At the center of the Holmes case was his infamous "Castle," a bizarre eight-thousand-square-foot three-story Victorian apartment building with storefronts on the ground floor. Holmes had custom-built the structure in 1888 in Chicago's south-side Englewood neighborhood, on the corner of West 63rd Street and Wallace Avenue, and he kept an office there. After Holmes's arrest, the building was allegedly discovered to contain "secret" soundproof rooms, some lined with asbestos; a system of gas pipes controlled from Holmes's office; hidden chutes; acid pits; and what looked like dissection tables and airtight gas chambers. In the basement, investigators found what looked like fragmentary remains of human bones mixed with animal bones and strands of human hair.

The notoriety of the case was heightened by allegations that Holmes converted the Castle into a temporary hotel during the 1893 World's Fair (World's Columbian Exposition) for the purpose of murdering tourists visiting Chicago for the fair.

After Holmes was arrested, the Castle was on the brink of becoming a tourist site when it burned down, in August 1895. New upper floors were built on top of the ground floor and foundation and the new building remained standing until the late 1930s, when it was torn down for a railway overpass and post office, obliterating that portion of Wallace Avenue. A utility tunnel in the post office appears to be built through a nineteenth-century brick foundation, very likely the original foundation of the Holmes Castle.[7]

But as a recent history of the case concludes, "Many of the stories of him and his 'Castle' are pure fiction. The castle never for one day truly functioned as a hotel, and the actual number of World's Fair tourists he's suspected of killing there has remained the same since 1895—a single woman, Nannie Williams. The "secret" rooms were almost certainly used more for hiding stolen furniture than for destroying bodies."[8] Moreover, many of the rooms, while hidden, were not exactly secret: employees knew about them and occasionally slept in them.

In the end "only" nine of the twenty-seven murders that Holmes confessed to were actually proven to have occurred, and only four were conclusively linked to Holmes. He was convicted and sentenced to death for one murder, of Pitezel. There is little doubt that he also murdered three of Pitezel's children. So Holmes was certainly a serial killer, but of what scale and magnitude?

While awaiting execution, Holmes confessed to 27 murders in an autobiography for which he was paid $7,500 (equivalent to $213,330 today) by the Hearst newspapers.[9] Some of the victims named by Holmes turned out to be alive, so perhaps his confession was his last scam before he went to the gallows. On the eve of his execution on May 16, 1896, Holmes retracted his confession and said he had killed only two victims, also an unlikely claim. Numerous people who had business or personal contact with the charming and affable Dr. Holmes vanished without a trace, leaving at least the *possibility* that he murdered as many as two hundred victims, which would certainly elevate him to the top of the pantheon of history's most prolific serial killers. But no conclusive evidence has ever been uncovered to confirm that any of the missing people were murdered by Holmes.

The interest in and fascination with Holmes was revived in the 1990s, with true-crime historian Harold Schechter's 1994 book *Depraved: The Shocking True Story of America's First Serial Killer*. (For subsequent editions, Schechter changed the subtitle to *The Definitive True Story of H. H. Holmes, Whose Grotesque Crimes Shattered Turn-of-the-Century Chicago*.) Recently, Chicago indie filmmaker John Borowski produced an award-winning documentary, *H. H. Holmes: America's First Serial Killer*,[10] while Erik Larson's bestselling account, *The Devil in the White City*, situated around the 1893 Chicago World's Fair, focused on two "architects"—Daniel Hudson Burnham, who designed the "White City" pavilions at the fair, and H. H. Holmes and his Castle.

Most recently, Chicago historian Adam Selzer has taken on the task of debunking the myth in his 2017 *H. H. Holmes: The True History of the White City Devil*, in which he argues that while Holmes was confirmed to have killed at least four victims, most of the narrative around his case is legend and myth.

The lore of H. H. Holmes has merged with the cult of *ripperology* to assert that Holmes committed the Jack the Ripper killings on a trip to London during the summer and autumn of 1888[11] (see more on Jack the Ripper and *ripperology* in chapter ten). Alas, there is absolutely no evidence that Holmes made any trips overseas in 1888 (or any other time). For one thing, he spent that year in Chicago supervising the complex construction of the Castle with its hidden passageways and secret rooms (apparently firing workers and contractors every few weeks so that nobody could get a full picture of the architecture and its sinister purpose). In the summer and autumn of 1888, when the Jack the Ripper murders were taking place, the historical record shows that Holmes was in the midst of a lawsuit over payments due for the construction of the Castle and was at risk of losing the property.[12] It's highly unlikely that Holmes would leave for a trip to England in the middle of the complex and troubled construction of the Castle.

Moreover, there are absolutely no signature similarities between the intricate murders that Holmes is accused of discreetly committing indoors, using gas, poison, battering, or strangulation of victims with whom he had prior personal or financial relationships, and the brutal outdoor "blitz-attack" evisceration of randomly selected stranger prostitutes on the sidewalks of London. You don't have to be an FBI behavioral scientist to see that there are absolutely no similarities between the two serial killers.

Further undermining the timeline, in his confession for Hearst newspapers, Holmes alleged that, with an accomplice, he murdered somebody by the name of Rodgers in Virginia on a fishing trip in the late summer of 1888 (during the same period Jack the Ripper was starting to kill in London). Holmes confessed that he struck the victim in the head with a boat oar and made the death appear as an accidental drowning.

I searched local American newspapers from that period and found no reported drownings of anyone named Rodgers in Virginia that summer, but typical of the daunting mystery of Holmes, there is a drowning reported on August 18, 1888, of a Joseph Seymour Rodgers in the Catskill

Mountains of New York. A local newspaper reported that Rodgers was in the company of a "Mr. Webster and his son" when he drowned after apparently having a heart attack while swimming.[13] Tantalizingly, Holmes's birth name was Herman Webster Mudgett. Beyond that, no further details of the death or about "Mr. Webster and his son" survive on the record.

No matter what Hollywood and the History Channel will claim, H. H. Holmes was by no means the "first American serial killer," any more than Jack the Ripper was the "first modern serial killer."[14] Holmes *might* have been the first "big number" serial killer, if his newspaper confessions are to be believed, but there were several cases before H. H. Holmes that fit the "traditional" sexual-lust murder pathology and thus make far better candidates for "America's first serial killer."

Jesse Pomeroy, the "Boy Fiend"—Boston, 1874

If we accept the FBI's new minimum-two-victim definition of a serial killer, then it can be argued that America's *first* modern pathological sex serial killer on the record, and perhaps the youngest, was fourteen-year-old Jesse Pomeroy in Boston, arrested in 1874 for the murder of two children. This case predates H. H. Holmes by twenty-one years.

Pomeroy was born in Charlestown, Massachusetts, on November 29, 1859, the second of two boys. His mother was a seamstress and his father was a laborer.[15]

Jesse was apparently a sickly baby, scrawny and frail. He also had a clouded cornea in one eye, which other children ridiculed as a "demonic eye" (and later helped in identifying him). Even his father would call his son a "goddamn jack-o'-lantern."

There are no stories of him as a child violently attacking other children, or committing typical acts of arson or cruelty to animals (other than one apocryphal account of him stabbing a cat and throwing it into the river when he was five years old and a report that he wrung the necks of two pet canaries). Jesse was, however, frequently horsewhipped and lashed with a belt by his father until one day Jesse's mother chased the father out of the house with a butcher knife after a particularly vicious beating. His father never returned.

Under his mother's protective supervision, Jesse grew up a lonely and aloof boy who was intelligent and enjoyed reading dime novels, which would be denounced by social critics after the Pomeroy case in the same way that crime comics would be denounced in the 1950s, for spawning juvenile delinquency. Pomeroy rarely played with other children except in games of cowboys and Indians, in which Pomeroy preferred to take the "villainous" Indians' part as long as it included play sessions of torture inflicted on "captives."

Jesse was a good student, but odd. One teacher stated that he was "peculiar, intractable, not bad, but difficult to understand." As an adolescent, Pomeroy was frequently truant and was on at least one occasion sent home from school for terrorizing younger children by sneaking up on them and making scary faces. On another occasion, he was reported for throwing firecrackers into a group of children at recess.

Typical of some serial-killer cases, Pomeroy apparently began his attacks a few months after he recovered from a serious medical episode, a case of pneumonia in October 1871. On December 26, 1871, the twelve-year-old Pomeroy lured four-year-old Billy Paine into an outhouse on top of Powder Horn Hill in Boston's Chelsea district. Once inside, Pomeroy threw a rope across an exposed rafter, tied the boy's hands together and suspended him from the beam, reminiscent of a dungeon-torture scenario. He then severely whipped the boy across his back. Passersby found the boy hanging by his arms where Pomeroy had left him. The boy was too traumatized to give police much information.

On February 21, 1872, a seven-year-old boy named Tracy Hayden was lured to the same outhouse by an offer to see soldiers on parade. His feet and arms were tied and a handkerchief was stuffed into his mouth, and he was suspended from the beams by rope. He was not only whipped across his back with a stick but severely beaten around the face, resulting in a broken nose, two front teeth knocked out, a split upper lip and severe battering around the eye sockets. The perpetrator, according to the boy, also threatened to cut his penis off. The only description that Hayden could give of his assailant was that he was "a big boy with brown hair."

On May 20, 1872, eight-year-old Robert Maier was approached by an older brown-haired boy on the street who invited him to come with him to the circus. They walked in the direction of Powder Horn Hill and near there the boy assaulted Maier and dragged him into another abandoned outhouse, suspended him from the rafters and beat the boy while forcing him to say obscenities. Apparently, the assailant climaxed and afterward untied the boy and released him.

On July 22, 1872, seven-year-old Johnny Balch was lured away from in front of a toy-store window by a brown-haired boy who offered him some money for running an errand. The boy was taken to the outhouse on Powder Horn Hill, suspended from the beam by rope and then beaten for approximately ten minutes on the chest, stomach, back, thighs, buttocks and finally his genitals. When it was over, the assailant took down the rope and coiled it, and warned the victim to remain in the outhouse or he would slit his throat. A passerby found the boy two hours later. By now these attacks were being reported in the newspapers and a five-hundred-dollar reward was posted for information leading to the arrest of the "Boy Torturer," as the mysterious perpetrator was dubbed in the papers.

On August 2, 1872, the family moved to South Boston, where they rented a house on West Broadway. The mother conveniently leased a small store across the street, where she opened a dress shop and sold small stationery items. On August 17, seven-year-old George Pratt was walking on a beach in South Boston Bay (Old Harbor), about a twenty-minute walk from the Pomeroys' store and apartment when an older boy approached him and offered him money to do an errand. The boy led him to an abandoned boathouse, where he struck him on the head and stuffed a handkerchief in his mouth. After stripping the victim naked, the boy tied his wrists and feet with two pieces of rope. He told Pratt that he was going to be "punished" and whipped him with the buckle end of his belt. He then kicked the restrained boy in the head, stomach and groin and afterward scratched him deeply on the abdomen and chest with his fingernails. Then the boy bit off a chunk of flesh from Pratt's cheek.

When Pratt began losing consciousness, the assailant revived him, and showed him a long sewing needle in his hand, asking, "Know what I am going to do now?" He then proceeded to torture the child with the needle, jabbing him in the arm, the chest, his wounded cheek and then between his legs. Then he began to attempt to attack the boy's eyes. Pratt managed to twist his face down into the ground to protect his eyes, and the assailant was unable to get a tight grip on his eyelids with all the blood and sweat pouring down Pratt's face. Frustrated, he took a bite from Pratt's buttocks and left. Pratt was found by a fisherman and rushed to the hospital.

Typically for serial offenders, there was an escalating arc in these attacks. They began with a simple beating with a stick but escalated to biting and the use of a belt and a needle. There was an obvious signature, the elaborate tying of the victims and their suspension from exposed beams (when available) in a ritualistic "dungeon" scenario, perhaps inspired by the dime novels Pomeroy was consuming. His attacks were also becoming more frequent.

A week later, on September 11, seven-year-old Joseph Kennedy was lured to a boathouse on South Boston Bay. The boy's head was slammed against the boathouse walls and he was stripped naked and severely beaten, resulting in a broken nose and knocked-out front teeth. The assailant, for the first time, now drew a knife; he forced the seven-year-old to kneel and, while slashing him on his face, his back and his thighs, made him repeat an obscene version of the Lord's Prayer. He then doused the boy in salty bay water.

Six days later, on September 17, five-year-old Robert Gould was found naked, lashed to a telegraph pole along a stretch of railway in South Boston. His scalp and face had been deeply cut and his face and hair were saturated with blood. He had been approached by an older brown-haired boy and invited to see soldiers on parade. Once on the railway line, the boy drew two knives, stripped Gould naked and tied him to the pole; he slashed the boy behind both ears, under his eyes and around his scalp, probably in an attempt to scalp him, again something he might have been inspired to do after reading dime novel Western stories of Indian torture. (Incidentally, scalping was a form of war-trophy taking practiced by both Europeans and pre-Columbian Indigenous peoples and other civilizations. It was not introduced to North American Indians by the British, as it is often claimed.)[16] He then put a knife to the boy's throat and told him that he was going to kill him but ran off when he saw workers approaching along the railway line. In this case, Robert Gould made a significant identification: he told police that the boy had a cloudy eye, like a "milky"—a white marble. Police now began taking one of the victims, Joseph Kennedy, around South Boston schools in an attempt to identify the assailant. At one point they came to Jesse's classroom, but the boy failed to spot his attacker.

Some sort of compulsion drove Jesse Pomeroy several hours later to pass by the local police station on his way home from school and pause at the doorway to stare at the police officer and Kennedy inside. He then turned and left toward home but it was too late. He had attracted the attention of the police officer, who took him into custody and brought him before Kennedy. This time, Kennedy identified Pomeroy.

Pomeroy was still only twelve years old, and on September 21 he was speedily sentenced to six years' detention in a juvenile reformatory, until the age of eighteen. Pomeroy, however, was intelligent and, when he wanted to be, a charming psychopath. He persuaded a senior South Boston police captain that he had "reformed," which earned him a "second chance." After the reformatory reported that Pomeroy's conduct had been excellent, a social-services inspector visited his mother and saw her and Jesse's brother diligently working at the dress shop and secured her promise that she would keep Jesse under strict supervision. With the police captain's endorsement, Jesse Pomeroy was paroled into his mother's custody on February 6, 1874, and put to work in her store across the street from their apartment and along the paper route that his brother had been working.

About six weeks later, on March 18, 1874, ten-year-old schoolgirl Katie Curran realized she needed a new notebook. Her mother gave her a few coins and sent her to Broadway to purchase a notebook from Tobin's, a neighborhood store. She warily cast her eye at the clock as her daughter ran off to get the notebook. It was 8:05 a.m.

That morning it had been Jesse's turn to open the store at 7:30 a.m. and prepare it for business. The shopkeeper at Tobin's would later testify that Katie had come in around 8:15 but left without finding a notebook she liked.

Rudolph Kohr, a neighborhood boy who earned pocket money by assisting in the Pomeroys' store, arrived at around 8:00 a.m. He would later testify that he was chatting with Jesse when a little girl came into the store seeking a school notebook. Jesse, he said, offered the girl a notebook at a discount because it had an ink spot on its cover. Just at that moment, the Pomeroys' cat came up from the cellar, meowing for food, and Jesse asked him to run over to the butcher for a few scraps of meat. When Kohr returned to the store, the little girl was gone and Jesse was nonchalantly sweeping up.

Katie never returned home. When Katie's mother began a frantic search of the neighborhood, another girl told her that she had seen Katie go into Pomeroy's store. Everybody in the neighborhood knew the story of Jesse Pomeroy, and Katie's mother rushed to the police station, where she was interviewed by the station commander, the same police captain who had endorsed Jesse's early release. The police officer assured her that Jesse had been "reformed," and moreover, he had a history of attacking little boys, not girls. In the meantime, to calm the woman down, the police agreed to make a search of Pomeroy's store. The search apparently turned up nothing suspicious or out of order.

A reward was offered for information on the missing girl, and a few weeks later a witness surfaced claiming he saw a weeping Katie lured into a closed carriage and taken away. Katie was a product of a mixed marriage between her Protestant mother and Catholic father. In the 1870s, sectarian tension between the Protestants and Catholics in the United States had not eased, and the consensus among Boston's Protestant ruling elite was that Katie's Catholic father had abducted his own daughter and sent her away to a convent.[17] The case went cold.

In the weeks that followed, several boys were approached by an older boy offering them either money for running an errand or to show them the circus or soldiers on parade. The now-wary children refused to go with him. None of these encounters were reported to the police.

On the morning of April 22, 1874, four-year-old Horace Millen was allowed by his mother to go to a bakery and buy himself a sweet. Numerous witnesses saw the boy share the pastry with an older boy on Dorchester Avenue and the two of them walking toward Boston's Savin Hill Beach. That afternoon Horace's corpse was found in a clambake pit surrounded by empty shells and scorched stones on the beach. The child was half-naked, his pants and underwear pulled down to his ankles; he was lying on his back with his face, hands and upper thighs and shirt caked in blood. The victim's heels had plowed deep furrows in the sand as he struggled. His fists were tightly clenched from the pain being inflicted upon him. His hands were slashed in defensive wounds from attempting to ward off the knife blows. Two cuts to the throat, one exposing the boy's windpipe and the other severing his jugular vein, were so deep that, despite being inflicted with a small knife, they nearly severed the boy's head. There were eighteen stab wounds to the chest and an attempt was made to castrate the victim, slashing open the scrotum so deeply that a testicle had fallen out nearby. The boy's right eye had been punctured by a knife stab through the eyelid.

With this murder, the Boston police's "linkage blindness" came to a speedy end. Senior police investigators immediately recalled the Jesse Pomeroy attacks and were shocked to learn that Pomeroy had been paroled several months earlier into the same neighborhood where Katie Curran disappeared. That same evening, police took Pomeroy into custody and cataloged the scratches and marks on his body. Shoes worn by Pomeroy would be matched to the two sets of footprints along the beach leading to the crime scene, and the knife that Pomeroy used was seized as evidence.

Police in Boston used the same technique as authorities in Bavaria attempted in 1808 to get a confession from serial killer Andreas Bichel: they brought Pomeroy to the mortuary to view the body of the victim.[18] Pomeroy quickly confessed in the mortuary but then recanted his confession, claiming police had tricked him into making it. He would maintain his innocence to the end. After an arraignment in which Pomeroy pleaded not guilty, his trial was scheduled for December.

In the meantime, Jesse's mother, who insisted that her son was framed and even went so far as to blame the victims' parents for allowing their children to roam around the city unsupervised, garnered so much hostility in the neighborhood that business dried up. On May 31 she vacated the store, and a neighboring business began expanding into the premises. On July 18 a worker was demolishing a dividing wall in the cellar near a corner where a heap of ash and refuse had accumulated. As he struck the earth with his pickax, he saw a round object suddenly fly up from the blow and roll into a dark corner. At first he paid no attention to it, assuming it was a discarded piece of broken crockery, but then his next pickax blow exposed a small human forearm draped in moldy clothing. Stunned, the worker glanced back at the round piece of "crockery" in the corner and realized it was a piece of human skull with tufts of hair adhered to a decomposing scalp. The body of Katie Curran had been discovered.

The case of the "Boy Killer" became a scandal of police incompetence for not only failing to properly search the premises of the store and therefore allowing the murder of Horace Millen, but also because of the police captain who had endorsed Pomeroy's early parole. The dime novels Jesse enjoyed reading were cited as an evil influence on juveniles. The judicial and juvenile penal systems came under attack for their "soft-on-crime" policies. There were cries for the fourteen-year-old Jesse Pomeroy to be tried in adult court and given the death sentence.

In the end Pomeroy was sentenced to life imprisonment. He served forty-one years in solitary confinement before he was transferred into the regular prison population in 1917, where he remained until his death in 1932 at the age of seventy-two, after a total of fifty-six years in prison.

Jesse Pomeroy is a good candidate for not only America's first modern serial killer but America's youngest serial killer on record. On a global scale, this serial killer's youth is surpassed only by Britain's eleven-year-old serial killer Mary Bell, who murdered and mutilated two boys in 1968. (Bell was released at the age of twenty-four and is now a grandmother, living in court-protected anonymity.)[19]

Joseph LaPage, the "French Monster"— Vermont–New Hampshire, 1875

Joseph LaPage (LaPagette) is also a good candidate for America's first serial killer, although technically he was a Canadian employed as an agricultural worker in Vermont and New Hampshire. Born in 1838, LaPage married at the age of twenty and fathered five children. He apparently attempted to rape his own daughters. In 1871, like one of those medieval werewolves, he attacked his sister-in-law in a pasture while disguised in the skin of either a buffalo or a bear. He raped her and attempted to strangle her, but she survived and LaPage fled across the Canadian border into Vermont to avoid arrest. A year later he returned to Canada, where he attacked and bludgeoned a young woman and attempted to lure a fourteen-year-old girl into the woods, before fleeing back to Vermont again.[20]

On July 24, 1874, he ambushed Marietta Ball, a young schoolteacher, bashed in her head with a rock, raped her and horrifically mutilated her. After being questioned by police as a suspect, LaPage fled Vermont to New Hampshire before they could complete the investigation.

LaPage went to work as a threshing-machine operator in Pembroke, New Hampshire. LaPage was a little peculiar, but nonetheless his boss, a Mr. Fowler, found him to be a good worker and even invited him to dine with his family. On one of these occasions, LaPage saw Fowler's teenage daughter, Litia, and immediately became obsessed with her. He questioned her brother as to what route she took to school, and over the next few days, at least one witness saw him lurking in the bushes on the road to the schoolhouse.

On October 4, 1875, a schoolmate of Litia's, seventeen-year-old Josie Langmaid, left on her usual two-and-a-half-mile walk to school but never arrived. A search party began looking for her, and at around nine p.m., her decapitated body was found about half a mile away from the school in a bush near the road. Her head was found the next morning about four hundred yards away, wrapped in her blue oilcloth cape. Her face had been slashed and battered, the killer's bootheel imprinted on her cheek. Nearby a bloodstained wooden club was found. An autopsy determined that Langmaid was raped, and her vagina had been partially excised.

The news of the murder reached Vermont, where authorities noted the similarity in the attack to the ambush-rape-murder of Marietta Ball the previous year and alerted the New Hampshire authorities, who then arrested LaPage. There was no linkage blindness in this case. LaPage was arrested, tried, convicted and executed in March 1878.

A fifteen-foot-tall monument and two stone hubs were erected at the site of one of America's earliest serial-killer crime scenes, on Academy Road in Suncook, New Hampshire. An inscription on the monument reads: "Death lies on her like an untimely frost upon the sweetest flow'r of all the field; Body found 90 ft north at stone hub, head found 82 rods north at stone hub." It's a popular geocaching site today.[21]

Thomas W. Piper, the "Boston Belfry Murderer" or the "Bat"—Boston, 1875

As the Jesse Pomeroy case was weaving its way through the courts in Boston, the city was shaken by another serial killer. The first homicide occurred on Friday, December 5, 1873, in the Uphams Corner neighborhood. At approximately nine p.m. witnesses working in a blacksmith shop at the corner of Hancock and Columbia Road heard a woman scream outside. When they emerged they saw a woman lying in a pool of blood by a brick wall with a man dressed in an opera cape and a tall silk hat standing over her (the way Jack the Ripper is frequently portrayed . . .). He ran off, his cape fluttering like the wings of a bat, according to some witnesses. The woman had been dealt a severe blow to the head with a sawed-off length of wagon shaft (the forklike frame that secures the horse to a wagon). The piece of wood was found resting on top of a wall next to where the victim lay; it was still wet with her blood, her blond hairs adhering to it.[22] The victim died at the scene from severe head trauma before she could say anything.[23] She was identified as Bridget Landregan, a servant girl "of good character" in her early twenties.

Several witnesses would describe the killer as a young, well-dressed "gentleman" in his early twenties. One remarked that the suspect ran with a "sailor's gait" and that he seemed to be short of breath, frequently pausing as he ran. The description of the caped suspect and the weapon was widely publicized. With Jesse Pomeroy newly put away in the reformatory for a series of assaults, this new outrage was the talk of the town that weekend.

On Monday, Thomas C. Piper, a prosperous house carpenter who had recently immigrated to Boston with his wife and nine sons from Yarmouth, Nova Scotia, Canada, appeared at a police station with a piece of wagon shaft, which he kept stored in the basement workshop of his house on West Cottage Street near Dudley Avenue, about twelve minutes' walk from the crime scene in the direction the assailant was seen fleeing.[24] Piper told police that over the weekend he'd discovered that a piece of his wagon shaft had been mysteriously sawn away without his knowledge. When police compared the shaft to the weapon used to murder Landregan, the two pieces matched.

Piper told police that during the day he rarely locked the basement door that led out into the backyard and that recently he allowed workers who had been laying new sewers on his street to store their tools behind his house. But police suspicion was aroused by the fact that the assailant had been seen running in the direction of the house. That week police descended on the house, searched it and interviewed the tenants, including T. C. Piper's sons.

The historical record does not indicate why the police first came to suspect T. C. Piper's second-oldest son, twenty-four-year-old Thomas W. Piper. Perhaps it was because he matched the descriptions given by several witnesses. Perhaps it was because Thomas claimed to have a kidney ailment that prevented him from running, or at least running any distance without pausing to catch his breath. Perhaps it was that Thomas had recently returned to Boston after spending five months working aboard a ship sailing to Liverpool, which might have explained the suspect's "sailor's gait" as reported by a witness. Perhaps there was something in his demeanor that set the police off.

The father, Thomas W. and some of his brothers were summoned that week to testify before the coroner's jury inquiring into the death of Landregan.

Piper was well-spoken and self-possessed. He stated that on Friday evening he had been to a church service with his brothers at the Dearborn Street Baptist Church, in the opposite direction from his house. He had returned home by horse-drawn streetcar but just before he reached his house he saw a crowd gathered watching a fire. He insisted that he alighted from the streetcar and watched the firemen combating the blaze. Several of his acquaintances from church and the neighborhood saw Piper there and would confirm his alibi. Piper said that after that he returned home and went to bed. Police could not shake his alibi.

Thomas Piper was born on April 22, 1849, in Yarmouth, Nova Scotia, where he worked with his father as a carpenter and on a farm that the family kept.[25] He joined his family in Boston in 1866, occasionally working with his father, but aspiring to better things. He apparently was literate and clever, and he took several clerking jobs, including work as a researcher on a directory of prominent businessmen in Boston. He was a churchgoing Baptist and volunteered at Sunday school at several churches in Boston. But there was an incipient dark side to Piper. He frequently changed jobs and had been dismissed from several positions for "dishonesty."

Piper also had a secret addiction to opium tincture—laudanum—which he would mix into whiskey as "treatment" for his kidney disorder. With a strength of 1 percent morphine, laudanum was an over-the-counter drugstore product, completely legal and unregulated. But it was highly addictive and, when mixed with whiskey, potentially hallucinogenic. Unknown to police as well, Piper was compulsively committing acts of arson, including the fire near his home on the night of Bridget Landregan's murder.[26]

In the previous winter, he signed up on a ship as a sailor and was away at sea until his return to Boston in August. Because a witness had reported the fleeing suspect as having a "sailor's gait" police began to get interested in Piper.

It is as frequent in serial-killer cases today as it was back then to find that when a serial killer is eventually apprehended he had already been interviewed as a suspect or a "person of interest." Ted Bundy, Peter Sutcliffe, Paul Bernardo and Gary Ridgway are particularly notorious examples of police having the needle already in their haystack of suspect files when the case is broken. Sutcliffe, the "Yorkshire Ripper," murdered thirteen women over a six-year period, all the while police questioned him on twelve separate occasions.[27]

In Piper's time, the science of forensic-evidence gathering was still in its early stages. Fingerprint identification would not come into use until 1891, when the first conviction based on fingerprints left at a crime scene was reached in a murder case in Argentina.[28] As far as DNA identification goes, that would have to wait until 1986, when it was first used in court in Britain.[29] Despite their suspicions, Boston police could not secure enough evidence to charge Piper, and when they discovered that Landregan had a jealous Irish suitor who had sailed to Ireland shortly after her murder, they arranged for the Irishman's arrest and extradition back to the United States. The process would take months, during which Piper was forgotten as a suspect.

Thomas W. Piper was the "perfect storm" of psychopathy. On the surface he wore a mask: the dutiful, hardworking son; the gracefully elegant young gentleman, eligible bachelor, pious churchgoer and Sunday-school volunteer. In April 1874, he would be hired as a church sexton and given the keys to the Warren Avenue Baptist Church, a massive building with a five-story-tall bell tower in the Columbus district of Boston (on the current site of James Hayes Park at Warren Avenue and West Canton Street).

Piper's duties included unlocking the church in the morning, firing up its six furnaces, setting out chairs and books for various events and services and assisting with the general maintenance of the building before locking up for the night. But behind the mask of respectable sanity was a raging, laudanum-drinking arsonist, petty thief and sex addict. Piper would often use his keys to sleep overnight in the church on a couch in the vestry, claiming that it was easier for him to fire up the furnaces early in the morning by staying overnight rather than returning home. A frequent customer of Boston's red-light district, Piper was on at least one occasion reprimanded for bringing a prostitute to the vestry, and after his final arrest, police would discover a stash of whiskey, opium and ether that he kept hidden in the church.[30]

On July 1, 1874, Piper took a hammer from the Warren Avenue church and proceeded to engage the services of prostitute Mary Tynan. She took him to her tenement at 34 Oxford Street, where they spent the night together. Early in the morning, as she slept, Piper struck her on the head with the hammer and then slipped out a window without being seen. According to his confession afterward, he returned to the Warren Avenue church, washed the hammer and scraped the dried blood off with a penknife and buried it in the church basement.[31]

Tynan was found in her blood-soaked bed in a semiconscious state and her jealous boyfriend, a woodworker who could not account for a missing hammer among his tools, was arrested for her assault but later released. Tynan, although she did not succumb to her injuries, remained incoherent and could not remember or identify her assailant. Her cerebral condition worsened, and within the year, she was hospitalized in a mental facility. (She was found dead in a Pitt Street hotel in 1889.)[32] As far as it is known, nobody in the Boston police thought of linking the hammer attack on Tynan with the murder of Bridget Landregan the previous December, especially as the police had identified other suspects in both cases. Even today, considering that Landregan had been ambushed in the street by a stranger, while Tynan had been battered inside her own apartment by somebody she knew or at least brought home with her, investigators might hesitate to link the two cases together.

Almost a year later, on Sunday, May 23, 1875, at approximately two p.m., Augusta Hobbs brought her five-year-old niece, Mabel Young, a pretty and precocious girl, to the Warren Avenue Baptist Church for Sunday school. On arriving at the church, little Mabel ran up to the sexton, Thomas Piper, in the vestibule and greeted him with a friendly hello. Augusta saw him stoop down and whisper something to the girl before she ran off to her class.

Augusta frequently taught Sunday school herself but on this day she took a desk near Mabel and sat in on the class. Just before it began, she noticed Piper standing in the doorway staring at her and Mabel. Augusta attempted to speak to Piper twice, but he walked away blankly and did not respond.

The class ended at three thirty p.m., and kids and their parents congregated in different parts of the church. As Augusta stood in the vestibule talking with another member of the congregation, she lost sight of Mabel. When five minutes later it came time to leave, Mabel was nowhere to be found.

A frantic search for Mabel now began inside the church and in the surrounding streets.

Suddenly the searchers outside the church heard a child's moaning emanating from the belfry. They rushed into the church to ask the sexton to unlock the doors leading to the belfry; some saw him at that moment sauntering in through a side door from the street, while other people testified that they saw him at a kitchen door with the pulpit pitcher in his hand and still others saw him setting up chairs in an assembly hall. In the frenzied search for the girl, witnesses lost track of time and place.

Several people rushed up to Piper, telling him that a child was trapped in the belfry and crying out, but he dismissed the idea, saying, "Impossible," that the doors had not been unlocked in six months. Several people demanded that he show them to the belfry door, which he did, but he fell behind, dragging his feet. As people tried the belfry door and found it locked, Piper remained behind them, watching from a lower stair landing. He said he would have to go back and look for the key to the doors, but he quickly returned, claiming he could not find the key. Piper told another witness asking about the key that "there were boys who have the key that opens the tower," and that perhaps he had left the key in the door when he recently went up there to clean out the pigeon droppings, contradicting his earlier statement that he had not been up there in at least six months. A locksmith would later testify that six weeks earlier, Piper had come in with the bell tower key, demanding urgently that he make a copy of it for him.

Approximately fifteen minutes after the girl went missing, a congregant used a pair of pliers to remove the door from its hinges, and several men rushed up the belfry stairs. At the second level, the so-called bell deck, a ladder led up to a trapdoor that opened to the "pigeon loft" under the peak of the tower. They made their way up the ladder, pushed open the trapdoor and found the unconscious Mabel lying on her back, a minute amount of blood at her nostrils. The girl was quickly bundled away in a carriage and taken home, and doctors were summoned. The assumption was that she had fallen while exploring the tower.

As police began to arrive and excited parishioners gathered, there was a general sense of annoyance with the sexton. Why was he unable to produce the key for the bell tower? Moreover, how was it that the girl was found on the other side of a locked door?

Searchers congregating on the bell deck, one level below the pigeon loft where the girl was found, lifted a scrap of newspaper from the floor and discovered a palm-sized pool of still-wet blood. The underside of the newspaper was stained with blood, not as if it had soaked up the blood from the floor but as if it had been used to wipe the blood off something. A police officer then noticed a loose floorboard. When he lifted it up he discovered an ash-wood cricket bat, two feet, six inches long, an inch and a sixteenth thick, weighing one pound and seven ounces.[33] (Baseball was still in its infancy and cricket was *the* game in Boston.) One of the parishioners was surprised at the sight of the bat because three hours earlier he had seen a cricket bat leaning up against the church library wall behind a door. He ran downstairs to look and ascertained that the bat he had seen was no longer there. When he mentioned this to Piper, Piper replied that there were many bats around the church, but none could be produced.

In the meantime, it began to dawn on people that had the girl been injured falling she would have been found on a lower level, not on the top level of the pigeon loft. Slowly people's gazes began to shift to the sexton. Several would remark that he seemed aloof and "disinterested" in what was transpiring. He stood apart from the milling crowd, quietly leaning against a closed door. Then Chief of Police Savage arrived at the scene. It wasn't long before the chief wanted to speak with the custodian of the premises. When he was directed to Piper, he immediately recognized the young man who had been a suspect in the bludgeoning murder of Bridget Landregan two years previously: Thomas W. Piper. It was one hell of a coincidence.

Savage approached Piper and immediately took from his hand a ring of keys. Piper was "invited" to accompany the police to a station house, where his clothes were taken from him and bagged as evidence and he was locked up. That Sunday evening, Savage returned to the church and began trying the lock in the bell tower door with the keys on the ring taken from Piper. Two of the keys worked in the lock; Piper had the keys all along.

In the meantime, Dr. B. E. Cotting, a physician from Harvard Medical School, arrived at Mabel's home and examined the girl. He immediately concluded that she was suffering from severe blunt trauma to the back of her head. Mabel Young died early the next morning without regaining consciousness. Cotting would conduct a historic (for its advanced wound-to-weapon comparison techniques) autopsy and determined that the girl had not been injured in a fall. Nor, as Piper eventually claimed, did she die accidentally when he took her up to the tower to "see the birdies" and the trapdoor, which he said he had propped open with the cricket bat, slipped and struck the girl on the head.[34] Cotting determined that the injuries to Mabel's skull had been deliberately inflicted with a blow from an object precisely shaped like a cricket bat.

Despite the evidence, it was not going to be an easy conviction. Two witnesses testified that they observed a man matching Piper's description exiting a lower window in the bell tower, dropping to the church grounds twelve feet below and reentering the church. One of the witnesses had a long criminal record and the other witness was a woman in an apartment with a view of the church 420 feet away. The first trial resulted in a hung jury, but Piper was convicted in the second trial, and sentenced to death by hanging.

On the eve of his execution, he confessed that since his return to Boston, he had been experiencing compulsions to rape and kill. On December 5, 1873, the day of Bridget Landregan's murder, he had gone to church in the evening with his two brothers but had sneaked away, purchased laudanum and whiskey and gotten high. He then went home, sawed off the piece of wagon shaft and hid it outside, underneath a fence, then set fire to a store nearby and watched the action in a state of excitement with his brothers and several friends. He was at his front steps when he saw the servant girl Bridget Landregan walking on the other side of the street. He went into the house, telling his brothers he was tired and going to bed, and then sneaked out the basement door in the back, retrieved the improvised wooden club and caught up with Landregan and followed her, intending to knock her unconscious and rape her.[35] When he found his opportunity, he struck her down but was interrupted before he could commit the rape.

He claimed disingenuously that he assaulted the prostitute Mary Tynan with a hammer to take back the money he had given her, and he drew for the police a map to the location where he buried the murder weapon in the church basement. The police successfully located it.

In the case of Mabel Young he claimed he was under a compulsion to kill a child, any child, and was in a delusional state from consuming laudanum and whiskey the previous night and from drinking or huffing ether (newspapers said "chloroform"). He stated that he lured the girl into the tower by offering to show her baby birds and then struck her twice with the bat. Contrary to the witness reports of him leaping out the window, Piper stated he slipped out the bell tower door and locked it behind him without anybody catching sight of him.[36]

The likely scenario is that Piper had developed a necrophilic compulsion to have sex with unconscious victims. He had intended to render his first known victim, Landregan, unconscious to sexually assault her; he likely raped the prostitute Mary Tynan after knocking her unconscious with the hammer; and it was probably his intention to do the same with Mabel, or to stash her corpse in the belfry so that he could return that night and engage in necrophilic sex with her. His plan went wrong when he failed to kill the girl and she convulsed and moaned so loudly that people in the street heard her cries.

Some contemporary newspaper accounts claim that Piper also confessed to the rape-murder of a twelve-year-old girl and the rape of a woman named Minnie Sullivan on Dennis Street the same night he killed Bridget Landregan, but neither of these two incidents appears in any searchable police records.[37]

Thomas W. Piper was executed on May 26, 1876.

Theodore "Theo" Durrant, the "Demon of the Belfry"—San Francisco, 1895

In a weird, synchronous footnote to the Boston belfry murder, nineteen years later, in 1895—slightly out of chronological order here, occurring *after* Jack the Ripper—another Canadian-born necrophile serial killer in the US, Theodore "Theo" Durrant, the "Demon of the Belfry," murdered and raped two women inside San Francisco's Bartlett Street Emanuel Baptist Church, where, like Piper in Boston, he too was a sexton.

A promising medical student at the Cooper Medical College in San Francisco, the twenty-five-year-old Durrant was a church sexton and taught Sunday school. In April 1895, he lured to the church a congregant he had been courting, twenty-year-old Blanche Lamont, and murdered her in the library. He then dragged her body up to the belfry. (Police found traces of her hair trapped in the splinters of the stairs.) He kept her naked corpse hidden on the bell deck of the belfry for two weeks, her head propped up with "corpse blocks," which he took from his school's anatomy department and which were designed to slow down the decomposition of a corpse.[38] An assortment of female clothing was later found in the belfry near the corpse. Presumably Durrant was dressing his victim like a doll during bouts of necrophilic sex, while at the same time visiting her family and assisting in the search for the missing woman. The affable and handsome Durrant commented to the family that Blanche was innocent and impressionable and might have been lured away into white slavery.

When after ten days Lamont's vagina had become infested with maggots, Durrant lost interest in her corpse. On Good Friday he lured twenty-one-year-old Minnie Flora Williams, another church member he had been courting, into the church and murdered and raped her. The next day, as women volunteers were preparing the church for Easter, one of the women found Williams's mutilated body stuffed in a closet of the church library. She had been strangled and stabbed, slashed on the head and face, and her wrists cut so deeply that the hands were almost severed from the body. Material torn from her undergarments had been shoved down her throat with a sharp stick. That discovery led to the subsequent discovery of Lamont's body in the bell tower, lying on her back, her hands folded over her chest.

Witnesses reported seeing the victims with Theodore Durrant shortly before each murder, and he was quickly arrested, tried and convicted of the two murders. Durrant never confessed, and he insisted on his innocence to the end. After he was arrested, several of Durrant's female Sunday school students came forward to report that before the murders Durrant had lewdly propositioned them; some reported that he had "ambushed" them stark naked in the library. There were also reports that Durrant frequented prostitutes, bringing with him a sack of live birds whose throats he would cut and cover himself in their blood while having sex.[39]

Durrant inspired perhaps the first reported instance of serial-killer "groupies." One of several young women infatuated with the "handsome-in-a-dark-sort-of-way" serial killer came to the trial bearing bouquets of sweet pea flowers for him. She became known as the "Sweet Pea Girl."[40]

Theodore Durrant was executed on January 7, 1898, at San Quentin Prison.

His younger sister, Beulah Maude Durrant, was the noted American actress, dancer and choreographer Maud Allan (1873–1956).

The "Servant-Girl Annihilator"—Austin, Texas, 1885

A still-unidentified perpetrator murdered seven women (five African-American and two white) and a black male in Austin, Texas, between 1884 and 1885. The victims were all attacked while asleep in their beds. Five of the women were dragged unconscious outdoors and killed there, three of them severely mutilated. Some of the victims were sexually assaulted and their heads cleaved open with an ax. Six of the victims were posed with a sharp object driven into their brain and protruding from their ears. Although the homicides were called the "servant-girl murders," two victims were housewives, one was a male and another a child. It's likely that the press latched onto this label because of the frequency of servant-girl murders over the century. The murders terrified Austin for an entire year, after which they inexplicably stopped. A 2014 episode of PBS's *History Detectives*, in which current psychological profiling and geoforensic profiling techniques were used, suggested that the perpetrator was a nineteen-year-old African-American cook named Nathan Elgin, who was shot dead by police in February 1886 during a knife assault on a girl.[41] This claim immediately sparked overenthusiastic claims that Elgin was "the first serial killer in the United States."[42]

If we go by the traditional three-or-more-victims definition, then Thomas Piper was America's first sexual serial killer; if we go by the more recent two-victims-or-more definition, then Jesse Pomeroy was. Both H. H. Holmes and the "Servant-Girl Annihilator" arrived on the scene too late to be America's "first."

NINE

Slouching Toward Whitechapel: Sex Crimes in Britain Before Jack the Ripper

Killed a young girl. It was fine and hot.
—JOURNAL ENTRY, CHILD KILLER FREDERICK BAKER, 1867

Baker was not mad. He was simply a monster.
—*POLICE NEWS*, LONDON, 1867

We are now approaching the Jack the Ripper case in 1888. But we are not there yet. Considering how many notorious serial killers Britain would contribute in the twentieth century, it's remarkable that there were no known sexual-lust serial killers prior to Jack the Ripper in the way they crop up in Germany, France, Italy, Spain and the US, as chronicled above. The legendary Sweeney Todd, the "Demon Barber of Fleet Street" in London who cut his customers' throats with a razor and tipped their bodies out of their chair down a chute into the basement of the barbershop, is just that: a legend. And a Broadway show.[1] The case of the Sawney Bean cannibal clan that supposedly killed a thousand victims in Scotland, salting some of the corpses for winter feeding, is apparently as much a myth as Sweeney Todd although not yet a Broadway show.[2] Sawney Bean is an artifact of a sixteenth-century *The Hills Have Eyes/The Texas Chainsaw Massacre* brand of war propaganda disseminated during England's conquest of the northlands. Not a myth were William Burke and William Hare in Edinburgh, Scotland, who perpetrated at least sixteen serial murders in 1828, but that was strictly business. They were selling corpses to medical schools.

There were many female serial killers using poison or suffocation to kill their husbands, lovers, children, siblings, parents, acquaintances or strangers of all ages for a variety of predatory, hedonistic, profit and psychopathological motives. Women were killing with poison so frequently that the British parliament in the 1850s debated introducing a law prohibiting the sale of arsenic to women.[3] Of 342 charges of murder by poisoning laid in England between 1750 and 1914, 210 were against women (62 percent).[4]

But there appear to be no "werewolf" or "vampire" serial killers on the record as there were all over France, Germany, Italy, Spain and the US. The closest things to Jack the Ripper were several historical cases that set the stage, so to speak, in the same way that the serial necrophile "vampire" Bertrand, although not a killer, set the forensic stage for serial killers to come on the European continent.

The "London Monster"—1790

Literary scholar Barbara Benedict writes about a man dubbed the "Monster" terrorizing women in London:

> Although he looked "normal," and thus did not fit into teratological categories [teratology is the study of physical abnormalities], he acted in a fashion at once human and inhuman that corresponded to traditional cultural conceptions of monstrosity. By his bloody violence, he resurrected earlier definitions of monstrosity that concentrated on perceptible elements: like the hybrids, human curiosities, giants, and demons of myth and popular "science," he abused language, reason, physicality, and space.[5]

Benedict could have been describing Jack the Ripper, but she wasn't. This was a case that took place almost a hundred years earlier, in the post-Versailles fluffy-wig-and-saucy-big-ass-dress era—fashion holdovers from France now in the throes of revolution. For two years, from 1788 to 1790, an incipient serial "werewolf" was stalking London's well-dressed women. He would approach them as they fumbled with their keys at their front doors, or he would suddenly rush up on them from behind, and drawing his head close to their ear and shoulder, he would mutter obscenities and viciously slash and stab them in the buttocks through their silken dresses.

The prosecutor in the case would later comment how shocking and confounding these crimes were to the authorities in London:

> In almost every crime we can trace a motive for committing it, but in the present case, what could induce the prisoner to such barbarous and cruel depredations; no motive to induce him, no revenge to be satisfied; he abused the most beautiful part of the fair sex.[6]

Indeed. The offender's erotic buttock *paraphilic partialism* was mutating with an emerging sadistic-destructive class-war silk-dress fetish, the kind hinted at in both the Bichel and Dumollard cases described in chapter seven.

More than fifty women reported being accosted and assaulted by the perpetrator. Some were hit across the back of the head by his fist; others he abused only verbally; some of those he slashed at escaped injury due to the fashion of the day, consisting of multiple thick petticoats, stays and bloomer-type underwear. But not all escaped unharmed.

Two sisters returning from the queen's birthday ball were at the front door of their London town house when the offender ran up on them and, pinning one between the door and front railing, mumbled obscenities and then drove a knife through her evening dress. The physician who treated her testified that the gash from her lower back to buttocks was nine inches in length and ran as deep as four inches at one point; it would have penetrated into her abdomen had her stays not deflected it.[7] It took effort for the offender to drive the edged weapon home, and in some of the cases he was reported to have dropped to one knee to force the blade deeper. These were raging, angry attacks, and potentially lethal.

London was as shocked and alarmed by these extraordinary and inexplicable attacks as they would be by Jack the Ripper a hundred years later. There was a newspaper-and-pamphlet feeding frenzy. A 100-pound reward (5,600 pounds, or 8,000 dollars, today) was offered for the capture of the Monster. The attacks escalated. Women on the street were approached by a man holding a small bouquet of artificial flowers who would ask them to smell it. Those who bent over to do so would be slashed in the face with something sharp hidden in the bouquet.

In June 1790, one of the victims and her companions thought they recognized their assailant, and he was pursued, brought to them, identified and arrested. He turned out to be a thirty-five-year-old Welshman named Renwick (Rhynwick) Williams. Unlike the brutal, ugly monster everyone expected, Renwick was a handsome gentleman who was popular with women, just like Ted Bundy would be in his day. Several young women would testify at his trial as to his good character and gentle nature. Working as an apprentice artificial-flower maker with a French master decorative florist, he was even androgynously cute in that British, Mick Jagger, girly-boyish way. The son of a prosperous Broad Street pharmacist from Wales, Renwick was so graceful as a youth that the great Italian dance master Giovanni Andrea Battista Gallini (Sir John Gallini) took him on as his disciple in his school. Williams was a talented violinist as well, playing second violin at concerts in Westminster Abbey and London's Pantheon Theater.[8]

But there were a few kinks in Renwick's past. Gallini dismissed him from his dance company after accusing him of stealing his watch. Renwick found work clerking for a solicitor running for Parliament, but then he lost the job through no fault of his own. When he began to have money troubles he found employment with the artificial-flower maker, and his delicate violinist fingers were so skilled that he was quickly promoted through the apprentice ranks. But then for unknown reasons, he lost that job shortly before his arrest. There were complaints that he was unusually obsessed with the opposite sex.

When he was apprehended, nobody knew what to charge him with. The prosecution spoke of "a crime that is so new in the annals of mankind, an act so inexplicable, so unnatural, that one might have regarded it, out of respect for human nature, as impossible." The judge in the case complained, "The legislature never looked forward to a crime of so diabolical a nature as that of wounding his Majesty's subjects in a most savage manner, for the mere purpose of wounding them, without any provocation to the party."

The press and noisy crowds outside the jail were calling for the Monster to be hanged, but due to the peculiarities of the criminal code at that time, assault, even with intent to murder, was a mere misdemeanor. Having been panicked for two years, however, the public was demanding stiff punishment for the Monster.

The prosecution was hard-pressed to find an appropriate felony with which to charge Renwick Williams. At first they considered the Coventry Act, which made it a felony to lie in wait with the purpose of maiming or disfiguring a person. But there was no evidence that the Monster had lain in wait for his victims. The Black Act made it a felony to go about armed while in disguise, but Williams was not obviously disguised. Finally, the prosecution discovered an obscure 1721 act that was passed when English weavers, in protest against cloth being imported from India, slashed the clothes of those they saw wearing it. The act made it a felony punishable by transportation (usually to Australia) for seven years to "assault any person in the public streets, with intent to tear, spoil, cut, burn, or deface the garment or clothes of such person, provided the act be done in pursuance of such intention."

Williams was convicted of the charge, but his lawyers successfully appealed, and a superior court overturned the conviction, ruling that it did not apply to his case. The tearing of the clothes had occurred as a result of the assault and was not in the high court's opinion the goal of Williams's offense. He was tried again on three counts of the misdemeanor assault, carrying a penalty of two years for each conviction, and was sentenced to six years in prison.

Frankly, when one reads the transcripts of the trial, there is little evidence that Renwick committed these assaults other than the word of the few good ladies who insisted they recognized him. (Not all the victims identified Renwick as their assailant.) Renwick's fellow workers at the artificial-flower factory testified that he had been with them at work the night of the attacks, but the witnesses were of a lower class than the upper-crust victims, and worse, foreigners: French refugees from the revolution, who had to give their testimony through an interpreter. Their testimony was discounted.

Even though no knife had ever been found in his possession, and Renwick had never been seen with one and had no record of attacks

against women, he was convicted and served the six years while proclaiming his innocence all the while. After his release, Williams married,
fathered a child and then vanished from history.

Whether Williams perpetrated the crimes is not the issue here;
someone did, and the attacks *almost* ceased entirely after Renwick
Williams's arrest. (There were several similar attacks reported while
Williams was held in jail awaiting trial.) But the climate of panic, and
the sales that the newspapers derived from fanning the flames of that
panic, set the stage for the frenzy that Jack the Ripper would inspire.
The case also framed the notion of the stalking serial monster that came
from within the community.

As Barbara Benedict concluded, "His real threat, however, seemed
to lie outside the perceptible and inside the body. Whereas teratology
located monstrosity corporeally, the Monster displayed an equally traditional metaphorical monstrosity that was enacted socially; his monstrosity, however, also hinted at an internal, private ontology beyond
social conditioning. Despite his notoriety, he remained an invisible con-
tainer of the hidden horror of mankind—indeed, specifically of men,
since his crimes were considered sexual."[9]

In the decades that followed, these "invisible containers of the hidden horror of mankind" cropped up in France and Germany, unleashing similar serial sprees of paraphilic fetish assaults. They were becoming
less unusual to authorities. In Paris in 1819, women on the street were
attacked and cut about the thighs and buttocks by *piqueurs* (from the
French for "to prick").

The term "piquerism" is still used today to indicate paraphilic stabbing or slashing committed as a substitute for sex. The attacks are most
often focused on the breasts, buttocks, genitals or torso and the offender
relishes the penetration, and the sight and smell of blood and abdominal viscera expelled through the wounds.

During this period, in Augsburg, Germany, a *Mädchenschneider*—"girl
cutter"—randomly stabbed and slashed young women in the buttocks,
arms and legs. His reign of terror lasted eighteen years, claiming some
fifty victims, until the arrest of a wealthy thirty-five-year-old wine mer-
chant named Carl Bartle. In his home, authorities discovered an exten-

sive collection of edged weapons. Bartle confessed an aversion to and disgust for women, and stated that since age nineteen he would have an orgasm at the sight of blood. He was sentenced to six years in prison.[10]

In the area of Bozen and Innsbruck, several women were stabbed with a small penknife in 1828 and 1829. The perpetrator, when arrested, also confessed to a sexual compulsion to stab women, which was enhanced by the sight of dripping blood. In Leipzig, similar attacks took place in the 1860s. In Bremen in 1880, twenty-nine-year-old Theophil Mary, a hairdresser with a history of sex offenses against girls and women, was charged with slashing the breasts of thirty-five women he had encountered on the streets. Previously he had committed a series of attacks in Strasbourg, but he moved when the authorities intensified their search for the offender.

When we put these phenomena together with the post-witch-hunt-era servant-girl serial killers and clothing fetishists like Bichel and Dumollard described in chapter seven, we begin to see a gathering storm of misogynistic "mimetic compulsions" stirring in Western society, brewing what will become Jack the Ripper.

BRITISH MONSTERS AND MURDERS

The next serial "monster" to trigger a public panic in England was the "Hackney Monster," a rapist targeting schoolgirls and children in the suburb of Hackney, London. William Cooper was convicted of "various acts of indelicacy" to females, and sentenced to two years' imprisonment in the house of corrections on April 27, 1805.[11]

On December 7 and December 19, 1811, two serial murders occurred in London's East End, the so-called Ratcliff [Ratcliffe] Highway Murders. In the first murder, a husband and wife, their fourteen-week-old son, an apprentice and a servant girl were battered to death late at night in their apartment behind their linen-drapery and hosiery shop. On December 19, the killer struck again, this time slaughtering the husband-and-wife owners of a pub and their servant after they had closed up the premises and gone to bed. These senseless nocturnal murders horrified

Londoners. John Williams, a sailor lodging in the neighborhood, was arrested as a suspect but committed suicide in his jail cell before he could be prosecuted and tried.

Although they were never linked together, a number of unsolved homicides of prostitutes and women in their homes and businesses plagued London in the nineteenth century. Some of the murders had pathological features to them, although there is no compelling evidence that they were serial murders perpetrated by predecessors of Jack the Ripper.

The most famous case that gripped the public's imagination was the murder of Eliza Grimwood on May 26, 1838. The twenty-five-year-old prostitute, nicknamed the "Countess" because of her beauty and poise, was seen bringing a well-dressed foreign "gentleman" home from a West End theater-district stroll. The next morning, she was found on the floor of her bedroom, still dressed and her bed unslept in, the nape of her neck with a deep stab wound, her throat cut ear to ear and three stab wounds present in her chest and abdomen.[12] It appeared as if somebody had attempted to sever Eliza Grimwood's head. Her pimp was suspected in the murder, but was later cleared.

The cry "Who killed Eliza Grimwood?" went up in the press and public and the unsolved murder figured prominently in the Victorian imagination of the dangers and risks of prostitution. The description of Eliza's supposed gentleman murderer, nicknamed "Don Wiskerandos," decked out for the theater in evening clothes and an opera cape, foreshadowed the popular image of Jack the Ripper as an upper-class gentleman with a Dr. Jekyll and Mr. Hyde complex. Charles Dickens was inspired by the Eliza Grimwood murder case when writing the graphic murder scene in *Oliver Twist*, in which Bill Sikes kills the prostitute Nancy.[13]

While these unsolved cases perplexed authorities, as individual homicides they were not particularly alarming, nor did they feature the kind of gross mutilation that characterized "werewolf" lust killings. They were often dismissed as crimes of passion.

Frederick Baker—Alton, Britain, 1867

The first seriously twisted, lycanthropic, sadistically pathological sexual-lust murder on the record in modern Britain occurred in 1867 in

Alton, Hampshire, a pastoral little paradise of an English market town, about fifty miles southwest of London's ugly, teeming slums. It was not a serial murder per se, but it set the tone for things to come.

It was a beautiful sunny Saturday afternoon, August 24. Eight-year-old Fanny Adams was out playing with her seven-year-old sister, Lizzie, and a friend, eight-year-old Minnie Warner. The little girls merrily made their way to a nearby grassy knoll called the Hollow, located in Flood Meadows, a green park on the River Wye that separated the center of the small town from the hop gardens that surrounded it. The park abutted Tanhouse Lane, where the girls lived, and was a familiar playground to them.

While playing on the green they were approached by twenty-nine-year-old Frederick Baker, a lawyer's clerk in the town. The clean-shaven Baker, who looked younger than his age, was a respectable gentleman, well-known in the town. He had been a member of a literary institute for twelve years and was a Sunday school teacher, the secretary of a debating society and a director of a penny savings bank. He might have even been a familiar figure to the girls. It had been reported that "he was known as a prowler among children" and that he habitually handed out halfpennies to them like crumbs to gathering flocks of pigeons.[14]

According to Minnie's testimony, Baker came up to them in the park at around two p.m. and said, "Ah, my little tulips, what are you playing at?" He gave two of the girls a halfpenny each to race each other, and then gave them all halfpennies to walk into the fields to pick berries with him. After that he told Lizzie and Minnie to go home and spend their money, and he lifted Fanny up in his arms, saying, "Come with me, and I will give you two pence more."

Fanny struggled in Baker's arms, crying out, "My mother wants me to go home," but Baker carried the girl off into the hop gardens bordering the park. Perhaps Fanny was more petulant than frightened. Neither Lizzie nor Minnie was particularly alarmed by what had just happened; it must have looked playful to them, and very few Victorian-era children would have dared to question their elders, which the young gentleman Mr. Baker clearly was.

When Lizzie and Minnie returned home, they said nothing to their mothers about Fanny not being with them. It was only after four o'clock when Fanny still had not returned, that Lizzie told her mother about the young man who had given them halfpennies and carried Fanny away. Her mother began a frantic search. This was before phones. It was going to be a word-of-mouth hue and cry in a town about the size of twenty city blocks, with a river, bridges, parks and hop fields for local breweries. About four thousand people lived in the Alton parish.

At around five p.m., Fanny's mother, with Minnie in tow, was joined in the search by a woman who had earlier that day seen Baker in the area, near the hop gardens, walking alone toward the town, although she did not know him by name. Suddenly they spotted the young man walking in the same direction again, from the hop gardens toward the town. Minnie and the woman recognized him.

They confronted him, the woman demanding, "What have you done with the child you took away?"

Baker politely replied that he had left the children at play. He had not carried anybody off. When he was asked if he had given the children money, he admitted he had indeed. The woman asked Minnie if that was the young gentleman who had given them pennies.

Minnie replied, "Yes, he gave me two pennies."

"No," corrected Baker, "three half-pence; and to the other two I gave a halfpenny each."

But when he was now asked for his name, Baker suddenly became impatient and curt, saying, "Never mind my name, you will find me at Clement's office." The women had found Baker so polite and unperturbed that when he became curt at their last question, they apologized for having spoken so disrespectfully to a gentleman. They resumed the search while Baker continued toward the town.

Later, witnesses were found who had seen Baker with the girls in the park, while others encountered him there alone later. Another witness saw him washing up in a creek. Nobody noticed anything particularly unusual about his behavior, except for one witness who stated that it appeared to him as if Baker was trying to avoid him.

That day Baker had been at work at his desk in the lawyer's office all morning, but at around eleven a.m. he stepped out for a drink. He returned, worked another hour or so and left in the early afternoon for lunch. He returned briefly to his desk at around three thirty p.m. and then left again, not coming back to the office until nearly six p.m. His fellow clerks noticed he had been drinking since morning, although that was not entirely unusual for him. He was excited and animated after lunch, but that was how he got when he drank. Baker remained working in the office until seven p.m., and then he and his colleagues went out for pints at the local pub.

According to witness testimony, as Baker chugged down his beer,

He said that a woman had told him that he had taken away a child, but he had told her that he knew no more about it than that he had given her some halfpence. He also said, "If the child is murdered or anything, I suppose I shall be blamed for it."

He afterward said, "I think I shall go away on Monday"; and asked the witness if he would go with him. When the witness asked what kind of work he could do in another town, Baker replied, "Well, I can go as a butcher."

That evening at eight thirty, while looking in one of the hop gardens, a searcher caught a glimpse of the girl's light blond hair. When he looked closer he couldn't believe what he was seeing: there was a severed child's head resting on a hop pole. Fanny Adams had been found.

A brief witness summary that appears in the court record reveals the scale of the horror the search party now faced:

Thomas Gates deposed to finding the head of the child in the hop-garden. It was lying exposed. He also found the trunk of the body, about sixteen yards from the head. He also noticed that the body was cut open and cleaned out.

Charles White corroborated the foregoing statement, and stated that he also found a girl's hat in the hedge, near where the remains were lying.

Harry Allen, a coach maker, deposed to finding a heart and an arm, in a field adjoining the hop-garden. They were under the hedge, covered with some hedge clipping. Witness also found the lungs.

Thomas Swain, a shoemaker, deposed to finding the left foot in a clover field on the opposite side of the Hollow.

Joseph Waters, a police constable, deposed to finding an eye near the bridge, over Brood Flood, on the Alton side, at the bottom of the river Way. Police constable Masterman found a second eye in the same river.

William Henry Walker, a painter, living at Alton, deposed to finding the stone produced, covered with blood, hair, and small piece of flesh.

The physician performing the autopsy reported:

There was a fracture of the skull. I found contused wounds, and two bruises, one on the right and the other on the left side of the head. The right ear was severed from the head, and there was a cut extending from the forehead above the nose to the end of the lower jaw, dividing the muscles and vessels of that part. The wound behind the head would cause death. Both eyes were cut out. On the left side a cut extending from above the ear to the end of the lower jaw, entering the cheek and dividing the muscles and vessels as far as the angle of the mouth . . . I found incisions piercing the walls of the chest, the largest incision three inches in length, the second two, and the third one. There was a cut in the armpit dividing the muscles. The forearm was cut off at the elbow joint. The left leg nearly cut off at the hip joint. In front deep incision dividing the muscles and vessels of the thigh. The left foot cut off at the ankle joint. A deep incision in the right side, entering the chest between the fourth and fifth ribs. A cut under the armpit in the right side, not dividing the muscles. The right leg was torn from the trunk at the part of the body where the sacrum joins the thigh. The whole of the contents of the pelvis and chest were completely removed. I found five incisions in the liver, three in the lungs, the heart cut out and separated from its large vessels, the spleen also separated, the sternum cut away and missing. I found a dislocation of the spine between the lumbar and dorsal vertebrae. The private parts were missing. They have not been found.

Baker was still drinking with his office buddies in the pub when people started drifting in from the search with news of the murder and that Baker was being sought. One villager came up to Baker and said straight out, "They say you murdered a girl and cut her head off and the police are after you." Advised to go down and report to the police, Baker replied that if the police wanted to speak to him they would have to come for him, which is precisely what they did.

When taken into custody Baker insisted he was innocent and stated that he was willing to go anywhere they wanted him. A knife was found on his person and taken from him. He admitted to giving the children halfpennies and stated that he was in the habit of doing so when out for a walk. Police noticed that Baker's trousers and socks were very wet, to which he said it was his habit to step through water when out for a walk. But he could not account for the recently dried bloodstains on his trousers and on the cuffs of his shirt. (Forensic science in that era was still unable to distinguish human blood from animal blood after it had dried.)

In the meantime, police searched his desk at work and found his journal. There was a fresh entry for August 24, 1867: "Killed a young girl. It was fine and hot."

Baker's lawyer, Mr. Carter, would later argue that he intended to write, "Killed, a young girl. [Today] it was fine and hot." The lawyer said, "'A child drowned in King's Pond,' is another entry. Suppose it had been 'Drowned a young child in King's Pond.' . . . The word 'fine' occurs in the diary 162 times, leaving only 74 days, though running over January, February, and March, which, according to the diary, were not fine."

Carter argued that Baker was insane; the nature of the crime itself showed that whoever did it must have been mad. The defense called witnesses to attest to Baker's mental health and his family history. Baker had grown up in the nearby town of Guildford. His family and acquaintances from Guildford testified that he had been a sickly and nervous child troubled by headaches and continually in the care of a doctor. He bled frequently from the nose. He was not sent to school until the age of twelve. At sixteen, he had typhus.

Working for a lawyer this last year, he often came home and said his duties were more than his head was able to bear. After breaking up with a girlfriend in 1865 he became despondent and talked of suicide. His nephew was in a mental asylum. His own father had had a violent outburst four years earlier and was still hospitalized.

An acquaintance who grew up with Baker in Guildford stated, "His manner was peculiar. He would make grim faces. He would break off in the middle of a conversation and go off laughing. I knew of his engagement with a young woman. He told me it was broken off. After that I have seen him walking along the street at the rate of five miles an hour . . . He had previously told me he would destroy himself. I never heard him threaten violence to anyone but himself."

The family physician testified that Frederick's father had shown violent behavior:

As a child the prisoner was very weakly. If I spoke to him on any subject he would blush and his lip would quiver. He was very sensitive . . . Just four years ago his father had an attack of acute mania. He was violent. He had delusions. On the day I saw him first he had attempted to strike his daughter with the poker, but he was restrained. He had also attempted to do violence to another woman. For the last year or two before he left Guildford I noticed a difference in the prisoner. I always thought him weak-minded, and that would be increased by the taint of insanity that was in the family.

He changed from being a very weak man to something swaggering. He had the look of an intemperate man. Homicidal mania is of two kinds. A man might murder his keeper, or he might have an intense desire to commit murder on any one. Both arise from disease of the mind.

In summing up his plea for Baker's insanity, his attorney argued:

Everyone who had heard of the case, or read it in the newspapers, must have said, "The man must be mad." Could they see any motive, any cause, anything impelling him to this act, anything like premeditation or forethought; could they see any of the ordinary circumstances that attend ninety-nine cases of murder out of a hundred? It was suggested that the crime was due to sexual desire, gratified or not gratified, and the murder was committed to hide the minor offense . . . The extraordinary, extravagant, and un-paralleled mutilation in the case, and the scattering of the members broadcast, did away with all notion of concealment.

The jury felt otherwise. He was convicted of murder and hanged December 24, 1867. Commentators at the time wrote:

The very phrase "fine and hot," found in the diary of this besotted and depraved wretch, is a sufficient key to his whole character. That sensuality combined with cruelty—the probable elements at work in the yet undetected assassin of Eliza Grimwood—may tend to the production of a state of mind bordering upon *dementia* we freely grant; but the mind may be diseased, and monomaniacally influenced, without a man's being absolutely distraught. Frenzied indulgence in the most hideous passion may be perfectly compatible with a capacity to distinguish between right and wrong.

That the wretch is a murderer is shown by the evidence; but that he is a madman we decline to admit. He is a monster. He satisfied first his carnal and then his bloodthirsty lust. He is of the same mental caliber as [Renwick Williams] who late in the last century, prowled about the streets of London, attacking only well-dressed young ladies, and piercing them on one particular part of the back—as bad as the ruffian known by the name of the "Hackney monster," who infested the suburban fields about fifty years since, assaulting only schoolgirls and young children—as the French vampire, the monstrous soldier, who, in 1848, used to lurk about the cemeteries of Montmartre and Pere La Chaise, satisfying his ghoul-like appetite on corpses—as Sawney Bean, in fine, who could not eat all the victims he had murdered, and so salted their mangled limbs down for winter consumption. Baker was not mad. He was simply a monster.[15]

From this commentary, it is clear that by then the press had already put the murder of Fanny Adams within the context of previous pathological murders and assaults, some of them sexual serial offenses, like those of the London Monster and the Vampire of Montparnasse. The pathological nature of these crimes did not elude the press.

As for the eight-year-old victim, the term "Fanny Adams" became British naval slang for tinned mutton rations, which disgruntled sailors joked were the butchered remains of the girl.[16] The term evolved over the century to "sweet Fanny A.," to "sweet F.A.," to "F.A.," which eventually became a Commonwealth military euphemism for "fuck all."[17]

At twenty-nine Frederick Baker was in that average age range when serial killers begin their killing. The only difference between him and a typical serial killer was that he did not get an opportunity to kill more than once. Had he perpetrated his first murder in densely populated London, with its anonymous crowds, instead of a small town where he was immediately recognized, he very likely would have gone on to kill again, just like Jack the Ripper twenty-one years later.

III

The New Age of
Monsters: The Rise of the
Modern Serial Killer

TEN

Raptor: Jack the Ripper and the Whitechapel Murders, 1888

I am down on whores and I shant quit ripping them till I do get buckled.

He is possibly living among respectable persons who have some knowledge of his character and habits and who may have grounds for suspicion that he is not quite right in his mind at times.

Even though he is mistakenly claimed by many to have been the "world's first serial killer," Jack the Ripper is nonetheless the Mount Everest of serial killers.[1] He is a serial killer's serial killer, with multiple "copycat" serial killers modeling themselves on what they thought Jack the Ripper was. It is safe to say that hundreds of books have been written about the Whitechapel murders or feature a fictional Jack the Ripper. At this writing Goodreads.com lists 358 currently available books "shelved" under "Jack the Ripper."[2] A recent search for "Jack the Ripper" in the "books" category on Amazon.com returns 1,985 results. Ask any person at random to name infamous serial killers, even if they have no particular interest in the phenomenon, and they will most likely rattle off Jack the

Ripper first, followed by Ted Bundy, John Wayne Gacy, the Son of Sam, the Boston Strangler and Jeffrey Dahmer before they slow down. These are the "whales," and Jack the Ripper stands among them as Moby-Dick, glimmering on the distant horizon of history and still to this day unidentified. All the rest of the herd—the Zodiac Killer, the Green River Killer, Andrei Chikatilo, the Hillside Stranglers, Ed Kemper, Arthur Shawcross, and so on—despite some of their astronomical body counts, are B- and C-listers compared with Jack the Ripper.

No serial killer has spawned a genre and industry of his own except Jack the Ripper. There are legions of *ripperologists* worldwide, comprising an obsessive subculture of armchair detectives and historians, sometimes even professional profilers, attempting to definitively identify and solve the mystery of Jack the Ripper, the ultimate cold case.

It is beyond the scope of this book to address the multiple theories about Jack the Ripper, some of which are very compelling, some completely harebrained, but all earnestly argued. The best I can do for you here is to pull back from the trees and gaze out at the forest itself. And the forest, but for the extraordinary violence, appears comparatively mediocre in terms of numbers: five or six murders, committed between early August and early November of 1888. (The dates are so close together that the murders could perhaps be classified as constituting a "spree series.") Unlike his legend, Jack the Ripper's actual killing "career" appears to be rather brief.

His biggest claim to fame is that he supposedly named himself "Jack the Ripper" in a series of taunting letters to the London press and that one letter enclosed a human kidney, allegedly from one of his victims. The idea that he corresponded with and taunted the authorities is part of Jack the Ripper's lore, but in fact there is no conclusive evidence that any of the letters were written by the murderer or that the human kidney came from one of his victims. (Police at the time concluded it was a prank by a medical student.) There are 210 letters from different sources claiming to be the Whitechapel murderer archived in the London Metropolitan Police file folder MEPO 3/142.[3] Not a single one has been authenticated as having come from the actual killer.

Other than a few witnesses claiming to have seen one of the victims in the company of a "gentleman," there is no persuasive evidence that

Jack the Ripper was from the upper class or that he was a physician or skilled surgeon or perhaps even a member of the royal family, a high-ranking Freemason, an artist or another famous serial killer like H. H. Holmes or Dr. Thomas Neill Cream, all of which claims have been argued by factions of ripperologists.[4] Recently it has been suggested that there was a "Dracula connection" to the author Bram Stoker, while the "Alice in Wonderland connection" points to author Lewis Carroll as Jack the Ripper, and somewhere I am sure there is a theory out there that these murders were actually committed by aliens.[5]

I will outline here what we know "for sure" and, based on that, and only that, what we might be able to conclude speculatively about Jack the Ripper from a big-picture point of view.

Firstly, a large body of literature—or *ripperature*—on Jack the Ripper was written before 1975, when the original letters and police files were first made accessible to the author of *The Complete Jack the Ripper*, Donald Rumbelow, who is considered the soberest of the ripperologists. Prior to that, during the first eighty-seven years after the case, no legitimate, primary source history of the Whitechapel murders could have been written.

Much of the earlier nonsense written about Jack the Ripper, some of it based on outright made-up sources, left behind a large body of secondary material that continues to contaminate the line between fact and fiction.[6] This is common in conspiracy literature: evidence is made to fit the theory (rather than the opposite) and gets incorporated into the overall historiography, and then is repeated from book to book until the original erroneous source is lost and forgotten.

Making matters harder, archives from other government departments involved in the investigation of the Whitechapel murders remained closed to researchers until 1992.[7] Moreover, the infamous "Dear Boss" letter written in bloodred ink and signed "Jack the Ripper," which introduced his moniker into the press, was pilfered in the 1880s and lost until its return in November 1987, when its anonymous possessor (probably a conscientious descendant of the police officer or functionary who took it home as a souvenir—a common occurrence in historical crime cases) mailed the letter back to the London police.

In 1888 the Whitechapel district in London's East End was basically skid row for the near-homeless, alcoholic, mentally ill and destitute. There were numerous daily rooming houses, doss-houses/flophouses, soup kitchens, pubs, taverns, sweatshops, small foundries, slaughter yards, rag merchants, street hawkers and pawnshops, and literally over a thousand desperate prostitutes plying their trade.

It was a dirty and primitively violent cesspool of a place, and a lot of crimes committed there were not reported to authorities, but nonetheless, there were no murders in Whitechapel in 1886 or 1887. Zero. London itself, with a population of 5.5 million, reported only 8 murders in 1886 and 13 in 1887.[8] So it's easy to see why, when Whitechapel was suddenly hit with 8 murders in 1888 (including the 5 or 6 Ripper murders), it raised alarms. It pushed London's overall murder total that year to a then-record high of 28. London was already experiencing a murder "epidemic"—and selling scads of newspapers—before Jack the Ripper came on the scene in August.

THE CANONICAL FIVE JACK THE RIPPER MURDERS

The five so-called "canonical victims" of Jack the Ripper were murdered from August 31 to November 9, 1888. (Most of the crime scenes have been obliterated in the reconstruction of London, but numerous websites and customized Google maps will show you the locations.)[9] Contrary to popular film portrayals of the victims as attractive, saucy young women dressed in shiny satin Hollywood-Victorian saloon-girl gowns, most of the prostitutes murdered by Jack the Ripper were diseased with tuberculosis, hepatitis or syphilis; derelict, alcoholic, middle-aged (and "middle-aged" in the nineteenth century was like seventy-five years old today) prostitutes with missing teeth, greasy hair, scarred and sagging skin covered in weepy pus sores, clothed in stinky, soiled Oliver Twist rags. Subtract a century of social progress and civilization from today's crack-and-meth-addicted hookers and truck-stop "lot lizards" who haunt the most forlorn corners of the American landscape, desperately selling themselves for a fix, the most degraded of the degraded, so frequently the preferred victims of serial killers to this day—the walking less-dead—and you'll get Whitechapel 1888.

Mary Ann Nichols, Friday, August 31, 1888, forty-three years old, was found between three forty and three forty-five a.m. in a footway at Buck's Row, Whitechapel. Nichols had been seen alive at two thirty a.m. in a state of drunkenness. She had no money for a doss-house room to flop the night in and went to the street to find a customer.

- The victim was lying on her back with her dress pushed up to her waist.

- Her throat had been cut from ear to ear, from left to right, so deeply that it nearly severed her head. The windpipe and spinal cord were cut through.

- Two distinct additional cuts were made on the left side of the throat.

- The abdomen had been jaggedly cut open along the center of her torso, beneath the ribs along the right side and under her pelvis to the left of her stomach, but no viscera or organs were extracted. There were two stab wounds to her genitals.

- There were no bruises or wounds consistent with a struggle.

- Wounds were made with a long-bladed and very sharp knife.

- Her throat wounds appeared to have been inflicted first, while she was already forced to the ground, and the remaining wounds were inflicted postmortem.

Annie Chapman, Saturday, September 8, 1888, about 47 years old, was found about five forty-five a.m. in the backyard of 29 Hanbury Street, Spitalfields in Whitechapel. She was seen in a drunken state at two thirty a.m. and by a witness at five thirty a.m. talking with a man near where she was later found.

- The victim was lying on her back, her legs drawn up and open, the feet resting on the ground and the knees turned outward. Her left arm was lying on her left breast.

- The throat was deeply cut from left to right and the wound reached around the neck. The muscular structures appeared as though an attempt had been made to separate the bones of the neck.

- The face was swollen and turned on the right side. The tongue protruded between the front teeth, but not beyond the lips. There was a bruise over the right temple. On the upper eyelid there was a bruise, and there were two distinct bruises, each the size of a man's thumb, on the top of the chest.

- There were two distinct, clean cuts on the left side of the spine. They were parallel with each other and separated by about half an inch.

- The abdomen had been entirely laid open, the intestines severed and lifted out of the body and placed on the shoulder of the corpse; whilst from the pelvis, the uterus and its appendages, along with the upper portion of the vagina and the posterior two-thirds of the bladder, had been entirely removed. No trace of these parts could be found.

- The incisions were cleanly made, avoiding the rectum, and dividing the vagina low enough to avoid causing injury to the cervix uteri.

- There was no evidence of a struggle or sexual assault.

- Two brass rings normally worn by the victim were missing and her ring fingers showed abrasions, indicating they were forcibly removed.

- The contents of the victim's pockets were emptied and arranged tidily at her feet.

- Wounds were made with a long knife with a thin blade six to eight inches in length, similar to a medical amputation knife or a slaughterhouse knife.

- The physical evidence indicated that the perpetrator seized the victim under the chin from behind and squeezed her throat until she was unconscious. The victim was then laid on the ground and her throat cut from left to right in two places, followed by the acts of mutilation.

• The physician examining the body stated that, *in his opinion*, the perpetrator showed anatomical knowledge and surgical skill in his mutilation.

A water-resistant leather apron of the kind worn by butchers and leatherworkers was found in the yard near a water tap, leading to the unidentified perpetrator—and later a suspect, John Pizer—being called "Leather Apron." There is no evidence that the apron was linked to the murder.

On Thursday, September 27, a London news agency received the infamous "Dear Boss" letter, the first of several signed "Jack the Ripper." It included the following passages: "I am down on whores and I shant quit ripping them till I do get buckled . . . I love my work and I want to start again . . . The next job I do I shall clip the lady's ears off and send to the police officers just for jolly wouldn't you . . . Keep this letter back till I do a bit more work then give it out straight. My knife's so nice and sharp I want to get to work right away if I get a chance. Good luck. Yours truly Jack the Ripper, Don't mind me giving the trade name."

It was treated as a joke at first, but on Saturday, September 29, the news agency forwarded the letter to the police literally hours before the "double event" of that night.

Elizabeth Stride, Sunday, September 30, 1888, about forty-five years old, was found at one a.m., inside the gates of Dutfield's Yard at No. 40 Berner Street, at the corner of Commercial Road East in St. George-in-the-East. Stride had been seen that evening in the company of, and soliciting, numerous men. Her attack had been witnessed by several people and a vague description emerged, something on the order of "a man with a mustache."

• The victim was found near a wall, on her back with her legs drawn up and her knees fixed near the wall. Her right arm was over the belly; the back of the hand and wrist had on it clotted blood. The left arm was extended and there was a packet of breath mints in her left hand.

- There was a clear-cut incision on the neck. It was six inches in length and commenced two and a half inches in a straight line below the angle of the jaw, one half inch in over an undivided muscle, and then becoming deeper, dividing the sheath. The cut was very clean and deviated a little downward. The arteries and other vessels contained in the sheath were all cut through. The cut through the tissues on the right side was more superficial, and tailed off to about two inches below the right angle of the jaw. The deep vessels on that side were uninjured. From this it was evident that the hemorrhage was caused through the partial severance of the left carotid artery.

- The victim had been forced to the ground and her throat cut as she lay on her back.

- No mutilation was evident, and the assumption is that the perpetrator was interrupted by passersby in the street.

Catherine Eddowes, Sunday, September 30, 1888, forty-six years old, was found at one forty-five a.m., at Miter Square, Aldgate, City of London. Eddowes was not working as a prostitute at the time but was severely alcohol dependent. She was detained for drunk-and-disorderly behavior and released by the police at twelve fifty-five, fifty minutes before being found dead. A witness claimed to have seen her at one thirty-five a.m. talking to a man about thirty years old, five feet, seven inches tall, with a fair complexion and mustache. He was wearing a pepper-and-salt-colored jacket which fit loosely and a gray cloth cap with a peak of the same color. He had a reddish handkerchief knotted around his neck.

- The victim was lying on her back with the head turned to the left shoulder. The clothes were drawn up over the abdomen and her thighs were naked. The arms were by the side of the body as if they had fallen there. Both palms faced upward, the fingers slightly bent. A thimble was lying off the finger on the right side. The left leg was extended in a line with the body.

- The throat was cut across to the extent of six or seven inches. A superficial cut commenced about an inch and a half below the lobe, and about two and a half inches behind the left ear, and extended across the throat to about three inches below the lobe of the right ear. The big muscle across the throat was divided through on the left side. The large vessels on the left side of the neck were severed. The larynx was severed below the vocal cord. All the deep structures were severed to the bone, the knife having marked intervertebral cartilages.

- The face was severely mutilated. There was a cut about a quarter of an inch through the lower left eyelid, dividing the structures completely through. There was a scratch through the skin on the left upper eyelid, near to the angle of the nose. The right eyelid was cut through to about half an inch. There was a deep cut over the bridge of the nose, extending from the left border of the nasal bone down near the angle of the jaw on the right side of the cheek. This cut went into the bone and divided all the structures of the cheek except the mucous membrane of the mouth. The tip of the nose was quite detached by an oblique cut from the bottom of the nasal bone to where the wings of the nose join the face. A cut from this divided the upper lip and extended through the substance of the gum over the right upper lateral incisor tooth. About half an inch from the top of the nose was another oblique cut. There was a cut on the right angle of the mouth as if made with the point of a knife. The cut extended an inch and a half, parallel with the lower lip. There was on each cheek a cut that peeled up the skin, forming a triangular flap about an inch and a half.

- The front walls of the abdomen were laid open from the breastbone to the pubes. Her intestines were drawn out and placed over her right shoulder and smeared with fecal matter. One piece of intestine was detached from her body and placed between her body and left arm. The body was missing the left kidney and the uterus. The left renal artery was also severed. Several stab wounds were present, one in the liver and another in the left groin. The vagina and cervix of the womb were uninjured, but the majority of the womb was removed.

- The weapon was a sharp, pointed knife about six inches in length.

- There were no signs of a struggle.

- The cause of death was hemorrhage from the left common carotid artery. The death was immediate, and the mutilations were inflicted postmortem as the victim lay on her back.

A piece cut from the victim's apron, wiped in blood, was found nearby in a passageway entry on Goulstone Street under some graffiti written in chalk on the brick wall:

The Juwes are
The men that
Will not
be Blamed
for nothing

Fearing an anti-Semitic outburst, police erased the graffito before it could be photographed. Because of the spelling of "Juwes," some schools of ripperology connect the graffito to Masonic terminology and allege that there was a conspiracy in a Mason-dominated police department to protect a fellow Mason and possibly a member of the royal family.[10] However, London was covered in graffiti at that time and there is not a shred of evidence that the killer chalked that line of graffiti or that it had any connection to the crime whatsoever.

On Monday, October 1, the double murder, along with the Jack the Ripper letter, was splattered on the front pages of every newspaper. It was a big story introducing the Whitechapel murderer's new moniker:

Jack the Ripper. The newspapers debated the authenticity of that letter and the hundreds of crank and prank letters that followed. No conclusive evidence links the letters to the actual unidentified perpetrator of the killings.

Mary Jane Kelly, Friday, November 9, 1888, about twenty-five years old, was found at ten forty-five a.m. in her ground-floor room in a lodging house on 26 Dorset Street by a rent collector. She was seen in the company of different men the night before and in the early morning. The last sighting was at two a.m. by a witness who was acquainted with Kelly and saw her in the company of a man with a pale complexion, a slight mustache turned up at the corners, dark hair, dark eyes, and bushy eyebrows. He was, according to this witness, of "Jewish appearance." The man was wearing a soft felt hat pulled down over his eyes, a long dark coat trimmed in astrakhan, and a white collar with a black necktie fixed with a horseshoe pin. He wore dark spats over light button-over boots. A massive gold chain in his waistcoat had a red stone hanging from it. He carried kid gloves in his right hand and a small package in his left. He was five feet six or seven tall and about thirty-five or thirty-six years old. Kelly and the man crossed Commercial Street and turned down Dorset Street. The witness followed them. Kelly and the man stopped outside Miller's Court and talked for about three minutes. Kelly was heard to say, "All right, my dear. Come along. You will be comfortable." The man put his arm around Kelly, who kissed him and said, "I've lost my handkerchief." At this, he handed her a red handkerchief. The couple then headed down Miller's Court.

- Unlike the other victims, this victim was found indoors, on her bed, lying on her back, wearing a linen undergarment pushed up to her waist, her legs wide apart and knees turned outward. The left arm was close to the body, with the forearm flexed at a right angle and lying across the abdomen. The right arm was slightly abducted from the body and rested on the mattress. The elbow was bent, the forearm supine with the fingers clenched. Her clothing was neatly folded on a chair by the bed.

- The throat was cut through right down to the vertebrae, the fifth and sixth being deeply notched. The air passage was cut at the lower part of the larynx through the cricoid cartilage.

- The face was gashed in all directions, the nose, cheeks, eyebrows and ears being partly removed. The lips were blanched and cut by several incisions running obliquely down to the chin. There were also numerous cuts extending irregularly across all the features.

- Both breasts were removed by circular incisions; the muscles down to the ribs were attached to the breasts. The skin and tissues of the abdomen from the coastal arch to the pubic area were removed in large flaps. The right thigh was denuded in front to the bone, including the external organs of reproduction and part of the right buttock. The left thigh was stripped of skin, fascia and muscles to the knee. The left calf showed a long gash through skin and tissues to the deep muscles and reached past the knee to five inches above the ankle. Both arms and forearms had extensive and jagged wounds. The right thumb had a superficial incision about one inch long and there were abrasions on the back of the hand. The lower part of the right lung was broken and torn away; the left lung was intact. The surfaces of her abdomen and of her thighs were removed, and her abdominal cavity had been emptied of viscera. The uterus and kidneys were found, along with one breast, under her head. Her other breast was found by her right foot, and her liver between her feet. Her intestines were placed by her right side and her spleen was placed by the left side of her body. The flaps removed from her abdomen and thighs were found on the table. Her face was mutilated beyond recognition and her neck was severed to the bone. Further examination revealed that the pericardium had been opened and her heart had been removed. It was not found.

- Death was due to the throat wound, and most of the mutilation was believed to be postmortem.

THE "SIXTH" FIRST VICTIM

Professional criminologists, police investigators and experienced profilers who review the eight Whitechapel murders—or the eleven Whitechapel murders if we include an additional two murders of women in 1889 and one more in 1891—conclude that there were six Jack the Ripper victims, not five.[11] Jack the Ripper's noncanonical sixth victim would really be his first victim, murdered three weeks before the first of the "canonical five."

> **Martha Tabram, Tuesday, August 7, 1888,** thirty-six years old, was found at about four forty-five a.m. on a first-floor landing of the George Yard Buildings tenement off a narrow north-south alley called George Yard connecting Wentworth Street and Whitechapel High Street. Tabram was last seen by a fellow prostitute after the two of them paired off with two soldiers in a pub and she left with her client at about eleven forty-five p.m. At about three thirty a.m., her body was seen by a witness returning home from a night job, but in the dimly lit landing, he mistook her for a sleeping vagrant and paid no attention to her. A person leaving for work in the morning called the police after finding Tabram. Despite numerous attempts, the two soldiers were not successfully identified.

- The victim was found lying on her back, with her dress pushed up to her waist. Her legs were drawn up and open, the feet resting on the ground and the knees turned outward.

- There were 39 stab wounds: 9 in the throat; 5 in the breast area—3 in the left lung, 2 in the right lung and 1 in the heart, which would have been fatal; 5 in the liver; 2 in the spleen; 6 in the stomach; and 9 in the genital area.

- Only one of the wounds, to the heart, was produced by a long dagger or bayonet, while the remaining wounds were inflicted with a smaller knife, possibly a folding penknife.

Because there were no facial wounds, no slashing of the throat or torso and no mutilation or organ harvesting, all of which characterized the later murders, many amateur ripperologists dismissed Martha Tabram from the canon of victims, but most professional investigators and criminologists today include the Tabram murder. The fact that the perpetrator might have stabbed Tabram in the throat rather than slashing her as he did the other victims does not automatically exclude her from the canon.

The anomalies in the Tabram murder when it is compared with the later five murders can be attributed to the possibility that this was Jack the Ripper's first murder. Unlike the other murders, it might not have been planned, which might account for why it occurred on a Tuesday, while the later murders each took place on a Friday, Saturday or Sunday. Perhaps something happened unexpectedly between the killer and the victim, sparking an unplanned murder and unleashing an addictive bloodlust for more, as often happens in serial-killer cases. After his first murder the killer embarks on a cycle of fantasy killings that are "improved upon" with every repetition in a learning process. But the first murder often looks like an anomaly in the series precisely because it is unplanned, unlike the murders that follow. The first murder is often closer to home than an offender would ever intend, and it may look hesitant and incomplete in its fantasy signature, disorganized and improvised.

PROFILING JACK THE RIPPER IN 1888

Are you wondering how Jack the Ripper might have been pursued in modern times with all the techniques available to law enforcement today? Certainly, the science of DNA analysis and identification could have narrowed the suspect list. But, perhaps surprisingly, criminal psychological and crime-scene profiling had been attempted back in 1888 and in more than just rudimentary form.

The first attempt to psychologically profile Jack the Ripper was in September, when the alienist Dr. L. Forbes Winslow inserted himself into the case, and wrote to the *Times*:

That the murderer of the three victims in Whitechapel is one and the same person I have no doubt. The whole affair is that of a lunatic, and as there is "a method in madness," so there was method shown in the crime and in the gradual dissection of the body of the latest victim . . . I think that the murderer is not of the class of which "Leather Apron" belongs, but is of the upper class of society, and I still think that my opinion given to the authorities is the correct one—viz., that the murders have been committed by a lunatic lately discharged from some asylum, or by one who has escaped . . . one who, though suffering from the effects of homicidal mania, is apparently sane on the surface, and consequently has been liberated, and is following out the inclinations of his morbid imagination by wholesale homicide.[12]

When referring to the "three victims" in his letter, Winslow was, as the newspapers did at the time, including the Martha Tabram murder with the two later, "canonical" murders of Mary Ann Nichols and Annie Chapman. Dr. Winslow in his time was so bitten by the ripperology bug and focused so tenaciously on his favorite suspect, the so-called "lodger" from Canada, G. Wentworth Smith, that police at some point began to suspect Winslow himself of being Jack the Ripper.

What arguably might be the first police-sponsored attempt in history to produce an official crime-scene profile of an unidentified serial killer came from police surgeon Dr. Thomas Bond on November 10, 1888, following the murder of Mary Jane Kelly.[13]

Dr. Bond concluded, "All five murders [he didn't include Martha Tabram] were no doubt committed by the same hand . . . the women must have been lying down when murdered and in every case the throat was first cut . . . in all the cases there appears to be no evidence of struggling and the attacks were probably so sudden and made in such a position that the women could neither resist nor cry out . . . in all the murders, the object was mutilation."

Dr. Bond then ventured a psychological profile of the serial killer:

The murderer must have been a man of physical strength and of great coolness and daring. There is no evidence he had an accomplice. He must in my opinion be a man subject to periodical attacks of Homicidal and erotic mania. The character of the mutilations indicate that the man may be in a condition sexually, that may be called satyriasis. It is of course possible that the Homicidal impulse may have developed from a revengeful or brooding condition of the mind, or that Religious Mania may have been the original disease, but I do not think either hypothesis is likely. The murderer in external appearance is quite likely to be a quiet inoffensive looking man probably middle aged and neatly and respectably dressed. I think he must be in the habit of wearing a cloak or overcoat or he could hardly have escaped notice in the streets if the blood on his hands or clothes were visible.

Assuming the murderer to be such a person as I have just described he would probably be solitary and eccentric in his habits, also he is most likely to be a man without regular occupation, but with some small income or pension. He is possibly living among respectable persons who have some knowledge of his character and habits and who may have grounds for suspicion that he is not quite right in his mind at times. Such persons would probably be unwilling to communicate suspicions to the Police for fear of trouble or notoriety, whereas if there were a prospect of reward it might overcome their scruples.[14]

Thomas Bond's historic attempt at criminal profiling was an admirable effort hampered only by the lack of statistical behavioral data to guide him. That would take another one hundred years, until John Douglas, Robert Ressler and Ann W. Burgess completed their sexual homicide survey, which established the first rudimentary statistical database on which FBI profiling techniques would be based.

Jack the Ripper's "Surgical Skill"

There was a lot of speculation at the time that, given the serial killer's "surgical skill," he could be a physician. Several physicians who examined the mutilated bodies, with the missing kidneys, uterus, heart and other organs, which the Ripper harvested, were quoted or described as commenting:

> There were indications of anatomical knowledge . . . I believe the perpetrator of the act must have had considerable knowledge of the position of the organs in the abdominal cavity and the way of removing them. It required a great deal of medical knowledge to have removed the kidney and to know where it was placed. The parts removed would be of no use for any professional purpose . . .
>
> He thought he himself [the examining physician] could not have performed all the injuries he described, even without a struggle, [in] under a quarter of an hour. If he had done it in a deliberate way such as would fall to the duties of a surgeon it probably would have taken him the best part of an hour.[15]

Of course this all depends on the assumption that Jack the Ripper was looking specifically for a kidney or a uterus when he cut those victims open; with more experience of serial killers, we can see the possibility that he just blindly "ripped" the victims, exposing a smorgasbord of organs like slimy appetizers on a tray, to take and taste what caught his eye without knowing what it was, snatching at whatever came into his hand or slipped and slid loose from under his knife's edge as he ripped and tore through a bloody stew of spilled guts, kidneys and liver. You don't have to be a surgeon to be a butcher, and before supermarkets and refrigeration, even in an urbanized center like London, you did not have to be a butcher to have butchered. Lots of people had experience with gutting and butchering fresh meat.

The London police surgeon Dr. Thomas Bond, who produced the November 1888 "official" profile of Jack the Ripper, dismissed all notions of the killer having surgical skills, or even a butcher's skill, arguing, "The mutilation was inflicted by a person who had no scientific nor anatomical knowledge. In my opinion he does not even possess the technical knowledge of a butcher or horse slaughterer or any person accustomed to cut up dead animals."[16]

PROFILING JACK THE RIPPER TODAY

One of America's veteran serial-homicide investigator-profilers, Robert Keppel, tackled the Jack the Ripper case in 2005. Keppel, today an academic, was an investigator with the Washington State Attorney General's office and was one of the investigators in the Ted Bundy and Green River Killer serial murders.[17] Keppel co-opted Bundy to help him profile the Green River Killer, an episode that partly inspired the scenes in *The Silence of the Lambs* between FBI trainee Clarice Starling and serial killer Hannibal Lecter.[18]

Keppel states that while a serial killer's method of operation (MO)—what he *needs to do* to accomplish the crime—changes as he learns and develops, and even the pathological "rituals" he performs at the crime scene can change, the fantasy "signature"—what he *does not need* to do, but compulsively does—behind the rituals will always be the same.

In his analysis Keppel points out that after killing his likely first victim, Martha Tabram, Jack the Ripper probably learned to manually strangle or choke the victims from behind, lower them to the ground in an unconscious state with their heads typically pointing to his left, kill them by cutting their throats and, finally, having gained complete possession and control of their bodies, proceed to mutilate them.[19] (We often forget that Jack the Ripper was a necrophile, a "warm-destructive" on Lee Mellor's scale of necrophilia [see chapter seven].) This strategy prevented him from being splashed by the victim's blood while her heart was pumping, as he must have been when he attacked his first victim, Tabram, from the front. Prior to the last victim, the murders all occurred outdoors in the darkest hours, between midnight and morning, and the victims were left at the scene. After he was interrupted by passersby in his attacks on Elizabeth Stride and Catherine Eddowes, he adjusted his MO, killing and mutilating his next victim, Mary Jane Kelly, indoors without risking interruption again.

The static signature of Jack the Ripper was his *piquerism*—his use of a knife to slash open and penetrate in a mimicry of sexual intercourse. According to Keppel, Jack the Ripper was gratified by violence, dominance, control, bleeding, penetration, evisceration, destruction and ultimately the complete possession of the victim, including the harvesting of their internal organs. That was what turned him on.

Jack the Ripper's static signature is evident in eleven characteristics that shift in and out of the evolving MO:

1. Except for the last one, the victims were all middle-aged prostitutes or former prostitutes with severe long-term alcohol addiction who were seen drunk in the hours before their murders. The victims, in investigative parlance, were in a "high-risk" category: they were already "less alive" before Jack the Ripper even laid eyes on them;

2. The crimes all displayed various degrees of *piquerism*, which escalated from the stabbing of the first victim's breasts and genital area to the "extravagant" mutilation and organ harvesting of the sixth victim. Not all the victims were exposed to the same amount and type of mutilation, but there was an escalation from the first to the last victim. The more he killed, the more he did things that were *not necessary* to perpetrate the murder, and did them in an escalating intensity;

3. The perpetrator immediately and completely incapacitated, subdued and took control of the victims in a "blitz" type of attack from behind, silencing them first through asphyxiation or strangulation, lowering them to the ground and then killing them by cutting their throats with such impatience and urgency that he nearly decapitated some of his victims. The killing was just a chore, a means to an end, the wringing of a chicken's neck in anticipation of a fine meal; the mutilation and evisceration were pure butchery—a Lycaon's Shepherd's Pie of guts—the sacrificial Abomination;

4. The perpetrator showed signs of "overkill" by inflicting an excessive number of potentially fatal wounds beyond the minimum necessary to incapacitate or kill his victims;

5. There was no primary penetrative sexual assault on the victims;

6. The victims were not tortured before being killed;

7. All the homicides occurred within a quarter mile of one another and, except for the first, noncanonical homicide, occurred late on weekend nights;

8. The perpetrator left his victims in the open with no attempt to cover or conceal the bodies or forestall their discovery. The one body that was left indoors was the one that was most excessively mutilated;

9. Except in the murder of Stride, during which he was interrupted, Jack the Ripper posed his victims lying on their backs with their legs apart and skirts hiked up in a degrading "sexual" position to be found in the open where they were killed and mutilated. The victims were posed as if they were having sexual intercourse. Some of the victims' clothes were rearranged, possessions were laid out near some of the victims' bodies and their internal organs and body parts were used in horrifically weird tableaus created by the killer;

10. The killer's objective was to spend more time alone with his victims to enjoy acting out his compulsion and to escalate his violence and postmortem mutilation and harvesting of body parts. He amputated the breasts of his last victim and attempted to sever her legs at the thigh and knee. Each uninterrupted killing was characterized by an escalation of the mutilation and violence. Aside from complete decapitation, amputation or dismemberment, by the sixth victim there was very little room left for further escalation. That may be why Jack the Ripper stopped, if he stopped of his own accord. (Serial killers have been known to "retire," as in the cases of Albert DeSalvo, Gary Ridgway and Dennis Rader, the "BTK Killer");

11. The attacks were organized, with the perpetrator bringing his own knife to the scene and leaving with it. Jack the Ripper probably had a serial killer's "kill kit" that contained the knife and possibly disguises and anything else he felt he would need to commit his mur-

ders. Jack the Ripper left behind at the scene no tangible evidence that was detectable in that era, no witness conclusively glimpsing him red-handed with knife in hand or fleeing. Having dismembered at least four women on sidewalks and pavements in spans of ten to fifteen minutes, he then slipped through highly trafficked and crowded areas unseen and somehow unbloodied (or covering the blood up). He appeared to have an intimate familiarity with the streets of Whitechapel and their traffic patterns and rhythms in the night hours in order to pass through them invisibly. Many people probably looked at him; very few saw him. This serial killer was comfortable in Whitechapel because he belonged in it, because it was his home, where he lived and worked.

In FBI parlance, Jack the Ripper would be a mixed category of "unsub" (unknown subject) showing both organized and disorganized personality traits: organized because he brought his weapon to the scene; disorganized because he struck at targets of opportunity by "blitzing" them; organized because he chose a hunting ground dense with the same targets of opportunity; disorganized because it was his own home ground; organized because he carefully chose the dark of night to strike; disorganized because he killed in open, public areas and was interrupted on multiple occasions; organized because he learned to take his last victim inside; disorganized because it took him so long to figure out to do that. Jack the Ripper was cunning but crazy.

In 1988, FBI profiler John Douglas took a crack at applying what the Behavioral Sciences Unit had recently learned from interviewing serial killers to profiling Jack the Ripper. Douglas ignored the "Jack the Ripper" letters because they were unauthenticated.

He developed the following profile of the unsub:

- Between the ages of twenty-eight and thirty-six;

- Does not look out of the ordinary;

- At the time of the assaults would not wear his everyday clothing, because he wanted to project to unsuspecting prostitutes that he had money;

- Raised by a domineering mother and weak, passive and/or absent father;

- Likelihood his mother drank heavily and enjoyed the company of many men;

- As a child did not receive consistent care and contact with stable adult role models;

- Detached socially and developed a diminished emotional response toward fellow humans;

- Asocial and prefers to be alone;

- Internalized anger and in younger years expressed through setting fires and acts of cruelty toward animals;

- Fantasies of domination, cruelty and mutilation of women;

- Employed in a trade where he could work alone and vicariously experience his destructive fantasies. Employment could include work as a butcher, mortician's assistant, medical examiner's aid or hospital attendant;

- Employed Monday through Friday, and on Friday night, Saturday and Sunday is off from work [Douglas was unaware of the six-day workweek of the Victorian era. This illustrates the pitfalls of profiling into the distant past.];

- Carried a knife routinely for self-defense;

- Paranoid-type thinking with poor self-image. Might have some physical abnormality although not severe. Might be below average weight or height, or have problems with speech, scarred complexion, physical illness or past injury;

- Probably not married but if married then to someone older than himself and the marriage lasting a short duration;

- Not adept in meeting people socially, and the majority of his heterosexual relationships would be with prostitutes. Likely infected with venereal disease, untreatable in that era, which could further fuel his hatred and disgust for women;

- Would be perceived as being quiet, a loner, shy, slightly withdrawn, obedient and neat and orderly in appearance and when working;

- Drinks in local pubs, and after a few drinks he becomes more relaxed and finds it easier to engage in conversation;

- He lives and works in the Whitechapel area. The first homicide should be in close proximity to either his home or workplace;

- Would not have committed suicide after the last homicide. Generally, when crimes like these cease it is because the perpetrator came close to being identified, was interviewed by police or was arrested for some other offense.[20]

In other words, in the view of an FBI profiler, it is unlikely Jack the Ripper was a top-hatted upper-class surgeon or physician, or prominent artist or Prince Albert, although he might have dressed up to lure his prostitute victims and perhaps even wore a cape to cover any bloodstains on his clothing. His social ineptitude meant that dressing well would have helped him draw women to himself rather than his having to approach them and risk being seen; however, it is unlikely that he dressed in formal evening wear as he is frequently portrayed doing in iconic imagery.

Jack the Ripper was most likely an anonymous denizen of Whitechapel, of a similar social class as his victims, a colorless and shy Gary Ridgway, as opposed to a charismatic, outgoing Ted Bundy. Since 1888 some five hundred suspects have been nominated as Jack the Ripper by amateur investigators, journalists, ripperologists, criminologists and both amateur and professional historians.[21] The London Metropolitan Police website identifies only four "official" suspects seriously considered by the original official investigation, all names familiar to any ripperologist:

- "Kosminski," a poor Polish Jewish local resident in Whitechapel, today identified as twenty-three- or twenty-four-year-old Aaron

Kosminski, a hairdresser residing in Whitechapel with a history of mental illness;[22]

- Montague John Druitt, a thirty-one-year-old barrister and schoolteacher who committed suicide in December 1888;

- Michael Ostrog, a Russian-born multipseudonymous thief and confidence trickster, believed to be fifty-five years old in 1888, and detained in asylums on several occasions;

- Dr. Francis J. Tumblety, fifty-six years old, an American quack doctor who was arrested in November 1888 for offenses of gross indecency, and fled the country later the same month, having obtained bail.[23]

The suspect Aaron Kosminski certainly fits the profile generated in 1988 by John Douglas at the FBI. But since the 1990s, a new generation of criminal profiling techniques has risen to the forefront: geoforensic profiling. When geoforensic techniques are applied to the Whitechapel murders, one of the suspects looks especially good.

RAPTOR: GEOPROFILING JACK THE RIPPER, AND OCKHAM'S RAZOR

One of the newest tools in serial-homicide investigation is geoprofiling, or geoforensic profiling, an investigative technique that began to gain traction in the 1990s with the ubiquitous availability of inexpensive but powerful computers. Interpretive-intuitive psychological profiling based on crime-scene analysis produces a hypothetical suspect profile only as good as the individual profiler. In contrast, geoprofiling relies on empirical data and mathematical algorithms, which ferret out where the actual suspect is most likely to be "anchored"—the location of his home or workplace—by following "bread crumbs" from the crime scenes back to the suspect's home base and comfort zone.

The premise behind forensic geoprofiling is that serial criminals tend to commit crimes not too close to their "anchor" for comfort, but not too far into unfamiliar territory either. Once the location of three or more serial offenses can be linked to a single perpetrator and triangulated, the place between too close and too far can be calculated with geoforensic algorithms. With multiple crime scenes, a probable anchor can sometimes be calculated down to a 150-square-yard area. (The algorithms were originally formulated in the 1940s by Gestapo mathematicians and psychologists to geoprofile the homes of individuals clandestinely distributing anti-Hitler leaflets and painting graffiti in Berlin. They worked very well.)[24]

In its early form, geoprofiling was based on a simple *circle hypothesis* that says serial offenders live within a circle whose diameter is equal to the distance between the two murder sites farthest from each other. Various studies confirm this hypothesis. For example, from a sample of 126 American serial killers, 89 percent lived within a circle defined by their two body disposal sites farthest from each other, and 86 percent of 26 British serial killers sampled also met the circle hypothesis.[25]

Kim Rossmo, one of the pioneers of geoforensic profiling, classifies serial offenders as either *stalkers*, who seek out their victims in a comfort zone territory, or *raptors*, who attack their victims more or less randomly upon encountering them in a territory they frequent.[26] These factors—combined with a serial killer's place of employment or lack of employment, marital status, children's age, entertainment and dining tastes, addictions, hobbies, sports activities, mode of travel, road system, geography, land use and zoning and infrastructure—all have an impact on where his home base gets centered. Some serial killers will go out specifically to hunt and stalk, while other serial killers keep an eye out for potential victims while they are routinely shopping, running errands or on their way to work, a factor that geoprofilers include in their algorithmic variables.

The behavioral mathematics involved in geoprofiling serial killers involves not only the perpetrator's movement, but the victim's as well. The movement of both victim and offender through different geographical spaces leading to their encounter has a social, cultural and historical dimension to it, shaping and nurturing not only the serial killer through time and geography but any individual's likelihood to be targeted by a serial killer. Geoprofilers have identified a matrix of five distinct, mutually exclusive offender-victim geographic encounter patterns:

1. Internal: victim and offender share the same territory;

2. Predatory: offender invades the victim's territory;

3. Intrusion: victim enters the offender's territory;

4. Offense mobility: victim and offender share the same territory but the offense takes place elsewhere;

5. Total mobility: victim and offender live in different territories and the offense takes place in a unique third territory.[27]

Offenders can be *marauders*, committing their crimes in areas that they frequent in the course of day-to-day life, or they can be *commuters*, traveling from their home base to a specific area that they do not otherwise visit in their routine activities.[28]

Today geoprofiling is highly evolved, and it is recognized that it is not only serial killers who move and strike in a mathematically discernible pattern but also terrorists, smugglers, illegal migrants (targeted today by LBIMP—Land Border Illegal Migration Profiling systems), sharks, mosquitoes and epidemic diseases.[29] Rossmo advocated to US forces during the Iraq War the utility of geoprofiling to link locations of urban insurgency graffiti to insurgent home bases.[30]

One of the compelling aspects of geoprofiling is its effectiveness in profiling cold cases of serial murder going back decades or even centuries. Jack the Ripper crime-scene data has been fed into the new generation of geoprofiling systems, which take into account variables of pre-automobile movement and all the other historical factors that would have influenced the algorithms. The big question remaining is whether Jack the Ripper was a stalker or a raptor, a marauder or a commuter.

Serial killers of prostitutes have historically been "commuters" who travel to areas frequented by them, and while London had many places like that, without a doubt Whitechapel had a highly concentrated number of the skid-row prostitutes the Ripper seemed to prefer. It is therefore possible he was a "commuter" into Whitechapel, and the potential suspect list therefore is large and unwieldy, as is his geoprofile.

But if he was a marauder-raptor, then current geoprofiling software locates the perpetrator of the five canonical Jack the Ripper murders in a 150-square-yard area with its anchor around Flower and Dean Street in the heart of Whitechapel.[31] And if you include the "first," perhaps unplanned murder, of Tabram, that just nails the anchor more tightly to that same location.

Add to that the age-old principle of *Ockham's razor* in problem-solving: "If there are a number of possible solutions, the simplest one, based on the fewest assumptions, is most likely to be correct." Aaron Kosminski, who lived in the heart of Whitechapel, or somebody very much like him, *most likely* was the serial murderer known as Jack the Ripper. It's *the simplest* solution, with *the fewest* assumptions. Robert House gives in "Aaron Kosminski Reconsidered," on casebook.org, a very detailed and persuasive argument for Kosminski's candidacy based on all the recent geoprofiling advances.[32]

Kosminski or not, Jack the Ripper as a serial killer was "special" in a very real way—not just because of his notoriety in the center of the newspaper capital of Britain, but by serial-killer behavioral standards even today. Robert Keppel, who designed a computer system for Washington State to track and link murder cases—Homicide Investigation Tracking System (HITS)—ran Jack the Ripper data through the system, comparing the Whitechapel murders signature and MO characteristics with 3,359 murder cases in the HITS database. In Washington, home to mega serial killers like Ted Bundy, the Green River Killer and Robert Yates, the HITS system found no match with the same combination of signatures and MO that Jack the Ripper had. Only by subtracting various characteristics did he find a rare few comparable murders. Keppel reported:

> There were only nine cases in the database in which the victim's body was probed, explored, or mutilated, six of them females, only one being a prostitute. There are only two cases, both females and neither a prostitute, that contain both characteristics of unusual body position and explored, probed, or mutilated body cavities. More significant, there are no cases where the body of a prostitute displayed both characteristics of unusual body position and explored, probed, or mutilated cavities.[33]

Jack the Ripper was indeed a rare monster. He was a unique necrophile lust serial killer deserving of the cult of ripperology so obsessed with identifying the man behind the monster. It is unlikely, however, that we will ever conclusively determine his identity.

Whether the investigation of the 1888 Whitechapel murders was bungled is debated by ripperologists familiar with the intricacies of the two rival police departments investigating the case (the London City Police and the London Metropolitan Police) and the frenzied competition among London's newspapers to cover the case. To all their credit, there was little linkage blindness in this case; the murders were quickly recognized as the work of a solo serial killer, even though the term was not available to describe him as such. How much better the London police might have been able to investigate the Whitechapel murders had current forensic sciences like fingerprinting, geoprofiling and DNA testing been available to them, one can easily speculate.

LUST KILLERS: "THE INSANE DIALOG OF LOVE AND DEATH IN THE LIMITLESS PRESUMPTION OF APPETITE"

What historical or social factors might account for the gathering storm of lust serial killers in the nineteenth century? Firstly, sex was driven underground. While prostitution itself was long condemned, sexuality in general before the mid-nineteenth century was much more open. As late as the 1860s it was still respectable for upper-class Victorians in Britain to bathe in the nude at public beaches, although "bathing booths" could be wheeled out into the sea for privacy.[34] Twenty years later, by the 1880s, such a thing would be unthinkable.

Author and social critic Colin Wilson suggests that two factors may have played a role in the rise of sadistic sexual serial murder in the late nineteenth century: the expansion of the female workforce and a new sexual sensibility reflected by the emergence of a certain type of pornographic literature.[35]

Wilson argued that today every man knows that most of the women he encounters in the city are unavailable to him. However, during much of the nineteenth century, the reverse was true. Thousands of impoverished, urbanized women turned to prostitution and were available to any man with a coin in his pocket. But by the last decades of the nineteenth century, it was discovered that women made better typists than men did, that they were excellent shop clerks, and so on. The new middle classes were also hiring thousands of young women as domestic servants. Now men were faced with a large population of gainfully employed and *unavailable* women, to which was added the Victorian-era philosophy that sex beyond procreation was something unnatural and unhealthy. Women became taboo objects of a forbidden desire—a guaranteed formula for a volatile cocktail of confused and lethally misdirected libido.

Furthermore, the nature of pornographic literature suddenly changed, reflecting the new, repressive Victorian antisex culture. In previous centuries, both erotic literature and images portrayed sex explicitly and freely. Sex was something to be indulged in sensually, with gusto, like a good meal. But in the nineteenth century, pornographic literature began to take its cue from the Marquis de Sade. It described sex as something forbidden—a taboo to be overcome only through voyeurism, illicit seduction, bondage, force and rape. In the nineteenth-century pornographic novel, the virtuous Victorian woman could enjoy sex only if she was overpowered and forced into it.

A common theme was the capture of traveling Victorian virgins by pirates or lustful Turks, the women discovering the pleasures of sex by being raped in a harem. Children were portrayed as sexual beings intent on seducing the family butler. Scenes of bondage, flogging and sex were intermixed; sex was almost always linked to pain and the loss of female virginity—often in childhood and accompanied by copious blood. Sold in cheap, popular, magazine-like multipart editions, in an age when print encompassed all available media, this literature had a tremendous impact on the imaginations of the bored, frustrated and repressed males among whom, no doubt, dwelled Jack the Ripper.

There is no evidence that pornography spawns serial killers, but it can function as a *facilitator*, in the same way as alcohol or drugs, or true-crime detective magazines or for that matter even passages in the Bible condemning harlots, and similar little pieces in a jigsaw puzzle that makes up the structural underpinnings of complex serial-killer fantasies, psychopathologies and behaviors. Pornography can also function as a *conditioner*. Unlike the Bible, pornography, especially pictorial, is not, as often claimed, "watched" or "read," but masturbated to. When women complain, "My man is watching porn on the Internet," one wants to snicker. The problem is not that he is "watching" porn; it's that he is compulsively masturbating to it. For somebody with a paraphilic addiction, pornography can become a sexual-response conditioner to self-selected sadistic or other transgressive fantasies.

It is interesting that while so many medical, psychiatric, sexual and philosophical terms derive from ancient Greek gods or Greco-Roman words, "sadism," although the fact of it has presumably always existed, is entirely modern as a term, deriving from the late-eighteenth-century figure the Marquis de Sade (as is "masochism," derived from Leopold von Sacher-Masoch [1836–95]). Or as French philosopher and social critic Michel Foucault argued,

> Sadism is not a name finally given to a practice as old as Eros; it is a massive cultural fact which appeared precisely at the end of the eighteenth century, and which constitutes one of the greatest conversions of Western imagination: unreason transformed into delirium of the heart, madness of desire, the insane dialog of love and death in the limitless presumption of appetite.[36]

ELEVEN

The French Ripper:
The Forensics of Serial Murder
in the Belle Epoch, 1897

Who sees always in the accused a fallen brother or one wrongfully suspected, he will question well.

—DR. HANS GROSS, *HANDBOOK FOR
EXAMINING MAGISTRATES*, 1893

Justice withers, prison corrupts and society gets the criminal
it deserves.

—DR. ALEXANDRE LACASSAGNE, FATHER OF SOCIAL
ENVIRONMENTAL CRIMINOLOGY

A decade after Jack the Ripper, police across the channel in France were
faced with a series of their own "ripper" murders. Unlike the British, the
French were already experienced with serial killers like Martin Dumollard, Louis-Joseph Philippe and Eusebius Pieydagnelle, not to mention
the serial necrophile vampire François Bertrand. Yet their seminal serial-
killer case was more daunting than the Jack the Ripper murders, within
the urban confines of Whitechapel. The French Ripper left a migratory
trail of murders covering a vast and mostly remote rural territory of
southeastern France. This case was thoroughly modern not only in
terms of its investigation (albeit without the benefits of fingerprinting
and DNA) but also in its psychiatric and legal debates about the killer's
sanity when, unlike Jack the Ripper, he was identified, apprehended and

put on trial. It can be classified among the earliest serial-killer cases successfully solved through modern forensic techniques and advanced investigative strategies.

Joseph Vacher—"Southeast Ripper"—"Killer of Little Shepherds"—France, 1897

In late-nineteenth-century France, young female textile workers lived and worked far from their rural homes, like Mexican *maquiladora* laborers or Chinese migrant factory workers today: in big suburban mills with dormitories and cafeterias where they labored, ate and slept. It was a grueling, wage-slave life, but it was better than anything they ever had before, the ultimate paradox of industrial-era disposable labor exploitation.

Eugénie Delhomme was a pretty twenty-one-year-old peasant girl, a single mother who found work in one of those textile mills in Beaurepaire, a small town south of France's industrial center of Lyon, the same city where Martin Dumollard trolled for his victims thirty years earlier. Eugénie worked six days a week in the deafening clatter of mechanical looms. It was an exhausting shift that began at five a.m. and ended fifteen and a half hours later at eight thirty p.m., with short breaks for lunch and supper in the communal dining hall. She earned just enough to send money to her aging father and her daughter back home in the country.

On Saturday, May 19, 1894, at about seven thirty p.m., an hour before her shift ended, Eugénie rose from her workstation and said she was taking a short break to get some air in the alley outside the doors. Her supervisor commented that it was beginning to rain but she was insistent. Eugénie was a reliable worker but she had a reputation for having several boyfriends in the nearby town, and the tolerant supervisor might have assumed she was stepping out to meet a boyfriend; or perhaps she wanted to sneak a smoke.

Nobody was alarmed when she did not return to her station; she might have left early in the last hour of the long workweek. No one was worried enough to search for her around the factory grounds in the rain and dark. The next morning, she was not in her dormitory nor did she make her usual appearance in church. Later that afternoon a shepherd woman came across Eugénie's body dumped under a hedge about two hundred yards from the factory door.

It was a horrific scene reminiscent of the probable first victim of Jack the Ripper, Martha Tabram. Eugénie was found nude except for a chemise pulled down and up to around her waist. It was immediately evident that her clothing did not get into a state of disarray as a result of her struggles, but because she was disrobed in a frenzy by her murderer.[1] The rest of her torn bloodstained clothing, corset and scarf were found nearby. The examining physician determined that Eugénie had been first grabbed by the throat and thrown to the ground and strangled. As evidenced by the trampled grass and the bruises on her hands, the young woman had put up a struggle. The killer forced his hand over her mouth to stifle her cries, leaving her lip torn and bruised, and cut off her oxygen supply while keeping her pinned down with his legs and other hand. He then cut her throat with his left hand, severing her jugular vein to hasten her death. When she was dead or nearly dead, the killer, then in a rage, kicked and stomped her torso, chest and pubic area, his boots leaving distinctive imprints on her body. Finally, he used his knife to excise the areola of one of her breasts and left it hanging by a strip of flesh about two or three inches in length. Afterward the killer dragged her body behind the hedge where she was found. There were no signs of vaginal rape, and the physician neglected to examine the victim for signs of anal rape.[2]

In 1894, forensic medical procedure had been reasonably well developed and systemized over the previous fifty years. We saw how in the Jack the Ripper case, physicians were able to reconstruct how the victims were attacked and in what order the various injuries and mutilations took place.

Over the next few weeks police arrested three different suspects, all of them men who were known to have some connection to the victim. The assumption was that this was a singular crime of passion. Even though shortly before the murder three women reported being stalked and approached menacingly near the crime scene by a stranger, a vagabond with a hideous grimace, the police for the next four months focused on the "crime of passion" motive before the case went cold.

During the Dumollard case in the 1860s French police were criticized for not having linked various murders in the region where Du-mollard used to sally forth to Lyon to stalk, lure back and kill his victims. Since then, police divisions endeavored to be aware of what was happening in the next division, but this awareness and sharing of infor-mation did not extend beyond bordering divisions.

But Eugénie's murderer was a different species of serial killer than Dumollard or presumably Jack the Ripper was. This was a migratory serial killer who, after killing Eugénie, washed up in a creek, spent the night sleeping concealed in a haystack and the next day tramped along the back roads an extraordinary distance of forty miles, several police districts away, where nobody was even aware of Eugénie's murder.

As the killer compulsively walked enormous distances, thirty to forty miles a day, thousands of miles a year, through remote villages in south-eastern France, carrying his hobo sack, seeking casual work or handouts of food and shelter, playing an accordion for coins, along the way he am-bushed, killed, raped and mutilated two women and at least nine teenagers—four boys and five girls ranging in age from thirteen to nine-teen—often shepherds tending their flocks alone in isolated locations.

His escalating mode of attack had some similarities to Jack the Ripper. He strangled his victims quickly as he forced them to the ground and cut their throats to kill them. As evidenced by the blood pools left at the crime scenes, he apparently first drained the blood from the victims before drag-ging the corpses away to dry ground. Then he would go at the victims' bodies, mutilating them, but unlike Jack the Ripper, he raped them vagi-nally and anally after they were dead, sometimes using lubricant to aid the necrophilic act. Sometimes he severed or excised the genitals completely and ripped their torsos open, pulling out the intestines and harvesting organs. The victims were all found with their throats cut and their genitals mutilated and exposed like the victims in Whitechapel. These were classic "warm," destructive, necrophilic "werewolf" lust serial killings.

Despite the horrific character of the killings, the French police were in a complete state of linkage blindness. After all, some of the crimes occurred six hundred miles apart. Considering that eighty years later, police in the US in the 1970s linked by telephone and telex were blind to the series of murders committed by Ted Bundy, it is hard to fault the French police in the 1890s when it came to interjurisdictional murders.

It was not as if the authorities had overlooked the incidence of these extraordinarily savage murders. One investigator in Dijon began cataloging the murders, but on the assumption that they were a viral, contagious phenomenon, a homicidal epidemic in a form of "copycat killings." While French police could conceive of a single perpetrator killing multiple victims, they could not conceive of him doing it over such vast distances. Unlike the place-specific Jack the Ripper, the French Ripper was a migratory-type serial killer, a Henry Lee Lucas without a car.

The "Killer of Little Shepherds," or "Southeast Ripper," as he was called in the French press, had another advantage working for him. As a vagrant, he was part of a huge anonymous population of rootless and destitute people overrunning France as a result of industrial labor practices. Industrial labor was "disposable" in the nineteenth century (like "contract" labor in the twenty-first century). There were no unions, job security or benefits. Workers could be summarily dismissed for the day, the week or forever, if they were not needed. There was no severance, unemployment insurance or welfare. Very few laid-off workers returned to their dead-end rural homes; most just hit the road, seeking a few days' more employment at their next destination, before being laid off again. It was an endless migratory cycle. With mechanization in agriculture increasing rural unemployment and a worldwide recession in the 1890s, an estimated 400 thousand vagrants were tramping the roads of France, looking for a meal in the next town or farmhouse—nearly 1 percent of the entire French population was dispossessed and homeless, ready to join the less-dead.[3] It was not just the industrial-age city that gave serial killers an anonymous crowd to hide in and feed on; the industrial-age country road did so too.

Eventually this serial killer made a mistake—in 1896 he circled back to the region around Lyon and began killing in several locations in that district. This would be like a modern American serial killer choosing the vicinity of Quantico, Virginia, where the FBI's training academy and Behavioral Analysis Unit are located. Lyon was the home of the Institute of Forensic Medicine, the premier research center in nineteenth-century forensic sciences and psychiatry not only in France, but in the world.

The institute was dominated by Dr. Alexandre Lacassagne, a pioneer in forensic anthropology, toxin analysis, blood-splatter analysis and criminal psychology. Some of forensic science's greatest pioneers emerged from the Lyon school, like Edmond Locard, who gave us "Locard's exchange principle": every criminal leaves some trace evidence at a crime scene while at the same time taking some trace away from it.

Lacassagne controversially challenged the predominant "born criminal" faction of criminology led by the Italian criminologist Cesare Lombroso, who argued that a person's hereditary and genetic makeup predetermined their criminality.[4] Lacassagne maintained that psychology and social environments bred criminals, not genetics. He declared, "Justice withers, prison corrupts and society gets the criminal it deserves"— a statement that US Attorney General Robert Kennedy famously quoted in 1963.[5]

ÉMILE FOURQUET AND LINKAGE ANALYSIS

In France police investigations were led by "examining magistrates" akin to district attorneys. In April 1897, an ambitious thirty-five-year-old attorney, Émile Fourquet, was hired as the examining magistrate in Belley, a small market town sixty miles west of Lyon. Fourquet inherited an unsolved murder. Two years previously, on August 31, 1895, Victor Portalier, a fifteen-year-old shepherd boy, was horrifically murdered, raped and mutilated. He was found lying on his back with his pants pulled down around his shins; he was completely eviscerated, his intestines hanging out through a gash opened in his torso from sternum to pubis, his sexual organs severed and tossed away near his body. Locals had reported a vagabond begging for milk in the vicinity that day, but as one of the thousands of vagrants wandering France, he was never identified. All that was left was the ghastly crime scene and a description of a suspect: a man aged thirty to thirty-five years, with thick black eyebrows and a pale and sickly complexion, wearing a panama-style straw hat, carrying a small bag and a club. The one distinguishing feature was his disfiguring facial grimace around his right eye, and a bad odor of decay reportedly emanating from his right ear. He was apparently suffering from some sort of chronic facial injury or festering wound.

Fourquet was particularly interested in this case because he was working on a personal project, a study of the criminality of vagabonds in France, and this unsolved case fit the bill perfectly. (He would eventually publish his book on the "vagabond problem" in 1908.[6]) Reading in the newspaper reports of similar shepherd mutilation-murders near Lyon perpetrated by "a new Jack the Ripper," Fourquet began reviewing his cold-case file and found correspondence in it from the magistrate in Dijon inquiring about similar murders as evidence for a homicidal "contagion" theory he was developing. The magistrate believed these were "copycat" killings. Fourquet had his own idea: the spate of murders was not a "contagion" but serial homicide perpetrated by one migratory killer. On a hunch, Fourquet now wrote to every magistrate in France, inquiring about similar vagabond "werewolf" ripper-type homicides in their jurisdictions, and before long he had seven additional cases with very similar crime-scene characteristics linked to a vagabond with similar descriptions.

Fourquet now created two charts on a grid, one cataloging various characteristics—such as body position, weapon used, types of mutilation, wounds, whether there were signs of rape, and other crime-scene details—and the other listing the descriptions of the suspects associated with each case. Fourquet began underlining in blue all the similar factors across the eight cases. Before long he had a sea of blue underlining, from the placement of the wounds, the mutilation and the MO of the perpetrator to the description of the suspect in each case. Fourquet became convinced he had a single migratory monster on his hands. The term did not exist for it, but Fourquet had himself a serial killer.

What Fourquet was doing in 1897, Los Angeles Police homicide investigator Pierce Brooks found himself having to do in 1958. Described by James Ellroy as "LAPD's philosopher-king," Brooks, a former naval officer and blimp pilot, became convinced that two separate homicides in the Los Angeles area might have been committed by the same perpetrator.[7] Surmising that if one killer had murdered two victims, he might have killed three or more as well, Brooks spent weeks thumbing through old crime files and newspaper reports at the public library. Eventually he linked three "glamor girl murders" to serial killer Harvey Glatman, who in 1957 to 1958 was luring aspiring models to pose for him in true-detective-magazine-style bondage photos, and raping and murdering them as he took the photos.[8]

Brooks called for the establishment of a shared, networked computer database of homicide cases. For decades nobody listened. Brooks would get his wish only in 1985, with the establishment of ViCAP (Violent Criminal Apprehension Program), a database of homicide cases and their characteristics (see chapter thirteen for more on ViCAP). It took twenty-seven years for Brooks to see his idea transformed into reality, eighty-eight years after Fourquet first used the strategy in his investigation of the Vacher murders. Today we rightly consider Brooks among the pioneers of linkage analysis for his rediscovery of what we had forgotten since Fourquet.

The Arrest

On July 10, 1897, Fourquet telegraphed (or "t-mailed") to the 250 magistrates in France what we would today call a BOLO (Be On the Lookout) for a vagabond with a grimace, a scarred right eyelid and a deformity around the mouth. A magistrate in nearby Tournon telegraphed back that he had recently sentenced a vagabond matching the description to three months in jail for attempted rape. Not only did he match the description, but he was also very violent and raging, so much so that the photographer in Touron was too frightened to photograph him.

The attacker was identified as Joseph Vacher, a twenty-eight-year-old former sergeant in the French army and apparently a mentally disturbed vagabond.

The victim had been an adult woman collecting pinecones in the forest with her husband and three children. She was about fifty yards away from her husband when she was suddenly ambushed and thrown to the ground by Vacher, who attempted to strangle her. The children's screams brought her husband running. After a struggle he managed to subdue Vacher and hold him prisoner until the gendarmes arrived. What struck a chord with Fourquet was the comment the prisoner made: "I would have preferred a thirteen-year-old girl . . . I'm a poor, miserable, handicapped man. I love women, but they find me repulsive, so I attack those I can. Even in a whorehouse the women won't have anything to do with me. I'm so pitiful . . . That bitch! If she hadn't screamed so much, it would be all over by now and I would be in another district."[9]

Fourquet had Vacher transported to him under escort by train to be interviewed in the unsolved Portalier murder. Deep down Fourquet had a hunch that the other seven similar murders had been committed by the same perpetrator. While today an investigator would tap into a suspect's cell phone account and credit card records to track their past movements, there were no such things in Fourquet's time. Continental Europe did have a robust system of passports, identity cards, local sojourning and residence registrations and hotel and guesthouse logs, but Vacher had been a homeless vagabond sleeping in barns and haystacks. Nor was there any security camera footage that might have incidentally caught a homeless person passing in its view for Fourquet to look for. The only way he was going to find out if Vacher was near any of the locations of the unsolved murders at the time in question was if Vacher told him he was. He needed a confession. Without it, his hunch was useless.

"The Jesuit"

Joseph Vacher was born in Beaufort, Isère, in western France, on November 16, 1869, to farmers Pierre Vacher and Marie-Rose (Rosalie) Ravit. Rosalie was forty-four years old when she had Joseph. She was fifteen years younger than Pierre and was his second wife. Joseph, the thirteenth of fifteen children (two from the previous marriage), was a twin whose brother Eugène (some sources claim sister Eugénie) was accidentally baked or smothered to death when a large, hot loaf of bread taken from the oven was carelessly laid on a bed in which the one-month-old infants were sleeping.[10]

Joseph's mother, Rosalie, was said to be ultrareligious and prone to hallucinations, and after the tragic death of one of her twins, she must have been prone to a lot more religion and hallucinations. Understandably, she was said to be overprotective of the surviving twin. A dominant, overprotective mother and a passive father are common factors in the childhoods of many serial killers. The theory is that a serial killer's behaviors are sometimes rooted in an inability to successfully negotiate his masculine autonomy from his mother. When a boy cannot achieve this autonomy, or when there is no solid foundation from which to negotiate this autonomy, a sense of frustrated rage develops in the child, and he subsequently carries the anger toward women into adolescence and adulthood.

For example, "Hillside Strangler" Kenneth Bianchi, who, with his cousin, raped, tortured and killed ten women snatched off the streets or lured to an auto upholstery shop. His adoptive mother was hysterically concerned with his health when he was a child, and she constantly dragged him to hospitals with ailments she imagined he had.

Canadian serial killer Peter Woodcock's foster mother was highly controlling and relished the challenge of her troubled foster child's behavioral problems. Upon being arrested for murdering three children, Woodcock worried about only one thing: "My fear was that Mother would find out. Mother was my biggest fear. I didn't know if the police would let her at me."

Peter Sutcliffe, the Yorkshire Ripper, is remembered as a normal child except for his strange need to constantly cling to his mother's skirt. Joseph Kallinger's mother refused to allow him to play outside, flogged him with a whip, beat him with a hammer, threatened to cut off his penis and selected his wife for him. Ed Gein so worshipped his widowed, religiously fanatic mother that he preserved her bedroom as a shrine in his otherwise filthy and disordered house (but not her mummified corpse, as in the Hitchcock movie *Psycho*).

Mother launched Jerry Brudos on his path to shoe-fetish murders when he was five. Edmund Kemper's mom used to force him to sleep in the basement under a floor hatch with a heavy dining table pushed over it. She was one of Kemper's last victims. Henry Lee Lucas's mom beat his father and sent little Henry to school dressed as a girl. She was one of his first victims. The "mommy dearest" school of serial-killer psychopathology is a familiar one.

When Joseph Vacher was ten he was licked by a stray dog and the hysterical Rosalie insisted he undergo a folk remedy against rabies. Family and neighbors would later say that Joseph's character changed after that incident. He himself would later claim he had been "poisoned" by the homemade antirabies medicine. Perhaps because of the hysteria associated with the dog incident, and psychologically tuning in to lingering werewolf legends, Joseph became bad-tempered and prone to violent, animal-like outbursts. He nearly choked his brother to death in one of his rages. Angry that he was asked one day to watch the family cattle, he broke the legs of several. Although a bright and intelligent student, he was a feared and violent bully at school. Playmates began to avoid him.

Vacher was also grandiose and pompous and, like his mother, driven by a religious messianic zeal. On a school trip into town when he was ten, while a teacher was distracted for a moment, Vacher took his fellow students into a church, seated them in the pews and climbed into the pulpit and gave a sermon. Vacher himself would later recount that he was obsessed with violent sexual fantasies of raping, mutilating and killing "like a werewolf" but that he would resist them by compulsively walking long distances, a compulsion that would enhance his future vagabond killing career.

Vacher's childhood rages and the fear other children had of him are reminiscent of the childhood of necrophile-cannibal serial killer Arthur Shawcross, the "Genesee River Killer," who murdered and raped a boy and a girl in two separate incidents in Watertown, New York, and was convicted and sentenced to twenty-five years but paroled after twelve. He then settled in Rochester, where he proceeded to murder twelve prostitutes. Like Vacher, Shawcross was remembered by family and friends as compulsively walking or biking enormous distances, usually to fishing holes, like the ones where he murdered the two children and later would take his prostitute victims to kill and conceal for sex with their corpses later. The principal difference between Vacher and Shawcross was that Shawcross appeared to have learning disabilities, while Vacher was remembered as intelligent and articulate.

Vacher was thirteen years old when his mother died in May 1882. The next year he went to work as a farmhand, like a typical rural boy his age. On June 18, 1884, a ten-year-old boy, Joseph Amieux, was found in a nearby barn, raped and murdered. At the time nobody suspected Vacher, and the murder of Amieux is the first of some of the sixteen murders later attributed to him in addition to the eleven he would confess to.

Still burning in the messianic light of Jesus, Vacher joined a Catholic monastery as a novice at the age of fifteen. At first the monks were impressed by his devotion, intelligence, beautiful handwriting and charismatic preaching abilities. They sent him out to teach children on several occasions, but he was expelled from the monastery two years later after he was caught masturbating fellow novices.

Vacher returned to his hometown to work in the fields but had to flee after he was accused of attempting to rape a twelve-year-old boy in 1888, the year that Jack the Ripper would do his thing. Vacher fled to his sister's house in Grenoble, where he contracted venereal disease while frequenting prostitutes. The venereal chancre sores became infected, and he had to undergo a painful removal of one of his testicles, which is said to have made him even crazier than he already was. A fellow patient at the hospital recalled that he was nicknamed the "Jesuit" for his clerical pretensions, his preaching and his propensity to attempt to fondle the nuns.

After his release from the hospital Vacher went to work in a stationery store in Lyon but was dismissed after attacking a fellow employee in a rage. Vacher found employment elsewhere but was dismissed for harassing women and children and for openly professing anarchist ideals.

On October 2, 1890, Vacher enlisted in the French army and showed sufficient intelligence and leadership to be sent to junior noncommissioned officers' school, from which he graduated near the top of his class. He was promoted to corporal. His fellow soldiers, however, recalled that he was prone to violent outbursts and abused soldiers under his command. His temper was so violent that his men feared to go to sleep at night without keeping their bayonets nearby. When Vacher was turned down for promotion to sergeant he flew into a rage and slashed his throat in an apparent suicide attempt. This episode did not prevent Vacher from being promoted to sergeant after his release from the military hospital.

Like the serial necrophile Sergeant Bertrand before him, Sergeant Vacher fit well into the ranks of the French army despite his stormy personality. At the same time, Vacher wanted to get out. He applied for a family-hardship discharge but was refused. His barrack mates would later testify that Vacher was already fantasizing about becoming a vagabond and was hoarding pieces of military equipment like canteens and field mess kits for his future wanderings.

In the spring of 1893 Vacher met nineteen-year-old Louise Barrand (Barant) while on a riverside promenade. He seemed charming, intelligent and gallant in his sergeant's dress uniform. She was smitten on the spot by the well-spoken military man and accepted his invitation for dinner that evening in a nearby café, where Vacher, to her horror, immediately proposed marriage while warning her that he would kill her if she ever betrayed him. Louise of course bolted, but Vacher now relentlessly pursued her for weeks with gifts, letters and unannounced visits. Eventually Louise was forced to escape Vacher by returning to her hometown, but Vacher stalked her there.

On June 25, 1893, he appeared unannounced at her door and confronted her. When she refused to leave with him, he drew his service revolver and shot her. The first shot went through her mouth, taking out several teeth and a piece of her tongue; two more shots grazed the top of her head as she collapsed to the floor into a pool of blood. Assuming he had killed her, Vacher pressed the handgun to his head and shot himself twice. Both Louise and Vacher survived his typically French-military marksmanship but were disfigured for the rest of their lives.

Vacher was declared insane, unable to stand trial, and was packed off to a mental hospital, where he had a bout of suicidal rage and paranoid ranting and raving and even escaped, trying to make his way back to Louise. He refused surgery to remove a bullet lodged behind his ear, accusing the doctors of conspiring to murder him. The bullet in his head provoked a constant flow of stinky pus seeping and bubbling out from his inner ear, which witnesses later reported smelling and seeing. Because of nerve damage from the gunshot wounds his right eyelid was left permanently open, the right side of his face was disfigured by a grimace and his speech was slurred. But the charismatic and articulate Vacher regained control of his situation. Failing to escape, he now resorted to an "I'm so sorry. I was temporarily crazy, and I will never do this again" performance in the psychiatric hospital; ten months later, on April 1, 1894, Vacher was set free as "cured."

Medically discharged from the French army, Vacher now had nothing to do except enjoy his fantasy of compulsively walking, wandering and killing. He melted away in the traffic of 400 thousand homeless vagabonds tramping the back roads and villages of France where the rural people's hospitality and charity often sheltered and fed this army of the destitute.

Six weeks later, on a rainy Saturday evening, May 19, 1894, about forty miles from the psychiatric hospital from which Vacher had been released, Eugénie Delhomme stepped out the silk factory door for a breath of fresh air as Vacher was randomly passing in the alley outside. And that's how it often happens, completely at random.

Vacher would later confess that he was suddenly overcome by rage, that he strangled, stomped and slashed the young woman on an impulse and that she was his first murder victim. No doubt the young woman reminded him of Louise. After this killing, Vacher began to wander and range thousands of miles between 1894 and his arrest in 1897, seeking casual labor or begging for food and shelter while killing on impulse along the way.

Many people ended up hosting him in their homes or on their farms and remembered the talkative and strange Vacher, who played an accordion and preached and pontificated like a mad prophet. He even befriended some of their children. But whenever nobody was looking and Vacher saw boys or girls alone during his travels, he fell on them, strangling them, cutting their throats and raping and mutilating their corpses. His extraordinary compulsive traveling kept him one step ahead of the authorities until the summer of 1897, when he was arrested in his failed rape attempt. Vacher probably considered himself lucky to escape with just a three-month prison sentence and was biding his time until his scheduled release when Fourquet ordered him to be brought before him for questioning in the unsolved Portalier murder.

INTERVIEWING SERIAL KILLERS: THE ART AND SCIENCE OF INTERROGATING PSYCHOPATHS

Today we make an easy and familiar assumption that Joseph Vacher was probably a psychopath, but in Fourquet's time that concept had not been fully developed or described adequately. In the same way serial killers had been around for ages but not described or labeled, psychopaths have been around forever. We did not adequately describe them until 1941, when American psychiatrist Dr. Hervey Milton Cleckley published *The Mask of Sanity: An Attempt to Clarify Some Issues About the So-Called Psychopathic Personality*. In it he described a rational, functioning, unfeeling, destructive personality type that appears sane and healthy behind a "mask of sanity." It was a personality type that had appeared in courtrooms throughout the nineteenth century, always described as rational and nondelusional, but obsessed with a *monomania* or a *homicidal mania*, like Sergeant Bertrand, or Jesse Pomeroy, or the two "belfry" killers. Before the term "psychopath" was adopted, they had been referred to sometimes as "moral imbeciles."[11]

Psychopaths can be very clever and manipulative, especially so of psychiatrists. There are a number of cases on record in which serial killers have been convicted of murder but persuaded prison psychiatrists and parole boards that they were "cured and reformed," were released and went on to kill more. (Arthur Shawcross and Edmund Kemper are the most notorious examples.) Having shot his girlfriend and attempted suicide, Vacher persuaded his psychiatrists that he was "cured" and fit to be released after only ten months' confinement.

When Joseph Vacher was brought to Émile Fourquet for questioning, the examining magistrate was immediately struck by his oddly pompous demeanor. Fourquet observed that Vacher was a stormy little spark plug of micro facial tics and wandering eye movements; with foul-smelling pus leaking out of his ear from his self-inflicted head wound; constantly shape-shifting his face from distorted, crazy-eyed, drooling monster to very normal, thoughtful, friendly and attractive. There was a theatrical grandiosity to the man. Like a disfigured male model he could freeze and pose his face to display his "good side"—which he did for many of the subsequent press photographs he sat still for, clutching in his hand the "keys to heaven" loaned to him by prison guards and wearing what became his trademark white rabbit-fur hat symbolizing innocence. Vacher had a slight difficulty speaking because of his facial tic, but otherwise he appeared to Fourquet smart but cagey in his steadfast denial of having committed any crime other than his "mischievous" attack on the woman, for which he felt his three-month sentence was much too harsh.

Medical sciences historian Douglas Starr, in *The Killer of Little Shepherds*, a recent and definitive account of the Vacher case, writes that it is not known if Fourquet had read the chapter on questioning psychopaths in Hans Gross's 1893 *Handbook for Examining Magistrates as a*

System of Criminology, one of the many manuals on forensic sciences and criminological techniques published by German and French forensic specialists who were beginning to standardize investigative techniques between 1870 and 1900. (Alexandre Lacassagne, for example, published a pocket-sized *"Vade-mecum"* ["come with me"] manual for medical examiners called out to crime scenes.)[12]

Torture had been throughout history a routine component of questioning by authorities, and while in many European countries torture had been recently abolished, the questioning of a suspect was still typically hostile and implicit with threats just short of torture. In his handbook, Gross advised interrogators to be firm but fair, friendly and dispassionate with the suspect, and above all nonjudgmental no matter how horrific the circumstances of the crime.

Gross advised that the investigator distance himself from threats, intimidation and any hostile emotional approaches to the prisoner: "Calm and absence of passion are also indispensable. The officer who becomes excited or loses his temper delivers himself into the hands of the accused, if the latter, wiser than the officer, preserves his *sangfroid*, or even with happy foresight, sets himself deliberately to exasperate his questioner so as to get the better of him."[13]

Gross advised the questioner to establish a bond with the prisoner and "help" him relieve himself of his burden of guilt by making confession a pleasure for the suspect: "We must smooth their way, render their task easy," Gross declared. "Who sees always in the accused a fallen brother or one wrongfully suspected, he will question well." It's a technique frequently used by American police today: "Man up, get this off your chest, you'll feel better about everything . . ."

Fourquet's interview of Vacher was going to be textbook perfect as advised back then by Gross, and as advocated by the FBI today.[14] According to the FBI's *Law Enforcement Bulletin* in 2012, the best strategy in questioning a psychopath and extracting a confession is to exploit his propensity for boredom and need for thrills by keeping him engaged. "Law enforcement officers should be aware of the psychopath's early-onset boredom and be prepared to incorporate strategies to keep the individual stimulated and interested." The recommended strategies include "letting suspects write down ideas and comments for discussion, or having the psychopath act as a teacher giving a course about criminal behavior and providing opinions about the crime."[15]

Investigators and psychologists all stress the importance of researching the suspect's life and especially the details of his crimes. Psychopaths can be insulted, offended and bored if an investigator makes a factual mistake about his life history or crimes, even if he denies having committed them. The FBI article urges investigators to be calm and collected, especially in the crucial first-impression stage of an interview. Any nervousness or fidgeting on the examiner's part is immediately perceived by the subject as a weakness, and the subject can lose interest in engaging in a "game" with the examiner. Keep switching things up and keep it interesting, the FBI urges, or else the subject can stop paying attention or cooperating. Because of his narcissistic, grandiose sense of self-worth the psychopath will always perceive the examiner as an inferior. The FBI advises interviewers to set aside their own egos.

> Premises in past successful interviews of psychopathic serial killers focused on praising their intelligence, cleverness, and skill in evading capture as compared with other serial killers . . . As distasteful as it might be, investigators should be prepared to stroke psychopaths' egos and provide them with a platform to brag and pontificate. It is better to emphasize their unique ability to devise such an impressive crime, execute and narrate the act, evade capture, trump investigators, and generate media interest about themselves.

As psychopaths tend to deny responsibility for their actions and blame the victim, the interviewer can minimize the seriousness of the charges by suggesting that the victim might have been "asking for it." Do not appeal to the suspect's feelings of pity or regret for the victims or their families, the FBI advises; he has no empathy or sense of guilt. Placing the victim at fault works much better. By keeping the psychopath amused, talking, bragging and preaching the interviewer can carefully collect contradictory statements or revealing evidence.

To rattle and disorient the psychopath, ask how he or she *felt* about the victim, or about being investigated and arrested. Psychopaths do not "feel" and are disoriented when asked to describe emotions which are foreign to them. Psychopaths can feign the outward appearance of emotions, but they don't know how to describe them effectively in words. Suggesting that mistakes were made in the crime can further upset a psychopath's balance and induce them to reveal just how smart and efficient the murder really was. Bonding or finding a common ground with a psychopath can work as long as the interviewer can maintain an illusion that the psychopath is in the center of the common ground. The experiences, opinions and character of the interviewer are of no interest to the psychopath; he is the center of his own universe.

Fourquet's Interview of Vacher

Fourquet carefully inspected the items Vacher carried in his bag; along with his accordion and camping gear, these included an assortment of sharp knives and a jar of lubricating oil. Fourquet made a mental note of the items, remembering that autopsy reports showed that lubricant was found on some of the victim's bodies. Rather than launching into a hostile, accusatory line of questioning, Fourquet mildly told Vacher that he was interested in the problems of vagabonds in France and asked him about the hardships of being on the road, about the items he had in his bag, where he had acquired them and how he used them while traveling. Vacher felt he had a rapport with gendarmes and other figures of authority because of his own service in the French army. By engaging him as a "military" man, Fourquet got Vacher easily and openly chatting about his military career and the shooting episode that ended it. As he was doing this, Fourquet was assessing Vacher's speech, body language and demeanor while he felt comfortable in order to later recognize Vacher's demeanor and "tells" when he was nervous or lying.

Fourquet questioned Vacher for three weeks, but every time he approached the subject of the unsolved Victor Portalier murder, Vacher vehemently denied being anywhere near the location of the murder and quickly clammed up. Fourquet in the meantime stayed mute about his suspicion that Vacher had committed a whole series of other murders. He did not have the slightest evidence indicating that Vacher had even been near the locations of the murders when they were committed. All he had was a hunch based on his own analysis of the signatures left at all the crime scenes. He needed a confession from Vacher, but Vacher was no fool and he evaded every trap set for him.

Finally, Fourquet resorted to a ploy. He told Vacher that he was now convinced that Vacher was innocent and, pending a few days of paperwork, he was going to be sent back to serve the rest of his three-month jail term in peace. Vacher's disappointment was almost palpable. No more lively duels of intellect with Fourquet; only the boredom of his jail cell. Fourquet humbly asked Vacher for help with his manuscript on vagabonds, asking if he would "do him the honor" before they parted ways of reading it and sharing with him his superior experience and observations of being on the road—perhaps he would even be mentioned in the forthcoming book.

Vacher was practically beaming with pride at the opportunity to pontificate on his days of vagabonding, and for the next three days he recounted his experiences. Fourquet would pose naïve questions or challenge Vacher's statements, manipulating the egotistical Vacher to draw on specific examples from his vast experiences on the road. Subtly and strategically Fourquet questioned and challenged Vacher's accounts, manipulating him to respond argumentatively with precise dates and locations. Not realizing that Fourquet was eyeing him for a whole series of murders rather than just the one unsolved murder in his district, Vacher babbled away about where he went and when, and what he observed during the last three years. By the end of the three days, Fourquet had secured Vacher's own admission of having been in the vicinity of the eight unsolved murders at the times they had occurred.

Then Fourquet suddenly turned on Vacher, coldly telling him that he was implicated in eight murders and, to Vacher's shock, meticulously rattling off the entire timeline, victim by victim, and listing in detail everything that Vacher had done. Vacher was taken back to his cell, "staggering like a drunk," according to Fourquet's memoirs.

Later that day Fourquet was brought a letter from Vacher. In it Vacher confessed,

> Yes, it was I who committed all the crimes you blame me for . . . and all of this in a moment of rage. As I said to the doctor from the prison medical service, I was bitten by a rabid dog around the age of seven or

eight, but I'm not so sure, although I remember taking a remedy. Only my parents can assure you of the bitings. As for myself I always believed . . . that it was the medicine that corrupted my blood.[16]

This was good but not enough. "Yes, it was I who committed all the crimes you blame me for" was not going to be sufficient to indict Vacher for trial on the various counts of murder. Fourquet spent several more weeks maneuvering and manipulating Vacher's ego to get him to confess in detail, case by case. Fourquet realized that Vacher was angling for an insanity plea and another short stay in a psychiatric hospital instead of the guillotine. Vacher's argument was basically, "Who in their right mind would kill eight children the way I did?"

Fourquet "advised" Vacher that to prove his insanity, he needed to give the details of all the murders, that without the details, Vacher would be charged in only the one murder in his district and his claims to insanity would go unheard. He cleverly put Vacher in the position of wanting to prove that he'd committed each of the eight murders.

Vacher at first was reluctant, but again Fourquet played on his narcissism. Seeing that Vacher had a huge ego and was a big newspaper reader, he assured Vacher that if he confessed he would arrange for the newspapers to print the confession along with his portrait, further advancing his insanity claim in a public forum. Vacher eagerly agreed. Suddenly the "Killer of Little Shepherds" had a name and a face. Jack the Ripper might have been the first unidentified modern celebrity serial killer, but Vacher was the first identified one. Of course once Vacher's account and photo appeared in the newspapers throughout France, there came a wave of new witnesses who recognized him.

Fourquet used the newspaper coverage to his advantage. When one newspaper questioned the authenticity of Vacher's confessions, Fourquet suggested he prove his serial-killing credentials by revealing murders that Fourquet was unaware of and therefore could not have tricked him into confessing. In the end, Vacher admitted to a total of eleven murders, including a victim who had never been discovered until Vacher described the well into which he threw the body.

Émile Fourquet handled Vacher as well as any investigator would handle a psychopath-serial-killer interview today. His profiling of the various crime scenes for their unique signature, linking them together, and questioning of the suspect were as modern and thorough as those of such American "pioneers" as James A. Brussel, Pierce Brooks and the FBI behaviorists of the 1970s and 1980s. As it's said of Thomas Edison, they did not "invent the lightbulb" of serial-murder case linkage and profiling as is often claimed, but they brilliantly improved upon it by applying modern research and statistical methodology to something we already knew and understood well by 1900 but seemed to later forget until the rise of the great serial-killer "epidemic" in the US in the 1970s and 1980s. Americans would then have to learn or relearn how to deal with serial killers, almost from the ground up. What had been a European phenomenon became uniquely American by the 1980s, to the point that books on serial murder were often prefaced with the observation that it was not exclusively an American phenomenon but sometimes even happened in Europe.

The Question of Sanity

Fourquet's job was still not done. Having successfully gotten Vacher to confess in detail not only to the eight suspected cases but to three other cases that Fourquet had been unaware of, he now needed to take the case through trial and overcome any claims Vacher might make to insanity. Vacher was already lobbying for an early release from any psychiatric facility he might be sent to by claiming that he had been "temporarily insane" and was now healed and ready to rejoin society. That this case was unfolding in the region of Lyon was a huge benefit to Fourquet, because he had convenient access to the Lyon Institute of Forensic Medicine's superstar, its dean, Dr. Alexandre Lacassagne.

Lacassagne and his colleagues happily agreed to examine Vacher to attest to his legal sanity. Contrary to the claims that the insanity plea was a nineteenth-century development, we've seen how in the Renaissance era the question of sanity was at issue in some of the "werewolf" trials. The 1843 McNaughton decision in Britain established the principle of insanity as the incapacity to discern the difference between right and wrong or perceive or understand the consequences of one's actions, which still today defines the parameters of an insanity plea.

In earlier cases of stark-raving-mad, "foaming-at-the-mouth," raging killers, the insanity question was limited to whether the accused was "faking it" or genuinely delusional. French forensic psychiatrists by the end of the nineteenth century developed a reputation for their ability to discern the difference between genuine and feigned insanity. Vacher, on the other hand, was lucid and clearly aware of everything he did and the criminality of it. Furthermore, there was no question of his faking his rages; numerous witnesses would testify to his having them since childhood.

But he claimed that he was not guilty because the irresistible volatile rages were a result of being exposed to rabies as a child, and were further aggravated by his self-inflicted gunshot wound to the head and his subsequent "sad" experiences being confined in the psychiatric hospital afterward and the traumas of the vagabond life he led.

To determine whether the bullet that remained in Vacher's head might be pressing on a nerve or a part of his brain, causing behavioral anomalies, Lacassagne had Vacher's head X-rayed, the first time this new technology had been used in a murder prosecution. The X-rays revealed the bullet was not located near any part of his brain known to be related to behavior. (By the 1850s, medical researchers had deciphered some of the different functions of the brain.)

The question of Vacher's sanity was framed at the time in the context of obvious delusional "total madness" versus a subtle "loss of reason" and "irresistible impulses." Lacassagne pointed out that while on the road, Vacher seemed to experience his rages only when he found himself alone with a child. He argued that Vacher had the presence of mind to choose the victim, time and place and to escape afterward in a preconceived, systematic and logical way, frequently disguising himself by shaving his beard and changing his clothing. His murders were performed coldly and precisely with the objective of taking possession of the body, as opposed to a raging kill. Noting that the Vacher crime scenes were characterized by large pools of blood a short distance away from where the bodies were found, Lacassagne concluded that Vacher would first drain the bodies of blood, then drag them away to rape and mutilate the victims. "The complete possession of the cadaver aroused him; then and only then, he freely delivered the wounds to the genital areas," Lacassagne reported.

According to Lacassagne, Vacher was a "sadist," a new term recently introduced to forensic psychiatry, but as such he was not legally insane. Despite his grandiosity, paranoia, episodes of suicidal melancholy and violent rages, Vacher was fully cognizant of and responsible for his criminal actions, Lacassagne concluded, after interviewing, examining and studying Vacher for four months.

Fifty years earlier in the case of the vampire necrophile, it was argued by Sergeant Bertrand's defense that he had been overwhelmed by a compulsion so irresistible that it was equivalent to legal insanity. Vacher was trying to make the same argument. In the 1960s and 1970s, American lawyers defending serial killers attempted to raise the "volition defense" until the Reagan-era Congress passed the Insanity Defense Reform Act that explicitly invalidated it (see chapter seven).

The Trial and Execution of Joseph Vacher

We've seen that once apprehended, serial killers were often put on trial within weeks, without many preliminaries. In the case of Joseph Vacher, however, it took a year before he went on trial in October 1898, for a single count of murder, of Victor Portalier, the fifteen-year-old shepherd boy. It was of course a huge public and media circus.

As Vacher had confessed to murdering Portalier, the trial was focused on the issue of his sanity. Vacher now shifted blame to the mental hospital that had certified him sane and released him ten months after his shooting of Louise Barrand. How could he have been sane if he murdered Eugénie Delhomme six weeks after his release from the psychiatric hospital? Vacher argued. If anybody was to be blamed for the subsequent murders, then it should be the psychiatrists who released him, Vacher insisted. At one point in the courtroom he held up a hand-lettered card that read, "Joseph Vacher, the great martyr of our turn-of-the-century society and instrument of divine will."

Lacassagne and his colleagues testified that Vacher carefully chose his victims, that he systematically and calculatingly killed them to gain possession of their corpses for his aberrant sexual fantasies and that afterward he would meticulously disguise himself and flee the region, completely aware of the wrongful acts he had perpetrated. He was not "alienated" but a sadistic antisocial offender criminally responsible for the horrific crimes he knowingly perpetrated. He dismissed Vacher's claim of having been transformed by a rabid dog's lick as impossible according to medical knowledge.

Lacassagne described Vacher as a "sanguinary sadist" like Gilles de Rais and the recent serial killers Vincenzo Verzeni in Italy, Jesse Pomeroy in the United States and the unidentified Jack the Ripper in Britain. Lacassagne referred to Krafft-Ebing's *Psychopathia Sexualis* and his description of the pathology of sexual lust fused with aggression and anger, i.e., "sadism." His two colleagues also testified to his self-awareness and to the X-ray confirmation that his head wound had no impact on his behavior. The defense called two of its own medical witnesses, who naturally testified to the contrary.

At the end of the three-day trial Vacher was convicted by a jury in the murder of Portalier and sentenced to death. His other murders would not be tried. After an appeal two months later, on December 31, 1898, Vacher was guillotined. His head was transported to the Lyon Institute of Forensic Medicine, where it joined Dumollard's head. No physical anomalies were found in his brain.

Vacher was our first celebrity sexual serial killer. He gave press interviews, and photos of him in his rabbit-fur hat were printed in newspapers, books and pamphlets and on postcards. Before the Vacher case, the investigation of serial killers was often improvised, with investigators shocked and surprised on discovering just how many murders their subjects had committed. The Vacher case was different. His arrest and conviction represented a concerted investigative effort based on the premise from the start that Vacher was killing a series of victims and that his type was a unique category of murderer, albeit not yet termed a "serial killer." In many ways Vacher was what Jack the Ripper is thought to be—our first modern serial killer—except unlike Jack the Ripper, he was identified and caught. Perhaps that was why he was mostly forgotten while Jack the Ripper still has a grip on our imagination.

TWELVE

Red Tide Rising: Serial Killers in the First Half of the Twentieth Century, 1900–1950

> How she did kick, bite and scratch. I choked her to death, then cut her in small pieces so I could take my meat to my rooms, cook and eat it.
>
> —CHILD KILLER AND CANNIBAL ALBERT FISH, IN AN
> ANONYMOUS LETTER TO A VICTIM'S MOTHER, 1934

> Everything a girl could wish for.
>
> —DR. J. PAUL DE RIVER, LAPD'S FORENSIC PSYCHIATRIST, ON THE
> "SERIAL *SADIST RAFFINÉ* (GENTEEL SADIST)"

By the time Joseph Vacher was brought to justice, we knew almost as much about serial killers as we do today, but we kept forgetting it. The investigation and trial of Vacher in 1897 to 1898 was conducted in much the same way as hundreds of serial-murder cases would be in the twentieth century: through case signature linkage, then with luck fingerprint or other forensic trace evidence; but for most of the century a successful suspect interview with a resulting confession remained key for a conviction.

The repertoire of forensic investigative techniques expanded slowly over the century: fingerprint and bite-mark identification, blood-content and splatter-pattern analysis, chemical analysis, hair and fiber identification. But serial murder's root causes continued to confound criminologists and psychologists.

Forensic sciences in the United States were late in their development, probably because of the American predilection for proactive gun-slinging-sheriff-style law enforcement as opposed to the plodding European investigative-magistrate approach. American forensic scientists are not as celebrated as France's Alexandre Lacassagne or Edmond Locard. For example, it was only recently that one of America's forensic pioneers, "Detective X," was identified as Dr. Wilmer Souder of the National Bureau of Standards in the US Department of Commerce (today the National Institute of Standards and Technology [NIST]). Souder helped the FBI set up its crime lab in the 1930s and provided forensic analysis to various federal agencies from the 1920s until his retirement in the 1950s. For the protection of his family he was typically referred to only as "Detective X."[1]

THE GLOBAL RISE OF SERIAL KILLERS

In my first book, *Serial Killers: The Method and Madness of Monsters*, I focused on the rise of early- to mid-twentieth-century serial killers and some of the more notorious cases in detail. I update and outline that history here, touching on some of the seminal cases in a more abbreviated form.

European serial killers continued to make their appearance in the twentieth century, with a "hot spot" of notorious lust serial killers in the chaos and degradation of post–World War I Germany. One of the earliest known gay serial killers, Fritz Haarmann, aged forty-five at his arrest, raped and murdered twenty-seven young men in Hanover between 1918 and 1924. Peter Kürten, the "Vampire of Düsseldorf," stabbed, strangled and battered at least nine and maybe as many as thirty women and girls between 1913 and 1930.

While Kürten's and Haarmann's cases are both well documented because they went to trial, several other cases in Germany during the same period are more obscure. In Berlin, Georg Karl Grossman is believed to have killed as many as fifty people between 1913 and 1920 and sold their flesh at a hot dog stand he kept at a railway station. Grossman was convicted in one murder and committed suicide on the eve of his execution. In Silesia in 1924, police found the remains of at least thirty men and women pickled in jars in the kitchens of serial killer Karl Denke's inn. Suspected in the murder of as many as forty-two victims, Denke committed suicide in police custody before he could be brought to trial.

There were two notorious sexual serial killers apprehended in Nazi Germany. Bruno Ludke is thought to have killed as many as fifty-one women between the late 1920s and 1943, when he was arrested for strangling a woman near his home. Ludke stabbed or strangled all his victims and had sex with the corpses. He was found not guilty by reason of insanity and was turned over to the Nazi SS for medical experiments, during which he died on April 8, 1944. Paul Ogorzov was a railway employee and a member of the Nazi Party's Brownshirt storm troopers in Berlin; he raped and murdered eight women, battering them with a length of railway cable and throwing some of them off moving trains. He was convicted of the murders and executed in 1941.

In Jack the Ripper's homeland of Britain between 1910 and 1914, George Smith killed three of his seven wives. During the blitz of London in 1942, Gordon Frederick Cummins, the "Blackout Killer," murdered and mutilated four women Jack the Ripper style under the cover of wartime darkness. In France, Henri Désiré Landru, "Bluebeard," killed eleven aspiring brides between 1915 and 1922. Dr. Marcel Petiot in Paris killed at least sixty-three Jewish refugees hiding from the Nazis between 1941 and 1944 and seized their belongings. His serial murders seemed to be profit motivated.

One can only imagine how many still-undigitized European newspapers from Holland, Belgium, Greece, Turkey, Norway, Sweden, Hungary, Romania, Bulgaria, Poland, Portugal, Russia and so on must contain reports of forgotten serial-murder cases from the nineteenth and twentieth centuries. Germany, Italy and France are well documented because of their robust forensic-sciences tradition, as are Britain's.

There is no reason, however, to assume that the rates of serial homicide in Africa, Asia and South and Central America were not comparable to Europe's. For example, newspapers in 1906 reported the execution of a serial killer in Morocco, Hadj Mohammed Mesfewi, for the murder of thirty-six women.[2] Francisco Guerrero Pérez, "El Chalequero," a Mexican "ripper," murdered twenty-one women between 1880 and 1908. Also in Mexico, twenty-seven-year-old chemistry student Gregorio "Goyo" Cárdenas Hernández lured to his "laboratory" and strangled three prostitutes and his girlfriend, the daughter of a prominent Mexican lawyer, in August and September 1942. There was evidence of torture, necrophilia, black magic and even mad-scientist medical experiments at the crime scenes. While in prison Hernández became a celebrity figure and the darling of psychologists, who maintained he could be reformed. In 1976 he was declared rehabilitated and was pardoned by the president of Mexico. He became a practicing lawyer in Mexico City, and in 1992 he successfully sued theater director Raúl Quintanilla for misrepresenting his life in a play. Hernández died in 1999.[3]

The Radford University/FGCU Serial Killer Database lists 126 serial killers outside of the United States between 1900 and 1950, but that number is very likely low and as more obscure foreign-language newspapers become digitized, searches will very likely reveal numerous serial-killer cases that were either forgotten, not recognized as such or simply underreported.[4]

SERIAL KILLING IN THE USA, 1900–1950

Between 1900 and 1950 the incidence of reported serial murder in the United States was slowly but steadily increasing. If we include female serial killers and profit killers, 171 serial killers made their appearance over the span of those 50 years, an average of about 3 new serial killers every year (3.4, precisely). There is, however, an ominous arc to that average. The number increased from about 20 serial killers per decade in the 1910s to as many as 40 serial killers per decade by the 1930s and 1940s (still low compared to the "epidemic" decades: 534 new serial killers appeared in the 1970s, 692 in the 1980s and 614 in the 1990s!).[5]

According to historian Philip Jenkins, the author of *Using Murder: The Social Construction of Serial Homicide*, the 1980s serial-killer "epidemic" was preceded in the first half of the century by two smaller serial-killer "epidemics." Jenkins identified two earlier surges of serial homicides in the United States: 1911–1915 and 1935–1941.[6]

The First American Serial-Killer Surge, 1911–1915

Looking through back issues of the *New York Times*, Jenkins found reports of 17 serial killers in just 5 years, between 1911 and 1915. Henry Lee Moore, for example, was a traveling serial killer who murdered more than 23 people—entire families. But little is known about him— he is a mere footnote. In September 1911, using an ax, Moore killed 6 victims in Colorado Springs—a man, two women, and 4 children. In October he killed 3 people in Monmouth, Illinois, and then he slaughtered a family of 5 in Ellsworth, Kansas, the same month. In June 1912, he killed a couple in Paola, Kansas, and several days later he killed an entire family of 8 people, including 4 children, in Villisca, Iowa. Moore then returned home to Columbia, Missouri, where he murdered his mother and grandmother. For this he was arrested and convicted in December 1912. But Moore was not immediately linked to the previous crimes until a federal agent investigating the Villisca homicides was informed by his father, a warden of the Leavenworth Penitentiary with contacts throughout the prison system, of the nature of Henry Lee Moore's crimes in Missouri. Another typical case of "linkage blindness."

In another case, 20 biracial or light-skinned African-American women were murdered on the streets of Atlanta, with mutilations similar to those perpetrated by Jack the Ripper. Between May 20 and July 1, 1911, the unknown killer murdered his first 7 victims like clockwork, one every Saturday night.

In Denver and Colorado Springs in 1911 and 1912, 7 women were bludgeoned to death by an unidentified perpetrator.

Between January 1911 and April 1912, 49 victims were killed in unsolved ax murders in Texas and Louisiana. Very similar to the Moore murders, entire families were wiped out: a mother and her 3 children hacked to death in their beds in Rayne, Louisiana, in January 1911; 10 miles away in Crowley, Louisiana, 3 members of the Byers family in February 1911; 2 weeks later, a family of 4 in Lafayette. In April the killer struck in San Antonio, Texas, killing a family of 5. All the victims were killed in their beds at night and nothing was stolen from their homes. In November 1911 the killer returned to Lafayette and killed a family of 6; in January 1912 a woman and her 3 children were killed in Crowley. Two days later, at Lake Charles, a family of 5 was killed in their beds. In February 1912 the killer murdered a woman and her 3 children in Beaumont, Texas. In March, a man and a woman and her 4 children were hacked to death in Glidden, Texas, while they slept. In April a family of 5 was killed in San Antonio again, and 2 nights later, 3 were killed in Hempstead, Texas. The murders were never solved and the case has only recently been explored in a book by Todd C. Elliot, *The Axes of Evil: The True Story of the Ax-Men Murders*.

In New York City a "ripper" killed a five-year-old girl, Lenora Cohn, inside her apartment building on March 19, 1915. The victim's mother received taunting letters afterward signed "H. B. Richmond, Jack-the-Ripper" and threatening to kill again. On May 3, he may have killed a four-year-old boy playing in a hallway and stuffed his body under a tenement staircase. The offender was never identified, nor were the two cases definitively linked.

Also in New York City, in 1915 the corpses of 15 newborn infants were recovered, suspected to be linked to some sort of "baby farm" operation. That same year 6 bodies with their skulls crushed were found hidden in a farmhouse being demolished in Niagara, North Dakota. The victims, who were dropped into the basement through a clever trapdoor, were all farmhands who had been employed by the former house owner, Eugene Butler, who had died in 1913. There were numerous hospital and nursing home serial murderers and female poisoners rounding out the number of serial killers in this period.

These murders were all spectacular crimes, some widely reported in their time, others not, but all are mostly forgotten today. Jack the Ripper with his 5 or 6 victims is immortalized, but the Louisiana-Texas ax murderer with 49 victims is mostly forgotten. The primary difference is that London in 1888 was the center of a huge global English-language newspaper industry while North Dakota, Louisiana and Texas were not. The story of Jack the Ripper was retold endlessly and entered popular myth and literature—while the Louisiana-Texas ax murderer faded from public consciousness. Like real estate, serial murder "epidemics" are as much about location, location, location as they are about the killing.

The Radford/FGCU Serial Killer Database lists a total of 34 new serial killers emerging in the decade of 1910 to 1919.

The 1916–1934 Serial-Killer "Interlude"

Once the United States went to war in Europe in 1917 there appeared to be a lull in reports of sexual serial killing, but other forms of serial killing thrived. After World War I the affluent "Roaring Twenties" were a Jazz Age of serial-killing celebrity gangsters, spates of kidnapping, lynching and wanton thrill killing like the infamous Leopold and Loeb murder of a boy in Chicago in 1924.

Domestic terrorism in the US supplanted serial killings in newspaper headlines. In April 1919, a shadowy anarchist group sent 36 mail bombs to prominent politicians and appointees across the United States. Then terrorists detonated what is sometimes said to be the first "car bomb," a horse-drawn wagon packed with TNT and metal slugs, on Wall Street in New York at lunch hour on September 16, 1920, killing 38 people and seriously wounding 143.

Overall murder in the United States increased by 77 percent between 1920 and 1933.[7] Sexual serial killing still went on, but it was no longer front-page news, despite the fact that it was becoming pathologically stranger, with increasing reports of necrophilia and cannibalism. Yet during this "interlude" period, some of the most shocking cases of serial homicide occurred. Necrophile serial killer Earle Leonard Nelson, the "Dark Stranger Gorilla Killer," was apprehended in 1927 after killing 22 women and having sex with their corpses; Gordon Northcott, the "Wineville Chicken Coop Murderer," raped and killed at least 3 children in California in 1928; and the notorious cannibal child murderer Albert Fish, the "Werewolf of Wisteria" or the "Gray Man," was active in New York from 1928 to 1935. In 1928 he lured ten-year-old Grace Budd from her parents, killed and ate her, and several years later infamously sent the victim's mother a letter in which he described how he'd killed and cooked her daughter. Fish admitted to killing, mutilating and cannibalizing two other children and was suspected in five other similar murders of male and female children and youths between the ages of four and seventeen.

The Second American Serial-Killer Surge, 1935–1950

By the 1930s, the American public was familiar with both the phenomenon and character of serial killers without using the term itself. The multiple murderer was becoming a stereotypical character, and even played for laughs, as in the 1939 play *Arsenic and Old Lace*, a black comedy about a family of serial killers, including two dotty aunts who murder lonely old men via homemade wine laced with arsenic, and their nephew, a migratory serial killer of twelve victims around the world. The play was adapted into a hit movie directed by Frank Capra.

From the twelve unsolved "Cleveland Torso Murders," mutilation killings of derelicts in the mid-1930s; to the twenty suspected murders by Joe Ball, the "Alligator Man" and "Butcher of Elmendorf," in Texas in the 1930s; to Jake Bird's "Axeman of Tacoma" murders of as many as forty-six victims between 1930 and 1947, the United States saw some 127 serial killers appear between 1900 and 1950, at an average rate of five new serial killers every two years.

DEFINING THE "TED BUNDY-TYPE" POSTMODERN *SADIST RAFFINÉ* (GENTEEL SADIST), 1949

New Orleans–born psychiatrist Dr. J. Paul de River was the first forensic psychiatrist permanently hired by a law enforcement agency in the United States. The LAPD assigned him to the Sex Offense Bureau in 1939; his job was to assist police in profiling unknown suspects and to prepare prosecutorial psychiatric assessments of accused offenders to preempt any potential insanity defense. In 1949, de River would publish *The Sexual Criminal: A Psychoanalytical Study,* his update of Krafft-Ebing's 1886 *Psychopathia Sexualis*. In it, de River described recent paraphilic sexual crimes in California and revised and expanded the psychiatric terminology, including the concept of the "mask of sanity" psychopath as described by Hervey Milton Cleckley in 1941.

De River stripped away the notions of vulgar, crude, foaming-at-the-mouth werewolf "monster" serial killers and introduced a new typology of offender that we recognize today in many postmodern serial killers. De River labeled this new species the *sadist raffiné* (genteel sadist). He described them thus:

> The genteel "nice boy" type, whose suave manner and smooth tongue ingratiates him in the favor of his victim. He may be studious and pedantic and often strives to give one the impression of being very religious. His genteel manner and fastidious appearance, together with a winning personality, dimpled chin, wavy hair, usually offset by dreamy, neuropathic eyes, are very often everything a girl could wish for.[8]

De River could have been describing the sadistic necrophile serial killer Ted Bundy when he wrote those lines, except Ted Bundy was only three years old at the time. That in itself is of great significance, because Bundy was part of a new generation of so-called "golden age" serial killers to come, and the society he was growing up in would have much, if not everything, to do with the murders he would perpetrate as an adult in the 1970s.

From 1950 to 2000, some 2,065 new serial killers would appear, overshadowing the relatively small but steady rise in serial killing in the first five decades of the twentieth century.[9]

THIRTEEN

American Gothic:
The "Golden Age" of Serial
Killers, 1950–2000

Big numbers are better than small numbers; official numbers
are better than unofficial numbers; and big, official numbers
are best of all.

—JOEL BEST, "MISSING CHILDREN, MISLEADING STATISTICS"

The years between 1950 and 2000 have sometimes been called the
"golden age" of serial killers.[1] While there had been numerous small
surges of serial killing in the past as described in these pages, their
scope and number were incomparable to the peak "epidemic" surge of
the 1970s to the 1990s. In the middle of that era, we coined the term
"serial killer," creating an entirely new phenomenon in our political,
social, psychological, forensic and cultural discourse. Prior to that,
serial killings were perceived as inexplicable, individual, monstrous acts
of personal aberration. Now they became a part of something bigger
than the individual perpetrator. As the number of serial killers began to
multiply exponentially, so did their individual body counts, in a kind of
macabre race to the top to see which serial killer would dominate news
headlines in what new bizarre way and with what unimaginable number of victims. Serial killers became front-page news.

By the 1990s real and fictional serial killing was a major genre in
literature, movies and television. Some serial-killer fictional characters
were even elevated to the status of "antiheros," like the movie versions

of Hannibal Lecter in *The Silence of the Lambs* and Patrick Bateman in Bret Easton Ellis's controversial *American Psycho*. (Female serial-killer partner Karla Homolka testified that she had been reading *American Psycho* snuggled up on the couch downstairs while her husband, Paul Bernardo, was upstairs in their bedroom raping a schoolgirl they had abducted. When asked in cross-examination at her trial how she could bring herself to read as a girl was being raped upstairs, Homolka was insulted and replied she was entirely capable of "doing two things at the same time."[2])

In the meantime actual serial killers like Ted Bundy, Kenneth Bianchi and Richard Ramirez were attracting followings of female groupies, although in view of the 1895 case of Theodore Durrant and the "Sweet Pea Girl," that was not necessarily something new. What was new was how crazed this new generation of groupies was.

Carol (or Carole) Ann Boone, for example, met Ted Bundy when the two of them worked at the Washington State Department of Emergency Services (DES) in Olympia. After his arrest for a series of brutal necrophile murders, she faithfully attended Bundy's trials in Florida, professing her undying love for him. During one of the televised trials, Bundy married Boone by taking advantage of an archaic Florida state law that allowed persons who declared marriage in front of a judge to be legally married. Despite Florida's strict prohibition of conjugal visits for death-row inmates, Bundy managed to impregnate Boone, who gave birth to a girl the couple named Rose. It's speculated that Boone had passed a condom to Bundy through a kiss and he later returned it to her the same way, with his sperm sealed inside.[3]

Kenneth Bianchi, who as one of the Hillside Stranglers abducted and killed ten women and killed another two on his own, began receiving letters in jail from Veronica Compton, a twenty-four-year-old fledgling playwright whose work was obsessed with sadomasochism and serial murder. Eventually she went to see him and they began a relationship. In the summer of 1980, Bianchi showed Compton how he strangled his victims, and he slipped her a sample of his sperm, secreted in the finger of a rubber glove. Compton then flew to Bellingham and lured a woman to her motel room, where she attempted to strangle her Bianchi-style. This was in an era before DNA testing, and the plan was to kill the woman in the same way Bianchi killed the others and make it look as if the killer was still at large by leaving a sperm trace with the same blood type as Bianchi's. The victim, however, was more powerful than Compton and managed to escape. Compton was arrested shortly afterward.[4]

While in jail, Compton fell into a relationship through letters with another serial killer—Doug Clark, the necrophile "Sunset Boulevard Killer," who murdered seven women. Compton was convicted of premeditated attempted murder and sentenced to life imprisonment. Compton was eventually paroled in 2003 and today is a writer, artist and musician working under the name Veronica Compton Wallace in Los Angeles.[5]

THE DAWN OF THE GOLDEN AGE

I would venture that the "golden age" of serial killers in the United States dawned metaphorically in 1945 to 1946 in Chicago with what is probably our first "self-aware" serial killer, seventeen-year-old William Heirens with his "For heaven's sake, catch me before I kill more—I cannot control myself" lipstick "signature" serial murders. When he was arrested, police found a stolen copy of Krafft-Ebing's *Psychopathia Sexualis* in his possession.[6] Heirens was closely followed by the serial-killing team of Raymond Fernandez and Martha Beck, the "Lonely Hearts Killers" or "Honeymoon Killers," in 1949, followed by Ed Gein (1957), Harvey Glatman (1958), Melvin Rees (1959), and then Albert DeSalvo, the "Boston Strangler," with his thirteen murders from 1962 to 1964, which were reported nationally in the media as they occurred, one by one.

After the Boston Strangler, there would be no turning back.

There was a kind of historical synchronicity with the Boston Strangler when he murdered one of his last victims on November 23, 1963, the day after the JFK assassination. As the nation mourned that Saturday afternoon in the somber gray light of black-and-white television, DeSalvo gained entry to twenty-three-year-old Sunday school teacher Joann Graff's apartment, raped her and then strangled her with two nylon stockings intertwined with a leg of her black leotard, which he tied tightly around her neck in an exuberant gift bow, his signature.

In that narrow-channeled television world of the 1960s, serial murder would creep up on us along with a dramatic rise of other types of violence and mayhem, from self-immolating Buddhist monks going up in flames in Vietnam to JFK's exploding head and Lee Harvey Oswald's gutshot on live television. Things were getting ugly really fast.

At first we did not quite distinguish serial killing from all the other crazy violence surging in American society in the 1960s. It was just a part of the madness seizing the nation. The TV series *Mad Men* got its sixties violence chronology right, recalling most of the historic moments that seized our televised collective consciousness in one big rainbow of death and horror:

- the Boston Strangler, 1962–1964;

- the threat of thermonuclear annihilation during the Cuban Missile Crisis in 1962;

- the JFK assassination and the televised murder of Lee Harvey Oswald in 1963;

- the 1964 civil-rights-worker murders in Mississippi;

- the 1965 Watts riots;

- the Richard Speck murder of eight nurses in Chicago in July 1966;

- the University of Texas sniper killing of sixteen people in Austin in August 1966;

- the Newark and Detroit riots in 1967;

- the 1968 Tet Offensive execution;

- the assassination of Martin Luther King in April 1968;

- the assassination of Robert Kennedy in June 1968;

- the Chicago police riot in August 1968;

- and in the last year of the waning sixties, the Manson Family murders in August 1969.

The sixties just *felt* more murderous than the fifties. It seemed like a man-made plague of violence in the middle of an apocalyptic siege, with serial killers being catapulted like diseased carcasses over the protective walls of civilization harboring the tattered remains of the illusory innocent America we had believed in the decade before.

From the late 1960s through the 1990s, notorious serial killers began rising up among us in shit and dark, like homicidal mushrooms: Jerry Brudos, Richard Chase, Edmund Kemper, Charles Manson, Ted Bundy, John Wayne Gacy, David Berkowitz, Dean Corll, William Bonin, Herbert Mullin, Robert Hansen, Wayne Williams, Richard Cottingham, Gary Heidnik, Randy Kraft, Leonard Lake, Chares Ng, Bobby Joe Long, Gerard Schaefer, Gerald Stano, Joel Rifkin, Kenneth Bianchi, Angelo Buono, Arthur Shawcross, Richard Ramirez, Danny Rolling, Ottis Toole, Henry Lee Lucas, Jeffrey Dahmer and literally hundreds more. They comprised a pantheon of "superstar" serial killers who captured our imaginations as if they were sports stars or celebrities. With that came the emergence of serial-killer trading cards, calendars, lunch boxes, action figures and coloring books, and ancillary industries like the trafficking of serial-killer artifacts, artworks and autographs in the form of *murderabilia*.

The first really big-number serial-killing case to be reported nationally since the Boston Strangler was in California in May 1971. Even by today's standards, the number was spectacular; police dug up twenty-five bodies in a peach orchard near Yuba City. Juan Corona, a green-card-holding Mexican labor contractor and father of four children, was charged with the murders. At the time, we did not "get it." How could someone kill that many people without anybody noticing? It just did not compute. Nor was there much follow-up in the media; it looked like Corona was simply insane, and to boot, according to the press, he was some kind of closeted homosexual, and the victims were all transient illegal Mexican agricultural workers and maybe even gay too, a complete pass to write them off as "less-dead" victims nobody cared about. Many remain unidentified to this day.

Likewise, two years later in 1973, reports of the Dean Corll "Candy Man" murders of twenty-seven transient male youths in Houston, Texas, also quickly faded, for he was a "homo" and he was dead (murdered by his serial-killing junior partner), as were his disposable, delinquent runaway victims—no trial, no story. Again, nobody cared. They too were all "less-dead."

The college town of Santa Cruz, California, with a population of only 135 thousand, had 26 killings at the hands of 3 local serial killers between 1970 and 1973, some kind of mad record for sure: John Linley Frazier, "Killer Prophet" (five victims); Herbert Mullin, "Die Song Killer" (thirteen victims); and Edmund Kemper, "Co-Ed Killer" (eight victims). In the wake of the 1969 Manson killings, the Santa Cruz murders were attributed to "drugged-out hippies."

It was only in the mid-1970s, after Ted Bundy started abducting and killing middle-class white college girls at schools, shopping malls, ski chalets, national parks and public beaches, that the media suddenly began paying close attention. When Bundy was identified and apprehended, his classic "handsome devil" good looks and Republican Party credentials made the story sizzle. His subsequent escape from jail, additional murders, televised trial and bestselling biography by Ann Rule elevated him as the first of our postmodern superstar serial killers. Say the words "serial killer" and usually Ted Bundy's name comes to mind.

In the 1970s an extraordinary 534 new serial killers appeared in the United States and another 692 in the subsequent 1980s and 614 more in the 1990s—a total of 1,840 serial killers between 1970 and 1999.[7] We experienced some of these cases in the news as collectively as we did the first moon landing or the first heart transplant; they were historical and cultural milestones we all acknowledged the significance of and were all familiar with.

Americans had no other channels to flip away to, no web pages to surf and shop on or YouTube kittens to distract us from the carnage. It was mainlined into our cultural vein by network television and Hollywood; we were forced to look at the horror, as if we were all strapped in, with our eyelids forced open like Alex's in the movie *A Clockwork Orange*, itself a cinematic artifact of the "ultraviolence" that would be drenching us for the next thirty years like blood from a fire hose.

THE MISSING MISSING AND THE GREAT
SERIAL-KILLER "EPIDEMIC"

The heightened fear of serial killers in the 1970s was magnified by a general concern over a rising rate of all kinds of violence compared to the 1960s, from familial violence to mass murder, predatory street crime, assassination, domestic terrorism, riot and cult, gang and race murders, and it all became worse by the 1980s.

That great serial-killer "epidemic" panic of the early 1980s that would inspire Congressional hearings hammered into the collective American brain a fear and loathing of a dark, hidden yet at the same time humanly monstrous and intimate source of danger: the human werewolf or vampire, the lust erotophonophiliac, the compulsively driven zombie serial killer necrophile cannibal. *The tenant upstairs with a roomful of severed heads.* A zombie indeed, but one inside the fence, one living disguised among us. One of *us*.

I have already cited the statistics, but I'll repeat them here. There was a tenfold increase in active serial killers per year in the 25-year period of 1970 to 1995, compared to the 169-year period of 1800 to 1969.[8] Of 2,236 identified serial killers in the United States on record between 1900 and 2000, 82 percent (1,840) made their appearance in the last thirty years, 1970 to 2000.[9]

In 2010, Enzo Yaksic, a criminal justice scholar and serial-murder investigative consultant, after ten years of researching serial homicide, established the Serial Homicide Expertise and Information Sharing Collaborative (SHEISC), which in 2013 partnered with professor Mike Aamodt at Radford University and Florida Gulf Coast University to assemble and populate the Radford/FGCU Serial Killer Database, currently the most comprehensive shared database on incidents of serial murder.[10]

The database includes serial killers under the new FBI definition of two or more victims, and currently lists a total of 2,743 US serial killers (2,537 males and 206 females) and 1,325 international serial killers (1,168 males and 157 females), for a grand total of 4,068 male and female serial killers. It also contains data on 11,680 serial-killer victims from around the world.[11]

According to the Radford/FGCU database, in the first five decades of the twentieth century there was a slowly rising average of twenty to forty new serial killers every decade in the United States. But after 1960 the number of new serial killers per decade went viral:

1950–1960: 51
1960–1970: 174
1970–1980: 534
1980–1990: 692
1990–2000: 614

These figures add up to 2,065 "golden age" serial killers in the United States.

Estimating the number of serial killers and the number of their victims, however, presents a very treacherous statistical minefield, with the potential for both exaggeration and underestimation.

Kenna Quinet, a professor in criminal justice studies, reviewed the statistics and was horrified to discover how many possible serial killings might be unreported due to wrongly classified deaths in institutions, unidentified victims, "throwaway kids" whose parents don't report them missing, missing foster children whose names are never published for privacy reasons (in some states the biological parents are prohibited from going to the media if their child was placed in foster care and goes missing), misidentified and elsewhere classified dead, and prostitutes who are not even reported missing. Quinet refers to this hidden subsurface stream of victims as *"the missing missing."* Nobody even knows they are missing.

Extrapolating based on all these possible margins of error in the statistics, Quinet concluded in 2007, "By counting potentially hidden serial murder victims, we add a minimum number of 182 annual serial murder deaths . . . and as many as 1,832 uncounted annual serial murder deaths [added to the existing counts]."[12]

When investigative journalist Thomas Hargrove reviewed FBI murder statistics over a forty-year period since 1976 and compared them to local police statistics and news reports, he discovered that roughly twenty-seven thousand murders were not reported by local authorities to the FBI Uniform Crime Reports (UCR) Program.[13] Hargrove is concerned that this underreporting of murders might be concealing current serial-killer cases and founded the Murder Accountability Project (MAP) to track the problem. He has written computer code that datamines homicide reports and statistics for anomalies that may reveal a serial pattern and lobbies local police agencies when MAP believes they are overlooking a possible serial killer at large.

CONGRESS AND THE "SERIAL-KILLER EPIDEMIC," 1981–1983

At the exact same time as the term "serial killer" was entering our popular vocabulary, Congress was embracing the concept of a "serial-killer epidemic." Coincidentally, the same guy who we think coined the term serial killer also coined "serial-killer epidemic" when in the 1980s FBI behaviorist Robert Ressler stated, "Serial killing—I think it's at an epidemic proportion. The type of crime we're seeing today did not really occur with any known frequency prior to the fifties. An individual taking ten, twelve, fifteen, twenty-five, thirty-five lives is a relatively new phenomenon in the crime picture of the U.S."[14]

There were three major committees on Capitol Hill from 1981 to 1983 that looked into the issues of increasing violence, linkage blindness, child abduction, child pornography, and serial killers: the Attorney General's Task Force on Violent Crime, the House Committee on Civil and Constitutional Rights and Senator Arlen Specter's Juvenile Justice Subcommittee of the Judiciary Committee of the US Senate.

The start of these hearings in 1981 was punctuated by several dramatic cases of child abduction murders in the US. In Atlanta, Wayne Williams was arrested for a series of thirty-one child murders; in New York, Etan Patz infamously vanished on his way to school (thirty-eight years later in February 2017, the boy's killer was convicted);[15] and in Florida, six-year-old Adam Walsh vanished in a shopping mall. Adam's severed head was found floating in a canal; his body was never recovered. Adam's father, John Walsh, became a vocal advocate for victims and missing children, and the host of *America's Most Wanted*. An out-of-state car was linked to the crime, but the perpetrator wasn't identified until more than a decade later when serial killer Ottis Toole, Henry Lee Lucas's partner, confessed to kidnapping and killing Adam. (Henry Lee Lucas dubiously claimed a total of 360 victims, some on his own, some with Toole as they roamed the highways.)

A year after his son's murder, the tragic figure of John Walsh was broadcast nationwide as he testified before the Senate committee describing recent cases of serial murder and suggested that missing children are in large measure murdered by serial killers. The problem, Walsh said, was linkage blindness and the failure of law enforcement agencies to coordinate information and intelligence across multiple jurisdictions. Because of this weakness, young people were disappearing without a trace, until they might be found in a mass grave somewhere. Using a controversial Department of Health claim that 1.8 million children go missing every year, Walsh stated that every hour 205 children go missing and that many of them would be found murdered. What Walsh failed to explain was that 95 percent of those missing were confirmed runaways, of whom 95 percent would return home within fourteen days. Instead, hysterical headlines screamed, quoting him: "205 MISSING CHILDREN EVERY HOUR!"[16]

Walsh later narrowed down the number to predatory "stranger" abductions, claiming in his testimony to Congress, "The unbelievable and unaccounted-for figure of fifty thousand children disappear annually and are abducted for reasons of foul play." Walsh claimed that organized rings of pedophiles were systematically abducting children: "The kidnappers are more organized than we are."[17] "This country is littered with mutilated, decapitated, raped and strangled children," he ominously warned.[18]

On February 3, 1984, in her nationally syndicated column, Ann Landers published a letter written by the executive director of the Adam Walsh Center. It opened, "Dear Ann: Consider these chilling statistics: Every hour 205 American children are reported missing. This means 4,920 per day and 1.8 million per year."[19]

It was spooky stuff and it frightened parents across the nation. But where did that fifty-thousand figure that Walsh cited come from? According to research by John Gill, it was Senator Claiborne Pell of Rhode

Island who in 1981 was the first public official to formally claim that the Department of Health and Human Services stated that fifty thousand children vanish each year. Officials at HHS denied making that estimate and Pell's staff "could not remember" which official they spoke to.[20] It was an early example of "fake news" in American public discourse.

As the hearing progressed, all kinds of ridiculously speculative statements were entered into the *Congressional Record* and presented at press conferences. The most prevalent gimmick was to combine the FBI's Uniform Crime Reports homicide categories of *unknown* and *stranger* into one figure, pumping up the percentage of killings that appeared to be motiveless murders by unknown perpetrators, presumably roaming serial killers. Using this kind of "fuzzy math," it was claimed that nearly 25 to 30 percent of all murders—some four thousand to five thousand each year—could be attributed to serial killers. The message was: the only thing that could save us now was increased funding from Congress.

These numbers were never realistic. The total *maximum* number of *all known* serial-killer victims in the United States over *a span of 214 years* from 1800 to 2014, as cataloged by Eric Hickey, is estimated at only 5,515.[21] (The low estimate is 3,740 victims.) Of this number, at most 1,878 victims were murdered between 1975 and 2004, at an average rate of 63 victims a year. The Radford/FGCU Serial Killer Database lists 11,680 victims identified *worldwide* over hundreds of years and the highest number of documented annual serial-killer victims in the United States was in 1987: 361.

Even if we allow for unknown or "missing missing" victims, the total number of serial-killer victims comes nowhere near the 3,500 to 5,000 *annual* number so often claimed even today. But in the quest for Congressional funding, 5,000 victims a year sells better to the public than 63. As Joel Best put it in his analysis of child abduction statistics in the 1980s, "Three principles seem clear: Big numbers are better than small numbers; official numbers are better than unofficial numbers; and big, official numbers are best of all."[22] Yet even today, some distinguished academic criminologists like Ronald M. Holmes and Stephen T. Holmes continue to cling to the ridiculous 5,000 annual victims.[23]

For the record, a study of 1,498 child murders in California between

1981 and 1990 determined that *parents and relatives* were the most frequent killers of children under the age of ten, not strangers who are serial killers as John Walsh claimed. Strangers were involved in only 14.6 percent of homicides of children between ages five and nine and 28.7 percent of those between ages ten and fourteen.[24]

Back in 1981 to 1983, as the committee hearings unfolded in Washington, the press darted like schools of fish to the Senate hearings and the various press conferences. Articles in large-circulation magazines such as *Time, Newsweek, Life, Omni, Psychology Today, Playboy* and *Penthouse* painted a picture of the United States plagued by an "epidemic" of random homicides committed by roaming monsters who often victimized our children.

To draw parallels between the Great Serial-Killer Epidemic in the 1980s and the Great Witch Hunt of 1450 to 1650 is not entirely gratuitous. In the same way that witch-hunting would become institutionalized by state and church in the 1450s, serial-killer hunting became institutionalized in the secular American state in the 1980s with the emergence of state-funded serial-killer-hunting bureaucracies and programs, databases, manuals, both state- and self-appointed profiler experts of varying degrees of competence and qualification, and a heightened and exaggerated awareness among the public of a "serial-killer threat." The only difference was that while there were no witches, serial killers, although rare, were very real.

THE RISE AND DECLINE OF ViCAP (VIOLENT CRIMINAL APPREHENSION PROGRAM)

All those fearful and exaggerated cries of roaming serial killers threatening our children paid off. In 1982 Congress passed the Missing Children's Act and in 1984 the Missing Children's Assistance Act. President Ronald Reagan personally announced in 1984 the establishment of the National Center for the Analysis of Violent Crime (NCAVC), to be housed at the FBI Behavioral Sciences Unit at Quantico, Virginia.

The data collected by the BSU sexual homicide study led by John Douglas, Robert Ressler and Ann Burgess were implemented into the

FBI's profiling system and into a homicide-data collection program called ViCAP (Violent Criminal Apprehension Program). LAPD detective Pierce Brooks had been calling for such a computerized interjurisdictional homicide database for twenty-seven years since having successfully identified the "Glamor Girl" serial killer Harvey Glatman in 1958 by linking newspaper reports of similar homicides.

Back in the late 1950s and early 1960s, Brooks proposed that California police install a computerized database of unsolved homicide descriptions, an astute idea in a time when most people were unfamiliar with computers. His plan called for every police department in California to have a computer terminal linked with a central mainframe that stored data on every unsolved homicide in the state. Every department would have access to shared data on homicides in other jurisdictions. Aside from the fact that most of his superiors had no idea what a computer was, back then computers were huge elephants costing millions of dollars. Nobody took his proposal seriously. Brooks put the idea aside and went on to become the head of the Los Angeles homicide unit, and later a chief of police in Oregon and Colorado during the 1960s and 1970s.

In the early 1980s FBI behaviorists Robert Ressler and John Douglas returned to the issue of linkage blindness during the "serial-killer epidemic" and lobbied for the establishment of a national homicide database system. Ressler learned that Pierce Brooks had retired from active police work and had just received a small grant of 35 thousand dollars to revive and update his original proposal of an unsolved-homicide computer data network. Brooks was now based at Sam Houston University in Texas, and Ressler went down to see him.

The following year, Brooks and the FBI joined forces and got a one-million-dollar research grant to design a data collection, analysis, and distribution system that today is known as ViCAP and is run out of the NCAVC. Pierce Brooks was appointed its first director.

From 1985 onward, local police could fill out a standard ViCAP questionnaire about their homicide case and submit it to the Investigative Support Unit and request a profile of the unknown offender and other possible cases linked to him. The questions on the form addressed information that ranged from the description of the location where the victim's body was found down to the details of the assault and mutilations, and if known, things like the condition of the suspect's car and his method of approaching the victim.

The problem was that it required a substantial amount of paperwork. Need I say more? Overworked cops and paperwork do not mix well. The ViCAP form was fifteen pages long with 189 detailed questions, many of them multipart. It was as painstaking as an income tax form, if not worse . . . and then it had to be put in the mail![25] (Before the ubiquity of fax and e-mail.)

To derive any benefit from ViCAP, a police agency not only had to file the form, but also had to make a formal request to the FBI to process it through their database and report back the results, if any. Of course, many local agencies were reluctant to allow an outside agency to get formally involved in their cases.

By 1990 things improved technologically: police agencies could fax the form rather than rely on snail mail. After 1995 almost everybody had a PC, and the FBI distributed ViCAP forms as computer software, so at least a police officer could fill out a digital form rather than manually write or type it up on paper. But again, to get any result from ViCAP, the police agency had to file an official request for the FBI to search their massive database and report back on possible hits in their system. There was no way for a police agency to log directly on to the FBI database and make a search of its own.

By the mid-2000s, after twenty-five years of operation, many American police departments had lost touch with ViCAP's existence. Many police officers who were first introduced to ViCAP in the 1980s had retired, and for a new generation of overworked officers it was easy to overlook the FBI's reminders of ViCAP. Nor did local police care to wait while the FBI looked for possible matches in the ViCAP database.

In 2007, only a last-minute referral to ViCAP led to a breakthrough in the Adam Leroy Lane "Hunting Humans 'Ninja' Truck Driver" serial killings.[26] As a result, the ViCAP database can now be directly queried online by authorized police agencies.

But all is not well with ViCAP.

It is rarely used by police in the US. An investigation in 2015 by journalists at ProPublica revealed the depth of ViCAP's dismal decline, despite the FBI's claims of success. While the FBI has an 8.2-billion-dollar yearly budget, ViCAP receives only 800 thousand dollars a year. Although ViCAP claims that 3,800 state and local law enforcement agencies have contributed to its databases since its founding, currently only 1,400 police agencies in the US, out of some 18 thousand, participate in the system. The database receives reports of less than 1 percent of the violent crimes committed annually.[27]

A review in the 1990s found ViCAP had successfully linked only thirty-three crimes in *twelve* years. More recently, in 2014 the FBI claimed that three serial killers were apprehended through ViCAP in the previous eight years and characterized this as "a success." In fact, in 2014 ViCAP provided analytic assistance to local law enforcement on only 220 occasions, with mixed results.

It is not even clear how many crimes the database has helped to solve, because the FBI does not release any raw data on ViCAP use. The FBI's Office of Public Affairs at Quantico declines to answer specific questions about ViCAP from journalists, academics and researchers, including my own. Instead they referred me to the FBI's website.[28] But on its website, the FBI misrepresents itself in its public statements on ViCAP. While the FBI claims that new data are "continually compared" to the case files on record, program officials have said elsewhere that does not happen. "We have plans for that in the future," said Nathan Graham, a crime analyst for the program.

The FBI subsequently said it would update the information on its website, according to ProPublica's report. Indeed, the FBI has "updated" its website on ViCAP advances, by changing nothing and only adding the following disclaimer: "This is archived material from the Federal Bureau of Investigation (FBI) website. It may contain outdated information and links may no longer function."[29]

The FBI claims on the same webpage that it has case data on "150,000 open and closed violent crime investigations submitted by some 3,800 state and local law enforcement agencies—and includes some 'cold cases' that go back to the 1950s." ProPublica reports that the FBI has only 89 thousand cases on file and only 1,400 police agencies currently contribute data to the system. ViCAP has a skeleton staff of only 12 people. Training of police officers in the use of the ViCAP interface has declined as well, from about 5,500 officers in 2012 to 1,200 by 2014.

In comparison, in the 1990s Canada set up its own federal database system called ViCLAS (Violent Crime Linkage Analysis System). Despite Canada's population of 36 million compared to the 325 million of the US, ViCLAS has an annual budget of 15 million dollars, a database of over 400 thousand case files and a staff of more than one hundred police officers and analysts. On average, ViCLAS analysts send 175 to 200 potential linkage reports each year.[30] This is similar to the ViCAP total number of linkage reports (220 reports in 2014) but the US has nine times the population and twenty-three times more murders than Canada.[31]

Dissatisfied with the FBI's lame ViCAP system, some jurisdictions have set up their own database systems, like HITS (Homicide Investigation Tracking System) in Washington State and TracKRS (Task Force Review Aimed at Catching Killers, Rapists and Sexual Offenders) in Orange County, California.

TWILIGHT OF THE GOLDEN AGE

Those of us from the baby boom generation who knew the names of the Apollo 11 astronauts Neil Armstrong and Buzz Aldrin, the first men to walk on the moon, would became just as familiar with the names of Ted Bundy, John Wayne Gacy and Jeffrey Dahmer, the "moonwalkers" of serial killing. But after Jeffrey Dahmer in the early 1990s, serial killing became one long, hazy Apollo 12 moon mission—who knows who was on it? How many cases can you name of the 782 new serial killers who appeared in the United States and the world after the year 2000 in the way most of us can rattle off the names of Ted Bundy, Jeffrey Dahmer, John Wayne Gacy, Edmund Kemper, Henry Lee Lucas, Richard Ramirez, and any other of the many "super serial killers" from the "golden age"?

The "golden age" arguably began to fade after the arrest and trial of Jeffrey Dahmer in 1991 to 1992, which was breathlessly covered by all the media at the time. Two years later, all that media attention turned to the O. J. Simpson celebrity murder case. As mentioned earlier, the trial of serial killer William Lester Suff, suspected in the murder of twenty-two women in Riverside, California, was barely covered when he went on trial at the same time O. J. Simpson did. Serial killers were no longer newsworthy, no matter the number of victims; enraged homicidal celebrities were now the new media flavor of the month.

We can perhaps nudge the end of the "golden age" slightly later, to the early 2000s, with the cold-case arrests of the serial killers Gary Ridgway, the "Green River Killer," in 2001 and Dennis Rader, the "BTK Killer," in 2005. Both had been killing back in the "golden age"; their reputations and fame as unidentified serial killers from that era had preceded their arrests. They had "retired" in the waning years of the century, Rader apparently killing his last victim in 1991 and Ridgway killing his in 1998. But when these cold cases made the news in the 2000s, the coverage was relatively muted and relegated to second and third place in the news lineups, compared to the lead coverage of the Jeffrey Dahmer case. Since then, the news media have become relatively blasé about serial killers.

Part of the waning interest in news reporting of serial-killer cases has to do with the decline of national network news and the rise of the Internet and specialty cable channels. When Jeffrey Dahmer was arrested in 1991, cable networks and the Internet were in their infancy, and there were only four dominant sources of national television news: NBC, CBS, ABC and CNN. FOX was just creeping up onto the channel lineup. They all covered the Dahmer case with a unified chorus of lead-story furor. Since the rise of the Internet and the emergence of the thousand-channel television universe in the mid-1990s, our culture is no longer blanketed by a few "high-concept" stories on the big four channels but instead is fragmented into thousands of subjects, each subscribed to by viewers with narrow interests and serviced by media focused on those interests to the exclusion of other subjects. Serial-killer news today is rarely "breaking news." Serial murder is matter-of-factly reported on the evening news, or featured in true-crime TV programing, which itself is subdivided between serial killers, cold cases, "snapped wives with knives," mass killers, teen killers, wife killers, family annihilators, CSI forensic cases, fugitive pursuits, reality policing and multiple other parallel but stand-alone true-crime subcategories, each with its own precise electronic "penny dreadful," pornlike paraphilic specificity. Now serial-killer news comes into our homes like hot and cold water and their novelty has worn thin.

The exaggerated reports in the 1980s of serial-killer zombie hordes swarming over us and our children left a deep impression on our paranoid public psyche, our culture and our fear-selling media and entertainment industry. With "ordinary" homicide rates escalating an astounding 300 percent in the twenty-year period between 1970 and 1990, there was an accompanying peak of unsolved stranger-on-stranger killings; it certainly *felt* as if there was an epidemic of serial killings; monsters seemed to lurk everywhere and Americans appeared to be dying in a plague of so many mysteriously unsolved homicides that even the Centers for Disease Control (CDC) began to look into the phenomenon of serial murder.[32]

The irony is that no exaggeration was necessary; the actual numbers are extremely disturbing. An increase from 51 serial killers in the 1950s to 692 in the 1980s is alarming, no matter how you look at it. In the next chapter, I will address the central question, still debated today: why were there *so many* serial killers so virally emerging in this period of the 1960s to 1990s? *Why?*

FOURTEEN

Diabolus in Cultura: Serial-Killing Rape Culture "Sweats," the "Greatest Generation," and Their Sons of Cain

Killing becomes like sex and sex like killing.

—LT. COLONEL DAVE GROSSMAN, *ON KILLING: THE PSYCHOLOGICAL COST OF LEARNING TO KILL IN WAR AND SOCIETY*

Every society gets the kind of criminal it deserves.

—ROBERT F. KENNEDY, US ATTORNEY GENERAL, QUOTING LACASSAGNE

I am an American, and I killed Americans. I am a human being, and I killed human beings; and I did it in *my* society.

—NECROPHILE SERIAL KILLER EDMUND KEMPER

My fantasy is a girl screaming . . .

—SERIAL KILLER LAWRENCE "PLIERS" BITTAKER

In trying to explain the mysterious surge of serial killers in the 1970s to 1990s, there has been much toying with the idea that somehow the radical transformation of society in the 1960s must have had a role in it. We keep searching for some direct sociohistorical phenomenon that triggered and unleashed the viral rise of serial killers. It is hard not to assume that the rise of serial killing was somehow nested in the decadelong surge of overall violence, chaos, rebellion, riot, sex, drugs and rock 'n' roll during the reboot of American society in the sixties.

It really was a *reboot* in all senses of the word. For those trapped in the very limited black-and-white world of American society up until the 1950s, the 1960s brought a saturated color wheel of opportunities and freedoms and ways of being unimagined in previous decades. From youth culture, civil rights and gender equality to the emergence of a more tolerant, progressive and pluralistic American culture, despite all the divisions that still trouble us today, America was fundamentally transformed. Anything became possible. But there was a dark side to it also.

For all the progressive things to come out of the sixties, a lot of previously repressed ugly things were also slipping off the leash. The transformation of American society from the 1950s to the 1960s freed a lot of people, but it also left a lot of casualties. *Leave It to Beaver*'s Wally Cleaver ended up in a rice paddy nursing a sucking chest wound while the Beaver put flowers in his hair and ran away on the magic bus with Charlie Manson at the wheel. And when Woodstock was stabbed and beaten to death by Hells Angels at Altamont and Wally came home from 'Nam with nightmares, penicillin-resistant gonorrhea and a heroin habit, the only things to hold on to through the disillusionment were the violence, greed, hedonism and serial killing of the next three decades, until Osama bin Laden brought the house down on 9/11 in 2001. That, in a nutshell, is the basic "social chaos" model offered to explain the surge of serial killers.

One can add to that Ginger Strand's observation of the dispossession and marginalization of vibrant low-income urban communities, which vastly increased the pool of "less-dead" potential victims for serial killers to feed on. It wasn't just that there were more serial killers; there were more available victims too. (See chapter four.) But these explanations, though plausible and helpful, in the long run are unsatisfactory.

DIABOLUS IN CULTURA

Anthropologist Simon Harrison, an expert on the necrophilic collection of body parts as war trophies by soldiers, wrote that just like the discordant tritone musical chords forbidden in the Medieval era, known as *diabolus in musica* ("Satan in music"), there are also discordant tones in culture, a type of "*diabolus in cultura*—a forbidden conjunction of cultural themes, each unexceptionable in itself, but highly disturbing when brought together."[1] This notion best describes a serial-killer culture or serial-killing "ecology" as I sometimes call it when I attempt to describe the ebbs and surges of serial killing at various points in history. At its root is never one thing, but a diabolical alchemy of several things that together drive and inspire the surges of sexual-fetish serial killers at certain times in history, like the example of the divisions in Christendom and the rise of witch hunting, or dense urbanization of the marginalized destitute and the rise of violent pornography, or the migration of impoverished female labor and the demands of the middle classes for well-dressed servant girls (see chapters six, ten and eleven). As I strove to figure out what *diabolus in cultura* could possibly trigger and inspire the epidemic increase of serial killing in the US starting in the 1970s, it dawned on me: we were looking into the wrong time period for the triggers!

If the psychopathology of evolving serial killers is shaped and formed when they are children, but they first kill when they are around twenty-eight years old, then the historical triggers we are seeking need to be *backed up* chronologically some twenty to twenty-five years, to when those killers were growing up, not when they began killing as adults.

A quick, selective thumbnail list of some of the notorious "golden age" American serial killers reveals a disturbing chronology.

SERIAL KILLER	BIRTH DATE	MAIN KILLING YEARS (earlier killings in brackets)
David Carpenter	1930	1979–1981
Juan Corona	1934	1970–1971
Angelo Buono	1934	1977–1979
Henry Lee Lucas	1936	1976–1983 [1960]
Joseph Kallinger	1936	1974–1975
Gary Taylor	1936	1972–1975
Carroll Edward Cole	1938	1971–1980 [1948]

SERIAL KILLER	BIRTH DATE	MAIN KILLING YEARS (earlier killings in brackets)
Jerry Brudos	1939	1968–1969
Dean Corll	1939	1970–1973
Patrick Kearney	1939	1965–1977
Robert Hansen	1939	1980–1983
Lawrence Bittaker	1940	1979
Samuel Dixon	1940	2000–2001 [1962, 1968]
John Wayne Gacy	1942	1972–1978
Rodney Alcala	1943	1971–1979
Lowell Edwin Amos	1943	1979–1994
Donald J. Beardslee	1943	1981 [1969]
Gary Heidnik	1943	1986–1987
John Ed. Robinson	1943	1984–2000
Robert Frederick Carr	1943	1972–1976
Richard Valenti	1943	1973–1974
Richard Tucker Jr.	1943	1978 [1963]
Anthony Scully	1944	1983
David James Roberts	1944	1974
Norman Parker Jr.	1944	1978 [1966]
Billy Richard Glaze	1944	1986–1987
Andre Rand	1944	1972–1987
James D. Canaday	1944	1968–1969
James E. Christian	1944	1970
Morris Solomon Jr.	1944	1986–1987
Ward Weaver Jr.	1944	1981
Robert Joseph Zani	1944	1967–1979
Vaughn Greenwood	1944	1974–1978 [1964]
Arthur Shawcross	1945	1988–1989 [1972]
Dennis Rader	1945	1974–1991
Robert Ben Rhoades	1945	1975–1990
Chris Wilder	1945	1984
Randy Kraft	1945	1972–1983
Manuel Moore	1945	1973–1974
James Emery Paster	1945	1980
Eugene Blake	1945	1982–1984 [1967]

SERIAL KILLER	BIRTH DATE	MAIN KILLING YEARS (earlier killings in brackets)
Wm. D. Christenson	1945	1981–1982
Fred Wm. Coffey	1945	1975–1986
Lawrence Dalton	1945	1977–1978
Bobby Joe Maxwell	1945	1978–1979
Donald Lang	1945	1965–1971
Edward D. Kennedy	1945	1981 [1978]
Wm. Luther Steelman	1945	1973
Eugene Spruill	1945	1972–1973
Paul Knowles	1946	1974
Ted Bundy	1946	1974–1978
Richard Cottingham	1946	1977–1980 [1967]
Gerald Gallego	1946	1978–1980
Gerard Schaefer	1946	1971–1972
William Bonin	1947	1979–1980
Ottis Toole	1947	1974–1983
John N. Collins	1947	1967–1969
Herbert Baumeister	1947	1983–1998
Herbert Mullin	1947	1972–1973
Eddie Lee Mosley	1947	1973–1987
Edmund Kemper	1948	1972–1973 [1964]
Charles Norris	1948	1979
Douglas Clark	1948	1980
Randy Greenawalt	1949	1978 [1974]
Gary Ridgway	1949	1982–1993
Robert Berdella	1949	1984–1987
Richard Chase	1950	1977
William Suff	1950	1986–1992 [1974]
Randy Woodfield	1950	1980–1981
Joseph Franklin	1950	1977–1980
Russell Elwood	1950	1991–1997
Lorenzo Gilyard	1950	1977–1993
Gerald Stano	1951	1970–1980
Kenneth Bianchi	1951	1977–1979
Gary Lee Schaefer	1951	1979–1983

SERIAL KILLER	BIRTH DATE	MAIN KILLING YEARS (earlier killings in brackets)
Robert Yates	1952	1975–1998
William Hance	1952	1978
Carlton Gary	1952	1977–1978
Larry Eyler	1952	1982–1984
Donald Harvey	1952	1970–1987
David Berkowitz	1953	1976–1977
Carl Eugene Watts	1953	1974–1982
Robin Gecht	1953	1981–1982
David A. Gore	1953	1981–1983
Bobby Joe Long	1953	1984
Vincent D. Groves	1953	1978–1988
Danny Rolling	1954	1980
Daniel Siebert	1954	1979–1986
Michael Swango	1954	1981–1997
Keith Jesperson	1955	1990–1995
Joseph Christopher	1955	1980–1981
Alton Coleman	1955	1984
Elton M. Jackson	1955	1987–1996
Michael Hughes	1956	1986–1993
Manuel Pardo	1956	1986
Eugene Victor Britt	1957	1995
David Leonard Wood	1957	1987
Wayne Williams	1958	1979–1981
Joel Rifkin	1959	1989–1993
Anthony Sowell	1959	2007–2009
Robert J. Silveria	1959	1981–1996
Richard Ramirez	1960	1984–1985
James Rode	1960	1991–1993
Jeffrey Dahmer	1960	1978–1991
Charles Ng	1960	1983–1985
Ángel Reséndiz	1960	1986–1999
Charles Cullen	1960	1984–2003

There is an enormous glut of serial killers who grew up either during World War II or in the first fifteen baby boom years following the war. The list is densely clustered with notorious serial killers born and raised in the postwar years who, increasingly near the average age of twenty-eight, began to kill for the first time between the 1970s and 1990s, at the height of the "golden age."

They all lived in the wake of a receding shock wave of humanity's biggest, most viciously primitive and most lethal war ever fought.

While most of us acknowledge that World War II was a war like no other and that it fundamentally changed our world, to this day we have not completely grasped the entire nature of that war and how American combatants experienced it. Our vision of how we fought that war, its history as told to us, is still fossilized in propagandistic necessities of the time, regarding how we defined ourselves—as a righteous democracy—and how we defined the enemy—as evil totalitarian states—and how *that* kind of enemy was going to be fought and defeated by us. To paraphrase Mark Seltzer's comment, "The Western was really about serial killing all along," I suggest that war in general is also really about serial killing all along, in the most primitive and savage way. And World War II arguably was humanity's largest orgy of state serial killing since the Great Witch Hunt.

WORLD WAR II AS THE LAST "GOOD WAR," AND THE "GREATEST GENERATION" WHO FOUGHT IT

Sixty to eighty million people, or 3 percent of the world's entire population, predominantly civilian women and children, were killed during World War II between the invasion of China by Japan in 1937 and the fall of Nazi Germany and Imperial Japan in 1945.

The Nazi German and Imperial Japanese enemies that American GIs—our fathers and grandfathers—were dispatched to fight were without exaggeration far more savage, sadistic and murderous than anything we see today in the form of the Taliban, al-Qaida or ISIS. In the span of six years between 1939 and 1945, the Nazis and their allies in

Europe murdered—that is, shot, gassed, tortured, hanged, battered, raped, bayoneted, immolated, mutilated, injected, X-rayed, drugged, poisoned, decapitated, massacred, subjected to medical experiments, worked and starved to death in captivity and enslavement—an astonishing eleven million people, of whom six million were Jews. This number of the criminally murdered does not include the unintentional or "negligent," collateral killing of millions more civilians by wanton bombing and deprivation at the hands of the German conventional armed forces and paramilitary during combat and pacification operations. ISIS are petty amateurs compared to the Nazis.

While our Nazi enemies were motivated in their state serial killing by kooky racial cult theory, our Imperial Japanese enemies killed wildly in a recently revived cult of *Bushido*—the "way of the warrior"—introduced in its bastardized form into Japanese military culture by fascistic imperialists who seized power as a junta in the 1930s. In 1937 these Japanese "warriors" captured the Chinese city of Nanking, where they tortured, raped, killed and horrifically mutilated an estimated 50 thousand to 300 thousand Chinese victims in a six-week orgy of mass murder.[2]

Young American men were catapulted overseas to fight these enemies in the most horrific four-year paroxysm of slaughter Americans have ever experienced. Yes, the 620 thousand casualties in the American Civil War in the 1860s were far more numerous than US casualties in World War II, but the Civil War slaughter took place mostly with a dumb chivalry on both sides, in which women and children were rarely targeted, but men were prepared to die en masse in heroic but futile charges in which they were, as one historian put it, "funneled like pigs into a slaughter pen."[3] During a suicidal charge up a slope by Union troops against dug-in Confederates at Marye's Heights in Fredericksburg in 1862, the Confederates were so impressed by the gallantry and courage of their enemy that they cheered and applauded them as they inflicted 8,600 Union casualties below them.[4] World War I was stupidly fought in the same way, devastating a "lost generation" of young American men. World War II, however, was worse: a "total war" of annihilation in which women and children were *explicitly* and murderously targeted by our enemy, way beyond the scope, focus and scale of our own aerial bombings of civilian populations. American Marines were not going to be cheering suicidal Japanese "banzai" charges. Americans had not fought a war like that before and haven't since.

Our fathers and grandfathers were the "good guys"—no question about that. It is more than just a cliché that World War II was the "last good war," because we clearly knew how sick and evil our enemy was and how truly noble a cause it was to destroy them. That is not historical myth. But today we forget that World War II was a *total war*, unlike the "limited wars" of "containment" we fought later—Korea, Vietnam, the Gulf War, even the War on Terror.

Our enemy in World War II was so evil and powerful that we were called upon not just to utterly annihilate its armies but to bomb and burn its cities along with its people, including the women and children, until their governments collapsed or surrendered. That kind of war could not have been fought anywhere near as nobly or gallantly as claimed. Unlike in the wars in Korea, Vietnam, Iraq and Afghanistan, in World War II we were not giving any lip service to "bringing democracy" to our German or Japanese enemies: we were just trying to kill as many of them as quickly as we could, until they unconditionally surrendered. Period.

After pounding Germany into rubble and dropping two nukes on Japan, we won total victory in that horrible war in 1945. But as we transitioned directly from World War II into the fear and paranoia of a possible new conflict with the Russians, we never had the time or a secure peace to catch our breath and consider the actual nature of the war we had just fought and what it took out of our soldiers. We welcomed home our World War II veterans with medals and parades as heroes who had just fought for democracy, as was right, but we posed no questions about what we had asked them to do, just in case we had to do it again soon in a war with Communist Russia.

We were told we had fought the war as noble, chivalrous liberators were expected to fight. Many of the vets coming back from their combat experience knew better. There was no nobility in the slaughter, and a lot of men returned home deeply disturbed by what they'd witnessed and experienced. Other than totally debilitating "shell shock" there was no PTSD (post-traumatic stress disorder, or "flashback syndrome") on the diagnosis books until after Vietnam. In 1945 there was no talking about the obscenity of total war. The wartime GI Joe–John Wayne–*Why We Fight* propaganda continued. Our returning soldiers were patted on the back and told they did their duty, given medals and a parade and tossed a GI Bill and then sent home to suck it up in sullen silence in the privacy of their own trauma. They couldn't even talk to their families about it. Nobody wanted to hear it . . . at least not the truth. Our traumatized World War II veterans were forever trapped in silence, like prehistoric life preserved in transparent amber as "the greatest generation any society has ever produced," a term journalist Tom Brokaw coined in his 1998 book, *The Greatest Generation.*[5]

THE POSTWAR SADISTIC TORTURE "SWEATS" AND TRUE-DETECTIVE PULPS: ". . . A WEIRD THING TO DO."

The first clue to something amiss carried home from the war into the *diabolus in cultura* of postwar America appears in the pages of popular men's magazines directed at returning veterans and at their young sons growing up in the years that followed the war. If there was ever a discernible "mimetic compulsion," a popular cultural phenomenon extolling woman-hunting, rape, torture, cannibalism, mutilation and killing, then it was garishly celebrated in the pages of true-detective and men's adventure magazines with monthly circulations in the millions and that sold openly on newsstands and in supermarkets everywhere from the late 1940s until the end of the 1970s. And it was an ugly thing to behold. Where did it ever come from, what dark and ugly part of the American male psyche?

Cave drawings, myths, popular lore, folk and fairy tales, fables and literature often reflect the hidden unspoken yearnings and deep, dark fears and hates in a society, as well as its traumas and triumphs. In the limited three-TV-channel-plus-Hollywood-movies world of postwar American popular culture, without cable and satellite TV, without video, without video games, DVDs and the Internet, many of the males returning from war, those that stayed at home, and their sons and grandsons read mainstream magazines, comics and paperbacks for entertainment. Other than movies, radio and later TV, there wasn't much of anything else in the way of popular narrative entertainment.

What entertained and came to obsess some boys of Ted Bundy's and John Wayne Gacy's generation, and their fathers at the time, was dozens of monthly pulp men's adventure magazine titles like *Argosy, Saga, True, Stag, Male, Man's Adventure, True Adventure, Man's Action, True Men, Man's Story, Action for Men, See for Men, Real Men, Man's Exploits, New Man, Men Today, Rugged Men, Man to Man, Man's Life, Men in Conflict, Man's Combat, Man's Epic, Man's Book, New Man, World of Men, All Man, Showdown for Men, Man's Daring, Rage for Men, Rage: The Magazine for Real Men, Fury: Adventure for Men, Peril: All Man's Magazine, Man's Age.*

Along with true-detective magazines, these men's magazines would increasingly be cited as favorite childhood and adolescent reading by "golden age" serial killers when they had been children, adolescents and young adults. By the 1980s this literature was denounced by FBI behaviorists as "pornography for sexual sadists" and would eventually be driven off the newsstands both by the failing economics of monthly magazine publishing and by a popular social revulsion to "rape culture" imbued in that sector of mainstream media.[6]

From the 1940s to the 1970s, one entertainment staple for men's adventure magazines was the salaciously exaggerated accounts of wartime Nazi rape atrocities. The magazine covers featured garish images of bound and battered women with headlines like SOFT NUDES FOR THE NAZIS' DOKTOR HORROR; HITLER'S HIDEOUS HAREM OF AGONY; GRISLY RITES OF HITLER'S MONSTER FLESH STRIPPER; HOW THE NAZIS FED TANYA SEX DRUGS; BRIDES OF TORMENT FOR THE S.S. BEASTS; CHAINS OF AGONY FOR THE BOUND BEAUTIES OF NORWAY; HITLER'S BABOON TORTURES IN MABUTI; THE NAZI MADHOUSE ZOO OF RAVAGED WOMEN; CAGED BEAUTIES IN THE NAZI DUNGEON OF THE DAMNED; DAMNED BEAUTIES FOR THE NAZI HORROR MUSEUM; STRIPPED VIRGINS FOR THE NAZIS' TORCH OF TORMENT; TORTURED BEAUTIES FOR THE NAZI BLOOD CULT; TORTURED BEAUTIES OF HITLER'S PRINCE OF PAIN; "SHRIEK FOR DEATH MY LITTLE

ONE"; HELPLESS MAIDENS OF THE NAZIS' TIMELESS CASTLE OF MADNESS AND HORROR; HELPLESS VIRGINS IN THE NAZIS' HARNESS OF TERROR; SCREAMING NUDES FOR HITLER'S MINISTRY OF HELL; STRIPPED FOR THE SWASTIKA; SOFT FLESH FOR THE NAZIS' GREATEST HORROR; SHACKLED NUDES OF THE MONSTER GENERAL; HELPLESS BEAUTIES OF THE NAZIS' CIRCUS OF AGONY; NAZI HORROR TORTURES OF THE RESISTANCE GIRLS; CRYPT IN HELL FOR HITLER'S PASSION SLAVES.[7]

Even today, nearly seventy years after the war, from *Ilsa, She Wolf of the SS, The Night Porter* and *Seven Beauties* to the recent *Inglourious Basterds* and *The Reader*, the Nazis and their psychosexual sadistic cruelty remain a major theme in our popular culture and imagination.

Known as the "sweats" for the luridly colored cover illustrations of male torturers and female victims glistening with sweat, an effect enhanced by casein paints and acrylics used by the cover artists, these pulp magazines featured not only a gamut of Nazi and Japanese World War II atrocities, but sweaty cannibal stories based in the South Seas and Africa; Middle East harem rape scenarios; and Cold War, Korean War and Vietnam War vice and torture themes.[8]

Parallel to the "sweats" was a genre of grotesque crime newsprint tabloids like the *National Enquirer* (before it turned to celebrity gossip) and titles like *Midnight, Exploiter, Globe, Flash* and *Examiner* and lurid true-detective magazines with staged bondage photos mixed in with horrific crime-scene photos and tales of sex, death and mutilation, featuring headlines like I LIKE TO SEE NUDE WOMEN LYING IN BLOOD; 39 STAB WOUNDS WAS ALL THE NAKED STRIPPER WORE; HE KILLED HER MOTHER AND THEN FORCED HER TO COMMIT UNNATURAL SEX ACTS; SEX MONSTERS! THE SLUT HITCHHIKER'S LAST RIDE TO DOOM; RAPE ME BUT DON'T KILL ME; BOUND AND GAGGED; STRIPPED AND ROPED; DUCT TAPED DAMSEL; THE MAN WHO DREAMED OF MUTILATING WOMEN; "DO IT TILL I SHOOT"; SECRETS OF THE SEX SADIST'S TORTURE CHAMBER; DEAD LITTLE GIRLS DON'T CRY; "LET'S RAPE THE GIRL NEXT DOOR"; THE KILLER LEFT HIS TEETH MARKS ON THE NAKED BARMAID; SHE'S MINE FOR THE TAKING; "SHE SAID I WASN'T MAN ENOUGH TO PLEASE HER"; DID

THE SEX TEASE DRIVE HER BOYFRIEND TO BEAT HER BRAINS OUT?; IF RAPE VICTIM YELLS, KILL HER!; NUDE MODEL WAS TOO SEXY TO LIVE!; HE BATHED HIS BEAUTIES BEFORE BUTCHERING THEM; MOLESTED AND MURDERED ON A MONDAY AFTERNOON; VIVIAN WAS ALMOST DEAD WHEN THEY BURIED HER; GREEDY HOOKER+ANGRY PIMP=MURDERED PIGEON; HOW MANY MOTIVES DOES A MAN NEED TO KILL A WOMAN?; WHILE HIS BUDDY CHEERED HIM ON—THE KIDNAPPING RAPIST STRANGLED THE LAS VEGAS BEAUTY WITH HER OWN PANTYHOSE; TORTURE, SODOMY AND RAPE ORDEAL OF THE BEAUTIFUL COED ROOMMATES; MONSTROUS CRIMES IN THE HUMAN BUTCHER SHOP; HE HACKED GIRLS TO DEATH WHENEVER HE GOT THE URGE!; RAPE IN A COFFIN; HIS KNIFE PLUNGED INTO THE YOUNG HOUSEWIFE'S BODY AGAIN AND AGAIN, THEN . . . HE TURNED CAROL INTO A HUMAN TORCH; I'LL TAKE OBSCENE PICTURES WHILE YOU'RE DYING; HE MADE ME WATCH HIM KILL GIRLS AGAIN AND AGAIN; SLAIN BLONDE WAS TRI-SEXUAL . . . TRY ANYTHING!; "RAPE TORTURE AND CHAIN THEM UP"; KILLERS WHO MADE LOVE TO THE DEAD; THE NUDE WAS VIOLATED AFTER DEATH!; NEVER SPURN A GUN-TOTING LOVER!; LUSTING NIGHTSTALKER SMASHED SUZANNA'S SKULL!; SLASHED CORPSES AND SHREDDED BRAS MARKED HIS TRAIL: SEX FREAK ON THE PROWL; FREAKY BATHING FETISH TRIGGERED A SEX SLAYING!; IT WAS HIS DUTY TO BUTCHER HER!; HE WANTS SLAVE GIRLS WAITING FOR HIM IN PARADISE; POSE IN THE NUDE OR I'LL KILL YOU; SAVAGE HOOKER KILLER; SHE SAW HER MOTHER & SISTER MUTILATED; 20-YEAR-OLD BEAUTY'S HEART HAD BEEN NAILED TO THE WALL!; MARYLAND SLEUTHS FOUND A PIN STUCK IN THE GIRL'S CHEST BUT THE REAL SHOCKER WAS THE HIDEOUS PHRASE SCRAWLED ON SHIRLEY'S BACK!; DECAPITATED FOR 14 SEXY CENTERFOLDS!; THE SOBBING GRANDMOTHER WAS SPARED NOTHING!; GO-GO DANCER SLASHED TO DEATH IN MOTEL SHOWER; HE MADE HOME HORROR MOVIES OF HIS VICTIMS: "STRIP AND START SCREAMING . . . BABY"; HIS TEETH MATCHED THE MARKS ON

HER MUTILATED BREASTS; I WATCHED MY BABY BURN ALIVE; RETARDED SON MADE OWN MOM PREGNANT—THEN HELPED HER KILL "SIN BABIES"; etc., etc.

All these hundreds of magazines had one thing in common: their covers featured a photograph of a professional model posing as a bound victim (detective magazines) or a lurid painted illustration of a bound woman (men's adventure magazines). She was inevitably scantily clad or her dress in disarray or tatters, her skirt hiked up, exposing her thighs or stockings, her breasts straining under the thin material of her torn clothing, her bronzed flesh glowing with a fine sheen of perspiration, often with chained or bound legs spread open, scratched and bruised, tied up in a torture chamber, in a basement, on the floor, on a bed, on the ground outside; tied to a chair, a table, a rack, a sacrificial pole; in a cage or suspended from a dungeon ceiling next to red-hot pokers and branding irons heating on glowing coals, turning on an iron roasting spit over a flame, lowered into a pot of boiling water to be cooked by lusty cannibals, strapped spread-eagle on surgical tables for mad Nazi scientists to probe and mutilate; her face contorted in fear and submission, sometimes gazing out from the magazine cover toward her unseen assailant, toward the male reader, as if she was the reader's personal slave who could be possessed for the price of the magazine.[9]

It all harked back to the gynocidal dungeons of the Great Witch Hunt of 1450 to 1650 at its most sadistic fantastic.

Norm Eastman, one of the cover artists for those magazines in the 1950s, recalled in 2003, "I often wondered why they stuck with the torture themes so much. That must have been where they were heavy with sales. I really was kind of ashamed of painting them, though I am not sure they did any harm. It did seem like a weird thing to do."[10]

Women in these blatantly misogynistic publications were portrayed in only two biblically paraphilic ways: either as captives bound and forced into sex against their will or as sexually aggressive, bare-shouldered women with a cigarette dangling from their lips, subject to punishment or death for their evil-minded sexuality. In this paraphilic world of the "sweats" women were either a sacred Madonna defiled or a profligate whore punished; there were no other options available.

These magazines were not squirreled away behind counters or in

adult bookstores or limited to some subculture; they were as mainstream as apple pie. Some had monthly circulations of over two million
copies at their height and were openly sold *everywhere*: on newsstands;
in grocery stores, candy stores, supermarkets; on drugstore magazine
racks, right next to *Time*, *Life*, *National Geographic*, *Popular Mechanics*
and *Ladies' Home Journal*.[11] They would be found lying around anywhere and everywhere men and their sons gathered, in workshops, bar-
bershops, auto shop waiting rooms, mail rooms, locker rooms and
factory lunchrooms. At their peak, there were over a hundred monthly
adventure and true-detective magazine titles, available to all ages.

All this in a country where it is still taboo to show even a glimpse of
a bare female breast or buttock on television.

In a colorless world, where photographs, movies and television were
mostly black-and-white, I remember in the late 1950s and the early
1960s going to the local supermarket with my mom and waiting for her
by the magazine and comic book racks, facing row after row of these
magazines with their candy-colored covers of bound women in distress,
offered up for the taking. "GIRLS PRICED TO SELL," as one headline
advertised.

I was five or six years old and had no notion of sex, but I remember
that those images stirred some kind of powerful primordial male reptilian euphoria. I recognize it today as entirely a sexual stirring for dominance and possession of my prim and bossy older-sister humans, from
babysitters and nurses to female store clerks and teachers towering over
me, under whose supervision and authority I constantly found myself as
a male child. These magazine images of prostrate females drew me into
a fantasy world in which women were tipped over into a so-powerless
and so-vulnerably-disheveled state.

I was one of those lucky kids who were given no reason to be hurt,
traumatized or angry, and was encouraged and raised to be independent and autonomous as an adolescent by both the men and women in
my young life. I was fortunate and had a trauma-free childhood with no
episodes of abuse. But I can only imagine now, if some severe abuse,
humiliation or trauma had been fused with that powerful, primitive,
reptilian sensation I describe, what might have happened and to what
dark place I potentially could have taken those impulses stirred by this

constant imagery had I been angry at women, or desperately craved control, revenge or even redemption, or as John William Money described sexual paraphilia, if I needed my "tragedy or trauma turned into triumph."

Why were our Greatest Generation and their sons feeding on this sadistically depraved popular literature after the war? Why did this illustrated literature even exist? What happened to our fathers and grandfathers in that war? What dark secrets were encoded in this literature, secrets that they came back with from the Last Good War but could not openly talk about?

It was only fifty years later, in the early 2000s, as most of the war generation started to pass away, that we began gathering the courage to ask those unaskable questions about what it meant for them to fight a primitive war to utterly exterminate an enemy. We did not like the answers coming back to us on several fronts.

"TSUNAMI OF LUST": AMERICAN GIs AND RAPE IN EUROPE DURING WORLD WAR II

What I will describe here is so taboo a topic, even today, that I feel I need to preface it with this disclaimer: this is not about what most of our fathers, grandfathers, and great-grandfathers *did* as GIs fighting in World War II; this is about what they *witnessed* a *minority* of GIs doing, and how they had to live with the memories without being able to talk about them with anybody.

Since the beginning of history rape has consistently been a characteristic of warfare and conquest. As Lt. Col. Dave Grossman writes in his magistral book *On Killing: The Psychological Cost of Learning to Kill in War and Society*:

> The linkage between sex and killing becomes unpleasantly apparent when we enter the realm of warfare. Many societies have long recognized the existence of this twisted region in which battle, like sex, is a milestone in adolescent masculinity. Yet the sexual aspects of killing continue beyond the region in which both are thought to be rites

of manhood and into the area in which killing becomes like sex and
sex like killing.[12]

This relationship between sex and killing in war is reflected by frequent
rape, which in itself is fueled less by sexual lust as by aggression in a
time and place where nothing is more valued and demanded of a soldier
than a capacity for lethal aggression of the most primitive kind.

While in the modern age wartime rape became punishable under
various military codes of conduct and criminal laws of certain countries, it was not explicitly outlawed in international conventions governing war crimes, laws and customs of war until 1996 and not until 2008
declared by the United Nations as being a war crime constituting an act
of genocide.[13]

During World War II we accused the Nazis and Japanese of wanton
rape, and after the war we blamed our Russian former allies for any
rapes perpetrated by "our side" in Germany. The democratic Western
Allies—USA, Britain, Canada and France—were portrayed as chivalrous liberators handing out chocolate bars and chewing gum. The enemy raped, but we seduced with gifts of nylon stockings and brought
home blushing war brides. It was all very romantic, the myth.

But then in the early 2000s, Northern Kentucky University's criminal sociologist J. Robert Lilly looked closely at the statistics of wartime
rapes committed by American GIs serving in Britain, France and Germany. To everyone's horror, Lilly reported that American "liberators"
raped fourteen thousand to seventeen thousand women between 1942
and 1945 in those three European countries alone.[14]

Some 16.5 million men (or 12 percent of the total US population),
mostly in their twenties, were mobilized into the military, deployed in
Europe or the Pacific or on wartime duty at home. About 990 thousand
young American men were thrown into combat, including some 100
thousand convicted felons who were inducted directly into the military
from prisons.[15]

To get some sense of the scale of the number of alleged rapes, consider there were about 1.5 million US troops in Europe in the four-year
period in question. Back home in the US, where most American males
had remained, about 4,700 rapes a year were being reported.[16] In 2014,

the US had a male population of about 150 million, 100 times the number of GIs deployed in Europe during the war; there were 84,041 reported rapes.[17] (Approximately 15 percent of the 2014 statistic were male victims.)[18] The World War II GI rape rate in Europe, prorated over the four years 1942 to 1945 and adjusted per capita to the current population of the US (14,000–17,000 x 100 / 4) would be equivalent today to 350 thousand to 425 thousand reported rapes a year in the United States! It was an unusually high rate.

No American publisher at first wanted to take on Robert Lilly's controversial book. It was the height of the Iraq war effort, but beyond that, negative revelations about the conduct of our "greatest generation" in the "last good war" were not something we collectively wanted to hear.[19] Robert Lilly's book was first published only in France and Italy, where the Europeans gleefully reveled in the accusations. It was finally quietly published by Macmillan in the United States in 2007 as *Taken by Force: Rape and American GIs in Europe.*

In April 2006, in the meantime, the British Home Office declassified wartime crime statistics which revealed that American GIs in Britain between 1942 and 1945 were convicted in 26 murders, 31 manslaughters, 22 attempted murders and more than 400 sexual offenses, including 126 rapes.[20] British newspapers ran headlines like "Wartime GIs went on rampage of rape and murder."[21]

Then University of Wisconsin–Madison history professor Mary Louise Roberts looked into rapes perpetrated by American GIs liberating France and published her results in 2013 in *What Soldiers Do: Sex and the American GI in World War II France.*[22] American troops raped so many women in France that French authorities begged the American military to set up brothels, but the United States prudishly refused. (One brothel was established, in September 1944, by Major General Charles H. Gerhardt, commander of an infantry division that landed at Omaha Beach, but it was closed after only five hours in deference to sentiments back home.)

Roberts argues that American troops were steeped in "rape culture" even before they arrived in France, pointing out that military recruiting propaganda and press accounts depicted going to war as an "exotic erotic adventure." *Life* magazine's Joe Weston reported from France that "the general opinion all down the line was that France was a tremendous brothel inhabited by 40 million hedonists who spent all their time eating, drinking and making love and in general having a hell of a good time."[23] In the meantime, the French phrase guide in the GI newspaper *Stars and Stripes* focused on handy "dating" phrases like "You are very pretty" and "Are your parents at home?"[24]

Frenchwomen were branded "sign language girls" because of rumors that they could be seduced by a simple series of hand gestures. An ironic joke circulating among the French in Normandy after D-day went: "With the Germans, the men had to camouflage themselves, but when the Americans arrived, we had to hide the women." As Roberts concluded, "Sexual fantasies about France did indeed motivate GIs to get off the boat and fight but such fantasies also unleashed a veritable tsunami of lust."[25]

J. Robert Lilly and Mary Louise Roberts point out other ways in which overseas rape statistics reflected American society back home. African-American soldiers were most likely to be charged and most severely punished for rape: of 29 US soldiers sentenced to death for rapes of Frenchwomen, 25 were African-Americans.[26] American GIs executed for crimes during the war were reported to their families as having "died due to willful misconduct" and were buried in "Plot E" in Oise-Aisne American Cemetery in France. According to Duke University historian Alice Kaplan, in Plot E there are 96 markers, of which 80 belong to African-Americans.[27]

From there it got worse. Historian Miriam Gebhardt, using German church records relating to illegitimate births, claimed in her book *Crimes Unspoken* that the Allies raped 860 thousand women in their conquest of Germany in 1945. The majority of rapes were typically ascribed to the Russians in the east, but Gebhardt attributed 190 thousand of the rapes to American GIs in Germany (and 45 thousand to British soldiers and 50 thousand to French troops).[28] Her book was published by Random House in Germany as *When the Soldiers Came* in 2015 and in the US in 2017.[29]

While these shocking numbers from a low of 14 thousand to a possible 190 thousand rapes are tenuous statistical projections—the higher numbers predicated on the notion that while peacetime rapes often go unreported, in wartime they are even less reported—even the lower numbers are deeply disturbing, especially as they represent rapes only in France, Britain and Germany. We do not have data from some of the other territories in which GIs fought, like North Africa, Italy, Belgium or the Pacific, which could significantly increase the number. Nor does it include, aside from the recent statistics from Britain, the noncombat zones to which Americans were sent around the world to serve. For example, in Australia in 1942 twenty-four-year-old US Army private Edward Joseph Leonski, the "Singing Strangler," killed three women with melodic voices to "get at their voices." Although he did not rape the victims, all three were found posed with their genitals exposed.[30]

Since the ugliness of the Vietnam War, we have desperately clung to the comforting notion that at least World War II was an unambiguously "good war"; we cling to it today with that naïve, childlike, Sgt. Rock, *Our Army at War* comic book yearning. Historian David M. Kennedy wrote, in the *New York Times*, "Our culture has embalmed World War II as 'the good war,' and we don't revisit the corpse very often . . ." *What Soldiers Do* is "a breath of fresh air," providing less of an "aha" than, as he put it, an "of course."[31]

As the journalist and historian Mark Kurlansky observed in 2008 in the *Los Angeles Times*, "World War II was one of the biggest, most carefully plotted lies in modern history."[32]

None of this is meant to disparage the overwhelming majority of American GIs who served courageously and honorably during the war, and who fought within the generally recognized parameters of the laws and customs of "civilized" warfare as best they could, considering the brutality and suicidal fanaticism of the enemy they faced.

The purpose of this digression here into World War II rape is to suggest that what we brought back home to the USA from the killing fields of Europe and the Pacific was a combat-amplified phenomenon of what had been incipiently unfolding in the repressed psychopathology and culture in America: the *diabolus in cultura*. Suddenly a million males, most of whom had been raised under the tenets of Western Judeo-Christian values but had rarely ventured beyond their hometowns, were catapulted thousands of miles overseas among strangers into a savagely primitive world of warfare stripped of the rules and inhibitions of civilization. It was a mini Stone Age war but with machine guns and flame-throwers, in which our soldiers were called upon to behave like our primitive ancestors in a reptilian state of killing for survival. Once that reptilian brain was suddenly freed from the bounds of civilization in the name of "military necessity," all sorts of dark and primitive things were going to happen. War is not a Hollywood movie. It's not even a sanitized documentary on the History Channel.

I repeat, the vast majority of American GIs *did not* perpetrate rape, but many witnessed it and knew about it and were forced to remain mute about what they saw. If the low estimate of 14 thousand to 17 thousand rapes is attributed to the approximately 1.5 million US troops serving in Europe, that means that roughly 1 percent of GIs committed rape. The other 99 percent may have witnessed their fellow soldiers committing these crimes, or at the very least were likely aware of them—crimes perpetrated by their "band of brothers" whose lives depended upon one another—resulting in a burden of truth that many had to swallow to get through the war in one piece. That in itself would have been a conflicted, shameful and demoralizing situation to find oneself in and to bring back home to their wives, mothers, daughters and sons. It was not something they were able to talk about.

American GIs in the Pacific and Necrophilic Fetish War Totems

It wasn't just wartime rape our soldiers might have witnessed or perpetrated. There was also primitive war-trophy harvesting of human heads and other body parts to contend with in another corner of the war—the one in the Pacific, where we were fighting a different enemy: the Japanese. The current leading authority on necrophilia, Dr. Anil Aggrawal, classifies such trophy taking as "Stage 5 fetishistic necrophilia" on his ten-stage scale of necrophilia[33] (see chapter seven).

As John Dower points out in his study of how World War II was waged in the Pacific, "War hates spawn war crimes."[34] We didn't take a lot of Japanese prisoners in the Pacific, and not just because the Japanese fought to the death or detonated hidden hand grenades after feigning surrender or because it was difficult to contain them in remote jungle-island battlefields. The war in the Pacific was a species of racial war of vengeance. Japanese wounded were often killed; those few attempting to surrender were shot; prisoners were assembled on airfields and machine-gunned and even sometimes thrown from air transports "while trying to escape."[35] The wanton killing of Japanese prisoners of war was of concern to the military high command, as it discouraged Japanese troops from surrendering. And of course, the even more brutal treatment that the Japanese meted out to American POWs from the beginning did not help the fate of Japanese prisoners in American hands.

As Confederate general Nathan Bedford Forrest, "That Devil Forrest," who massacred surrendering African-American Union soldiers at Fort Pillow, famously said, "War means fighting, and fighting means killing."

And worse. In the Pacific, US troops frequently mutilated Japanese corpses, cutting off ears, pulling teeth and even shrinking heads, collecting skulls and other body parts to take home with them. This would have been unacceptable conduct against a fellow white Christian enemy, which was precisely what the Germans were, despite their Nazi pretensions to neo-paganism. But in our war against the Japanese, mutilation of the dead (and sometimes even the wounded) was so ubiquitous that an edition of *Life* magazine proudly featured a photo of a young American woman sitting at a table with a skull on it. The caption read: "Arizona war worker writes her Navy boyfriend a thank-you note for the Jap skull he sent her."[36] President Roosevelt was presented with a letter opener with a handle made from a Japanese soldier's arm bone (which he ordered to be decently buried).[37]

In his classic memoir of fighting with the Marines in the Pacific, *With the Old Breed*, E. B. Sledge writes:

> It was a brutal, ghastly ritual the likes of which have occurred since ancient times on battlefields where the antagonists have possessed a profound mutual hatred. It was uncivilized, as is all war, and was carried out with that particular savagery that characterized the struggle between the Marines and the Japanese. It wasn't simply souvenir hunting or looting the enemy dead; it was more like Indian warriors taking scalps.

While I was removing a bayonet and scabbard from a dead Japanese, I noticed a Marine near me. He wasn't in our mortar section but had happened by and wanted to get in on the spoils. He came up to me dragging what I assumed to be a corpse. But the Japanese wasn't dead. He had been wounded severely in the back and couldn't move his arms; otherwise he would have resisted to his last breath.

The Japanese's mouth glowed with huge gold-crowned teeth, and his captor wanted them. He put the point of his kabar [a combat knife] on the base of a tooth and hit the handle with the palm of his hand. Because the Japanese was kicking his feet and thrashing about, the knife point glanced off the tooth and sank deeply into the victim's mouth. The Marine cursed him and with a slash cut his cheeks open to each ear. He put his foot on the sufferer's lower jaw and tried again. Blood poured out of the soldier's mouth. He made a gurgling noise and thrashed wildly. I shouted, "Put the man out of his misery." All I got for an answer was a cussing out. Another Marine ran up, put a bullet in the enemy soldier's brain, and ended his agony. The scavenger grumbled and continued extracting his prizes undisturbed.[38]

This is what the Last Good War was like for dad and grandpa. How do you come back the same from something like that?

At one point in his memoir, Sledge describes how he himself was on the brink of extracting a gold tooth from a Japanese corpse, when another GI admonished him and talked him out of it. While we can be comforted by the knowledge that most of our men in that war were somewhere between Sledge and the GI admonishing him, this is what the Greatest Generation had to witness and endure just the same.

The harvesting of Japanese body parts as necrophilic trophies and totems became so acute that in January 1944 the US Joint Chiefs of Staff issued a high-level directive to all theater commanders in the Pacific, ordering them to adopt measures to prevent US soldiers from collecting and curing Japanese body parts as trophies and importing them into the United States.[39] US Customs inspectors were mobilized to confiscate both Japanese trophy weapons and human body parts from homeward-bound GIs. The way we are asked by customs today whether we are bringing home any tobacco or alcohol, returning personnel from the Pacific were routinely asked if they were bringing home with them any human body parts.

American poet Winfield Townley Scott was working as the book editor for the *Providence Journal* in Rhode Island in January 1944 when a GI recently returned from the Pacific showed up at the newspaper's office with a Japanese skull. He recalled how everyone stopped what they were doing and rushed down to see and touch the gruesome war trophy. Scott must have had a particularly acute sense of the macabre—he was among the first literary critics to appreciate the works of horror writer H. P. Lovecraft, whom he extolled in several essays and articles—but that day he was horrified by the conduct of his fellow Americans as they gathered around a human skull, cracking jokes and heaping ritual abuse on it. It inspired Scott to later write his shocking 1962 poem "The US Sailor with the Japanese Skull," in which he meticulously describes the beheading of the dead Japanese soldier, the skinning, scalping, boiling, cleaning, curing, polishing and shellacking of his skull.[40]

Japanese war-trophy skulls are now showing up all over the United States as their original possessors die and family members seem inclined to dispose of them in horror or ignorance or both. Since as early as 1983, forensic experts have been warning that these skulls will be turning up in forensic labs throughout the country "as a generation was passing and that such materials were being discarded or redistributed to others."[41]

These skulls are now literally floating up in American lakes. One was recently pulled out of Lake Travis in Texas, having been carefully tied to a rock with fishing line in an attempt to "exorcise" it from somebody's possession. Police at first suspected a Mexican narco-cult homicide until the skull was identified by forensic anthropologists as a war-trophy Japanese skull. Another was found in a lake in Illinois. The skull had been spray-painted gold, and police feared they had a cult killing on their hands until it was identified as a World War II trophy skull. It was eventually traced to the teenage grandson of a veteran. He found the item among forgotten family possessions, spray-painted it gold, tied a bandanna around it and kept it as a decoration in his bedroom until he suddenly became frightened of it and dumped it into the lake.

A recent article in the American Institute of Forensic Science's journal described a spate of skulls turning up in forensic labs across the nation:

funeral director received the skull from the former wife of a deceased U.S. Navy veteran; reported to the police by the widow of a veteran who had them since his WWII service; found among the belongings of a deceased U.S. Army veteran and was turned over to police by a grandson; reported by a veteran's son who was told by his now deceased father that he had buried a trophy skull from WWII in their yard about 40 years previously; family members of a deceased WWII veteran discovered the skull among his possessions and turned it over to local law enforcement; discovered in a locked shed during a drug and gun raid by a northern California sheriff; found inside a wooden crate by a relative of a recently deceased U.S. veteran while cleaning out the individual's house; remains reportedly appeared in a box on an individual's front porch and were turned over to authorities; received them from a retired WWII U.S. Navy veteran residing in California; encountered by hikers off a trail in a Pennsylvania State Forest, [etc., etc.][42]

In Holden, Maine, local collectors had been reselling to each other a female Japanese trophy skull originally acquired in an estate sale, until one of the collectors finally contacted Japanese authorities who arranged for its repatriation to Japan.[43]

In the meantime, police in Colorado seized a decorated Japanese trophy skull they found in a trunk during a drug raid. It had been a family heirloom since the great-grandfather had brought it home from Guadalcanal, where he had fought with the Marines. It had been signed by him and other soldiers in his unit and the family knew it by its nickname, "Oscar." The family sued for the skull's return but it was turned over to the Japanese government for burial despite the family's protests.[44]

In 2010, Derrick Shaftoe in Phoenix, Arizona, found twenty Japanese skulls among his grandfather's possessions after he passed away. The grandfather had smuggled them home in a footlocker after serving with the 3rd Marine Division in the Pacific on Bougainville, Guam, and Iwo Jima. Shaftoe had no idea his grandfather had the grisly trophies stored in his attic, and said he vividly remembers finding the skulls, because "my wife heard me screaming from all the way in the front yard."[45]

These finds are now so frequent that there are standard protocols by which trophy skulls are repatriated to the Japanese government.[46] Forensic anthropologists working in the 1980s on the repatriation of Japanese war remains on the battlefields of the Mariana Islands reported that an extraordinary 60 percent of the dead were missing their heads.[47]

In his study of human war trophies (which includes a look at the collection of skull and bone trophies during the American Civil War and the Vietnam War), *Dark Trophies: Hunting and the Enemy Body in Modern War*, Simon Harrison describes case after case of American veterans keeping enemy skulls in their bedrooms or living rooms to the dismay of their wives and families, to the point that they sometimes led to divorce. (Harrison even reports a case of a World War II veteran still serving in the Marines who brought his Japanese war skull with him on a tour of duty in Vietnam.) Harrison notes that during the American Civil War, soldiers sometimes sent home to their fiancées pieces of enemy bones or skulls, as did soldiers in World War II and the Vietnam War. Such necrophilic "love gifting" can be anthropologically linked to primitive warrior-hunters bringing home game to their women, or head trophies symbolic of victory in a war of survival. It could even go deeper, in that "four-Fs" triune brain of ours, perhaps to those cannibal times when dead enemy warriors were not only a threat prevented but a source of a coming celebratory feast as well.

In Washington, D.C., at the National Museum of Health and Medicine on the grounds of the Walter Reed Army Medical Center, in File Cabinet 24, the museum stores human skulls confiscated by the military from soldiers during the Vietnam War. Some are decorated with graffiti and doodles including a peace sign and marijuana pipe. One skull (Inventory No. 1987.3017.23) is painted in Day-Glo colors and a fat black candle is melted into place at its top. There are drill marks in the skull indicating it was used as a hanging skull-candle. Another skull (No. 1987.3017.09) bears the inscriptions "Stay High Stay Alive" and "Viet Nam que loco."[48]

Professor Lawrence Miller recently reported, "Eating one's enemy to assimilate his strength and power, or the taking of body parts as trophies, has characterized victorious warriors in every age; as recently as September 2010, US Army soldiers were charged with keeping leg bones, finger bones, and teeth from slain Afghanis."[49]

Our GI ancestors were steeped in some seriously dark, savage territory during World War II—over a million of them, if we include both Europe and the Pacific—and now in 1945 the million were coming home, some of them in a state of trauma and shock and repressed in sullen silence, unable to speak about the unspeakable. They were coming home to collectively raise a new generation of American sons—both literally and metaphorically. From traumatized fathers raising sons at home to the nation's "fathers" in corporate boardrooms, Congress and the White House, from Eisenhower and JFK and all the way to George H. W. Bush, the World War II–veteran generation of males would shape and lead America and its sons of Cain through its *diabolus in cultura* well into the 1990s.

THE WORLD WAR II PATERNAL-TRAUMA-INDUCED SERIAL-KILLER EPIDEMIC HYPOTHESIS

I found on record no World War II combat veteran who returned home to become a serial killer. The reality of death in war probably preempted any "fantasy" veterans may have nurtured previously as civilians. It was their sons and grandsons who became the serial killers in the 1960s to 1990s.

Accounts of "golden age" serial killers rarely detail the biographies of the fathers (when they were around) but sometimes they do briefly touch on them. In his biography of the necrophile serial killer Arthur Shawcross, who killed two children and twelve women and was born in 1945, Jack Olsen describes the father, Roy Shawcross, as a corporal serving with the First Marine Division at Guadalcanal, where he barely survived being buried alive under tons of coral sand after being hit by a Japanese shell. His buddy next to him suffocated to death. Dug out by fellow Marines, Roy later ended up lost in the jungle, separated from the

US forces for four months, surviving on abandoned, maggot-ridden Japanese rations. He earned four battle stars but was never the same when he returned home from the war.[50] His son Arthur would later falsely claim he was transformed into a serial killer by atrocities he perpetrated while serving in combat in Vietnam. It turned out Shawcross had served at a supply depot and never saw any combat of the kind he fantasized about.

Necrophile serial killer Edmund Kemper was born in 1948 and murdered his grandparents when he was fifteen, later telling police he "just wanted to see what it felt like to kill Grandma." He was released after a brief incarceration in a psychiatric facility and went on to kill, behead and have sex with the corpses of six college-aged women, his mother and her friend. His biographer Margaret Cheney writes, "His father E. E. Kemper, Jr., had served in Europe during World War II in a Special Forces unit, which his son recalled as having included suicide missions." Cheney quotes Kemper's mother as telling her son, "The war never ceased. Upon his return he tried college under the G.I. Bill, couldn't get back into studying, argued like a staff sergeant with the instructors, dropped out . . ."[51] The family broke apart when Edmund was a child.

In her study of serial killer Dennis Rader, the "BTK Killer," born in 1945, Katherine Ramsland quotes him as saying briefly, "My dad, William Elvin Rader, a Marine, was still in the Pacific when I was born, on Midway Island."[52]

"Golden age" serial killers Douglas Clark, Herbert Mullin, Carl Eugene Watts and Chris Wilder reportedly had fathers in the military during World War II. Mostly, however, the biographies of the fathers of serial killers are not detailed to any great extent.

Derrick Shaftoe, who found the twenty skulls in his grandfather's attic, is not a serial killer, but he described his childhood memories of his grandfather. He said that after returning from the war his grandfather became a Lutheran minister and primary school teacher. He remembered his grandfather as a kind, quiet man who rarely talked about the war and was friendly to everybody.

But he had a dark side.

When Derrick was ten, he invited his grandfather to talk about his wartime experiences to his fourth-grade class. He recalled, "My teacher asked him if he ever missed home during the war. So he started telling us about this time on Bougainville he had to bulldoze a hundred Japanese corpses into a mass grave and then incinerate them for health reasons. He talked about sitting there in the jungle, reading love letters from my grandmother, by the light of the burning bodies. It was genuinely the most fucked-up thing I've ever heard in my life. Then he mentioned something about a giant lizard and the story went completely off the rails."[53]

My "war trauma" hypothesis invites an ambitious undergraduate or graduate student to collect and analyze the military histories of the fathers and grandfathers of "golden age" serial killers.

I suspect that the veteran fathers bringing up the sons in the 1940s and 1950s who became serial killers were not only traumatized by the war more than we realize, but also by the social catastrophe of the Great Depression that preceded it. The Depression destroyed a generation of male breadwinners and devastated families for decades to follow. No doubt some of the fathers of "golden age" serial killers never went overseas into combat, or did not even serve in the military. But they all lived through the Dirty Thirties, which broke the pride and spine of that generation of men and their families.

Not all veterans returned from the war disturbed and traumatized, but many more than we acknowledge did indeed come home alienated and damaged and in no state to raise healthy and productive sons. This hidden surge of war-traumatized fathers, either in unbearably conflicted relationships with their children or emotionally and physically withdrawn or unavailable to them, spawned that surge of serial-killing sons. There were enough degraded men after the Great Depression and those few of the most traumatized from the more than a million who saw combat, to afterwards have easily fathered the 2,065 "golden age" serial killers from the 1950s to the 1990s. The numbers are not wildly out of proportion.

The FBI's *Sexual Homicide* study of the "golden age" serial killers from that generation of sons revealed that only 57 percent of serial killers had both parents at birth, and 47 percent had their father leave before age twelve. A mother as the dominant parent was reported in 66 percent of the cases, and a negative relationship with the father or male parental figure was reported by 72 percent of the convicted sex killers. The FBI study also indicated that 50 percent of the offenders had parents with criminal pasts and 53 percent came from families with psychiatric histories.[54]

My hypothesis is that a broken generation of men either raised or abandoned a dysfunctional generation of boys who would emerge as epidemic serial killers—the sons of Cain.

KILLING FOR CULTURE

Popular culture that emerged in the wake of the Great Depression and the war had a part to play as well. In fact, it is not an exaggeration to say that from the 1940s to the 1970s, a large segment of mainstream popular entertainment focused on the abduction, restraint, torture and rape of women. That too inspired, or as the FBI would say, facilitated, a generation of budding serial killers and the fantasies that kept them up at night.

As the 1950s dawned, the sick sons of the sick fathers, along with some of the men who never went to war but remained home and fantasized about it, began to stir in the chemistry of their puberty. They fingered their knives and knotted ropes as they browsed the semen-sticky pages of their drugstore pulp magazines, with thousands of bound and prostrate women subjected to fantasy rape and torture. In this cultural ecology of repetitive visual cuing and masturbatory conditioning of their angry fantasies of revenge, they were in a state of mimetic compulsion, humming like a tuning fork, in harmony with the world of disorder and chaos that began descending on them by the mid-1960s. All deeply held values and authority were thrown open to question, presidents were caught lying, and old-school propriety and decency went out the window. The boundaries between the sacred and the profane, between love and lust, between good and evil, were smashed and scrambled in total hedonistic social breakdown, a perfect storm of repressed madness infecting an already sick and seeping wound, a fever in which these incipient dark fantasies were increasingly coming to reality in secret pulp-adventure dungeons of their own making. And because these misogynistic rape-and-torture magazines were sold next to *Better Homes and Gardens* and *Toy Train Hobbyist*, the message was, a desire to rape and torture is as mainstream as a desire to garden or collect toy trains.

Diabolus in cultura.

Following the war, forensic psychiatrists began routinely reporting among the characteristics of sexual murderers and serial killers their obsession with Nazis, concentration camp atrocities and photos of the naked, emaciated dead bodies their GI fathers had encountered when the death camps were liberated.[55]

When they arrested William Heirens, the "Lipstick Killer"—the first of the "golden age" serial killers—along with that stolen copy of *Psychopathia Sexualis*, police also found a scrapbook of Nazi officials. Ian Brady, who with his female partner, Myra Hindley, raped and murdered five victims between the ages of ten and seventeen from 1963 to 1965, was fixated on accounts and images of Nazi crimes. The necrophilic, grave-robbing Ed "Psycho" Gein murdered at least two women from 1954 to 1957 and made furniture of human bones and skin, including a chair upholstered in female breast skin with a visible nipple. He also rolled about in the grass under a full moon, his naked body clad in a female "skin suit" with breasts. He later confessed that he had gotten his ideas from images of Nazi and Japanese atrocities and tales of Pacific cannibalism and shrunken heads as portrayed in pulp adventure and true-detective magazines. (*Life* magazine published a series of photos of the squalid interior of Gein's house, cluttered with stacks of true-detective and adventure pulp magazines.)[56]

Thirty-year-old lonely mama's boy, TV repairman and amateur photographer Harvey Glatman was obsessed with true-detective magazine cover photos featuring bound women. Having already served time for kidnapping and raping a woman when he was eighteen, Glatman learned not to leave surviving witnesses. In 1957 in Los Angeles he began contacting models through their agencies or classifieds pretending to be a detective-magazine photographer. Glatman later described to police what happened when he successfully lured nineteen-year-old Judith Ann Dull to his apartment "photo studio" for what he claimed was a modeling assignment: "I told her that I wanted to take pictures that

would be suitable for illustrations for mystery stories or detective magazine stories of that type, and that this would require me to tie her hands
and feet and put a gag in her mouth and she was agreeable to this, and
I did tie her hands and feet and put a gag in her mouth and I took a
number of pictures."

Once she was bound and pinned in a pose matching his magazine-
cover fantasy, he "stepped into it" and raped and murdered her, photo-
graphing the process along the way, creating his own set of custom-made
true-detective magazine images to satisfy his obsession.[57] Glatman photographed, raped and murdered three women this way before a fourth
victim escaped and alerted police. Glatman is also suspected in a fourth
homicide committed earlier in Colorado, the victim of which was identified only in 2009 through DNA testing.[58] Glatman is among the earliest of the many serial killers who would later record their murders on
film, audiotape or videotape in order to relive them again and again.

From 1957 to 1959, the Nietzsche-steeped, pill-popping jazz musician Melvin "Sex Beast" Rees forayed from a cinder-block shack in the
woods papered in sadistic pornographic images to force cars off Virginia and Maryland country roads, dragging away the female passen-
gers, whom he would rape, torture and kill. He killed nine victims. In
one case, after kidnapping a mother and her daughter and raping and
killing them, he wrote in his personal journal, "Now the daughter and
mother are all mine."[59]

John Joubert, the "Nebraska Boy Snatcher," who murdered three
young boys from 1982 to 1983, stated that when he was eleven or twelve
he had seen true-detective magazines in the local grocery store and become aroused by the depiction of bound women on the covers. He began acquiring these magazines and masturbating to the images, eventually
superimposing the fantasy of bound young boys over the images of the
women. While a facilitator, detective magazines or porn on its own does
not make people into serial killers. Joubert stated that when he was six
or seven, at least six years *before* he saw his first detective magazine, he
fantasized about strangling and eating his babysitter. He could not recall
whether these images brought on the masturbation or the masturbation
brought on the fantasies.[60]

Serial killer Dennis Rader, the "BTK Killer," in his recent interviews with forensic psychologist Katherine Ramsland, described to her his adolescent obsession with illustrations of bound women. Rader said, "I was soon addicted to them and was always looking for 'strung-up' models in distress."

Rader described fantasizing about attacking women: "she became a *True Detective* Horror Magazine' hit and fantasy. Her bedroom appeared to be in the center east. I was planning on tying her up on the bed, either half naked or totally. Then I would either strangle her or suffocate her. Her hands would be bound in front and tied to her neck—like a *True Detective Magazine* model I had seen. I used to fantasize about women on the cover, showing terror in their eyes, bound hands up near her neck, a man with a threatening knife overhead."

Rader said, "I quit buying detective magazines when they dropped the B/D women from the covers. I still read books about serial killers if they related to the style I was into. I always cut photos out of ads from places like Dillard's and J. C. Penney's."[61]

So some serial killers are as easily inspired by J. C. Penney catalogs as by sadistic imagery and literature.

Or by the Bible.

In 1959 German lust killer Heinrich Pommerenke committed four mutilation murders after watching the movie *The Ten Commandments*. John Haigh, the British "Acid Bath Killer," was raised in an ultra-Christian cult known as the Plymouth Brethren, and while suffering from religious nightmares, he loved to quote and debate passages from scripture between his murders. A serial killer in Glasgow known as "Bible John" would quote scripture as he murdered women he lured from dance halls. In 1911 an unidentified serial killer who slaughtered a family of five in Texas left behind a note at the scene quoting Psalm 9:5: "When He maketh the Inquisition for Blood, He forgetteth not the cry of the humble."

John Wayne Gacy, as he raped and strangled his male teen victims, reportedly recited Psalm 23: "Even though I walk through the valley of the shadow of death, I will fear no evil . . ."

Albert Fish, who described his cannibal murder of Grace Budd as an act of "Holy Communion," would frequently quote Jeremiah 19:9:

And I will cause them to eat the flesh of their sons and the flesh of
their daughters, and they shall eat every one the flesh of his friend
in the siege and straitness, wherewith their enemies, and they that
seek their lives, shall straiten them.

The Pentecostal-raised necrophile serial killer Earle Nelson quoted
from a well-thumbed Bible he carried as he murdered twenty-two land-
ladies and raped them postmortem. Nelson's favorite passage was from
the book of Revelation:

So he carried me away in the spirit into the wilderness: and I saw a
woman sit upon a scarlet-colored beast, full of names of blasphemy,
having seven heads and ten horns. And the woman was arrayed in
purple and scarlet color, and decked with gold and precious stones
and pearls, having a gold cup in her hand full of abominations and
filthiness of her fornication: and upon her forehead was a name written, Mystery, Babylon the Great, The Mother of Harlots and Abominations of the Earth. And I saw the woman drunken with the blood
of the saints, and with the blood of the martyrs of Jesus.[62]

Misogynistic literature, myths and religious tracts and illustrations
existed long before even Heinrich Kramer's 1486 *Malleus Maleficarum*
accused women of sexual liaisons with the Devil. Pulp magazines alone,
no more than the war alone, or pornography or the Bible alone, made
the serial-killer epidemic. The "sweats" were a mirror of things already
infecting society. The proliferation of lurid images of bound, victimized
women began creeping onto the covers of mainstream detective magazines in America back in the 1920s and 1930s, soon after women had
gained the vote, entered the male domain of the factory floor during
World War I and partied elbow to elbow in speakeasies.

The misogynistic fear of independently mobile and unsupervised
women was the same fear and anger reflected in the tale of Little Red
Riding Hood, in the Victorian rape pornography on the eve of Jack the
Ripper and in the increased targeting of young, single servant girls and
prostitutes in the nineteenth century described in previous chapters.
Combine the Great Depression that destroyed hundreds of thousands of

families, the horrors of the most murderous war in history, the Cold War fear of nuclear annihilation in the 1950s, the destruction of thriving minority communities in urban "renewal," the breakdown of traditional old-world patriarchal values in the 1960s, America's first defeat in a war (in Vietnam) and a growing mass of the dispossessed class of the "less-dead" to victimize, and you have certain children who "turned" like infected zombies into serial killers as they approached their late twenties in the 1970s to the 1990s.

While indeed these magazines and images did not "make" serial killers, they did reflect a collective misogynistic cultural imperative which normalized the fantasy of abducting, raping, torturing and killing women. The widespread availability of these magazines was a touchstone to a dark, reptilian fantasy subculture, the foundation to a serial-killing ecology. These totems facilitated and shaped the fantasies of a very small minority (a few thousand) of dangerously damaged males who felt compelled to act them out under the pressures of a variety of disruptive and traumatic historical and social forces along with their own personal experiences.

Economic ruin in the 1930s and total war in the 1940s crippled a generation of fathers and together sowed the seeds for a popular adventure-detective magazine rape culture of pathological, vengeful and highly misogynistic aggression that matured to plague our society in very real ways by the 1960s: the *diabolus in cultura* behind the serial-killer epidemic.

As necrophile serial killer Edmund Kemper summed it all up, "I am an American and I killed Americans. I am a human being, and I killed human beings; and I did it in my society."

Or to paraphrase that famous quote from Pogo: we have met the serial killer and he is us.

CONCLUSION

Pogo Syndrome: Thinking Herds of Crazies in the Twilight of the Golden Age of Serial Killers

People like me don't come from films. Films come from people like me.

—CANNIBAL DAVID HARKER, 1998

These children that come at you with knives, they are *your* children. *You* taught them.

—CHARLIE MANSON

In a 2011 article in *Slate* magazine entitled "Blood Loss: The Decline of the Serial Killer," Christopher Beam quoted historical true-crime author Harold Schechter as saying, "It does seem the golden age of serial murderers is probably past."[1] What Schechter meant tongue in cheek is that there is no longer a wide-eyed, "breaking news" fascination with serial killers today, in the way there once was in the 1980s and 1990s. While in the past there was intense news coverage of cases of serial murder like Jack the Ripper and the surges in early-twentieth-century America, each case was reported as an individual and rare aberration of multiple murder. There was no unifying concept of "serial killers" as a unique, identifiable phenomenon. Today, while serial killers, especially fictional, are still a staple in popular entertainment, we are less impressed by or concerned about actual serial killers. As Eric Hickey concludes, "Between 2000 and 2014 serial killers have emerged more slowly and

quietly. In fact, over the past 15 years there has been a dearth of head-
line-grabbing killers like the Dahmers, Gacys, Kempers, Raders . . .
Many serial killers have emerged in recent years who receive little media
attention. Part of the reason is that most of the new cases do not carry
the social drama, social class, or high body counts to be of serious public interest."[2]

These are strange times, these first two decades of the twenty-first
century. The 2000s perhaps are as different and transformational from
the 1990s as the 1960s were from the 1950s. There is no doubt that 9/11
was an epoch-changing reboot of our state of the union in the same way
Pearl Harbor was in 1941 and the JFK assassination in 1963. Our 1980s
visceral collective fear of serial killers and child abductors has been supplanted by a new fear of terrorists since 9/11.

Serial killers always were, and still are today, a statistically rare phenomenon. And then on top of that, overall homicide rates in the US,
which have always underpinned serial murder, have plummeted dramatically from a historic high of 24,760 homicides in 1993 down to a record
low of 13,472 by 2014.[3]

By 2014 the raw statistics indeed looked promising and optimistic
until that twenty-year decline in the national murder rate turned the
other way in 2015, rising to 15,696[4] (adjusted to 15,181 subsequently).
The FBI's preliminary Uniform Crime Report (UCR) for 2016, released
in September 2017, indicates 16,459 murders, an 8.4 percent increase
nationally over 2015. The most dramatic surge in murder was in cities
with over a million inhabitants, where murders soared 20.3 percent.[5]

The party might be over.

Yet despite the recent surge, we need to believe that the murder rate
will never return to the extraordinary 1993 level, if the technohumanitarian balance hypothesis (chapter two) is correct. We can *hope*. Hope
that the world makes sense and *must* as a rule of natural law become
progressively less violent, albeit in surges and waves, and that this
twenty-year-long decrease in murders has swept away many serial killers with it into the trash bin of human history. Hope is perhaps that one
new natural survival instinct that humans have been uniquely endowed
with to transcend all the necessities of the primitive survivalist four Fs.
That as a "thinking herd of crazies" species that dominates the earth, we

must become a gentler species *if* we are to survive: because there is no enemy left threatening our existence, other than us.

There are other signs of a decline in serial murder. A recent study identified "only" 63 serial-killer apprehensions in the US from 1997 to 2007, although these 63 serial murderers were responsible for a yearly average of 75 victims over that ten-year span—hardly the "thousands" some claimed, but still an unsettling number of victims. (Of these 63 serial killers, 19 had been killing unimpeded for more than 10 years and 8 for more than 15 years before being apprehended.)[6]

The Radford/FGCU Serial Killer Database also indicates that there has been a significant drop in the number of new serial killers appearing in the 2000s, from the 614 in the 1990s down to 337 in the 2000s, and currently 93 so far in the 2010s.[7] If somehow this new era represents the end of a "golden age" of serial killers, then few will lament it.

Eric Hickey has a different take from his sets of serial-killer data. While an all-time high of 234 serial-killer cases reported in his database occurred in the 34 years between 1970 and 2004, a total of 270 new cases emerged in just the recent 14 years between 2000 and 2014. Hickey states, "We have more cases of serial killers in fourteen years than we did in the previous twenty-five years [1975–2000]."[8]

Hickey believes that this rise in his statistical data is accounted for by our new definition of the term "serial killer," following the San Antonio Symposium of 2005, as anyone who kills two or more victims in separate events for any reason. But at the same time, Hickey emphasizes that "*What we do know for certain is that the modern-day serial killer as portrayed in the media had declined significantly.*"[9]

Hickey has also identified another declining serial-murder statistic: the average number of victims. From 1970 to 1980, the average hovered around 10 to 13 victims per serial killer. Today the number has declined significantly to 3 to 4 victims on average, and there have not been any recent cases in the United States of "big-number" serial killers of the scale of Ted Bundy, John Wayne Gacy or Gary Ridgway.[10]

The frequency of serial killers will always vary depending upon how we define them. If we define as serial killers the "werewolves" and gyno-cidal functionaries who raped, tortured and killed women accused of witchcraft, then we had more serial killers in 1450–1650 than we have today. Thousands of Nazi paramilitary murderers, who criminally killed millions of victims during the Holocaust in separate events with cooling-off periods in between, would mean we had more serial killers and victims in the 1940s than in the 1980s, according to the new FBI definition. Serial killers were, are and will be what we define them to be, under the prerogatives of history, politics, society, psychology, criminology, commerce, public order, power and natural evolution, which are constantly changing and shifting beneath our feet, like tectonic plates that sometimes catch on one another in that elusive historic synchronicity, and release earthquakelike shock waves in the form of serial-killing surges in their many forms.

Even if the emergence of new serial-killer cases appears to be slowing down, murders by "relationship unknown" perpetrators combined with "murder by stranger" have steadily continued to creep up. They were just over 50 percent at the height of the murder rate in the 1990s. That number increased to 58 percent by 2015. This is disconcerting, although one should not overemphasize the significance of the "relationship unknown" segment, as it indicates only that police have not conclusively determined the relationship between the victim and perpetrator—not that the perpetrator was necessarily a stranger to the victim.[11] (It was misinterpretation of the "relationship unknown" statistic that contributed to the "serial-killer epidemic" panic in the 1980s and the exaggerated claims of thousands of serial-murder victims a year.[12])

Nonetheless, at least some of the homicides in the "relationship unknown" category can be linked to currently unidentified serial killers on the loose, like the "Long Island Serial Killer" LISK (also known as the "Gilgo Beach Killer" or the "Craigslist Ripper") suspected in as many as thirteen recent murders; the "Bone Collector" linked to eleven female victims found buried together in West Mesa, New Mexico; the "Seven Bridges Road Killer" in North Carolina linked to the murder of eleven African-American prostitutes; the "Jeff Davis 8 Killer" in Jennings, Jefferson Davis Parish, Louisiana, suspected in eight murders; the "Daytona Beach Killer" in Florida with four murders; the "February 9 Killer," who has killed at least two women in Salt Lake City on the same date in different years; and the "Eastbound Strangler Foot-Fetish Killer" near Atlantic City, who left his four strangled female victims carefully posed facing east, stripped of their shoes and socks, and who some suspect might be the same person as the Long Island serial killer. At this writing, there is a cluster of women reported missing and found murdered in the small town of Lumberton, North Carolina, that could be the work of a local serial killer.

A 450-mile stretch of highway in British Columbia, Canada, has been dubbed the "Highway of Tears" for the number of unsolved murders of women that have taken place on it. Police officially list nineteen victims, of whom thirteen were teenagers and ten were Indigenous women, although activists list as many as forty murders.[13] So far, only one murder has been solved, attributed to serial killer Cody Legebokoff.

The ditches and roadsides of the American interstate freeway system alone have been the scene of almost five hundred unsolved homicides over the last thirty years, and at least twenty-five truckers have been convicted in serial-homicide cases. In 2009 the FBI launched a special Highway Serial Killings Initiative (HSKI) targeting serial killers suspected to be working as truckers.[14] While the majority of truckers are hardworking, decent people, the lonely anonymity of a trucker's life and constant mobility are conducive to the personality of serial killers.

EXPLAINING THE APPARENT DECLINE IN THE NUMBER OF SERIAL KILLERS

In his blog, serial-homicide researcher Enzo Yaksic, recently nicknamed "Profiler 2.0" by *Boston* magazine, offers a persuasive menu of reasons why serial killing might be in decline for good, rather than just following the decline of overall murder rates. The reasons run the gamut from social, technological and forensic to psychological, cultural and historical.[15]

Technological-Social

Since the 1990s, the ubiquitous use of cell phones has not only added some margin of safety for potential victims but has also made the tracking of suspected serial killers' movements substantially easier for police.

Today police routinely track cell-tower pings on a suspect's cell phone account, easily disassembling any false alibi. Obviously an intelligent, highly organized serial killer will adopt countermeasures or use an anonymous "burner" cell phone, but not all serial killers are organized or even know that they are going to kill again, until they kill again. Some kill targets of opportunity spontaneously, without planning.

The ubiquitous presence of surveillance cameras can capture the movements of a suspect. Surveillance cameras can even routinely record a suspect's movements before the suspect has decided to perpetrate a murder. There are no countermeasures for something you do not know you are going to do.

While social media can expose users to targeting by strangers, it mostly focuses users into personal networks in which interaction with strangers is restricted and where strangers can be screened before any interaction is initiated. Furthermore, cell phones, the Internet and video games have reduced the number of vulnerable children and adolescents playing outdoors unsupervised. Potential offenders are also exposed through their own posts on social media, and there have been cases of terrorism and mass murder being prevented when the would-be perpetrators were apprehended before they committed their acts because they posted their intentions on social media.

Cell phone, text and social media transactions assist police in identifying and understanding relationships and contacts between suspects and victims, so essential to any homicide investigation. Erasing these records locally on a cell phone or computer changes nothing, as service providers store this data on their remote servers. An attorney defending a client accused of serial murder complained to me that it has become impossible for him to match the resources available to police to "vacuum up" enormous volumes of cell phone, text and Internet data. To analyze the massive amounts of highly technical data and develop a defense to police interpretations of what it means is impossible for the average defendant.

Beyond the resources of law enforcement, true-crime "as it happens" reality TV and social media "cloud sourcing" allow for the dissemination of information about serial-murder cases and invite the public to contribute to the investigation of a case. While much of the information and speculation is useless or amateurish, police can sometimes cherry-pick valuable leads from the mass of "noise." For example, recently in the case of the LISK murders, the true-crime online forum Websleuths and the A&E series *The Killing Season* led to a significant identification of a LISK victim's remains that police had overlooked in their own investigation[16] (or at least did not disclose to the public). In the same way that amateur astronomical observers contribute to the detection of stellar phenomena in "cloud-sourced astronomy," police can tap into similar "cloud investigative analysis" contributed by amateurs and filter the signal from the noise. As one police officer said to me recently, "In a homicide investigation, there is no such thing as 'too much information.'"

Forensic Advances

Law enforcement is more experienced and better equipped now to deal with pathological serial murder than it was thirty-five years ago when the term "serial killer" did not even exist in the popular vocabulary or imagination. When the FBI first devised their profiling system in the 1980s, they based it on data gathered from only twenty-nine convicted serial killers and seven solo sexual murderers. It was criticized for not having a large enough data sample to make conclusions. The FBI's most recent study, from 2014, is based on 480 cases of sexual serial murder involving 92 male offenders.[17] (Unfortunately, the FBI has kept the raw data and the identities of the serial killers inaccessible to serial-homicide researchers outside the agency.)

The pathology of serial killers has become so familiar to investigators that often "serial killers" can be apprehended after one or two murders, cutting short their future "careers" and notoriety. As researchers Enzo Yaksic, Lindsey DeSpirito and Sasha Reid observe,

> Terms such as "budding," "potential," "becoming," "obsessed," "in-training" and "possible" are often used in conjunction with the phrase "serial murderer" to describe offenders that either admit to maintaining serial "tendencies" or outwardly display a desire to murder additional people upon capture for their first attempted or completed offense.[18]

The introduction of forensic DNA technology, unavailable for much of the "golden age" epidemic period, was a huge game changer and continues to be so. Currently the controversial technique of gathering familial DNA from a suspect's relatives to link that suspect to a crime has been on the leading edge of a new investigative strategy. It's especially useful in closing cold cases where the suspect might be long dead. Opponents argue that it subjects innocent family members to an unconstitutional search if done without their permission.

Geoforensic profiling, as described in chapter ten, is continually becoming more accurate, able to pinpoint a suspect to a 150-square-yard "anchor" with increasing efficiency. Brain-scanning technology is promising a new generation of lie-detecting polygraphs that can detect which part of the brain a suspect is using during an investigative interview, the "memory" part or the "storytelling imaginative" part.

Databases like ViCAP and communication nets, although still not perfect, have reduced some of the linkage blindness that in the past prevented serial murders from being recognized as such. Linkage blindness has been reduced even among murders committed in different parts of the country.

Police investigators are today better versed and better educated in interview techniques with suspects in pathological crimes and are better trained in how to manage interviews with a deceptively unfeeling psychopath. And of course, police in general have become more open at the initial stages of an investigation to considering the possibility of a serial killer than they had been in the 1980s when such offenders were perceived to be extremely rare and exotic. That too can contribute to an early arrest in a serial-homicide case. Furthermore, some police departments, especially at the state level, have employed criminal analysts to crunch data essential in identifying serial crimes, and have selected officers for supplementary training or graduate degrees in psychopathology or psychological and geographic profiling.

Cultural-Psychological

While light-years from a mission completed, American males since the 1960s have been continually socialized, cultured and sensitized to women's rights and issues. The sadistic rape magazine covers I described, still viable and mainstream as late as the 1970s, would be unthinkable from the 1990s onward anywhere other than on the Internet.

Misogyny still lives on in the more reptilian recesses of college-aged male brains, which still apparently fantasize about rape if "they can get away with it."[19] Misogynist commentary has spewed forth from a presidential candidate on an *Access Hollywood* "hot mic," but it has become significantly less excused or dismissed or joked off than it was, say, twenty or thirty years ago. (But not enough to change the electoral result in this case.)

Psychologically too, people are less repressed regarding unconventional sexual impulses that were once considered evil or sick or shameful. There is less impetus to act out these impulses secretly with the use of force and killing. Jerry Brudos's fetish for women's shoes would be less likely today to shame him sufficiently to kill women for it. The trauma and angst resulting from a single act of college-student oral sex that Philip Roth describes in his book *Indignation*, set in 1951, would have been inconceivable twenty years later, in 1971.

As I described in chapter three, psychiatry has destigmatized and delisted "happy paraphilics" whose compulsions do not lead them to hurt themselves or others. Culture today is pervasively more tolerant, more live-and-let-live and inclusive and less repressive and judgmental, allowing people to be more accepting not only of others but, more importantly, of themselves. This permissiveness increases the chance for sexual paraphilics to find willing partners with a compatibility of paraphilias, and the Internet further enhances their ability to find one another (although the Internet, of course, also enhances the ability of a deceptive serial killer to troll, stalk and trap victims).[20]

Yes, I know I am writing in a new political age, which is testing the limits of progressive and inclusive thought in America, and there are vast holdouts of bigotry, racism and sexism, but since the 1960s, despite the clamor of the "Moral Majority," they have been steadily losing ground. There is less trauma, shame and loneliness today in being different from one's peers, and therefore less need for fantasies of vengeance and control that sometimes are expressed in serial killing.

Nor is a serial killer today the rebel "antihero" he once was at the

height of the "golden age," and serial killing is no longer an easy ticket
to celebrity in the way it had been up until the 1990s. Transgressive, rebellious, pathological antiheroics today are more likely to be expressed
as suicidal episodes of mass murder and, more recently, as acts of self-
radicalized terrorism, the new career path for the lonely, isolated and
once-bullied misfit.

Moreover, mental health institutions, no matter how underfunded
and despite horror stories of having overlooked potentially dangerous
subjects, are generally better equipped and better educated to recognize
symptoms of budding violent serial offenders.

Availability of Pornographic Media

There is still no agreement as to whether pornography stimulates, shapes
and facilitates transgressive behavior or acts as a "safety valve" alternative to acting out a fantasy. Since the 1990s pornography has become
more easily available on the Internet and often for free. Its range of paraphilic specificity is also significantly expanded on the Internet. Online
porn can economically sustain a broader selection of specific and narrow paraphilic genres than brick-and-mortar retail-store porn. Moreover, those compelled to consume pornography, often a compulsion
bred in shame, no longer need to risk going out in public to storefronts
to acquire it. It is discreetly and conveniently available via the Internet.

A study of the sex crime statistics in four countries—the United
States, Denmark, Sweden and West Germany—during the twenty-year
period from 1964 to 1984, when there was a significant growth in the
availability of pornography "from extreme scarcity to relative abun-
dance," including violent pornography, found that there was no increase
in sexual offenses at any rates higher than increases in nonsexual violent crimes, and in some cases, there were actual declines in sexual offenses.[21] A more recent study, from 2009, concludes, "Evidence for a
causal relationship between exposure to pornography and sexual aggression is slim and may, at certain times, have been exaggerated by
politicians, pressure groups and some social scientists. Some of the debate has focused on violent pornography, but evidence of any negative

effects is inconsistent . . . Victimization rates for rape in the United States demonstrate an inverse relationship between pornography consumption and rape rates. Data from other nations have suggested similar relationships . . . it is time to discard the hypothesis that pornography contributes to increased sexual assault behavior."[22]

Typically, there are recent studies which argue the opposite: "Exposure to pornography helps to sustain young people's adherence to sexist and unhealthy notions of sex and relationships. And, especially among boys and young men who are frequent consumers of pornography, including of more violent materials, consumption intensifies attitudes supportive of sexual coercion and increases their likelihood of perpetrating assault."[23]

It should be pointed out that the mainstream rape imagery in American men's adventure and true-detective magazines described in the previous chapter was not pornographic.

It was something much worse.

The rape was *implicit* in the imagery, not explicit. It called upon the observer to complete the fantasy in his imagination, in the advanced cerebral cortex sitting atop his reptilian male brain. It worked on a different part of the brain than explicit imagery does. Moreover, in the 1950s to the 1980s, it was endorsed by mainstream consumer culture because it was sold everywhere from grocery stores to newsstands.

Today there is a copious amount of explicit rape pornography and even a small number of available videos made by serial killers and wannabe serial killers recording their murders. It does not titillate the viewer or beckon him to contemplate the fantasy in his head in the way the adventure magazine covers did. Instead it hammers one in the face with its ugliness and brutality. While implicit rape imagery stimulates the unfulfilled fantasy part of the male brain, the explicit imagery fulfills the perceptual part and might work in a different way.

One might argue that explicit fantasy rape and bondage porn or reality snuff porn preempt the fantasy in the same way serial killers often report being disappointed or depressed by the actualization of a fantasy they long held. The reality is never as appealing or as controllable as the fantasy, serial killers often complain, and their addiction to killing, until some burn out, is rooted in their repeatedly attempting to shorten the time between their fantasy and its attempted realization. Others will argue, however, that viewing ultraviolent porn desensitizes perpetrators and stimulates them to escalate in their compulsive fantasies from porn to reality.

The consumer grocery-store bondage magazines vanished in the 1980s and 1990s, destroyed not so much by changing values and social consciousness as by the economic challenges of publishing a monthly hard-copy magazine in the face of the Internet. Twenty years later, some statistics suggest that the number of cases of serial homicides has declined. The chicken or the egg?

Yes, sadistic content has been moved from the grocery store to the Internet, where it is much more readily available in much more horrifically explicit genres. What changed perhaps is that unlike when the sadistic grocery-store-and-barbershop torture-rape "sweats" were distributed and consumed *on par* with *Time* magazine and *Sports Illustrated*, today that material is "penned in" on the Internet unambiguously as a vice. Moreover, it needs to be proactively sought out, in an adult sector of the Internet, a place understood as what it is, rather than stumbled across in a barbershop among the fish-and-game magazines.

Despite numerous anecdotal instances of violent or pornographic material inspiring viewers to act out, unfortunately to this day we have still not determined the exact relationship between such viewing and acting out, and whether it defuses and preempts sexual aggression or facilitates and inspires it. We just don't know.

Serial Killers Are Better at Getting Away with It

There might be one fly in the ointment: maybe there are fewer cases of serial murder on the record simply because serial killers are better at concealing their crimes now. Many serial killers, especially organized ones, have always been aware of investigative techniques and what police look for. As advances in investigative forensics begin to plateau, serial killers adopt countermeasures that have a longer effective life span. Serial killers who read up on geoforensic profiling, for example, might adopt counterintuitive patterns of movement and selection of crime sites and body dumps to counteract detectable predatory behavioral links.

Serial killers with highlighter pens in hand carefully read and study FBI manuals, academic articles and highly specialized forensic literature on the psychology, pathology and investigation of serial homicide. For pleasure, they read popular true-crime accounts of serial murder. Serial killing is both a compulsion and a learning process.

Dennis Rader, the "BTK Killer," ran out and bought my first book on the history of serial killers almost as soon as it came out in October 2004. When Rader was arrested five months later in February 2005, he already had the book covered in a rainbow of sticky-notes.[24] As homicide specialist Vernon J. Geberth points out, "We are not the only people watching *Forensic Files*, *CSI*, *The New Detectives*, the Discovery Channel, and all of the other programs devoted to criminal investigation."[25]

A new generation of serial killers might be not only more educated and skilled at avoiding apprehension, but more aware of what they are, less confused and conflicted about it, now that the term "serial killer" has been given to us and they grew up with it like TV's Dexter did. Maybe serial killers are hiding as "happy paraphilics" in today's permissive culture of psychiatry.

While some argue that law enforcement has become better at confronting serial homicide, others argue the opposite, that today law enforcement is underfunded, assigns low priority to cases involving inner-city "less-dead" victims and is primarily focused, especially so in the Federal sector, on the threat of terrorism.

CONCLUSION: THE POGO SYNDROME

When we ask why some children become serial killers, we are asking the wrong question. We should be asking why children don't become serial killers more often.

Considering the way Mother Nature equipped us to evolve, I might argue most of us—at least the males—are naturally born serial killers and are "unmade," or socialized away from our instincts, by the necessary evolutionary techno-humanitarian balance impulse. As the Big Historians say, humans are a "thinking herd of crazies."[26]

The crazy part comes out in that circular self-referential process, the dark mimetic compulsion, in which emerging pathological killers, including serial killers, fantasize about and mimic not only the reality of one another's previous murders, but the cultural and entertainment-industry fantasy treatments of that reality, reflected back at them in a wilderness of media mirrors.

Cannibal killer David Harker, who in 1998 murdered a woman, decapitated and dismembered her and cooked and ate parts of her body with pasta and cheese, was asked by a psychiatrist whether he was inspired by the fictional serial killer Hannibal "the Cannibal" Lecter in the film *The Silence of the Lambs.*

Harker replied, "People like me don't come from films. Films come from people like me."[27]

It's the Pogo syndrome: the enemy is us. We as an organized species unleash serial killers on ourselves.

Probably the best analogy for the notion of the serial-killing historical-cultural ecology I am attempting to describe is our current crisis of self-radicalization in terrorism. Twenty years ago the notion that young Americans or even recent immigrants to New York, Detroit, Los Angeles, Miami or Boston would choose to perpetrate mass murder in the name of an overseas non-Christian radical religious agenda would have been unthinkable. The existence of jihadi terrorist groups, the Internet, radical Islamic propaganda, foreign military intervention, alienation and marginalization at home, mental illness and the easy availability of firearms—each of these elements on their own did not create the current phenomenon of self-radicalizing terrorists plaguing Western societies. It was only when a perfect storm of these things combined with a kind of historical dark energy of synchronicity, a *diabolus in cultura,* that these surges hit civilized societies.

These self-radicalized, mass-killing terrorists today come from the same place that rampaging postal workers came from in the 1980s (35 people were killed in 11 post office shootings between 1983 and 1993),[28] the same place the bullied 1999 Columbine massacre perpetrators Eric Harris and Dylan Klebold came from.

If they were around today, Harris and Klebold, instead of bullied loser pseudo-Goths, would be bullied loser pseudo-self-radicalized Islamic converts to ISIS. They would be dressed for it too. Our rising new breed of mass-killing zombies are basically impatient wannabe serial killers, greedily trying to get it all done in one big blowout without the patience to serially kill one victim at a time.

The same with serial killers, who in a sense are self-radicalized, evolutionarily pathological social terrorists, feeding on their own personal unhappiness and traumas and on the vulnerability and marginalization of their victims in a climate that glorifies and hails them as counterculture monster celebrities and their violence and sexual assault as staples of the entertainment industry and cultural expressions of masculine prowess and strength.

Count the kids today who are lapping all that up like kittens warm milk, and twenty years later you'd better duck and cover.

From the time of Jack the Ripper to that of Jeffrey Dahmer, an enormous body of true-crime literature, theater, movies and television created a complex and vast serial-killing genre that serial killers are drawn to, and sometimes mimic and learn from. But serial killers are not the primary consumers of this genre—it would not be financially viable if only serial killers consumed this form of entertainment media. A vast population of nonhomicidal consumers like you and me testifies to the draw of these dark narratives and their meaning. They are the true tales of horror as familiar as the Brothers Grimm.

Go figure why *you* are reading this book all the way to the end here, but you are, and that is why I felt the compulsion to write it.

Maybe for those of us who are not killers, Plato said it all 2,350 years ago when he commented on "the pleasures mixed with pains, which we find in mournings and longings" in Greek tragic theater. It's why people slow down by a crime scene or a roadside accident, a kind of primitive conditioning to a profanely lustful "Thank God it was not me" or a more sacredly loving "There but for the grace of God go I."

We love and we kill with a paraphilic dichotomy of the sacrificial sacred and selfish profane; it dogs the human condition in the Western world.

There is a troubling, foretelling, mirrorlike synchronicity, the *diabolus in cultura*, in the rise of werewolf killers, the emerging divisions among the elites of Western European society during the Great Witch Hunt of 1450 to 1650 and the religious wars; in the chaos and dispossession of generations of humans in the industrial revolution when serial killers like Martin Dumollard and Jack the Ripper made their presence felt; in the hedonistic affluence and greed of the 1920s, the social devastation that followed in the Great Depression of the 1930s, the brutality of the war our forefathers were called upon to fight in the 1940s, and the repressed grasp at an illusion of "normalcy" in the 1950s, followed by transcendent revolutionary cultural and political transformation in the 1960s, along with a rebirth of hedonism and in its wake, in the 1970s and 1980s, a viral surge of serial murder: the golden age of serial killers.

Looking back from the second decade of the new millennium, I see trailing behind us like smoke from a burning engine the renewed greed and exponential affluence of the post–Cold War "normalcy" of the New World Order in the 1990s, the shock and awe of 9/11, the social devastation of the 2008 financial meltdown and the brutality of the new enemy that not only American fathers, but mothers too now, have been called to fight in the still-ongoing catastrophic War on Terror, that apocalyptic "clash of civilizations" prophesied by Samuel P. Huntington back in 1993.[29] History really does repeat itself, but not in the way Karl Marx claimed, "first as tragedy and then as farce." No, it repeats itself with the same thing: our failure to imagine just how bad everything is going to get and how fucking fast. About as fast as the American body politic has suddenly become precariously divisive, not only among its people but dangerously among its elites too. About as fast as we are contemplating perhaps having to incinerate the people of North Korea, perhaps by the time this book comes out.

Where and how soon do we crash-land? If history has taught us anything, things can get a lot worse than they already are. I worry about what our recent generation of warriors brought home to the children they are raising in a newly traumatized and so divided Western world today. If my World War II + 20 years hypothesis has any validity for the killing surge from 1970 to 1990, considering our recent history, we may easily be facing another viral pandemic of serial killing unless we raise our children better now.

During his murder trial in 1970, Charlie Manson said, "These children that come at you with knives, they are *your* children. *You* taught them. I didn't teach them. I just tried to help them stand up."

Manson of course had a way of taking the truth and turning it into a lie, as somebody once said. Manson didn't help anybody to "stand up" other than to stand up as vicious cult killers. But just the same, his statement is probably the best summary of the forces behind the perfect storms of serial-killer surges, and it came from Manson, somebody who *really* knew about raising children to kill, not from some ivory-tower bookworm like me.

That elusive X-factor standing between us and serial killers of the future is teaching children and helping them to stand up. That's a truth.

We must care for the children *today*, before they come at us tomorrow with knives.

Because the monsters are us, and we need to stop or be stopped.

AFTERWORD

"Serial Killers Need Hugs Too"

My life as an author and a historian was defined in some ways by my brief random encounter with serial killer Richard Cottingham in New York in 1979, when I was twenty-three years old. For the next twenty-five years, I continued to work in film and television, never touching on the subject of serial killers, but I kept abreast of recent developments and cases in serial homicide out of personal interest. Much changed over those years, from the coining of the term "serial killer" to the emergence of serial killers and behavioral profilers in popular culture.

In wasn't until 1998, when I was in my early forties, that I finally tried my hand at writing a book about the history of serial homicide. *Serial Killers: The Method and Madness of Monsters* was published in 2004, and I followed it up with *Female Serial Killers: How and Why Women Become Monsters* in 2007. Both books focused primarily on the history from Jack the Ripper onward.

After the two books came out, I went back to school and earned a PhD in history, and after that, I figured maybe I had one more book in me about serial killers, this time a broader chronicle going back to the early beginnings, long before Jack the Ripper, and encompassing recent developments since my first book came out.

I finished writing *Sons of Cain* in the spring of last year, and that summer my editor Tracy Bernstein sent me her edited version of my manuscript for a final look over and approval. I had a month to review it and make last-minute revisions, and then I would be forever done with Cottingham, serial killers and all the weird and twisted connections they entailed. Having gone as far back as the Stone Age, I was satisfied that there was nowhere left for me to go. I intended this to be my last book on the history of serial killers.

But John Lennon knew what he was talking about when he wrote, "Life is what happens to you while you are busy making other plans."[1]

Just as I was rereading the last pages of my manuscript, a text message dinged in from an unfamiliar number.

The sender introduced herself as Jennifer Weiss and she wanted urgently to talk to me about Richard Cottingham. I don't know if I would have responded had it been about any other serial killer, but this was about "my guy"—Richie.

We set up a FaceTime call.

Jennifer spoke with that familiar brash Jersey-girl accent and actually was a *real* housewife of New Jersey, raising four children in an affluent subdivision on a golf course in Princeton. On-screen, she had dark and smoky good looks that reminded me of Demi Moore in her late thirties, but with exotic almond-shaped eyes, about which there was something hauntingly familiar.

She told me she was the biological daughter of Deedeh Goodarzi, one of the victims that Cottingham had murdered and beheaded in the hotel room and whose head was in the bag he had bumped me with on his way out. Jennifer was the infant girl Deedeh had given up for adoption nineteen months prior to her murder, the girl whose fate I had occasionally wondered about all these decades.

I was struck by her remarkable resemblance to Deedeh, whose face I had seen so many times over the last thirty-eight years among the photos of Cottingham's victims. Of course the eyes were familiar. It was almost as if Deedeh herself had come calling on me.

Jennifer had been adopted as an infant by a couple in New Jersey who had three sons but wanted a daughter. She was four when her parents first explained to her that she had been adopted. Later, when she was an adolescent, they told her that her birth mother had been a prostitute who couldn't keep her, but they did not know her name, the circumstances, her story or her fate.

Despite being raised in a loving and supportive family, Jennifer began to lose her way after graduating high school. She had been rebellious; there were typical teenage sprees of delinquency. She dropped out of college after her first year and ended up working as an exotic dancer until she married, settled down and had children.

When Jennifer was twenty-six she decided to make a search for her adoption records in the hope of identifying and perhaps contacting and meeting her birth mother. To her dismay, she discovered the identity and circumstances of her mother's horrific death as one of Cottingham's murder victims. Such is the wreckage left behind by serial killers; you never know what might float to the surface.

In the ensuing years, Jennifer was primarily focused on being a wife and mother raising four daughters, but her birth mother's history and fate nagged at her. She eventually found Deedeh's father and reconstructed her mother's history from her Iranian roots (Deedeh had been mistakenly described in the media as Kuwaiti) to her arrival in the United States as a fourteen-year-old to her eventual life as a prostitute in New York, Florida, Nevada and California. Jennifer discovered from the adoption file that Deedeh had been forced to give her up for adoption by her African-American pimp and lover, who thought the baby's skin was "not dark enough" for her to be his child.

Jennifer felt mostly rage toward Cottingham for robbing her of an opportunity to meet her birth mother. She was also haunted by the specter of her mother's headless torso, buried in an anonymous mass grave among the more-than-one-million unwanted, abandoned or unidentified dead interred in New York City's historic potter's field on Hart Island, offshore of the Bronx, her mother's severed head and hands still secreted someplace elsewhere by her murderer, where perhaps they can still be found, recovered and reunited with the rest of her remains.

It was surviving an early onset of breast cancer that galvanized Jennifer to act upon her preoccupation with her birth mother's fate.

Incarcerated since 1980, Cottingham for decades had steadfastly refused to talk about his crimes, primarily in deference to his three children's opinion of him, until suddenly in 2009 he was persuaded by

Canadian author Nadia Fezzani to do an interview for French television on the condition that it would not be broadcast in the United States. (He was not familiar with the global reach of YouTube.)

Cottingham appeared in the documentary looking like Santa Claus, roly-poly with a huge white beard and long gray hair. He spoke with that familiar, friendly New Jersey accent and there was an underlying amiability and good-humored charm to him. It was precisely this friendly persona that had facilitated him in luring so many women to their horrific deaths at his hands.

After seeing Cottingham in the documentary on YouTube and hearing him say that he was willing to help families of his victims toward closure, Jennifer contacted him in April 2017 and introduced herself as the daughter of his victim Deedeh Goodarzi, taking him up on his offer.

Cottingham agreed to see her and she began visiting him twice a week in the New Jersey State Prison in Trenton, where he has so far served 37 years of his 191-year sentence. He is never coming out. During the visits Jennifer had been urging Richie, as he tells her to call him, to describe to her in detail how and why he killed her mother and Jane Doe and what he did with their heads and hands.

Cottingham is seventy-two and in a wheelchair now, overweight and in a state of rapidly declining health, and believes he has little time left to live. Raised in a strict Catholic family and educated at Catholic schools, Cottingham is contemplating confession as a path to some degree of redemption for everything he has done. Some self-reflective psychopaths by late middle age, as their testosterone levels decline, begin to shed their behavioral compulsions and obsessions, and perhaps that is why some serial killers, if they have not been identified and arrested over a long period, start to "retire" from their killing (like Dennis Rader and Gary Ridgway, for example). They remain incurably psychopaths, but either the compulsions that drove their behavior fade or they develop intellectually the will to resist them.

I suspect, in that same process, incarcerated serial killers like Cottingham may find themselves "awakening" from their compulsions, perhaps even finding a path to some rudimentary sense of remorse and regret for everything they have perpetrated, but only in an intellectual context. They will not be *feeling* remorse or regret; they will only have some intellectual understanding of how they *should* feel and behave. They will try to be that way, not because they *feel* they should be, but because they *know it*. That's the closest we get to an incarcerated psychopath serial killer "reforming." Cottingham might now be going through such a process. In 2010, he suddenly confessed to an earlier murder he had committed in Bergen County, New Jersey, in 1967, when he was only twenty-one years old. The victim, twenty-nine-year-old Nancy Schiava Vogel, with whom Cottingham was acquainted, had been a cold-case murder for forty-three years until he suddenly confessed.

The sight of Jennifer, who so much resembles his victim Deedeh, unnerved Cottingham after all these years. Moreover, as a former exotic dancer she exudes the same seductive persona that drew him to her mother and other victims like her, and now triggers memories of his "best of times" when he was young and free as a serial killer. Rejected by his own children, who do not visit him, the lonely and aging serial killer took to Jennifer's prison visits.

Gradually, Cottingham revealed to her that Deedeh was not a random prostitute he had picked up and lured to his room, but had been one of his "favorite girls" for several years. He described her as an "upscale escort" he had met in a downtown club in New York. This was an unknown element in the case. Apparently, he had specifically called her to come to New York from New Jersey when he booked a "sex weekend" at the hotel. Witnesses reported to police that Deedeh had left Trenton on the Friday prior to the weekend, the same day that Cottingham checked into the hotel. Cottingham then lured from the nearby neighborhood the second victim to the hotel room. Cottingham said he regretted killing Deedeh and blamed the inexperience of the unidentified teenage prostitute he had picked up, claiming that she was an "amateur" causing him to "go too far" and resulting in the deaths of both women. In that, he remains typically a serial killer; it's not his fault, but the victim's. In this case, one victim is held responsible for both her own and another victim's death.

We know that Cottingham was killing random women he picked up, while at the same time maintaining relationships with two mistresses in New York, all the while he had a wife in New Jersey. He also had a series of more casual girlfriends, "friends with benefits" and regular escorts he favored. Most of them survived his bouts of sadistic sex and torture;

however, sometimes he ended up killing the women, including those he knew, indeed "going too far" as he had put it. In addition to Deedeh, Cottingham had been acquainted with at least two of his other victims, Nancy Schiava Vogel and Maryann Carr, prior to their murders.

It wasn't necessarily that Cottingham set out to kill; killing was not his fantasy—torture was. He simply just couldn't care less whether his victims lived or died. Several of his victims were found dumped by roadsides or in parking lots, bruised, cut and battered and drugged into an unconscious state, but alive. Others were found in similar conditions, but dead. He would rape and torture until he was satisfied, and if the victim survived, then fine; if not, then fine too. Cottingham probably is not much help to police in closing many more cold cases because he does not know himself how many of his victims he left dead or alive. He never cared enough about it to know.

Between what we think was his first murder, in 1967, and his arrest in 1980, there could be hundreds of women who were lured, drugged, raped and tortured by Cottingham but never reported it, especially if they were prostitutes. And among them, several dozen in New York and New Jersey and elsewhere in the vicinity could have been murdered and remain cold cases to this day. For example, on August 9, 1974, seventeen-year-old Mary Ann Pryor and sixteen-year-old Lorraine Kelly vanished while on their way to a mall in Bergen County. Their bodies were found five days later. They had been tortured with a lit cigarette, raped and strangled. Cottingham has been long suspected in this double murder, but if he did it, he might not ever admit to it because of the young ages of the victims. It could potentially affect his status in prison, where fellow inmates might become hostile to somebody who killed teenage girls.

Cottingham's revelation that he knew Deedeh answers one of the questions forensic psychologists have been puzzling over for decades about this case. His beheading and mutilation of the two victims in the hotel was not his usual signature. This appeared to be the first time he perpetrated that level of mutilation. Was he escalating? Was it "pathological" or was the mutilation "functional," to conceal the victims' identities? The severing of the heads and hands (along with the fingerprints that came with them) pointed in the "functional" direction, but if he had picked the women up at random on the street, why bother concealing their identities? They could never be linked to him. But if indeed he knew Deedeh for several years as he claims, then it made sense to remove the head and hands.

Complicating matters for forensic psychologists and profilers, Cottingham's next murder was in New Jersey, but the victim was not mutilated like the two in New York. Then Cottingham returned to kill another prostitute in New York, at the Seville Hotel, again setting the room on fire, but this time he cut her breasts off and left them behind on the bed board. Why do that? All this now, with his revelation, suggests that Cottingham staged the mutilation in the Seville Hotel to persuade police that the beheading of the victims in the previous double murder was the work of a crazy, pathological "ripper" rather than a "functional" act to disguise their identities. Cottingham was a deranged serial killer posing as a different type of deranged serial killer. It worked. Until his arrest, police had not linked his murders in New Jersey with those in New York, and until Cottingham revealed to Jennifer the extent of his previous relationship with Deedeh we were never sure what exactly had motivated the mutilations in New York.

Since discovering the identity and fate of her birth mother, and that Cottingham had actually known Deedeh for several years before killing her, Jennifer had been struck by not only her own close physical resemblance to her biological mother and even to some of her reported behavioral traits, but to her killer's as well. As Cottingham began recounting his friendship and long relationship with Deedeh before and after her pregnancy, Jennifer came to be haunted by the possibility that Cottingham actually might be her biological father. She produced a number of photomontages revealing a disturbing combination of similarities between her own face and both Deedeh's and Cottingham's.

When she broached the topic with Cottingham, he thought it was unlikely, but acknowledged that it was a remote possibility. Cottingham recalled that Deedeh had contacted him to tell him she was pregnant, which he thought at the time was an unusual thing for an escort to do. Back then he did not give it any further thought, but now he too wonders whether Jennifer is his own daughter. It is not outside the realm of possibility. Cottingham has agreed to supply her with a DNA sample for a paternity test.

Jennifer had asked Cottingham to reveal to her where he secreted her mother's severed head and hands and she pledged to him that she would forgive him for what he had done and be his friend (perhaps even daughter, if the DNA test is positive) until his death in prison.

Although obviously wary of his past and his capacity as a psychopath to deceive and manipulate, Jennifer has in a way "adopted" Cottingham and taught him how to address, write and send e-mails. They correspond almost daily. She told me it is hard for her to continue to hate this aged, seemingly helpless man confined in a wheelchair behind bars. The closer she comes to forgiving him, the more liberating of her past it becomes. Forgiveness and kindness heal, she said, not only the recipient but the giver as well.

Recently she had been approved for contact visits. Unlike regular visits, where inmates interact with visitors through glass windows and speak through monitored phone handsets, contact visits allow for a brief hug and direct private conversation and contact without glass. On her first contact visit, Jennifer sat with Cottingham, holding the hand of the serial killer who had killed and beheaded her mother. She affectionately calls the white-bearded monster "Snowflake" and the two sometimes quarrel like a cantankerous father and his restless daughter. It's a modern tale of Beauty and the Beast.

Jennifer started up a Facebook page called "Serial Killers Need Hugs Too" on which she shared with followers (and Cottingham) brief accounts of her visits with him and her suspicions that he may be her birth father and her willingness to forgive him for the murder of her mother, which she sees as a way of freeing herself from her past. One of her coping mechanisms is her irreverent "serial killers need hugs too" sense of humor. She shares "inappropriate" pictures and serial-killer jokes with Cottingham, many heavily laced with innuendo and crude locker-room humor. She sends him Photoshopped gag images of them together arm in arm, vacationing at a casino or her sitting on the lap of Santa Claus, with Cottingham's white-bearded face pasted in. She sends him pictures of her modeling "serial-killer design" T-shirts she produced featuring Cottingham quotes, like "With a hacksaw, very easy" (a comment he had made about cutting off the heads of his victims).

When Cottingham was at large as a serial killer, he had a history of illicit relationships with women, including several prostitutes. He spoke of "tutoring" them in their business and partnering in scams with some of them. Something drew Cottingham to troubled and nonconformist women, but if they crossed him or somehow "betrayed" his friendship with them by lying to him, he tortured and killed them. Cottingham once described how a simple thing like a woman lying to him about being a vegetarian resulted in his torturing and killing her. Whatever it was that drew Cottingham to befriend those troubled women is no doubt drawing him to Jennifer, herself a tortured soul. He warns her, however, if he catches her lying to him, he will cut off all contact, the closest he can come to "killing" her, should Jennifer betray him.

While Cottingham is both amused and titillated by Jennifer, he is also disarmed by her black sense of humor and has been made to feel that nothing he says will shock her or result in judgmental condemnation from her. She speaks with him in the same locker room vernacular that Cottingham uses, persuading him that nothing that he admits to having done to her mother will shock her or change her friendship and willingness to forgive him.

Because of my own encounter with Cottingham in the hotel when he was fleeing the scene, I found myself drawn to Jennifer's unfolding story. Being among the last people near whom Deedeh's head had passed on the way to its current secret hiding place, I feel a need for some closure myself, and perhaps this is it: to help Jennifer recover her mother's head.

Jennifer has told Cottingham that she is communicating with me about her visits with him and has cleared the way to my having exchanged several e-mails with him in which he has assured me he would do almost anything for her, but he himself is not seeking any notoriety. I told him it was too late for that. After her visits with Cottingham, Jennifer calls me to recount what they talked about, and I caution her on the propensity of psychopaths to dissemble and lie, to connive and control those around them. In assessing his accounts, we try to fish out anomalies contradicting the record and my own recollections of the timeline of the fire in the hotel, trying to ascertain whether Cottingham is genuinely confessing the truth (or confessing the truth as he may remember it and think it was), or just plain making up things that he thinks Jennifer wants to hear.

I was writing these last lines of this book when Jennifer called in a more excited state than usual. Cottingham had just revealed to her where her mother's head and hands are buried.

Cottingham said he wanted to find a respectful way to part with Deedeh's severed head and hands the morning after killing her. He intended to put them in a river so that they would float out into the ocean. He said, "I thought that would be something nice that she would have appreciated." Arriving at his chosen location, a riverside parking lot at the end of a dead-end road, Cottingham decided that the tide was not favorable for the remains to float out to the ocean. Instead, he chose to bury Deedeh's severed head under a nearby "beautiful tree." (He did not say whether he buried the other victim's head and hands, the unidentified "Jane Doe," in the same place, but it is likely he did for convenience.)

It is a location I am coincidentally very familiar with, one that I had scouted years before as a possible film location, lonely and isolated but easily accessible by car, with a dramatic vista of the city near a prominent New York landmark. The location would be ideal to bury severed heads on a cold December Sunday morning. There would have been nobody there, and any approaching vehicles could only come from one direction and be visible at a distance. Historical weather reports indicate no major cold spells before that December 2, 1979, and the ground would not have been frozen hard, although Cottingham said it was difficult to dig because "The soil was tough, full of rocks."

Cottingham could of course be lying, because that's what serial killers do, but if he's not, and if animals did not get to the remains, there is no reason that the skeletal heads and hands of both women cannot be found and recovered. Cadaver dogs specially trained in scenting traces of old human remains and decomposition absorbed by soil decades previously have been successfully locating the resting places of missing US soldiers killed as long ago as seventy years, during World War II, and are being used in the search for the remains of the pilot Amelia Earhart, who went missing in the Pacific in 1937.[2] Perhaps, although a long shot, "Jane Doe" could still be identified.

Jennifer contacted the law enforcement agencies that had prosecuted Cottingham; however, they have not responded enthusiastically to her information. Cottingham has already been convicted for the murders, and for the authorities, there is no upside to spending resources to recover heads buried nearly forty years ago in a closed case.

Jennifer is now intent on recovering her mother's head and reuniting it with the rest of her body on Hart Island, one way or another. She invited me to come down, meet Richie in person and write one more time about him and her mission. In February 2018 I flew to meet Jennifer and to visit with Richard Cottingham in prison, a kind of "reunion" since briefly running into him at random thirty-nine years ago that fateful morning in 1979 which had so much changed my life. I suppose now, there is going to be another book after all.

BIBLIOGRAPHY

BOOKS

Affaire Dumollard. Lyon: Darment et Guerin, 1862.

Aggrawal, Anil. *Necrophilia: Forensic and Medico-legal Aspects*. New York: CRC Press, 2011, p. xv.

Aldrich, Richard James. *The Faraway War: Personal Diaries of the Second World War in Asia and the Pacific*. New York: Doubleday, 2005.

The Alton Murder: The Police News Edition of the Trial and Condemnation of Frederick Baker. London: 1867.

American Psychiatric Association. *Diagnostic and Statistical Manual of Mental Disorders*, fifth edition *(DSM-5)*. Arlington, VA: American Psychiatric Publishing, 2013.

The Annual Register for the Year 1805. London: 1807.

Anonymous. *My Secret Life: An Erotic Diary of Victorian London*, c. 1890. New York: Penguin Random House, Kindle edition.

Asbury, Herbert. *The Barbary Coast: An Informal History of the San Francisco Underworld*. New York: Alfred A. Knopf, 1933.

Attorney General of Massachusetts. *The Official Report of the Trial of Thomas W. Piper for the Murder of Mabel H. Young in the Supreme Judicial Court of Massachusetts*. Boston: 1887.

Backderf, Derf. *My Friend Dahmer*. New York: Abrams, 2012.

Baring-Gould, Sabine. *The Book of Were-Wolves*. London: Smith Elder & Co., 1865.

Barrère, Albert, and Charles Godfrey Leland. *A Dictionary of Slang, Jargon & Cant*. London: The Ballantyne Press, 1889.

Beavan, Colin. *Fingerprints: The Origins of Crime Detection and the Murder Case That Launched Forensic Science*. New York: Hyperion, 2001.

Behringer, Wolfgang. *Witches and Witch-hunts: A Global History*. Cambridge: Polity Press, 2004.

Blainey, Geoffrey. *Triumph of the Nomads: A History of Ancient Australia*. London: Macmillan, 1976.

Bodin, Jean. *De la demonomanie des sorciers*. Paris: n.p., 1587.

Bollough, Vern L., and James A. Brundage (eds.). *Handbook of Medieval Sexuality*. New York: Garland Publishing, Inc., 1996.

Bondeson, Jan. *The London Monster: A Sanguinary Tale*. London: Free Association Books, 2000.

Bonn, Scott. *Why We Love Serial Killers: The Curious Appeal of the World's Most Savage Murderers*. New York: Skyhorse Publishing, 2014.

Borowitz, Albert. *Blood & Ink: An International Guide to Fact-Based Crime Literature*. Kent, OH: The Kent State University Press, 2002.

Boston Directory. Boston: 1873.

Bourrie, Mark. *Peter Woodcock: Canada's Youngest Serial Killer* St. John's, Newfoundland: VP Publication—R. J. Parker Publishing, 2016.

Brady, Ian. *The Gates of Janus: Serial Killing and Its Analysis.* Los Angeles: Feral House, 2001.

Brinkman, Tom. *Bad Mags 2.* London: Headpress, 2009.

Brokow, Tom. *The Greatest Generation.* New York: Random House, 1998.

Brownmiller, Susan. *Against Our Will: Men, Women, and Rape.* New York: Ballantine Books, 1993. (First published 1975.)

Burgess, Glyn Sheridan. *The Lais of Marie de France: Text and Context.* Athens, GA: University of Georgia Press, 1987.

Chang, Iris. *The Rape of Nanking.* New York: Basic Books, 1997.

Chauvincourt, Beauvoys de. *Discours de la lycantropie* [sic] *ou de la transmutation des hommes en loups.* Paris: n.p., 1599.

Cheney, Margaret. *Why: The Serial Killer in America.* Lincoln, NE: Back Imprint Books, 2000.

Collins, Max Allan, George Hagenauer, and Steven Haller. *Men's Adventure Magazines in Postwar America.* Köln: Taschen, 2004.

Daley, Christopher. *Murder & Mayhem in Boston: Historic Crimes in the Hub.* Charleston, SC: Arcadia Publishing Inc., 2015.

Daly, Mary. *Gyn/ecology: The Metaethics of Radical Feminism.* Boston: Beacon Press, 1978.

Dashu, Max. *Reign of the Demonologists: The Diabolist Logic of Torture Trials in Early Modern Europe.* 1998.

Davidenkov, S. N. *The Problems of Evolution and Genetics in Neuropathology.* Leningrad: Volodarsky Edit., 1947. (In Russian)

Davido, Roseline. *The Davido-CHaD in Practice: A Clinical and Projective Personality Test.* Brussels: *Editions du Cugne,* 2015.

De River, J. Paul. *The Sexual Criminal.* Burbank, CA: Bloat, 2000. (Originally published by Charles C. Thomas, Springfield, IL, 1949.)

Diamond, Jared. *The Third Chimpanzee: The Evolution and Future of the Human Animal.* New York: HarperCollins, 1992.

Dobash, R. Emerson, and Russell P. Dobash. *When Men Murder Women.* New York: Oxford University Press, 2015.

Dower, John W. *War Without Mercy: Race & Power in the Pacific War.* New York: Random House, 1989.

Downing, Walter Hubert. *Digger Dialects: A Collection of Slang Phrases Used by the Australian Soldiers on Active Duty.* London: Lothian Book Publishing Company, 1919.

Dreyer, John Louis Emil. *A History of Astronomy from Thales to Kepler.* New York: Dover Publications, 1953.

Egger, Steven A. *The Killers Among Us: An Examination of Serial Murder and Its Investigation.* Upper Saddle River, NJ: Prentice-Hall, 1998.

Ehrenreich, Barbara, and Deirdre English. *Witches, Midwives, & Nurses: A History of Women Healers.* New York: Feminist Press at City University of New York, 1973.

Eisler, Robert. *Man into Wolf: An Anthropological Interpretation of Sadism, Masochism, and Lycanthropy.* London: Routledge and Kegan Paul, Ltd., 1951.

Ellroy, James. *LAPD '53.* New York: Abrams, 2015.

Evans, Ruth (ed.), *A Cultural History of Sexuality in the Middle Ages.* New York: Berg, 2011.

Evans, Stewart P., and Keith Skinner. *Jack the Ripper: Letters from Hell.* Gloucestershire: Sutton Publishing, 2001.

Feuerbach, Anselm Ritter von (trans. by Lady Duff Gordon). *Narratives of Remarkable Criminal Trials.* London: John Murray, 1846.

———. *Merkwürdige Criminal-Rechtsfalle,* vol. 2. Giessen: 1811.

Fezzani, Nadia. *Through the Eyes of Serial Killers: Interviews with Seven Murderers*. Toronto: Dundurn Press, 2015.

Foucault, Michel. *Abnormal: Lectures at the Collège de France, 1974–1975*. London: Picador, 2007.

———. *Madness and Civilization*, trans. R. Howard. New York: Pantheon, 1965.

Fourquet, Émile. *Les vagabonds. Les vagabonds criminels. Le Problème du vagabondage*. Paris: Marchal et Billard, 1908.

Fox, James Alan, and Jack Levin. *Extreme Killing: Understanding Serial and Mass Murder*. Sake Publications, 2011.

Freud, Sigmund, and J. Strachey et al. (ed. and trans.). *The Standard Edition of the Complete Psychological Works of Sigmund Freud*, 23 vols. London: Hogarth, 1953–1966.

Gebhardt, Miriam. *Als die Soldaten kamen (When the Soldiers Came)*. Munich: DVA/Random House, 2015.

———. *Crimes Unspoken: The Rape of German Women at the End of the Second World War*. Malden, MA: Polity Press, 2017.

Gerbeth, Vernon. *Practical Homicide Investigations*. Boca Raton, FL: CRC Press, 1996.

———. *Sex-Related Homicide and Death Investigation*. Boca Raton, FL: CRC Press, 2003.

Giannangelo, Stephen J. *Real-Life Monsters: A Psychological Examination of the Serial Murderer*. Santa Barbara, CA: Praeger, 2012.

Gibb, David A. *Camouflaged Killer*. New York: Berkley, 2011.

Gibson, Dirk C. *Legends, Monsters, or Serial Murderers? The Real Story Behind an Ancient Crime*. Santa Barbara, CA: Praeger, 2012.

Godtland, Eric, and Dian Hanson. *True Crime Detective Magazines 1924–1969*. Köln: Taschen, 2013.

Golden, Richard M. (ed.). *Encyclopedia of Witchcraft: The Western Tradition*. Santa Barbara, CA: ABC-CLIO Inc., 2006.

Goldstein, Jan E. *Console and Classify: The French Psychiatric Profession in the Nineteenth Century*. Chicago: University of Chicago Press, 2002.

Gollmar, Judge Robert H. *Edward Gein: America's Most Bizarre Murderer*. New York: Pinnacle Books, 1981.

Gross, Hans. *Criminal Investigation: A Practical Handbook for Magistrates, Police Officers, and Lawyers*. English edition translated and adapted to Indian and Colonial practice. Madras: 1906.

———. *Handbuch für Untersuchungsrichter als System der Kriminalistik (Handbook for Examining Magistrates as a System of Criminology)*, 2 vols.: 1893.

Grossman, Dave. *On Killing: The Psychological Cost of Learning to Kill in War and Society*. New York: Open Road Media, 1995.

Guislain, Joseph. *Leçons Orales sur les Phrénopathies*. Paris, 1852.

Hannum, Alberta. *Spin a Silver Dollar: The Story of a Desert Trading Post*. New York: Viking Press, 1945.

Harrison, Simon. *Dark Trophies: Hunting and the Enemy Body in Modern War*. New York: Berghahn Books, 2012.

Hedgepeth, Sonja M., and Rochelle G. Saidel, eds. *Sexual Violence Against Jewish Women During the Holocaust*. Lebanon, NH: Brandeis University Press, 2010.

Hickey, Eric W. *Serial Murderers and Their Victims*, fifth edition. Belmont, CA: Thomson/Wadsworth Publishing Company, 2010.

———. *Serial Murderers and Their Victims*, sixth edition. Belmont, CA: Thomson/Wadsworth Publishing Company, 2013.

———. *Serial Murderers and Their Victims*, seventh edition. Boston: Cengage Learning, 2016.

Holmes, H. H. (H. W. Mudgett). *Holmes' Own Story: In Which the Alleged Multi-Murderer and Arch Conspirator Tells of the Twenty-two Tragic Deaths and Disappearances In Which He is Said to be Implicated.* Philadelphia: Burke & McFetridge Co., 1895.

Holmes, Ronald M., and Stephen T. Holmes. *Murder in America.* Thousand Oaks, CA: Sage, 1994.

———. *Profiling Violent Crimes: An Investigative Tool.* Thousand Oaks, CA: Sage Publications, 2009, Kindle edition.

Hudson, Valerie M., Bonnie Ballif-Spanvill, Mary Caprioli, and Chad F. Emmett. *Sex and World Peace.* New York: Columbia University Press, 2012.

Jacobs, Don E. *Criminal Psychology: Sexual Predators in the Age of Neuroscience.* Dubuque, IA: Kendall Hunt Publishing Company, 2006.

Jenkins, Nathan. *The Trial of Renwick Williams (Commonly Called the Monster).* London: 1790.

Jenkins, Philip. *Using Murder: The Social Construction of Serial Homicide.* New York: Aldine de Gruyter, 1994.

Keppel, Robert D., PhD, with William J. Birnes. *The Psychology of Serial Killer Investigations.* New York: Academic Press, 2003.

———. *The Riverman: Ted Bundy and I Hunt for the Green River Killer.* New York: Simon & Schuster, 1995.

———. *Signature Killers: Interpreting the Calling Cards of the Serial Murderer.* New York: Simon & Schuster, 1997.

Knight, Stephen. *Jack the Ripper: The Final Solution.* London: George G. Harrap, 1976.

Kors, Alan Charles, and Edward Peters. *Witchcraft in Europe, 400–1700: A Documentary History.* Philadelphia: University of Pennsylvania Press, 2001.

Krafft-Ebing, Robert von. *Psychopathia Sexualis,* twelfth edition, authorized English edition. New York: Rebman Company, n.d.

Kramer, Heinrich. *Malleus Maleficarum.* 1486.

Lacassagne, Alexandre. *Vacher L'Eventreur et les Crimes Sadiques.* Lyon: A. Storck, 1899.

———. *Vade-mecum du médecin-expert.* Lyon: A. Storck, 1892.

Ladwig, Dane. *Dr. H. H. Holmes and the Whitechapel Ripper.* Chicago: Ink Slinger Enterprises, 2004.

Lancre, Pierre de. *L'incredulite et mecreance des sortileges.* Paris: n.p., 1622.

———. *Tableau de L'inconstance des Mauvais Anges et Demons (On the Inconstancy of Witches and Demons).* 1612.

Lasseter, Don. *Dead of Night: A True Crime Thriller.* Crime Rant Books, 2014.

Laval, Claude de Prieur. *Dialog de la Lycanthropie, ou transformation d'hommes en loups, vulgairement dit loups-garous, et si telle se peut faire.* Louvain, 1596.

Layton, Elliot. *Compulsive Killers: The Story of Modern Multiple Murder.* New York: New York University Press, 1986; later published as *Hunting Humans: The Rise of the Modern Multiple Murderer.* New York: McClelland & Stewart, 2005. [Second edition]

Lea, Henry Charles. *Materials Toward a History of Witchcraft,* 3 vols. Philadelphia: University of Pennsylvania Press, 1939; New York: Thomas Yoseloff, 1957.

Leatherman, Janie. *Sexual Violence and Armed Conflict.* Malden, MA: Polity, 2011.

Levenstein, Harvey. *We'll Always Have Paris: American Tourists in France Since 1930.* Chicago: University of Chicago Press, 2010.

Lilly, J. Robert. *Taken by Force: Rape and American GIs in Europe During World War II.* New York: Palgrave Macmillan, 2007.

Lorenz, Konrad. *Das sogenannte Böse zur Naturgeschichte der Aggression.* Verlag Dr. G. Borotha-Schoeler, 1963 ("On Aggression" or "So-called Evil: Toward a Natural History of Aggression").

MacLean, Paul D. *The Triune Brain in Evolution: Role in Paleocerebral Functions*. New York: Plenum, 1990.

McCarter, William. *My Life in the Irish Brigade: The Civil War Memoirs of Private William McCarter, 116th Pennsylvania Infantry*. Da Capo Press, Incorporated: 1996.

McCarthy, Katherine. *Invisible Victims: Missing and Murdered Indigenous Women*. St. John's, Newfoundland: VP Publications, 2017.

McClellan, Janet. *Erotophonophilia: Investigating Lust Murder*. Amherst, NY: Cambria Press, 2010.

McLaren, Angus. *A Prescription for Murder: The Victorian Serial Killings of Dr. Thomas Neill Cream*. Chicago: University of Chicago Press, 1993.

McNamara, Robert P. *The Times Square Hustler: Male Prostitution in New York City*. London and Westport, CT: Praeger, 1994.

Mellor, Lee. *Cold North Killers*. Toronto: Dundurn Press, 2012.

Mellor, Lee, Anil Aggrawal, and Eric Hickey (eds.). *Understanding Necrophilia: A Global Multidisciplinary Approach*. San Diego: Cognella Academic Press, 2017.

Money, John William. *Lovemaps: Sexual/Erotic Health and Pathology, Paraphilia, and Gender Transposition in Childhood, Adolescence, and Maturity*. Prometheus Books, Kindle edition, 2011 (originally published 1986).

Morton, Robert J., Jennifer M. Tillman, and Stephanie J. Gaines. *Serial Murder: Pathways for Investigation*. Washington, DC: Federal Bureau of Investigation, Behavioral Analysis Unit, National Center for the Analysis of Violent Crime, US Department of Justice, 2014.

Muehsam, Gerd. *French Painters and Painting from the 14th Century to Post-Impressionism*. New York: Ungar, 1970.

Newton, Michael. *Century of Slaughter*. New York: ToExcel, 1992.

———. *The Encyclopedia of Serial Killers*. New York: Facts on File, 2000.

———. *Rope: The Twisted Life and Crimes of Harvey Glatman*. New York: Pocket Books, 1998.

Odell, Robin. *Ripperology: A Study of the World's First Serial Killer and a Literary Phenomenon*. Kent, OH: Kent State University Press, 2006.

Olsen, Jack. *The Misbegotten Son: The True Story of Arthur J. Shawcross*. New York: Island Books, 1993.

Pardoe, Blaine L. *Sawney Bean: Dissecting the Legend of the Scottish Cannibal*. London: Fonthill, 2015.

Parker, R. J. *Forensic Analysis and DNA in Criminal Investigations*. St. John's, Newfoundland: R. J. Parker Publishing, 2015.

———. *Social Media Monster: Internet Killers*. St. John's, Newfoundland: R. J. Parker Publishing, 2015.

Peixotto, Edgar D. *Report of the Trial of William Henry Theodore Durrant*. Detroit: Collector Publishing, 1899.

Pettit, Mark. *A Need to Kill*. New York: Ballantine Books, 1990.

Pistorius, Micki. *Strangers on the Street: Serial Homicide in South Africa*. Johannesburg: Penguin Books, 2002.

Purcell, Catherine, and Bruce A. Arrigo. *The Psychology of Lust Murder: Paraphilia, Sexual Killing, and Serial Homicide*. New York: Elsevier Press, 2006, Kindle edition.

Ramsland, Katherine. *Confession of a Serial Killer: The Untold Story of Dennis Rader, the BTK Killer*. Lebanon, NH: University Press of New England, 2016.

———. *The Human Predator: A Historical Chronicle of Serial Murder and Forensic Investigation*. New York: Berkley, 2005.

——. *Inside the Minds of Serial Killers: Why They Kill*. Westport, CT: Greenwood Publishing Group, 2006.

——. *The Sex Beast* (Crimescape). New York: RosettaBooks, 2013.

Ressler, Robert K., Ann W. Burgess, and John E. Douglas. *Sexual Homicide: Patterns and Motives*. Lexington, MA: Lexington Books, 1988.

Ressler, Robert K., and Tom Shachtman. *Whoever Fights Monsters*. New York: St. Martin's Press, 1992.

Roberts, Mary Louise. *What Soldiers Do: Sex and the American GI in World War II*. Chicago: University of Chicago Press, 2013.

Rodriguez, Teresa. *The Daughters of Juarez: A True Story of Serial Murder South of the Border*. New York: Atria Books, 2007.

Rossmo, D. Kim. *Criminal Investigative Failures*. Boca Raton, FL: CRC Press, 2008.

——. *Geographic Profiling*. Boca Raton, FL: CRC Press, 2000.

Rumbelow, Donald. *The Complete Jack the Ripper*. London: Penguin Books, 1988.

Salisbury, Joyce E., ed. *Sex in the Middle Ages: A Book of Essays*. New York: Garland Publishing, Inc., 1991.

Saunders, David. *Norman Saunders*. St. Louis, MO: The Illustrated Press, 2008.

Schechter, Harold. *Fiend: The Shocking True Story of America's Youngest Serial Killer*. New York: Pocket Books, 2000.

——. *Hell's Princess: The Mystery of Belle Gunness, Butcher of Men*. New York: Little A, 2017.

——. *The Serial Killer Files*. New York: Ballantine Books, 2003.

Schmid, David. *Natural Born Celebrities: Serial Killers in American Culture*. Chicago: University of Chicago Press, 2005.

Schurman-Kauflin, Deborah. *The New Predator: Women Who Kill*. New York: Algora, 2000.

Sconduto, Leslie A. *Metamorphoses of the Werewolf: A Literary Study from Antiquity Through the Renaissance*. Jefferson, NC, and London: McFarland, 2008.

Scot, Reginald. *The Discoverie of Witchcraft*, 1584. Brinsley Nicholson, ed. London: Elliot Stock, 1886.

Select Criminal Trials at Justice Hall in the Old Bailey. Edinburgh: Peter Hill and Longman & Rees, 1803.

Seltzer, Mark. *Serial Killers: Death and Life in America's Wound Culture*. New York: Routledge, 1998.

Selzer, Adam. *H. H. Holmes: The True History of the White City Devil*. Skyhorse Publishing, 2017.

Shumaker, Robert W., Kristina R. Walkup, and Benjamin B. Beck. *Animal Tool Behavior: The Use and Manufacture of Tools by Animals*. Baltimore: Johns Hopkins University Press, 2011.

Sidky, Homayun. *Witchcraft, Lycanthropy, Drugs and Disease: An Anthropological Study of the European Witch-Hunts*. Eugene, OR: Wipf & Stock, 1997.

Singular, Stephen. *Unholy Messenger: The Life and Crimes of the BTK Killer*. New York: Simon & Schuster, 2006.

Sledge, E. B. *With the Old Breed: At Peleliu and Okinawa*. New York: Random House Publishing Group, 1981.

Snape, Michael. *God and Uncle Sam: Religion and America's Armed Forces in World War II*. Woodbridge, UK: Boydell Press, 2015.

Standage, Tome. *The Victorian Internet: The Remarkable Story of the Telegraph and the Nineteenth Century's Online Pioneers*. London: Phoenix Books, 1998.

Starr, Douglas. *The Killer of Little Shepherds: A True Crime Story and the Birth of Forensic Science.* New York: Knopf Doubleday Publishing Group, 2010.

Stearne, John. *A Confirmation and Discovery of Witchcraft.* 1648.

Stein, et al., Sigmund Freud. *The Sexual Life of Human Beings,* standard ed. London: Hogarth Press, 1917/1963.

Stout, Harry S. *Upon the Altar of the Nation: A Moral History of the Civil War.* New York: Penguin Books, 2006.

Strand, Ginger. *Killer on the Road: Violence and the American Interstate.* Austin: University of Texas Press, 2012.

Strange, Carolyn. *Toronto's Girl Problem: The Perils and Pleasures of the City, 1880–1930.* Toronto: University of Toronto Press, 1995.

Stubley, Peter. *1888: London Murders in the Year of the Ripper.* Stoud, Gloucestershire: History Press, 2012.

The Trial of Joseph LaPage the French monster, for the murder of the beautiful school girl Miss Josie Langmaid. Also, the account of the murder of Miss Marietta Ball, the school teacher, in the woods, in Vermont, Philadelphia: Old Franklin Publishing House, 1876.

Tucker, Thomas, and Pia Seija Seagrave, eds. *The History of the Irish Brigade: A Collection of Historical Essays.* Fredericksburg, VA: Sergeant Kirkland's Museum and Historical Society, 1995.

Turner, Kay, and Pauline Greenhill (eds). *Trangressive Tales: Queering the Grimms.* Detroit: Wayne State University Press, 2012.

US Department of Justice, FBI Behavioral Analysis Unit, National Center for the Analysis of Violent Crime. *Serial Murder: Pathways for Investigations.* Washington, DC: 2014.

Vandam, Albert. D. *Masterpieces of Crime.* London: Eden, Remington & Co., 1892.

Vronsky, Peter. *Female Serial Killers: How and Why Women Become Monsters.* New York: Berkley, 2007.

———. *The Ken & Barbie Killers: Paul Bernardo and Karla Homolka.* St. John's, Newfoundland: R. J. Parker Publications, 2015.

———. *Serial Killers: The Method and Madness of Monsters.* New York: Berkley, 2004.

———. *Times Square Torso Ripper: Sex and Murder on the Deuce.* St. John's, Newfoundland: R. J. Parker Publications, 2017.

Waller, S., ed. *Serial Killers—Philosophy for Everyone: Being and Killing.* Wiley, 2010.

Warren, Alan R. *Above Suspicion: The True Story of Serial Killer Russell Williams.* St. Johns, Newfoundland: VP Publication, 2017.

Watson, Katherine D. *Forensic Medicine in Western Society: A History.* London and New York: Routledge, 2011.

———. *Poisoned Lives: English Poisoners and Their Victims.* London: Hambleton and London, 2004.

Weaver, Gina Marie. *Ideologies of Forgetting: Rape in the Vietnam War.* Albany: State University of New York Press, 2010.

Wilson, Colin. *A Criminal History of Mankind.* New York: Carroll & Graff, 1990.

———. *Written in Blood: A History of Forensic Detection.* London: Grafton Books, 1989.

Wilson, Edward O. *On Human Nature.* Cambridge, MA, and London: Harvard University Press, 1978.

Wilson, Larry. *Criminal Major Case Management: Persons of Interest Priority Assessment Tool.* Boca Raton, FL: CRC Press, Taylor & Francis Group, 2012.

Young, Michelle. *Images of America: Broadway.* Charleston, SC: Arcadia Publishing, 2015.

Zaccone, Pierre. *Histoire des bagnes depuis leur creation jusqu'a nos jours.* Clichy: Paul Dupont, 1878.

FORENSIC AND ACADEMIC JOURNAL ARTICLES, CHAPTERS, NEWS MEDIA AND OTHER SOURCES

Aamodt, Mike G. Radford/FGCU Serial Killer Database (23 November 2015). *Serial Killer Statistics* (retrieved 25 Feb 2016 from http://skdb.fgcu.edu/info.asp).

Adcock, John. "Who Murdered Eliza Grimwood?" *Yesterday's Papers*, October 20, 2010.

Aggrawal, Anil. "A New Classification of Necrophilia." *Journal of Forensic and Legal Medicine*, no. 16, 2009, pp. 316–20.

Ajello, Nello. *"L'Assassino ha un dito in piu." La Repubblica*, September 2, 1988.

Archivo del Reino de Galicia. C-8938—AHP Ourense (Judiciary, File 1852) "Case 1788, the Werewolf," 1852.

A true discourse. Declaring the damnable life and death of one Stubbe Peeter, a most wicked sorcerer who in the likenes of a woolfe, committed many murders, continuing this diuelish practice 25. yeeres, killing and deuouring men, woomen, and children. Who for the same fact was taken and executed the 31. of October last past in the towne of Bedbur neer the cittie of Collin in Germany. Trulye translated out of the high Duch, according to the copie printed in Collin, brought ouer into England by George Bores ordinary poste, the xi. daye of this present moneth of Iune 1590. who did both see and heare the same.

Atti del processo, tribunale di Ivrea, sentenza del 15 dicembre 1823 ("Court records, Tribunal at Ivrea, sentence December 15, 1823").

Auckland Star. "A Murderous Monster—Ordinary Confessions of Crime by A Sexton," vol. VII, issue 1984, June 19, 1876.

Collin, brought ouer into England by George Bores ordinary poste, the xi. daye of this present moneth of Iune 1590. who did both see and heare the same. At London: Printed [by R. Ward?] for Edward Venge, and are to be sold in Fleet-street at the sign of the Vine [1590].

Barstow, Anne L. "Women, Sexuality, and Oppression: The European Witchcraft Persecutions." Paper presented at the Conference of the American Historical Association, Washington, DC, December 1987.

Basset, Nikki A. "Neanderthals and Modern Behavior: Did They Bury Their Dead?" *UMASA Journal*, vol. 33, 2015.

Bauer, Heike. "Scholars, Scientists and Sexual Inverts: Authority and Sexology in Nineteenth-Century Britain." In David Clifford, Elisabeth Wadge, Alex Warwick, and Martin Willis, eds., *Repositioning Victorian Sciences: Shifting Centers in Nineteenth-Century Scientific Thinking*. London: Anthem Press, 2006.

Becker, Peter. "The Criminologists' Gaze at the Underworld," in Peter Becker and Richard F. Wetzell, eds., *Criminals and Their Scientists: The History of Criminology in International Perspective*. New York: Cambridge University Press, 2006.

Bell, Donald. "Jack the Ripper: The Final Solution." *The Criminologist*, Summer, 1974.

Benedict, Barbara. "Making a Monster: Socializing Sexuality and the Monster of 1790," in Helen Deutsch and Felicity Nussbaum, eds., *"Defects" Engendering the Modern Body*. Ann Arbor: University of Michigan Press, 2000.

Bennell, C., and S. Corey. "Geographic Profiling of Terrorist Attacks" in R. N. Kocsis (ed.), *Criminal Profiling: International Theory, Research, and Practice*, Totowa, NJ: Humana Press, 2007, pp. 189–203.

Best, Joel. "Missing Children, Misleading Statistics." *Public Interest*, 92, 1988.

Bianchi, G. N., J. E. Cawte, J. Money, and B. Nurcombe. "Sex Training and Traditions in Arnhem Land." *British Journal of Medical Psychology*, no. 43: 1970, pp. 383–99.

Blécourt, Willem de. "The Werewolf, the Witch, and the Warlock: Aspects of Gender in the Early Modern Period," in Allison Rowland (ed.), *Witchcraft and Masculinities*. New York: Palgrave Macmillan, 2009.

Blom, Jan Dirk. "When Doctors Cry Wolf: A Systematic Review of the Literature on Clinical Lycanthropy," *History of Psychiatry*, vol. 25, no. 1, 2014, pp. 87–102.

Bonfiglio, Maurizio, and Maddalena Serazio. "La Iena di San Giorgio," *Il Punto*, Torino, 2003.

Branson, Allan L. "African American Serial Killers: Over-Represented Yet Underacknowledged," *The Howard Journal*, vol. 52, no. 1., February 2013, pp. 1–18.

Brittain, R. P. "The Sadistic Murderer," *Medicine, Science and the Law* (1970), vol. 10, pp. 198–207.

Buffalo Medical Journal and Monthly Review of Medical and Surgical Science, vol. 5. Buffalo: Jewett, Thomas & Co., 1850.

Canadian Medical Association Journal, vol. 90: March 7, 1964.

Cavallini, Letizia. *"Le sepolture anomale in Italia: dalla lettura tafonomia all'interpretazione del gesto funerario, in Pagani e Cristiani. Forme e attestazioni di religiosità del mondo antico,"* in *Emilia*, vol. X, Edizioni All'Insegna del Giglio, Firenze, 2011, pp. 47–105.

"Cenozoic Formation of S.E. Shansi." *British Journal of Social Science*, vol. XII, 1933.

Chardin, Pierre Teilhard de, and C. C. Young. "The Late Cenozoic Formation of S. E. Shansi," *Bull. Geol. Soc. China*, XII, 1933.

Charnock, Richard Stephen. "Cannibalism in Europe," *Journal of the Anthropological Society of London*, vol. 4, 1866, pp. xxii–xxxi.

Chase, Richard, Jr., and David Teasley. "Little Red Riding Hood: Werewolf and Prostitute," *The Historian*, vol. 57, no. 4, Summer 1995.

Chew, Kenneth S. Y., Richard McCleary, Maricres A. Lew, and Johnson C. Wang. "The Epidemiology of Child Homicide in California, 1981 Through 1990," *Homicide Studies*, vol. 3, no. 2, May 1999, pp. 151–169.

Coid, Jeremy, Min Yang, Simone Ullrich, Amanda Roberts, and Robert D. Hare. "Prevalence and Correlates of Psychopathic Traits in the Household Population of Great Britain," *International Journal of Law and Psychiatry*, vol. 32, issue 2, 2009.

Compte Rendu L'Assemblee Nationale Legislative, vol. 10, from July 21 to October 10, 1849. Paris: Panckoucke, 1849.

Cotting, B. E., MD. "The Belfry Murder Case: Reported to the Roxbury Society for Medical Improvement, February 17, 1876," *The Boston Medical and Surgical Journal*, vol. 94, no. 15, April 13, 1876.

Crepault, C., and M. Couture. "Men's Erotic Fantasies," *Archives of Sexual Behavior*, vol. 9, issue 6, 1980. pp. 565–81.

Datta, Vivek, MD, MPH. "When Homosexuality Came Out (of the DSM)," *Mad in America Science, Psychiatry and Community*, December 1, 2014, http://www.madinamerica.com/2014/12/homosexuality-came-dsm/

Delmas, Guillaume, Sarah-Marie Maffesoli, and Sébastien Robbe. *Le traitement juridique du sexe in Actes de la journée d'études de l'Institut d'Etudes de Droit public (IEDP)*, dir. Paris: L'Harmattan, 2010.

Dickens, Charles, ed. "The French Wolf," *All the Year Round Weekly Journal*, no. 162, May 31, 1862, pp. 280–88.

Dietz, P. E., B. Harry, B., and R. R. Hazelwood. "Detective Magazines: Pornography for the Sexual Sadist?" *Journal of Forensic Sciences*, vol. 31, issue 1, January 1986, pp. 197–211.

Douglas, John E., Supervisory Special Agent. *Unsub; AKA: Jack the Ripper*, NCAVC Homicide (Criminal Investigative Analysis). Department of Justice, FBI: July 6, 1988.

Downing, Lisa. "John Money's 'Normophilia': Diagnosing Sexual Normality in Late-Twentieth-Century Anglo-American Sexology," *Psychology & Sexualit*, vol. 1, issue 3, 2010.

Egger, S. A. "A Working Definition of Serial Murder and the Reductions of Linkage Blindness," *Journal of Police Science and Administration*, 12, 1984, pp. 348–57.

Eigen, Joel Peter. "Delusion in the Courtroom: The Role of Partial Insanity in Early Forensic Testimony," *Medical History*, vol. 35, no. 1, January 1991, pp. 25–49.

The Examiner, Catskill, NY, Saturday, August 25, 1888, p. 3, col.1.

Fahy, T. A. "Lycanthropy: A Review," *Journal of the Royal Society of Medicine*, vol. 82, January 1989.

Farber, M. A. "Leading the Hunt in Atlanta's Murders," *New York Times*, May 3, 1981.

Faria, João Ricardo. "What Happened to the Neanderthals?—The Survival Trap," *KYKLOS*, Vvl. 53—2000—Fasc. 2, pp. 161–72.

Federal Bureau of Investigation (FBI). *Serial Murder: Multidisciplinary Perspectives for Investigators*. Behavioral Analysis Unit, National Center for Analysis of Violent Crime (NCAVC), Department of Justice, Washington, DC: 2008.

Fenton, Ben. "Wartime GIs Went on Rampage of Rape and Murder," *The Telegraph*, April 25, 2006.

Féray, Jean-Claude. *"Histoire événementielle, Les grands procès qui ont marqué l'histoire de l'homosexualité au XIXe siècle, III: L'affaire du sergent Bertrand," Bulletin mensuel Quintes-feuilles*, no. 17, May 2014.

Flood, Michael. "The Harms of Pornography Exposure Among Children and Young People," *Child Abuse Review*, vol. 18, no. 6, 2009, pp. 384–400.

Foran, W. Robert. "Lycanthropy in Africa," *African Affairs*, vol. 55, no. 219, April 1956, pp. 124–34.

Frazer, J. G. "On Certain Burial Customs as Illustrative of the Primitive Theory of the Soul," *Journal of the Anthropological Institute of Great Britain and Ireland*, no. 15, 1886, pp. 63–104.

Ferguson, Christopher J., and Richard D. Hartley. "The Pleasure Is Momentary . . . the Expense Damnable?: The Influence of Pornography on Rape and Sexual Assault," *Aggression and Violent Behavior*, vol. 14, no. 5, 2009, pp. 323–29.

Gargett, R. H. "Grave Shortcomings: The Evidence for Neanderthal Burial," *Current Anthropology*, vol. 30, no. 2, 1989, pp. 157–90.

———. "Middle Paleolithic Burial Is Not a Dead Issue: The View from Qafzeh, Saint-Césaire, Kebara, Amud, and Dederiyeh," *Journal of Human Evolution*. no. 37, 1999, pp. 27–90.

Garland, Anna. "The Great Witch Hunt: The Persecution of Witches in England, 1550–1660," *Auckland University Law Review*, vol. 9, no. 4, 2003.

Gaskill, Malcolm. "The Pursuit of Reality: Recent Research into the History of Witchcraft," *The Historical Journal*, vol. 51, no. 4: 2008, pp. 1069–88.

Gibbons, Jenny. "Recent Developments in the Study of the Great European Witch Hunt," *The Pomegranate*, issue 5, Lammas: 1998.

Gill, John. "Missing Children: How Politics Helped Start the Scandal," FatherMag.com, 2000.

Goldstein, Laurence. "'The Imagination Problem': Winfield Townley Scott and the American Wars," *WTA (War Literature and the Arts) Journal*, vol.14, nos. 1–2, 2002, pp. 59–77.

Green, Richard E., et al. "A Draft Sequence of the Neandertal Genome, *Science*, vol. 328, no. 5979, May 7, 2010, pp. 710–22.

Grimak, L. P. "Faith as a Component of Hypnotism," *Applied Psychology*, no. 6 (2001), pp. 89–96. (In Russian).

Harley, D. "Historians as Demonologists: The Myth of the Midwife-witch," *Social History of Medicine*, no. 3, 1990, pp. 1–26.

Harrison, Simon. "Skull Trophies of the Pacific War: Transgressive Objects of Remembrance," *Journal of the Royal Anthropological Institute*, vol. 12, issue 4 (2006), pp. 817–36.

Home Office, Freedom of Information Records Release, April 2006: HO 45/25603 *WAR: Offenses Committed by US Forces Personnel in the UK; Liaison Between the Police and the US Military*, National Archives, UK.

Home Office Correspondence 1782–1979, HO 144/221/A49301C, ff. 220–23, National Archives, UK.

House of Commons. *Report from the Select Committee of Anatomy*, London: July 22, 1828.

Huntington, Samuel P. "The Clash of Civilizations?" *Foreign Affairs*, Summer 1993.

Institute of Criminal Science, University of Copenhagen, Denmark, "Pornography and Rape: Theory and Practice? Evidence from Crime Data in Four Countries Where Pornography Is Easily Available." *International Journal of Law Psychiatry*, vol. 13, nos. 1–2, 1991, pp. 47–64.

I'on, J. L. "Postmortem Appearance of Eliza Grimwood," *The Lancet*, vol. 30, no. 772, June 16, 1938.

Jenkins, Philip. "Serial Murder in the United States 1900–1940: A Historical Perspective," *Journal of Criminal Justice*, vol. 17, 1989, pp. 377–92.

Jones, Owen D. "Sex, Culture, and the Biology of Rape: Toward Explanation and Prevention," *California Law Review*, vol. 87, issue 4, July 1999, pp. 827–939.

Julini, Milo. "Le feroci malefatte in Provenza di Antoine Galetto, nipote della 'Jena'," *Il Canavesano 2012*, Ivrea: 2011.

Kaplan, Alice. "A Hidden Memorial to the Worst Aspects of Our Jim Crow Army," *Chicago Tribune*, September 25, 2005.

Kennedy, Robert, in *Statement by Attorney General Robert F. Kennedy to the Permanent Subcommittee on Investigations of the Senate Government Operations Committee*, Washington, DC: September 25, 1963.

Keeney, B. T., and K. Heide. "Gender Differences in Serial Murderers," *Journal of Interpersonal Violence*, vol. 9, no. 3, September 1994, pp. 383–98.

Keppel, Robert D., Joseph G. Weis, Katherine M. Brown, and Kristen Welch. "The Jack the Ripper Murders: A *Modus Operandi* and Signature Analysis of the 1888–1891 Whitechapel Murders," *Journal of Investigative Psychology and Offender Profiling*, no. 2, 2005, pp. 1–21.

Kiverstein, Julian, and Mark Miller. "The Embodied Brain: Toward a Radical Embodied Cognitive Neuroscience," *Frontiers in Human Neuroscience*, May 6, 2015.

Ko, Kwang Hyun. "Hominin Interbreeding and the Evolution of Human Variation," *Journal of Biological Research-Thessaloniki*, vol. 23, no. 17, December 2016.

Koning, Niek. "Witchcraft Beliefs and Witch Hunts: An Interdisciplinary Explanation," *Human Nature*, no. 24, 2013, pp. 158–81.

Kurlansky, Mark. "Days of Infamy 'Smoke' and Mirrors," *Los Angeles Times*, March 9, 2008.

"La leyenda del 'hombre lobo' Romasanta resucita en Allariz," *La Voz de Galicia*, October 30, 2011.

Lalueza-Fox, Carles. "Agreements and Misunderstandings Among Three Scientific Fields Paleogenomics, Archeology, and Human Paleontology," *Current Anthropology*, vol. 54, no. S8, *Alternative Pathways to Complexity: Evolutionary Trajectories in the Middle Paleolithic and Middle Stone Age*, December 2013, pp. S214–S220.

Langevin, R., M. Ben-Aron, H. P. Wright, V. Marchese, and L. Handy. "The Sex Killer." *Annals of Sex Research*, Clark Institute of Psychiatry, Toronto, 1988, vol. 1, issue 2, pp 263–301.

Leafe, David. "Oliver's Murderous Twist: The Bloody Killing of the Real-life Nancy That So Obsessed Charles Dickens It Drove Him to an Early Grave," *Daily Mail*, April 18, 2009.

Le Comber, S. C., B. Nicholls, D. K. Rossmo, P. A. Racey. "Geographic Profiling and Animal Foraging," *Journal of Theoretical Biology*, no. 240, 2006.

Le Comber, S. C., D. K. Rossmo, A. N. Hassan, D. O. Fuller, D.O., and J. C. Beier. "Geographic Profiling as a Novel Spatial Tool for Targeting Infectious Disease Control," *International Journal of Health Geographics*, no. 10, 2011, pp. 35–42.

Levack, Brian P. "The Horrors of Witchcraft and Demonic Possession," *Journal of Social Research*, vol. 81, no. 4, Winter 2014, pp. 921–39.

Life magazine, May 22, 1944; December 10, 1945.

Livi, Carlo, Cesare Trevvi, and Gaetano Riva, eds. *"L'Uccisore dei Bambini Carlino Grande,"* *Revista di Freniartria e di Medician Legale*, vol. 3, Reggio-Emilia: Stafano Calderini, 1877.

London Evening News, "Jack the Ripper's Predecessor," October 12, 1888.

Lundrigan, Samantha, and David Canter. "Spatial Patterns of Serial Murder: An Analysis of Disposal Site Location Choice," *Behavioral Sciences and the Law Journal*, no. 19, 2001, pp. 601.

MacLean, Paul D. "New Findings Relevant to the Evolution of Psycho-sexual Functions of the Brain," *Journal of Nervous and Mental Disease*, vol. 135, issue 4, 1962, pp. 289–301.

Mackie, Amy. "Part 3: I Am the Real Veronica Compton," *Pelican Bomb*, August 23, 2016.

MacPherson, Myra. "The Roots of Evil," *Vanity Fair*, May 1989.

Malivin, Amandine. *"L'article 360 du Code pénal, ou l'inextricable question de la nécrophilie en droit,"* in Guillaume Delmas, Sarah-Marie Maffesoli et Sébastien Robbe, *Le traitement juridique du sexe in Actes de la journée d'études de l'Institut d'Etudes de Droit public (IEDP)*, dir. Paris: L'Harmattan, 2010.

Malone, P. "Macabre Mystery: Coroner Tries to Find Origin of Skull Found During Raid by Deputies," *Pueblo Chieftain*, 25 August 2003.

Martin, R. A., D. K. Rossmo, and N. Hammerschlag. "Hunting Patterns and Geographic Profiling of White Shark Predation," *Journal of Zoology*, no. 279, 2009, pp. 111–18.

McAuley, James. "A Tsunami of Lust: American's Liberation of France Was Not Innocent," *Prospect*, May 31, 2013.

McCall, Grant S., and Nancy Shields. "Examining the Evidence from Small-scale Societies and Early Prehistory and Implications for Modern Theories of Aggression and Violence," *Aggression and Violent Behavior*, issue 13, 2008, pp. 1–9.

Meade, Everard. "From Sex Strangler to Model Citizen: Mexico's Most Famous Murderer and the Defeat of the Death Penalty," *Mexican Studies/Estudios Mexicanos*, vol. 26, issue 2, Summer 2010, pp. 323–77.

Meehan, Brian. "Son of Cain or Son of Sam? The Monster as Serial Killer in *Beowulf*," *Connecticut Review*, Connecticut State University, Fall issue, 1994.

Mehlman, Peter, and Carol Leifer. "The Masseuse," *Seinfeld*, NBC TV, episode first aired November 18, 1993.

Mellor, Lee. "Necrophilic Homicide Offenders," in Lee Mellor and Joan Swart, eds., *Homicide: A Forensic Psychology Casebook*. New York: CRC Press, 2016.

Metzger, Nadine. "Battling Demons with Medical Authority: Werewolves, Physicians and Rationalization," *History of Psychiatry*, vol. 24, no. 3, 2013, pp. 341–55.

Miller, Laurence. "The Predator's Brain: Neuropsychodynamics of Serial Killing," in Louis B. Schlesinger, ed., *Serial Offenders: Current Thought, Recent Findings* (pp. 135–66). Boca Raton, FL: CRC Press, 2000, p. 158.

———. "Serial Killers: I. Subtypes, Patterns, and Motives," *Journal of Aggression and Violent Behavior*, no. 19, 2014, pp. 1–11.

Moeliker, C. W. "The First Case of Homosexual Necrophilia in the Mallard Anas Platyrhynchos (Aves: Anatidae)." *DEINSEA—Annual of the Natural History Museum Rotterdam*, November 2001, pp. 243–48.

Money, John. "Forensic Sexology: Paraphilic Serial Rape (Biastophilia) and Lust Murder (Erotophonophilia)," *American Journal of Psychotherapy*, January 1990, vol. 44, pp. 26–36.

Moores, Patrick. *(Re)Covering the Missing Women: News Media Reporting on Vancouver's "Disappeared,"* master's dissertation, University of British Columbia, 2006.

Morrison, Helen. *Mind of a Killer*, CD. Chicago: Kozel Multimedia, 1995–1998.

Murphy, Eileen M., ed. *Deviant Burial in the Archeological Record*. Oxford: Oxbow Books, 2008.

Nasirian, Mansoureh, MD, Nabi Banazadeh, MD, and Ali Kheradmand, MD. "Rare Variant of Lycanthropy and Ecstasy," *Addict Health*, vol. 1, no. 1, Summer 2009, pp. 53–56.

Nazaretyan, Akop P. "Fear of the Dead as a Factor in Social Self-Organization," in *Journal for the Theory of Social Behavior*, vol. 35, no. 2, 2005, pp. 155–69.

———. "Power and Wisdom: Toward a History of Social Behavior," *Journal of Social Behavior*, vol. 33, no. 4, 2003.

Neumann, Craig S., and Robert D. Hare. "Psychopathic Traits in a Large Community Sample: Links to Violence, Alcohol Use, and Intelligence," *Journal of Consulting and Clinical Psychology*, vol. 76, issue 5, 2008.

New York Times. "A Mania for Killing, Thomas W. Piper's Confession," May 13, 1876.

———. "The Murderer Piper: Card from Sheriff Clark of Boston—He Will Not Make Public the Detailed Confession," June 1, 1876.

———. "Piper, the Murderer: Another Statement from the Culprit," May 27, 1876.

———. "Telegraphic Brevities," March 21, 1889.

Nobus, Dany. "Over My Dead Body: On the Histories and Cultures of Necrophilia," in Robin Goodwin and Duncan Cramer (eds.), *Inappropriate Relationships: The Unconventional, the Disapproved, & the Forbidden*. London: Lawrence Erlbaum Associates, 2002.

Osborne, Jeffery R., and C. Gabrielle Salfati. "Re-Conceptualizing 'Cooling-Off Periods' in Serial Homicide," *Homicide Studies*, vol. 19, no. 2, 2015.

O'Toole, Mary Ellen, Matt Logan, and Sharon Smith. "Looking Behind the Mask: Implications for Interviewing Psychopaths," *FBI Law Enforcement Bulletin*, vol. 81, no. 7, July 2012, pp. 14–19.

Ottawa Citizen, "A Horrid Chapter of Crime," July 25, 1866.

Pearl, Jonathan L. "French Catholic Demonologists and Their Enemies in the Late Sixteenth and Early Seventeenth Centuries," *Church History*, vol. 52, no. 4, December 1983.

Pennisi, Elizabeth. "Cannibalism and Prion Disease May Have Been Rampant in Ancient Humans," *Science*, new series, vol. 300, no. 5617, April 11, 2003, pp. 227–28.

Philip, Rajeev, Prem P. Patidar, Praveen Ramachandra, and Keshav K. Gupta. "A Tale of Nonhormonal Hairs," *Indian Journal of Endocrinology and Metabolism*, vol. 16, no. 3, May–June 2012.

Phillips, Robert Anthony. "Mayor: No Reward in Missing Hookers Case," *APB News*, April 9, 1999.

Poulakou-Rebelakou, E. Tsiamis, C. G. Panteleakos, and D. Ploumpidis. "Lycanthropy in Byzantine Times (AD 330–1453)," *History of Psychiatry Journal*, vol. 20, no. 4, 2009.

Quinet, Kenna. "The Missing Missing: Toward a Quantification of Serial Murder Victimization in the United States," *Homicide Studies*, vol. 11, no. 4, November 2007, pp. 319–39.

Rendu W., C. Beauval, I. Crevecoeur, P. Bayle, A. Balzeau, T. Bismuth, L. Bourguignon, G. Delfour G, J. P. Faivre, F. Lacrampe-Cuyaubère, C. Tavormina, D. Todisco, A. Turq, B. Maureille. "Evidence Supporting an Intentional Neanderthal Burial at La

Chapelle-aux-Saints," *Proceedings of the National Academy of Sciences*, vol. 111, no. 1, January 2014, pp. 81–86.

Rendu, W., et al. "Let the Dead Speak . . . Comments on Dibble et al.'s Reply to "Evidence Supporting an Intentional Burial at La Chapelle-aux-Saints," *Journal of Archeological Science*, no. 69, 2016, pp. 12–20.

Riedel, Mark. "Counting Stranger Homicides," *Homicide Studies*, vol. 2, no. 2, May 1998, pp. 206–19.

Renneville, Marc. *"Les transformations du droit pénal et les progrès de la médecine légale, de 1810 à 1912,"* Archives d'anthropologie criminelle, 1913.

Rodrigues, Javier. "A Real-life *Silence of the Lambs*," *The Houstonian*, September 19, 2006.

Rossmo, D. Kim, Heike Lutermann, Mark D. Stevenson, and Steven C. Le Comber. *Geographic Profiling*, presentation at the NCIS Conference 1998.

———. "Geographic Profiling in Nazi Berlin: Fact and Fiction" [Unclassified], *Geospatial Intelligence Review*, National Geospatial-Intelligence Agency, Washington, DC, vol. 12, no. 2, 2014, pp. 54–67.

Salinas, Rebecca. "A Look Back at the Serial Killer That Terrorized Austin in the 1880s," *My San Antonio*, April 28, 2015.

Schuessler, Jennifer. "The Dark Side of Liberation," *New York Times*, May 20, 2013.

Seneca, Lucius Annaeus (the Younger). *L. Annaei Senecae, Ad Novatum De Ira*, Liber III, xvii–xviii (*Essays on Anger, Book III*).

Sigmond, G. "Impulsive Insanity: The Case of the French Vampire," *Journal of Psychological Medicine and Mental Pathology*, vol. 2. London: John Churchill, 1849.

Sledzik, P. S., and S. Ousley. "Analysis of 6 Vietnamese Trophy Skulls," *Journal of Forensic Sciences*, vol. 36, no. 2, 1991, pp. 520–30.

Stevenson, M. D., D. K. Rossmo, R. J. Knell, and S. C. Le Comber. "Geographic Profiling as a Novel Spatial Tool for Targeting the Control of Invasive Species," *Ecography*, no. 35, 2012, pp. 704–15.

Sublimi Saponetti, S., F. Scattarella, A. De Lucia, and V. Scattarella. "Paleobiology, Palaeopathology and Necrophobic Practices in Early Iron Age Burials (IX–VII Century BC) in Capo Colonna, Trani, Apulia, Southern Italy—The State of Health of a Small Sample from Iron Age, *Coll Antropol*, vol. 31, no. 1, March 2007, pp. 339–44.

Thorpe, B., ed. *Ancient Laws and Institutes of England*. London: Commissioners on the Public Records of the Kingdom, 1840.

The Times. L. Forbes Winslow, "To the Editor," September 12, 1888.

Tita, George, and Elizabeth Griffiths. "Traveling to Violence: The Case of a Mobility-Based Spatial Typology of Homicide, *Journal of Research in Crime and Delinquency*, vol. 42, no. 3, August 2005, pp. 277–78.

Travis, John. "Sea-bathing from 1730 to 1900," in Stephen Fisher, ed., *Recreation and the Sea*. Exeter: University of Exeter Press, 1997.

Tsaliki, Anastasia. "Unusual Burials and Necrophobia: An Insight into the Burial Archeology of Fear," in Murphy, ed. http://works.bepress.com/anastasia_tsaliki/13.

United Nations, Security Council Resolution 1820, Adopted by the Security Council at Its 5916th meeting, on June 19, 2008.

United States Court of Appeals, *UNITED STATES V. FREEMAN*, 804 F.2d 1574 (11th Cir. 1986).

US Department of Justice. "Psychopathy," *FBI Law Enforcement Bulletin*, vol. 81, no. 7, July 2012.

US Department of Justice. *Uniform Crime Reports [United States], 1930–1959*. Republished by Inter-University Consortium for Political and Social Research.

US Department of Justice. *Uniform Crime Reports*, Expanded Homicide Data 2013, 2013.

US Department of Justice, Federal Bureau of Investigation. *ViCAP Crime Analysis Report* (FD-676 [Rev. 3-11-86]) OMB No. 1110-0011, Quantico, VA, 1986.

US Department of Justice, Office of Justice Programs, Bureau of Justice Statistics. *Violent Victimization Committed by Strangers, 1993–2010*, NCJ 239424, Washington, DC, December 2012.

Vick, Karl. "Violence at Work Tied to Loss of Esteem," *St. Petersburg Times*, December 17, 1993.

Vronsky, Peter. "Necrophilia: The Case of François Bertrand 'The Vampire of Montparnasse,'" in Eric Hickey, Anil Aggrawal, and Lee Mellor (eds.), *Understanding Necrophilia: A Global Multidisciplinary Approach*, Cognella, 2016.

———. "Zebra! The *Hunting Humans* 'Ninja' Truck Driver Serial Killer," in *Serial Killers True Crime Anthology 2015*, vol. 2, R. J. Parker Publishing, 2014.

Walters, Guy. "Did Allied Troops Rape 285,000 German Women?" *Daily Mail*, March 25, 2015.

Weingartner, James J. "Trophies of War: U.S. Troops and the Mutilation of Japanese War Dead, 1941–1945," *The Pacific Historical Review*, vol. 61, no. 1, February 1992, pp. 53–67.

Westall, William. "A Precedent for the Whitechapel Murder," *Pall Mall Gazette*, Friday, September 7, 1888.

Willey, P., and Paulette Leach. "The Skull on the Lawn: Trophies, Taphonomy, and Forensic Anthropology," in Dawnie Wolfe Steadman (ed.), *Hard Evidence: Case Studies in Forensic Anthropology*. New York: Routledge, 2009.

Wilson, David. "The Secret War," *The Guardian*, March 27, 2007.

Yaksic, Enzo, Lindsey DeSpirito, and Sasha Reid. "Detecting an Observable Decline in Serial Homicide: Have We Banished the Devil from the Details?" Unpublished paper in progress, 2017.

Yucha, Josephine M., James T. Pokines, and Eric J. Bartelink. "A Comparative Taphonomic Analysis of 24 Trophy Skulls from Modern Forensic Cases," *Journal of Forensic Sciences*, September 2017, vol. 62, no. 5.

Zollikofer Christoph, P. E., Marcia S. Ponce de León, Bernard Vandermeersch, and François Lévêque. "Evidence for Interpersonal Violence in the St. Césaire Neanderthal," *Proceedings of the National Academy of Sciences of the United States of America*, vol. 99, no. 9, April 30, 2002, pp. 6444–48.

WEBSITES

http://abcnews.go.com/Nightline/dating-game-serial-killer-rodney-alcala-guilty-murder/story?id=9949007

http://www.absolutecrime.com/married-to-murder-the-bizarre-and-true-accounts-of-people-who-married-murderers.html#.WZdvlRuWw8w

http://www.academia.edu/7307390/Larticle_360_du_Code_penal_ou_linextricable_question_de

http://adb.anu.edu.au/biography/leonski-edward-joseph-10814_la_necrophilie_en_droi
http://adb.anu.edu.au/biography/leonski-edward-joseph-10814

http://altereddimensions.net/2013/african-muti-medicine-murders-hospitals-sell-body-parts-murderers-harvest-organs-from-live-victims-witch-doctors-black-magic-spells

http://www.annalsofcrime.com/04-05.htm; http://www.historicalcrimedetective.com/killer-theodore-durrant/

https://archives.fbi.gov/archives/news/stories/2008/august/vicap_080408

http://www.atlasobscura.com/places/josie-langmaid-monument

http://www.bbc.com/news/science-environment-32804177

http://news.bbc.co.uk/2/hi/programs/newsnight/8245312.stm

http://www.becominghuman.org/node/news/earliest-stone-tool-evidence-revealed

http://blogs.berkeley.edu/2010/06/16/a-crime-puzzle-violent-crime-declines-in-america/

http://www.canada.com/news/Researchersquestioneffectivenesshightechpolicedatabase
     violence/6164630/story.html

http://www.casebook.org/dissertations/robhouse-kosminski.html

http://www.casebook.org/suspects/

http://www.cbsnews.com/pictures/michael-gargiulo-under-arrest/

http://www.chicagotribune.com/news/local/breaking/ct-chicago-homicides-study-met
     -20160726-story.html

https://commons.wikimedia.org/wiki/File:Bois_de_la_Morte_%C3%A0_Pizay_(Ain).JPG

https://commons.wikimedia.org/wiki/File:Martin_Dumollard_-_v%C3%A9ritable
     _peau_reconstitu%C3%A9e_-_mus%C3%A9e_Testut-Latarjet_-_32.JPG

http://content.met.police.uk/Article/The-Suspects/1400015320719/1400015320719

http://content.met.police.uk/Site/jacktheripper

http://criminologiaediritto.altervista.org/callisto-grandi/

http://www.dailymail.co.uk/news/article-1110123/Child-killer-Mary-Bell
     -grandmother-51-But-I-left-grief-says-victims-mother.html

http://www.dailymail.co.uk/news/article-2241334/Was-Chicago-doctor-serial-killer
     -Londons-Jack-Ripper-Descendant-American-murderer-investigates-links
     -notorious-criminals.html

http://www.dispatchlive.co.za/news/2013/10/29/sangoma-killing-people-with
     -muti-is-my-job/

https://www.duffelblog.com/2012/06/man-unsure-grandfathers-wwii-japanese-skull
     -collection/

http://www.eastlondonadvertiser.co.uk/news/dracula_may_have_been_jack_the_ripper
     _whitechapel_society_is_told_1_3214396

https://en.wikipedia.org/wiki/List_of_serial_killers_by_number_of_victims#Serial_kill
     ers_with_the_highest_known_victim_count

https://www.fbi.gov/about-us/cjis/ucr/crime-in-the-u.s/2014/crime-in-the-u.s.-2014/ta
     bles/table-12

https://www.fbi.gov/stats-services/publications/serial-murder

https://www.fbi.gov/news/stories/latest-crime-statistics-released

http://www.fumento.com/exploit.html

http://gallica.bnf.Fr./ark:/12148/bpt6k6115200z/f481.image

http://www.gettyimages.ca/detail/news-photo/filthy-cluttered-kitchen-of-alleged-mass
     -murderer-ed-gein-news-photo/50425931

https://www.geocaching.com/seek/gallery.aspx?guid=269a94da-8da7-4452-a2e8
     -aco2e28791c3

http://www.globalresearch.ca/the-terrorism-statistics-every-american-needs-to-hear
     /5382818

https://www.goodreads.com/shelf/show/jack-the-ripper

https://www.google.com/maps/d/u/o/viewer?mid=znNfXxzuBPKU.k7defDElF7Ic&hl
     =en_US

http://gw.geneanet.org/antistar?lang=Fr.&pz=marcel+andre+henri+felix&nz=petiot&
     ocz=0&p=pierre&n=vacher&oc=1

http://harpers.org/sponsor/thewar/harpers-index-wwii-edition/index.html

http://www.hhholmesthefilm.com/

http://www.huffingtonpost.com/kathy-freston/shattering-the-meat-myth_b_214390
     .html

http://www.huffingtonpost.com/entry/leonardo-dicaprio-hh-holmes-scorsese_us
    _55ca08fee4b0f1cbf1e63768
http://www.icpsr.umich.edu/icpsrweb/NACJD/studies/3666
http://www.independent.co.uk/news/africa-witchcraft-returns-to-haunt-new-south
    -africa-1139937.html
http://www.iol.co.za/news/south-africa/muti-killings-is-a-way-of-life-in-rural-areas
    -470603
https://it.wikipedia.org/wiki/Giorgio_Orsolano
http://www.jack-the-ripper.org/
http://jezebel.com/1-in-3-college-men-admit-they-would-rape-if-we-dont-ca-1678601600
http://www.kersplebedeb.com/mystuff/feminist/gibbons_witch.html
https://www.longislandpress.com/2016/12/30/how-websleuths-sparked-revelation-in-long
    -island-serial-killer-case/
http://www.medical.theclinics.com/article/S0025-7125(05)70029-8/abstract#bibliography
http://medind.nic.in/icd/t12/i3/icdt12i3p483.htm
http://www.missingpeople.net/updatenoreward.htm
http://www.murderpedia.org/male.G/g/glatman-harvey-photos-2.htm
http://mysteriouschicago.com/the-murder-castle-today-or-good-grief
    -more-hh-holmes-2/
http://www.nationmaster.com/country-info/compare/Canada/United-States/Crime
http://news.nationalgeographic.com/2017/07/forensic-dogs-amelia-earhart-spot-where
    -died/
http://www.newsweek.com/campus-rapists-and-semantics-297463
https://www.nist.gov/featured-stories/who-was-detective-x
http://www.nydailynews.com/news/world/suspected-serial-killer-appeared-celebrity
    -masterchef-uk-article-1.2407560
http://www.nytimes.com/1996/06/28/world/un-court-for-first-time-defines-rape-as-war
    -crime.html
http://www.nytimes.com/2014/10/09/science/ancient-indonesian-find-may-rival-oldest
    -known-cave-art.html
http://online.liebertpub.com/doi/pdf/10.1089/vio.2014.0022
http://www.orangecoast.com/features/center-of-the-universe/?src=longreads/
http://www.paris-normandie.Fr./detail_article/articles/PN-1047332
    /necrophile-et-necrosadique-au-havre-1047332#.VA3EiGdow8E
http://www.pbs.org/kqed/demonbarber/penny/index.html
http://www.pitt.edu/~dash/type0333.html
http://pressfortruth.ca/top-stories/what-are-your-chances-being-killed-terrorist-attack/
https://www.propublica.org/article/the-fbi-built-a-database-that-can-catch-rapists
    -almost-nobody-uses-it
https://www.psychologytoday.com/blog/shadow-boxing/201611/boys-dressed-girls-who
    -became-serial-killers
https://www.psychologytoday.com/blog/shadow-boxing/201410/who-coined-serial-killer
http://quod.lib.umich.edu/cgi/t/text/text-idx?c=eebo;idno=A13085.0001.001
http://quickfacts.census.gov/qfd/states/00000.html
http://radaronline.com/celebrity-news/sean-penn-talks-about-serial-killer-richard
    -ramirez/
http://repository.countway.harvard.edu/xmlui/handle/10473/1827
http://ricerca.repubblica.it/repubblica/archivio/repubblica/1988/09/02/as
    sassino-ha-un-dito-in-piu.html

http://serialhomicidecollaborative.blogspot.ca/2013/08/an-attempt-to-explain
-decline-in.html
http://www.servantgirlmurders.com/
http://www.science20.com/hawkins_science/blog/could_story_cain_abel_be_story
_genocide_neanderthals
http://www.silviapettem.com/books.html
http://skdb.fgcu.edu/info.asp
http://www.slate.com/articles/briefing/articles/1997/05/skull_session.html
http://www.slate.com/articles/news_and_politics/crime/2011/01/blood_loss.html
http://www.spokesman.com/stories/1996/jul/14/it-was-a-match-made-in-prison-ewu
-professors/
http://www.statista.com/statistics/191137/reported-forcible-rape-cases-in-the-usa-since
-1990/
http://www.suppressedhistories.net/secrethistory/demonologists.html
http://www.telegraph.co.uk/culture/music/music-news/8191211/Blondies-Debbie-Harry
-claims-serial-killer-Ted-Bundy-lured-her-into-car.html
http://www.telegraph.co.uk/news/uknews/10880601/We-know-where-Jack-the-Ripper
-lived-experts.html
http://www.telegraph.co.uk/news/worldnews/europe/bulgaria/11153923/Vampire-grave
-found-in-Bulgaria.html
https://theodorerobertcowellnelsonbundy.wordpress.com/tag/carole-ann-boone/
http://time.com/4635049/chicago-murder-rate-homicides/
http://time.com/4607059/murder-rate-increase-us-cities-2016/
http://www.torinoscienza.it/anatomia/le_collezioni/aprieed6eed6.html?obj_id=2375
http://torontoist.com/2014/09/historicist-h-h-holmes-in-toronto/
http://www.txstate.edu/gii/projects/jack-the-ripper.html
http://www.txstate.edu/gii/projects/land-border-illegal-migration-profiling.html
http://www.usmarshals.gov/usmsforkids/fingerprint_history.htm
https://www.vice.com/en_us/article/the-haunting-photography-of-a-serial-killer
http://www.visualnews.com/2015/07/28/the-rape-statistics-you-need-to-know/
https://whitechapeljack.com/jeff-mudgett-bloodstains-hh-holmes-book-review/
https://web.archive.org/web/20140220060641/http://www.suntimes.com/6482474-417/la
-detective-murder-suspect-could-have-killed-10-women.html
http://www.wesleyenglish.com/geoprofile/infamous-cases/jack-the-ripper/
http://www.xares.es/index.html?body39.html
https://www.youtube.com/watch?v=HNW1JWq2oIc

ENDNOTES

1. SERIAL KILLERS: A BRIEF INTRODUCTION TO THE SPECIES

1 Prostitution Task Force et al. *Prostitution in New York City: Answers to Some Questions.* New York: New York Women in Criminal Justice, 1977, p. 2.
2 http://www.disastercenter.com/crime/nycrime.htm.
3 Michelle Young. *Images of America: Broadway.* Charleston, SC: Arcadia Publishing, 2015, p. 70. And Robert P. McNamara. *The Times Square Hustler: Male Prostitution in New York City.* London and Westport, CT: Praeger, 1994, p. 21.
4 http://www.oed.com/viewdictionaryentry/Entry/121738.
5 Robert D. Keppel, PhD, with William J. Birnes. *Signature Killers: Interpreting the Calling Cards of the Serial Murderer.* New York: Simon & Schuster, 1997, p. 82.
6 Elliot Layton. *Compulsive Killers: The Story of Modern Multiple Murder.* New York: New York University Press, 1986. Later published as *Hunting Humans: The Rise of the Modern Multiple Murderer,* second ed. New York: McClelland & Stewart, 2005.
7 M. A. Farber. "Leading the Hunt in Atlanta's Murders." *New York Times,* May 3, 1981; *New York Times Online,* Proquest search, December 31, 2012.
8 Ann Rule. Foreword to Keppel, *Signature Killers,* p. xv.
9 Michael Newton. *The Encyclopedia of Serial Killers.* New York: Facts on File, 2000, p. 205.
10 https://www.psychologytoday.com/blog/shadow-boxing/201410/who-coined-serial-killer.
11 Robert Eisler. *Man into Wolf: An Anthropological Interpretation of Sadism, Masochism, and Lycanthropy.* London: Routledge and Kegan Paul, Ltd., 1951, p. 78, *n.* 10. Date of lecture from e-mail correspondence with Brian Collins, Ohio University, Classics and World Religions, e-mail communication, March 25, 2016—https://ohio.academia.edu/BrianCollins.
12 Robert K. Ressler and Tom Shachtman. *Whoever Fights Monsters.* New York: St. Martin's Press, 1992, pp. 32–33.
13 Robert K. Ressler, Ann W. Burgess, and John E. Douglas. *Sexual Homicide: Patterns and Motives.* Lexington, MA: Lexington Books, 1988.
14 Mike G. Aamodt. Radford/FGCU Serial Killer Database (23 November 2015). *Serial Killer Statistics* (retrieved 25 February 2016 from http://skdb.fgcu.edu/info.asp).
15 Eric Hickey. *Serial Murderers and Their Victims,* seventh ed. Boston: Cengage Learning, 2016, pp. 335–36.
16 D. Kim Rossmo. *Geographic Profiling.* Boca Raton, FL: CRC Press, 2000, p. 14.
17 R. Emerson Dobash and Russell P. Dobash. *When Men Murder Women.* New York: Oxford University Press, 2015, p. 109.
18 *New York Times Online.* Proquest searches, 31 December 2012.

19   https://en.wikipedia.org/wiki/List_of_serial_killers_by_number_of_victims#Serial
_killers_with_the_highest_known_victim_count.

20   See photo at: http://en.wikipedia.org/wiki/File:Johnwaynegacyrosalynncarter.jpg.

21   Derf Backderf. *My Friend Dahmer.* New York: Abrams, 2012, pp. 96–97.

22   Peter Vronsky. *Female Serial Killers: How and Why Women Become Monsters.* New York: Berkley, 2007, p. 230.

23   See for example: https://www.vice.com/en_us/article/the-haunting-photography-of-a
-serial-killer. *And* http://abcnews.go.com/Nightline/dating-game-serial-killer-rod-
ney-alcala-guilty-murder/story?id=9949007. I have never been able to confirm conclusively that Alcala was a student of Polanski's at NYU or that Polanski taught there or
gave a seminar during the time in question.

24   https://www.youtube.com/watch?v=HNW1JWq2oIc.

25   http://www.nydailynews.com/news/world/suspected-serial-killer-appeared-celebrity
-masterchef-uk-article-1.2407560.

26   Don Lasseter. *Dead of Night: A True Crime Thriller.* Crime Rant Books, 2014, Kindle
ed. (Kindle locations 549–50).

27   http://radaronline.com/celebrity-news/sean-penn-talks-about-serial-killer-richard
-ramirez.

28   http://www.telegraph.co.uk/culture/music/music-news/8191211/Blondies-Debbie
-Harry-claims-serial-killer-Ted-Bundy-lured-her-into-car.html.

29   http://www.cbsnews.com/pictures/michael-gargiulo-under-arrest/. *And* https://web.
archive.org/web/20140220060641/. *And* http://www.suntimes.com/6482474-417/la
-detective-murder-suspect-could-have-killed-10-women.html.

30   See Alan R. Warren. *Above Suspicion: The True Story of Serial Killer Russell Williams.*
VP Publication, 2017. *And* David A. Gibb. *Camouflaged Killer.* New York: Berkley,
2011.

31   http://www.orangecoast.com/features/center-of-the-universe/?src=longreads.

32   Stephen Singular. *Unholy Messenger: The Life and Crimes of the BTK Killer.* New York:
Simon & Schuster, 2006, pp. 101–2. *And* Katherine Ramsland. *Confession of a Serial
Killer: The Untold Story of Dennis Rader, the BTK Killer.* Lebanon, NH: University
Press of New England, 2016, Kindle ed. (Kindle location 4418).

33   Allan L. Branson, "African American Serial Killers: Over-Represented Yet Underacknowledged." *The Howard Journal*, vol. 52, no. 1, February 2013, pp. 1–18. *And*
Mike G. Aamodt, *Serial Killer Statistics.*

34   Vronsky, *Female Serial Killers,* pp. 4, 15, 41–42.

35   R. Holmes and S. Holmes, *Murder in America.* Thousand Oaks, CA: Sage, 1994.

36   S. A. Egger. "A Working Definition of Serial Murder and the Reductions of Linkage
Blindness." *Journal of Police Science and Administration*, vol. 12, 1984, pp. 348–57.

37   Vernon Gerbeth. *Practical Homicide Investigations.* Boca Raton, FL: CRC Press, 1996.

38   B. T. Keeney and K. Heide. "Gender Differences in Serial Murderers." *Journal of Interpersonal Violence*, vol. 9, no. 3, September 1994, pp. 383–98.

39   Helen Morrison. *Mind of a Killer,* CD. Chicago: Kozel Multimedia, 1995–1998.

40   Deborah Schurman-Kauflin. *The New Predator: Women Who Kill.* New York: Algora,
2000.

41   Federal Bureau of Investigation. *Serial Murder: Multidisciplinary Perspectives for Investigators.* Behavioral Analysis Unit, National Center for Analysis of Violent Crime
(NCAVC), Department of Justice, Washington, DC: 2008, p.10; and https://www.fbi
.gov/stats-services/publications/serial-murder.

42   Eric W. Hickey. *Serial Murderers and Their Victims,* fifth ed. Belmont, CA: Thomson/
Wadsworth Publishing Company, 2010, p. 27.

43 Jeffery R. Osborne and C. Gabrielle Salfati. "Reconceptualizing 'Cooling-off Periods' in Serial Homicide." *Homicide Studies*, vol. 19, no. 2, 2015, pp. 188–205.

44 Eric W. Hickey. *Serial Murderers and Their Victims*, sixth ed. Belmont, CA: Thomson/ Wadsworth Publishing Company, 2013, p. 157.

45 Janet McClellan. *Erotophonophilia: Investigating Lust Murder*. Amherst, NY: Cambria Press, 2010, Kindle ed. (Kindle locations 173–78).

46 http://www.independent.co.uk/news/africa-witchcraft-returns-to-haunt-new-south -africa-1139937.html. *And* http://www.iol.co.za/news/south-africa/muti-killings -is-a-way-of-life-in-rural-areas-470603. *And* http://altereddimensions.net/2013/afri can-muti-medicine-murders-hospitals-sell-body-parts-murderers-harvest-organs -from-live-victims-witch-doctors-black-magic-spells. *And* http://www.dispatchlive .co.za/news/2013/10/29/sangoma-killing-people-with-muti-is-my-job. *And* Micki Pistorius. *Strangers on the Street: Serial Homicide in South Africa*. Johannesburg: Penguin Books, 2002, Kindle ed. *And* Teresa Rodriguez. *The Daughters of Juarez: A True Story of Serial Murder South of the Border*. New York: Atria Books, 2007.

2. *GENESIS:* THE STONE AGE REPTILIAN ZOMBIE SERIAL-KILLER TRIUNE BRAIN

1 For an excellent summary description of these many theories, see the recent edition of: Eric W. Hickey, *Serial Murderers and Their Victims*, seventh ed., pp. 68–116.

2 The age of 27.5, according to: Mike G. Aamodt, *Serial Killer Statistics*. While Hickey in his current seventh edition has moved his previous estimate of thirty down to 29.5 for recent serial killers. See Hickey, *Serial Murderers and Their Victims*, seventh ed., p. 238.

3 Nadia Fezzani. *Through the Eyes of Serial Killers: Interviews with Seven Murderers*. Toronto: Dundurn Press, 2015, Kindle ed., Kindle locations 2985–89.

4 Craig S. Neumann and Robert D. Hare. "Psychopathic Traits in a Large Community Sample: Links to Violence, Alcohol Use, and Intelligence." *Journal of Consulting and Clinical Psychology*, vol. 76, issue 5, 2008, pp. 893–99.

5 J. Coid, M. Yang, S. Ullrich, and R. Hare. "Prevalence and Correlates of Psychopathic Traits in the Household Population of Great Britain." *International Journal of Law and Psychiatry*, vol. 32, issue 2, 2009. pp. 65–73.

6 Paul D. MacLean. *The Triune Brain in Evolution: Role in Paleocerebral Functions*. New York: Plenum, 1990.

7 Paul D. MacLean. "New Findings Relevant to the Evolution of Psychosexual Functions of the Brain." *Journal of Nervous and Mental Disease*, vol. 135, issue 4, 1962, pp. 289–301.

8 Julian Kiverstein and Mark Miller. "The Embodied Brain: Toward a Radical Embodied Cognitive Neuroscience." *Frontiers in Human Neuroscience*, May 6, 2015, https://doi .org/10.3389/fnhum.2015.00237.

9 John Money. "Forensic Xexology: Paraphilic Serial Rape (Biastophilia) and Lust Murder (Erotophonophilia)," *American Journal of Psychotherapy*, vol. 44, January 1990, pp. 26–36.

10 L. Miller. "The Predator's Brain: Neuropsychodynamics of Serial Killing." In Louis B. Schlesinger, ed. *Serial Offenders: Current Thought, Recent Findings*. Boca Raton, FL: CRC Press, 2000, p. 158.

11 In the name of full disclosure, I acknowledge that not all scientists agree that *Homo sapiens* deliberately raped and killed off the Neanderthals. Nobody in the sciences agrees or disagrees unanimously on anything I cite in this chapter. I have not, however, cited obscure or highly controversial schools of anthropology and psychology. These days, one school is as plausible as an opposing one. Again, the more we discover, the less we realize we know and understand, especially in the origins of humans.

12 Carles Lalueza-Fox. "Agreements and Misunderstandings Among Three Scientific Fields Paleogenomics, Archeology, and Human Paleontology." *Current Anthropology*, vol. 54, no. S8, *Alternative Pathways to Complexity: Evolutionary Trajectories in the Middle Paleolithic and Middle Stone Age*, December 2013, pp. S214–S220.

13 Richard E. Green et al. "A Draft Sequence of the Neandertal Genome." *Science*, vol. 328, no. 5979, May 7, 2010, pp. 710–22.

14 For example: Owen D. Jones. "Sex, Culture, and the Biology of Rape: Toward Explanation and Prevention." *California Law Review*, vol. 87, issue 4, July 1999, pp. 827–39. *And* Jared Diamond. *The Third Chimpanzee: The Evolution and Future of the Human Animal*. New York: HarperCollins, 1992, p. 45. *And* João Ricardo Faria. "What Happened to the Neanderthals?—The Survival Trap." *KYKLOS*, vol. 53—2000—fasc. 2, pp. 161–72. *And* Kwang Hyun Ko. "Hominin Interbreeding and the Evolution of Human Variation." *Journal of Biological Research-Thessaloniki*, vol. 23, no. 17, December 2016. *And* Grant S. McCall and Nancy Shields. "Examining the Evidence from Small-scale Societies and Early Prehistory and Implications for Modern Theories of Aggression and Violence." *Aggression and Violent Behavior*, issue 13, 2008, pp. 1–9

15 Valerie M. Hudson, Bonnie Ballif-Spanvill, Mary Caprioli, and Chad F. Emmett. *Sex and World Peace*. New York: Columbia University Press, 2012. *And* Susan Brownmiller. *Against Our Will: Men, Women, and Rape*. New York: Ballantine Books, 1993 (first published 1975). *And* Janie Leatherman. *Sexual Violence and Armed Conflict*. Malden, MA: Polity, 2011. *And* Sonja M. Hedgepeth and Rochelle G. Saidel, eds. *Sexual Violence Against Jewish Women During the Holocaust*. Lebanon, NH: Brandeis University Press, 2010. *And* Iris Chang. *The Rape of Nanking: The Forgotten Holocaust of World War II*. New York: Basic Books, 2012. *And* Gina Marie Weaver. *Ideologies of Forgetting: Rape in the Vietnam War*. State University of New York Press, 2010. *And* J. Robert Lilly. *Taken by Force: Rape and American GIs in Europe During World War II*. New York: Palgrave Macmillan, 2007. *And* Mary Louise Roberts. *What Soldiers Do: Sex and the American GI in World War II*. Chicago: University of Chicago Press, 2013. *And* Miriam Gebhardt. *Als die Soldaten kamen* (*When the Soldiers Came*); in English: *Crimes Unspoken: The Rape of German Women at the End of the Second World War*.

16 Marlise Simons. "UN Court, for First Time, Defines Rape as War Crime." *The New York Times*, June 28, 1996, http://www.nytimes.com/1996/06/28/world/un-court-for-first-time-defines-rape-as-war-crime.html (retrieved March 17, 2016). *And* United Nations, Security Council Resolution 1820. Adopted by the Security Council at its 5916th meeting, on June 19, 2008.

17 James Hawkins. "Could the Story of Cain & Abel Be the Story of the Genocide of Neanderthals?" *Science* 2.0, March 27, 2009, http://www.science20.com/hawkins_science/blog/could_story_cain_abel_be_story_genocide_neanderthals.

18 Christoph P. E. Zollikofer, Marcia S. Ponce de León, Bernard Vandermeersch, and François Lévêque. "Evidence for Interpersonal Violence in the St. Césaire Neanderthal." *Proceedings of the National Academy of Sciences of the United States of America*, vol. 99, no. 9, April 30, 2002, pp. 6444–48.

19 Richard Stephen Charnock. "Cannibalism in Europe." *Journal of the Anthropological Society of London*, vol. 4, 1866, pp. xxii–xxxi; *And* Elizabeth Pennisi. "Cannibalism and Prion Disease May Have Been Rampant in Ancient Humans." *Science*, new series, vol. 300, no. 5617, April 11, 2003, pp. 227–28.

20 Akop Nazaretyan. "Fear of the Dead as a Factor in Social Self-organization." In *Journal for the Theory of Social Behavior*, vol. 35, no. 2, 2005, pp. 155–69 [citing M. K. Mamardashvili. *Moe ponimania filosofii*. Moscow: Nauka, 1990].

21 http://www.telegraph.co.uk/news/worldnews/europe/bulgaria/11153923/Vampire
-grave-found-in-Bulgaria.html (retrieved February 13, 2016). *And* Eileen M. Murphy,
ed. *Deviant Burial in the Archeological Record.* Oxford: Oxbow Books, 2008.

22 Anastasia Tsaliki. "Unusual Burials and Necrophobia: An Insight into the Burial Archeology of Fear," in Murphy, ed. [http://works.bepress.com/anastasia_tsaliki/13 (accessed October 25, 2014), p. 1.

23 Pierre Teilhard de Chardin and C. C. Young. "The Late Cenozoic Formation of S.E.
Shansi." *Bull. Geol. Soc. China,* vol. XII, 1933. *And* "Cenozoic Formation of S.E.
Shansi." *British Journal of Social Science,* vol. XII, 1933.

24 Tsaliki, "Unusual Burials," p. 8.

25 Letizia Cavallini. *"Le sepolture anomale in Italia: dalla lettura tafonomia
all'interpretazione del gesto funerario, in Pagani e Cristiani. Forme e attestazioni di
religiosità del mondo antico."* In Emilia, vol. X, *Edizioni All'Insegna del Giglio,* Firenze,
2011, pp. 47–105.

26 S. Sublimi Saponetti, F. Scattarella, A. De Lucia, V. Scattarella. "Paleobiology, Palaeopathology and Necrophobic Practices in Early Iron Age Burials (IX–VII century BC)
in Capo Colonna, Trani, Apulia, Southern Italy—The State of Health of a Small Sample
from Iron Age. *Coll Antropol,* vol. 31, no. 1, March 2007, pp. 339–44.

27 Nazaretyan, "Fear of the Dead as a Factor in Social Self-Organization," p. 157.

28 J. G. Frazer. "On Certain Burial Customs as Illustrative of the Primitive Theory of the
Soul." *J. Anthropol. Inst. Great Brit. Ireland,* no. 15, 1886, pp. 63–104.

29 There are anthropologists who argue that Neanderthals practiced similar ritual burials.
But evidence for Neanderthal ritual burials is currently still scarce and controversial.
See: W. Rendu, C. Beauva, I. Crevecoeur, P. Bayle, A. Balzeau, T. Bismuth, L. Bourgui-
gnon, G. Delfour G, J. P. Faivre, F. Lacrampe-Cuyaubère, X. Muth, S. Pasty, P. Semal,
C. Tavormina, D. Todisco, A. Turq, and B. Maureille. "Let the Dead Speak . . . : Comments
on Dibble et al.'s Reply to "Evidence Supporting an Intentional Burial at La Chapelle-
aux-Saints." *Journal of Archeological Science,* no. 69, 2016, pp. 12–20. *And* R. H. Gargett.
"Middle Paleolithic Burial Is Not a Dead Issue: The View from Qafzeh, Saint-Césaire,
Kebara, Amud, and Dederiyeh." *Journal of Human Evolution,* no. 37, 1989, pp. 27–90.
And R. H. Gargett. "Grave Shortcomings: The Evidence for Neanderthal Burial." *Current
Anthropology,* vol. 30, no. 2, 1989, pp. 157–90. *And* W. Rendu, C. Beauval, I. Crevecoeur,
P. Bayle, A. Balzeau, T. Bismuth, L. Bourguignon, G. Delfour, J. P. Faivre, F. Lacrampe-
Cuyaubère, C. Tavormina, D. Todisco, A. Turq, and B. Maureille. "Evidence Supporting
an Intentional Neanderthal Burial at La Chapelle-aux-Saints." *Proceedings of the Na-
tional Academy of Sciences,* vol. 111, no. 1, January 2014, pp. 81–86. *And* Nikki A. Basset.
"Neanderthals and Modern Behavior: Did They Bury Their Dead?" *UMASA Journal,* vol.
33, 2015, http://umanitoba.ca/publications/openjournal/index.php/mb-anthro/article
/download/249/80.

30 Robert K. Ressler, Ann W. Burgess, and John E. Douglas, *Sexual Homicide,* Kindle
locations 1281–282.

31 Robert J. Morton, Jennifer M. Tillman, Stephanie J. Gaines. *Serial Murder: Pathways
for Investigation.* Washington, DC: Federal Bureau of Investigation, Behavioral Analysis Unit, National Center for the Analysis of Violent Crime, US Department of Justice,
2014, p. 47.

32 C. W. Moeliker, "The First Case of Homosexual Necrophilia in the Mallard Anas
Platyrhynchos (Aves: Anatidae)." *DEINSEA—Annual of the Natural History Museum
Rotterdam,* November 2001, pp. 243–48.

33 Sigmund Freud. In J. Strachey et al., ed. and trans. *The Standard Edition of the Complete Psychological Works of Sigmund Freud,* 23 vols. London: Hogarth, 1953–1966. Vol.

7: "Three Essays on the Theory of Sexuality," pp. 161, 231. Freud's essay was originally published in 1905.

34 Akop Nazaretyan. "Fear of the Dead as a Factor in Social Self-Organization." *Journal for the Theory of Social Behavior*, vol. 35, no. 2, 2005, pp. 155–69. See also S. N. Davidenkov. *The Problems of Evolution and Genetics in Neuropathology*. Leningrad: Volodarsky Edit., 1947. *And* John E. Pfeiffer. *The Creative Explosion: An Inquiry into the Origins of Art and Religion*. New York: Cornell University Press, 1985. *And* L. P. Grimak. "Faith as a Component of Hypnotism." *Applied Psychology*, no. 6, 2001, pp. 89–96.

35 "Earliest Stone Tool Evidence Revealed," August 11, 2010—http://www.becominghu man.org/node/news/earliest-stone-tool-evidence-revealed (retrieved March 15, 2016). *And* Robert W. Shumaker, Kristina R. Walkup, and Benjamin B. Beck. *Animal Tool Behavior: The Use and Manufacture of Tools by Animals*. Baltimore: John Hopkins University Press, 2011.

36 Konrad Lorenz. *Das sogenannte Böse zur Naturgeschichte der Aggression*. Verlag Dr. G Borotha-Schoeler, 1963 ("On Aggression" or "So-called Evil: Toward a Natural History of Aggression").

37 Rebecca Morelle. "Oldest Stone Tools Predate Earliest humans." *BBC News*, May 20, 2015, http://www.bbc.com/news/science-environment-32804177.

38 Akop P. Nazaretyan. "Power and Wisdom: Toward a History of Social Behavior." *Journal of Social Behavior*, vol. 33, no. 4, 2003.

39 Christoph P. E. Zollikofer, Marcia S. Ponce de León, Bernard Vandermeersch, and François Lévêque. "Evidence for Interpersonal Violence in the St. Césaire Neanderthal."

40 http://www.nytimes.com/2014/10/09/science/ancient-indonesian-find-may-rival -oldest-known-cave-art.html.

41 Edward O. Wilson. *On Human Nature*. Cambridge, MA, and London: Harvard University Press, 1978. *And* Geoffrey Blainey. *Triumph of the Nomads: A History of Ancient Australia*. London: Macmillan, 1976.

42 http://blogs.berkeley.edu/2010/06/16/a-crime-puzzle-violent-crime -declines-in-america/ (retrieved March 31, 2016).

43 http://www.chicagotribune.com/news/local/breaking/ct-chicago-homicides-study -met-20160726-story.html.

44 http://time.com/4635049/chicago-murder-rate-homicides.

45 See for example, Catherine Ramsland. *Inside the Minds of Serial Killers: Why They Kill*. Westport, CT: Greenwood Publishing Group, 2006, p. 101.

3. *PSYCHOPATHIA SEXUALIS*: THE PSYCHOLOGY OF THE LUST SERIAL KILLER IN CIVILIZED SOCIETY

1 Cited in Stein et al. *Sigmund Freud, The Sexual Life of Human Beings*, standard ed. London: Hogarth Press, 1917/1963, 16, pp. 303–19.

2 Robert von Krafft-Ebing. *Psychopathia Sexualis*, twelfth ed., authorized English ed. New York: Rebman Company, n.d., p. 79.

3 American Psychiatric Association. *Diagnostic and Statistical Manual of Mental Disorders (DSM-5)*, fifth ed. Washington, DC: American Psychiatric Publishing, 2013.

4 Krafft-Ebing. *Psychopathia Sexualis*, twelfth ed., p. 79.

5 Catherine Purcell and Bruce A. Arrigo. *The Psychology of Lust Murder: Paraphilia, Sexual Killing, and Serial Homicide*. New York: Elsevier Press, 2006, p. 26, Kindle ed.

6 G. N. Bianchi, J. E. Cawte, J. Money, and B. Nurcombe. "Sex Training and Traditions in Arnhem Land." *British Journal of Medical Psychology*, no. 43, 1970, pp. 383–99.

7   Robert K. Ressler, Ann W. Burgess, and John E. Douglas. *Sexual Homicide*, Kindle locations 1049–51.

8   Vronsky, *Serial Killers*, p. 169.

9   American Psychiatric Association, *Diagnostic and Statistical Manual of Mental Disorders (DSM-5)*, fifth ed., pp. 685–86.

10 Vivek Datta, MD, MPH. "When Homosexuality Came Out (of the *DSM*)." *Mad in America Science, Psychiatry and Community*, December 1, 2014, http://www.madin america.com/2014/12/homosexuality-came-dsm.

11 Lisa Downing. "John Money's 'Normophilia': Diagnosing Sexual Normality in Late-Twentieth-Century Anglo-American Sexology." *Psychology & Sexuality*, vol. 1, issue 3, 2010.

12 John William Money (2011-11-15). *Lovemaps: Sexual/Erotic Health and Pathology, Paraphilia, and Gender Transposition in Childhood, Adolescence, and Maturity.* Buffalo, NY: Prometheus Books, 1986, Kindle ed. (Kindle locations 88–89; 1233–39).

13 Money, *Lovemaps*, Kindle locations 1316–18.

14 "Interview: John Money." *PAIDIKA: The Journal of Paedophilia*, Spring 1991, vol. 2, no. 3, p. 5.

15 Catherine Purcell and Bruce A. Arrigo. *The Psychology of Lust Murder*, p. 26. And Robert K. Ressler, Ann W. Burgess, and John E. Douglas, *Sexual Homicide*, Kindle locations 1048–49.

16 C. Crepault and M. Couture. "Men's Erotic Fantasies." *Archives of Sexual Behavior*, vol. 9, issue 6, 1980. pp. 565–81. And http://www.newsweek.com/campus-rapists-and -semantics-297463. And http://jezebel.com/1-in-3-college-men-admit-they-would -rape-if-we-dont-ca-1678601600. And http://online.liebertpub.com/doi/pdf/10.1089 /vio.2014.0022.

17 Myra MacPherson. "The Roots of Evil," *Vanity Fair*, May 1989.

18 R. Langevin. "A Study of the Psychosexual Characteristics of Sex Killers: Can We Identify Them Before It Is Too Late?" *International Journal of Offender Therapy and Comparative Criminology*, vol. 47, issue 4, 2003, pp. 366–82.

19 Mark Bourrie. *Peter Woodcock: Canada's Youngest Serial Killer.* St. John's, Newfoundland: VP Publication—R. J. Parker Publishing, 2016.

20 Ian Brady. *The Gates of Janus: Serial Killing and Its Analysis.* Los Angeles: Feral House, 2001, pp. 87–88.

21 Hickey, *Serial Murderers and Their Victims*, sixth ed., p. 226.

4. THE DAWN OF THE LESS-DEAD: SERIAL KILLERS AND MODERNITY

1   For more on de Rais and Báthory, see Peter Vronsky, *Serial Killers: The Method and Madness of Monsters* and *Female Serial Killers: How and Why Women Become Monsters*.

2   J. P. Rosman and P. J. Resnick. "Sexual Attraction to Corpses: A Psychiatric Review of Necrophilia." *The Bulletin of the American Academy of Psychiatry and the Law*, vol. 17, no. 2, 1989, pp. 153-63 (citing H. von Huber, "*Nekrophilie,*" *Kriminalistik*, no. 16, 1962, pp. 564–68, and Ernest Jones, *On the Nightmare*, New York: Liveright, 1931, pp. 109–12).

3   Tractate Sanhedrin. Folio 66b, n. 18; *Tractate Baba Bathra*, Folio 3b http://www.come -and-hear.com/bababathra/bababathra_3.html#PARTb.

4   Lucius Annaeus Seneca (the Younger). *L. Annaei Senecae, Ad Novatum De Ira*, Liber III, xvii–xviii (*Essays on Anger, Book III*).

5   St. Augustine. *Confessions*, book 6, chapter 8, c. 397 and 400 AD.

6 Seneca. *De Clementia*. 1.25.1.

7 Plato. *Philebus*, 48a. In Harold N. Fowler, trans. *Plato in Twelve Volumes*, vol. 9. Cambridge, MA, Harvard University Press and London, William Heinemann Ltd., 1925.

8 St. Augustine. *Confessions*, book 3, chapter 2, c. 397 and 400 AD.

9 Kenna Quinet. "The Missing Missing: Toward a Quantification of Serial Murder Victimization in the United States." *Homicide Studies*, vol. 11, no. 4, November 2007, pp. 319–39.

10 Steven A. Egger. *The Killers Among Us: An Examination of Serial Murder and Its Investigation*. Upper Saddle River, NJ: Prentice-Hall, 1998, pp. 74–75.

11 Angus McLaren. *A Prescription for Murder: The Victorian Serial Killings of Dr. Thomas Neill Cream*. Chicago: University of Chicago Press, 1993, p. xiii.

12 Mark Seltzer. *Serial Killers: Death and Life in America's Wound Culture*. New York: Routledge, 1998, p. 1.

13 Robert Kennedy. In *Statement by Attorney General Robert F. Kennedy to the Permanent Subcommittee on Investigations of the Senate Government Operations Committee*. Washington, DC: September 25, 1963.

14 Peter Mehlman and Carol Leifer. "The Masseuse," *Seinfeld*, NBC TV, episode first aired November 18, 1993.

15 D. Kim Rossmo. *Criminal Investigative Failures*. Boca Raton, FL: CRC Press, 2009, p. 31.

16 Lora Grindlay. "Police Don't Think a Reward Would Help." *Province*, April 7, 1999, p. A18.

17 Patrick Moores. *(Re)Covering the Missing Women: News Media Reporting on Vancouver's "Disappeared."* Master's dissertation, University of British Columbia, 2006, p. 62.

18 Hickey, *Serial Murderers and Their Victims*, sixth ed., p. 237.

19 Ginger Strand. *Killer on the Road: Violence and the American Interstate*. Austin: University of Texas Press, 2012, Kindle ed.

20 Ginger Strand, *Ibid.*, Kindle locations 892–94.

21 Ginger Strand, *Ibid.*, Kindle location 939.

22 Ginger Strand, *Ibid.*, Kindle locations 927–28.

23 Eric Hickey, *Serial Murderers and Their Victims*, seventh ed., p. 222. *And* Mike G. Aamodt, *Serial Killer Statistics*.

24 http://quickfacts.census.gov/qfd/states/00000.html.

5. *LUPINA INSANIA*: CRIMINALIZING WEREWOLVES AND LITTLE RED RIDING HOOD AS VICTIM, 1450-1650

1 Brian Meehan. "Son of Cain or Son of Sam? The Monster as Serial Killer in *Beowulf*." *Connecticut Review*, Connecticut State University, Fall issue, 1994, p. 2.

2 Willem de Blécourt. "The Werewolf, the Witch, and the Warlock: Aspects of Gender in the Early Modern Period." In Allison Rowland, ed. *Witchcraft and Masculinities*. New York: Palgrave Macmillan, 2009, p. 207.

3 Eric Hickey, *Serial Murderers and Their Victims*, seventh ed., pp. 335–36.

4 B. Thorpe, ed. *Ancient Laws and Institutes of England*. London: Commissioners on the Public Records of the Kingdom, 1840, pp. 160–61.

5 Leslie A. Sconduto. *Metamorphoses of the Werewolf: A Literary Study from Antiquity Through the Renaissance*. Jefferson, NC, and London: McFarland, 2008, Kindle ed. (Kindle locations 3084–85).

6 Robert Eisler and W. Robert Foran. "Lycanthropy in Africa." *African Affairs*, vol. 55, no. 219, April 1956, pp. 124–34.

7   Alberta Hannum. *Spin a Silver Dollar: The Story of a Desert Trading Post*. New York: Viking Press, 1945, p. 86.

8   T. A. Fahy. "Lycanthropy: A Review." *Journal of the Royal Society of Medicine*, vol. 82, January 1989, pp. 37–39.

9   E. Poulakou-Rebelakou, C. Tsiamis, G. Panteleakos, and D. Ploumpidis. "Lycanthropy in Byzantine Times (330–1453 AD)." *History of Psychiatry Journal*, vol. 20, no. 4, 2009, p. 470.

10   Robert Eisler.

11   Kathy Freston. "Shattering the Meat Myth: Humans Are Natural Vegetarians." http://www.huffingtonpost.com/kathy-freston/shattering-the-meat-myth_b_214390.html.

12   Robert Eisler, p. 48.

13   Robert K. Ressler, Ann W. Burgess, and John E. Douglas, *Sexual Homicide*, Kindle location 4151.

14   John Louis Emil Dreyer. *A History of Astronomy from Thales to Kepler*. New York: Dover Publications, 1953, pp. 20, 37–38.

15   Leslie A. Sconduto, *Metamorphoses of the Werewolf*, Kindle location 219.

16   St. Augustine, *The City of God*, Book XVIII.17.

17   Wolfgang Behringer. *Witches and Witch-hunts: A Global History*. Cambridge: Polity Press, 2004, p. 30.

18   Glyn Sheridan Burgess. *The Lais of Marie de France: Text and Context*. Athens: University of Georgia Press, 1987, p. 175.

19   Henry Charles Lea. *Materials Toward a History of Witchcraft*, 3 vols. Philadelphia: University of Pennsylvania Press, 1939. New York: Thomas Yoseloff, 1957, vol. 1, pp. 179–80.

20   Brian P. Levack. "The Horrors of Witchcraft and Demonic Possession." *Journal of Social Research*, vol. 81, no. 4, Winter 2014, pp. 921–39.

21   Richard M. Golden, ed. *Encyclopedia of Witchcraft: The Western Tradition*. Santa Barbara, CA: ABC-CLIO Inc., 2006, pp. 713–15.

22   E. Poulakou-Rebelakou et al., and Nadine Metzger. "Battling Demons with Medical Authority: Werewolves, Physicians and Rationalization." *History of Psychiatry*, vol. 24, no. 3, 2013, pp. 341–55.

23   Jan Dirk Blom. "When Doctors Cry Wolf: A Systematic Review of the Literature on Clinical Lycanthropy. *History of Psychiatry*, vol. 25, no. 1, 2014, pp. 87–102.

24   Mansoureh Nasirian, MD, Nabi Banazadeh, MD, and Ali Kheradmand, MD. "Rare Variant of Lycanthropy and Ecstasy." *Addict Health*, vol. 1, no. 1, Summer 2009, pp. 53–56.

25   Sconduto, *Metamorphoses of the Werewolf*, chapters 3–7.

26   Eva Shield. *What Are Your Chances of Being Killed in a Terrorist Attack?* http://pressfortruth.ca/top-stories/what-are-your-chances-being-killed-terrorist-attack. *And Terrorism Statistics Every American Needs to Hear*, http://www.globalresearch.ca/the-terrorism-statistics-every-american-needs-to-hear/5382818.

27   Jonathan L. Pearl. "French Catholic Demonologists and Their Enemies in the Late Sixteenth and Early Seventeenth Centuries." *Church History*, vol. 52, no. 4, December 1983, pp. 457–67.

28   Anna Garland. "The Great Witch Hunt: The Persecution of Witches in England, 1550–1660." *Auckland University Law Review*, vol. 9, no. 4, 2003, p. 1154. Contrary to popular claim, the *Malleus Maleficarum* was not the standard manual for witch-hunters everywhere, but it was highly influential. It was most used as a guide in the Germanic territories.

29   Richard M. Golden, *Encyclopedia of Witchcraft*, p. 720.

30   Heinrich Kramer. *Malleus Maleficarum*. 1486, part 1: 63A–63C.

31 Kramer, *Malleus Maleficarum*, part 1: 7C; Sconduto, *Metamorphoses of the Werewolf*, Kindle location 1849.

32 On the nature of the charges against de Rais and Báthory, see Peter Vronsky, *Serial Killers* and *Female Serial Killers*, respectively.

33 *A true discourse. Declaring the damnable life and death of one Stubbe Peeter, a most wicked sorcerer who in the likenes of a woolfe, committed many murders, continuing this diuelish practice 25. yeeres, killing and deuouring men, woomen, and children. Who for the same fact was taken and executed the 31. of October last past in the towne of Bedbur neer the cittie of Collin in Germany. Trulye translated out of the high Duch, according to the copie printed in Collin, brought ouer into England by George Bores ordinary poste, the xi. daye of this present moneth of Iune 1590. who did both see and heare the same.* At London: Printed (by R. Ward?) for Edward Venge, and are to be sold in Fleet-street at the sign of the Vine (1590). Early English Books Online: http://quod.lib.umich.edu/cgi/t/text/text-idx?c=eebo;idno=A13085.0001.001.

34 Sconduto, *Metamorphoses of the Werewolf*, Kindle locations 1926–29.

35 Jean Bodin. *De la demonomanie des sorciers*. Paris: n.p., 1587, pp. 106–7.

36 Katherine Ramsland. *The Human Predator*. New York: Berkley, 2005.

37 Pierre de Lancre. *Tableau de L'inconstance des Mauvais Anges et Demons* (*On the Inconstancy of Witches and Demons*), 1612.

38 Pierre de Lancre and Sabine Baring-Gould. *The Book of Were-Wolves*. London: Smith Elder & Co., 1865.

39 Sconduto, *Metamorphoses of the Werewolf*, Kindle locations 2607–11.

40 Nadine Metzger.

41 Pierre de Lancre. *L'incredulite et mecreance des sortileges*. Paris: n.p., 1622.

42 Claude de Laval Prieur. *Dialog de la Lycanthropie, ou transformation d'hommes en loups, vulgairement dit loups-garous, et si telle se peut faire*. Louvain, 1596.

43 Beauvoys de Chauvincourt. *Discours de la lycantropie* [sic] *ou de la transmutation des hommes en loups*. Paris: n.p., 1599.

44 Reginald Scot. *The Discoverie of Witchcraft*, 1584. Brinsley Nicholson, ed. London: Elliot Stock, 1886.

45 *Canadian Medical Association Journal*, vol. 90, March 7, 1964, p. 648.

46 See for example: illustrations accompanying Rajeev Philip, Prem P. Patidar, Praveen Ramachandra, and Keshav K Gupta. "A Tale of Nonhormonal Hairs." *Indian Journal of Endocrinology and Metabolism*, vol. 16, no. 3, May–June, 2012, pp. 483–85, http://medind.nic.in/icd/t12/i3/icdt12i3p483.htm.

47 Homayun Sidky. *Witchcraft, Lycanthropy, Drugs and Disease: An Anthropological Study of the European Witch-Hunts*. Eugene, OR: Wipf & Stock, 1997; Mansoureh Nasirian.

48 Harold Schechter. *Hell's Princess: The Mystery of Belle Gunness, Butcher of Men*. New York: Little A, 2017.

49 Kay Turner and Pauline Greenhill. *Trangressive Tales: Queering the Grimms*. Detroit: Wayne State University Press, 2012, p. 129; Anil Aggrawal. *Necrophilia: Forensic and Medico-legal Aspects*. New York: CRC Press, 2011, p. xv.

50 D. L. Ashliman. *Little Red Riding Hood and Other Tales of Aarne-Thompson-Uther Type 333*. University of Pittsburg, http://www.pitt.edu/~dash/type0333.html (retrieved December 5, 2015).

51 Richard Chase Jr. and David Teasley. "Little Red Riding Hood: Werewolf and Prostitute." *The Historian*, vol. 57, no. 4, Summer 1995, p. 769. Citing Charles F. Fort. *Medical Economy During the Middle Ages*. New York and London: J. W. Bouton, 1883, pp. 337–38.

52 D. L. Ashliman, *Little Red Riding Hood and Other Tales of Aarne-Thompson-Uther Type 333.*

53 See for example: Katherine Ramsland, *The Human Predator.* And Dirk C. Gibson. *Legends, Monsters, or Serial Murderers? The Real Story Behind an Ancient Crime.* Santa Barbara, CA: Praeger, 2012.

54 Vern L. Bollough and James A. Brundage, eds. *Handbook of Medieval Sexuality.* New York: Garland Publishing, Inc., 1996. *And* Ruth Evans, ed. *A Cultural History of Sexuality in the Middle Ages.* New York: Berg, 2011. *And* Joyce E. Salisbury, ed. *Sex in the Middle Ages: A Book of Essays.* New York: Garland Publishing, Inc., 1991.

6. *MALLEUS MALEFICARUM*: THE GREAT WITCH HUNT AS A SERIAL-KILLING-WOMAN HUNT

1 Angus McLaren.

2 Mark Seltzer, *Serial Killers,* p. 1.

3 Barbara Ehrenreich and Deirdre English. *Witches, Midwives & Nurses: A History of Women Healers.* New York: Feminist Press at City University of New York, 1973. *And* D. Harley. "Historians as Demonologists: The Myth of the Midwife-witch." *Social History of Medicine,* vol. 3, 1990, pp. 1–26.

4 Jenny Gibbons. "Recent Developments in the Study of the Great European Witch Hunt." *The Pomegranate,* issue 5. Lammas: 1998, http://www.kersplebedeb.com/my stuff/feminist/gibbons_witch.html. *And* Brian A. Pavlac. "Ten Common Errors and Myths About the Witch Hunts, Corrected and Commented," http://www.brianpavlac .org/witchhunts/werrors.html. *And* Malcolm Gaskill. "The Pursuit of Reality: Recent Research into the History of Witchcraft." *The Historical Journal,* vol. 51, no. 4, 2008, pp. 1069–88. *And* Alan Charles Kors and Edward Peters. *Witchcraft in Europe, 400–1700: A Documentary History.* Philadelphia: University of Pennsylvania Press, 2001, p. 17. *And* Niek Koning. "Witchcraft Beliefs and Witch Hunts: An Interdisciplinary Explanation." *Human Nature,* no. 24, 2013, pp. 158–81.

5 Robert J. Morton, Jennifer M. Tillman, and Stephanie J. Gaines. *Serial Murder: Pathways for Investigation.* Washington, DC: Federal Bureau of Investigation, Behavioral Analysis Unit, National Center for the Analysis of Violent Crime, US Department of Justice, 2014.

6 Garland, "The Great Witch Hunt: The Persecution of Witches in England, 1550–1660," pp. 1168–69.

7 Kramer, *Malleus Maleficarum,* part 3, 211D, 214A.

8 Sonja M. Hedgepeth and Rochelle G. Saidel, eds. *Sexual Violence Against Jewish Women During the Holocaust.* Lebanon, NH: Brandeis University Press, 2010.

9 Mary Daly. *Gyn/ecology: The Metaethics of Radical Feminism.* Boston: Beacon Press, 1978, p. 136.

10 Anne L. Barstow. "Women, Sexuality, and Oppression: The European Witchcraft Persecutions." Paper presented at the Conference of the American Historical Association, Washington, DC, December 1987.

11 Max Dashu. *Reign of the Demonologists: The Diabolist Logic of Torture Trials in Early Modern Europe.* 1998, http://www.suppressedhistories.net/secrethistory/demonolo gists.html.

12 Gibbons, "Recent Developments in the Study of the Great European Witch Hunt," p. 1172.

13 John Stearne. *A Confirmation and Discovery of Witchcraft.* 1648.

7. THE RIPPERS BEFORE JACK: THE RISE OF MODERN SERIAL KILLERS IN EUROPE, 1800–1887

1 Transcripts of the Bertrand court-martial reproduced in Pierre Zaccone. *Histoire Des Bagnes Depuis Leur Creation Jusqu'a Nos Jours.* Clichy: Paul Dupont, 1878, pp. 488-502 [hereinafter, "IIe Conseil de Guerre de Paris"] (Accessed August 2, 2014 at http://gallica.bnf.Fr./ark:/12148/bpt6k6115200z/f481.image), p. 494.

2 IIe Conseil de Guerre de Paris, p. 500. *And* G. Sigmond. "Impulsive Insanity: The Case of the French Vampire." *Journal of Psychological Medicine and Mental Pathology,* vol. 2. London: John Churchill, 1849, p. 578.

3 Michel Foucault (2007-04-01). *Abnormal: Lectures at the Collège de France, 1974–1975.* Picador, Kindle ed. (Kindle locations 4409–14).

4 *London Lancet.* In Austin Flint, ed. *Buffalo Medical Journal and Monthly Review of Medical and Surgical Science,* vol. 5. Buffalo: Jewett, Thomas & Co, 1850, pp. 341–42. *And The Medical Times,* p. 53.

5 http://www.medical.theclinics.com/article/S0025-7125(05)70029-8/abstract#bibliography [accessed August 13, 2014].

6 Jan E. Goldstein. *Console and Classify: The French Psychiatric Profession in the Nineteenth Century.* Chicago: University of Chicago Press, 2002. pp. 155–56. *And* Joel Peter Eigen. "Delusion in the Courtroom: The Role of Partial Insanity in Early Forensic Testimony." *Medical History,* vol. 35, no. 1, January 1991, pp. 25–49.

7 IIe Conseil de Guerre de Paris, p. 500-1.

8 *UNITED STATES V. FREEMAN.* United States Court of Appeals, 804 F.2d 1574 (11th Cir. 1986)

9 Vronsky, p. 243.

10 Jean-Claude Féray. "Histoire événementielle, Les grands procès qui ont marqué l'histoire de l'homosexualité au XIXe siècle, III: L'affaire du sergent Bertrand." *Bulletin mensuel Quintes-feuilles,* May 17, 2014, p. 5.

11 Anil Aggrawal. "A New Classification of Necrophilia." *Journal of Forensic and Legal Medicine,* no. 16, 2009, pp. 316–20.

12 Lee Mellor. "Necrophilic Homicide Offenders." In Lee Mellor and Joan Swart, eds. *Homicide: A Forensic Psychology Casebook.* New York: CRC Press, 2016.

13 Dany Nobus. "Over My Dead Body: On the Histories and Cultures of Necrophilia." In Robin Goodwin and Duncan Cramer, eds. *Inappropriate Relationships: The Unconventional, the Disapproved & the Forbidden.* London: Lawrence Erlbaum Associates, 2002, pp. 171, 175, 186.

14 Joseph Guislain. *Leçons Orales sur les Phrénopathies.* Paris, 1852, p. 257.

15 *Compte Rendu L'Assemblée Nationale Legislative,* vol. 10, July 21 to October 10, 1849. Paris: Panckoucke, 1849, p. 45. See the review of French Penal Code Article 360 in the *Report from the Select Committee of Anatomy.* London: House of Commons, July 22, 1828. The language of the law remained unchanged in 1849. See also Amandine Malivin. "L'article 360 du Code pénal, ou l'inextricable question de la nécrophilie en droit." In Guillaume Delmas, Sarah-Marie Maffesoli, and Sébastien Robbe. *Le traitement juridique du sexe in Actes de la journée d'études de l'Institut d'Etudes de Droit public (IEDP).* Paris: L'Harmattan, 2010, pp. 121–38, http://www.academia.edu/7307390/Larticle_360_du_Code_penal_ou_linextricable_question_de_la_necrophilie_en_droit [accessed September 2, 2014].

16 http://www.paris-normandie.Fr./detail_article/articles/PN-1047332/necrophile-et-necrosadique-au-havre-1047332#.VA3EiGdow8E [accessed August 29, 2014].

17 Peter Vronsky. "Necrophilia: The Case of François Bertrand 'The Vampire of Montparnasse.'" In Eric Hickey, Anil Aggrawal, and Lee Mellor, eds. *Understanding Necrophilia: A Global Multidisciplinary Approach*. San Diego, CA: Cognella, 2016, pp. 357–66.

18 Charles Dickens, ed. "The French Wolf." *All the Year Round Weekly Journal*, no. 162, May 31, 1862, pp. 280–88.

19 Tom Standage. *The Victorian Internet: The Remarkable Story of the Telegraph and the Nineteenth Century's Online Pioneers*. London: Phoenix Books, 1998.

20 https://commons.wikimedia.org/wiki/File:Bois_de_la_Morte_%C3%A0_Pizay_(Ain) .JPG.

21 https://commons.wikimedia.org/wiki/File:Martin_Dumollard_-_v%C3%A9ritable _peau_reconstitu%C3%A9e_-_mus%C3%A9e_Testut-Latarjet_-_32.JPG.

22 *Affaire Dumollard*. Lyon: Darment et Guerin, 1862, p. 171.

23 Elliott Leyton. *Hunting Humans: The Rise of the Modern Multiple Murderer*. Toronto: McLelland-Bantam, 1987.

24 Carolyn Strange. *Toronto's Girl Problem: The Perils and Pleasures of the City, 1880–1930*. Toronto: University of Toronto Press, 1995.

25 Anonymous. *My Secret Life: An Erotic Diary of Victorian London*, c. 1890. New York: Penguin Random House. Kindle ed. https://www.amazon.com/My-Secret-Life -Victorian-Classics-ebook/dp/B001R9DHQC.

26 Albert Borowitz. *Blood & Ink: An International Guide to Fact-Based Crime Literature*. Kent, OH: The Kent State University Press, 2002, p. 97.

27 Gerd Muehsam. *French Painters and Painting from the 14th Century to Post-Impressionism*. New York: Ungar, 1970, p. 382. Cited in Borowitz.

28 Anselm Ritter von Feuerbach, trans. by Lady Duff Gordon. *Narratives of Remarkable Criminal Trials*. London: John Murray, 1846, p. 301.

29 Judge Robert H. Gollmar. *Edward Gein: America's Most Bizarre Murderer*. New York: Pinnacle Books, 1981, p. 35.

30 Feuerbach (Gordon), *Narratives of Remarkable Criminal Trials*, pp. 310–12.

31 Feuerbach (Gordon), *Ibid.*, p. 312.

32 Anselm Ritter von Feuerbach. *Merkwürdige Criminal-Rechtsfalle*, vol. 2. Giessen: 1811, pp. 3–33.

33 Peter Becker. "The Criminologists' Gaze at the Underworld." In Peter Becker and Richard F. Wetzell, eds. *Criminals and Their Scientists: The History of Criminology in International Perspective*. New York: Cambridge University Press, 2006, pp. 125–27.

34 Becker, "The Criminologists' Gaze at the Underworld," p. 127.

35 Robert von Krafft-Ebing. *Psychopathia Sexualis*, twelfth ed., p. 88.

36 William Westall. "A Precedent for the Whitechapel Murder." *Pall Mall Gazette*, September 7, 1888.

37 Heike Bauer. "Scholars, Scientists and Sexual Inverts: Authority and Sexology in Nineteenth-Century Britain." In David Clifford, Elisabeth Wadge, Alex Warwick, and Martin Willis, eds. *Repositioning Victorian Sciences: Shifting Centers in Nineteenth-Century Scientific Thinking*. London: Anthem Press, 2006, p. 198.

38 https://it.wikipedia.org/wiki/Giorgio_Orsolano citing *Atti del processo, tribunale di Ivrea, sentenza del 15 dicembre 1823* (Court records, tribunal at Ivrea, sentence 15 December 1823).

39 Milo Julini. *"Le feroci malefatte in Provenza di Antoine Galetto, nipote della 'Jena.'" Il Canavesano 2012*. Ivrea: 2011, www.criminiemisfatti.it/fd.php?path=Galetto-Sito.pdf.

40 http://www.torinoscienza.it/anatomia/le_collezioni/aprieed6eed6.html?obj_id=2375 (retrieved 10 Febuary 2016).

41 Maurizio Bonfiglio e Maddalena Serazio. *"La Iena di San Giorgio." Il Punto*, Torino, 2003, www.criminiemisfatti.it/fd.php?path=01.Orsolano.pdf.

42 http://www.xares.es/index.html?body39.html.

43 Catherine Ramsland. "Boys Dressed As Girls Who Become Serial Killers." *Psychology Today*, November 29, 2016, https://www.psychologytoday.com/blog/shadow-boxing /201611/boys-dressed-girls-who-became-serial-killers.

44 C-8938—AHP Ourense (Judiciary, File 1852) "Case 1788, the Werewolf," 1852. *Archivo del Reino de Galicia.*

45 *"La leyenda del 'hombre lobo' Romasanta resucita en Allariz." La Voz de Galicia*, 30 October 2011, http://www.lavozdegalicia.es/ocioycultura/2011/10/30/0003_201110 G30P44991.htm.

46 "Jack the Ripper's Predecessor." *London Evening News*, October 12, 1888.

47 Albert D. Vandam. *Masterpieces of Crime.* London: Eden, Remington & Co., 1892, p. 15.

48 "A Horrid Chapter of Crime." *Ottawa Citizen,* July 25, 1866, p. 2.

49 Lombroso Goltdammer's *Archiv*, p. 13. Cited in Richard von Krafft-Ebing. *Psychopathia Sexualis*, trans. Charles Gilbert. Chaddock, Philadelphia: F. A. Davis Company, 1894, p. 67.

50 Nello Ajello. *"L'Assassino ha un dito in piu." La Repubblica*, September 2, 1988, http:// ricerca.repubblica.it/repubblica/archivio/repubblica/1988/09/02/as sassino-ha-un-dito-in-piu.html.

51 Carlo Livi, Cesare Trevvi, and Gaetano Riva, eds. *"L'Uccisore dei Bambini Carlino Grande." Revista di Freniartria e di Medician Legale*, vol. 3. Reggio-Emilia: Stafano Calderini, 1877, pp. 352–643; http://criminologiaediritto.altervista.org/callisto -grandi. And Maria Conforti. *"Infanticidi, 'degenerati' e assassini: alcuni libri recenti su medicina e vita pubblica in Italia." Laboratorio dell'ISPF*, http://www.ispf-lab.cnr.it /system/files/ispf_lab/documenti/saggio_infanticidi_conforti.pdf.

8. BACK IN THE USA: THE RISE OF THE MODERN AMERICAN SERIAL KILLER

1 See Vronsky, *Female Serial Killers.*

2 Mark Seltzer. *Serial Killers: Death and Life in America's Wound Culture*, p. 1.

3 Michael Newton. *Century of Slaughter.* New York: ToExcel, 1992, p. xiv.

4 https://www.google.ca/?gws_rd=ssl#q=first+serial+killer (retrieved February 5, 2016).

5 http://www.huffingtonpost.com/entry/leonardo-dicaprio-hh-holmes-scorsese_us _55ca08fee4bof1cbf1e63768.

6 http://torontoist.com/2014/09/historicist-h-h-holmes-in-toronto.

7 http://mysteriouschicago.com/the-murder-castle-today-or-good-grief -more-hh-holmes-2.

8 Adam Selzer. *H. H. Holmes: The True History of the White City Devil.* New York: Skyhorse Publishing, 2017, Kindle ed. (Kindle locations 69–72).

9 H. W. Mudgett (H. H. Holmes). *Holmes' Own Story: In Which the Alleged Multimurder and Arch Conspirator Tells of the Twenty-two Tragic Deaths and Disappearances in Which He Is Said to Be Implicated.* Philadelphia: Burke & McFetridge Co., 1895.

10 http://www.hhholmesthefilm.com.

11 Dane Ladwig. *Dr. H. H. Holmes and the Whitechapel Ripper.* Chicago: Ink Slinger Enterprises, 2004. *And* http://www.dailymail.co.uk/news/article-2241334/Was-Chicago -doctor-serial-killer-Londons-Jack-Ripper-Descendant-American-murderer -investigates-links-notorious-criminals.html; *and* https://whitechapeljack.com/jeff -mudgett-bloodstains-hh-holmes-book-review.

12 Selzer, *H. H. Holmes: The True History of the White City Devil* (Kindle locations 776–79).

13 *The Examiner*, Catskill, NY, Saturday, 25 August 25, 1888, p. 3, col. 1, http://www.genealogy.com/ftm/w/a/l/Janet-B-Walker-GA/WEBSITE-0001/UHP-0009.html.

14 For more detailed accounts of the American female serial killers, see Vronsky, *Female Serial Killers*, pp. 111–34.

15 The master account of the Jesse Pomeroy case is: Harold Schechter. *Fiend: The Shocking True Story of America's Youngest Serial Killer*. New York: Pocket Books, 2000.

16 Simon Harrison. *Dark Trophies: Hunting and the Enemy Body in Modern War*. New York: Berghahn Books, 2012, Kindle ed. (Kindle locations 889–91).

17 Harold Schechter, *Fiend*, p. 59.

18 Schechter, *Fiend*, p. 81.

19 http://www.dailymail.co.uk/news/article-1110123/Child-killer-Mary-Bell-grandmother-51-But-I-left-grief-says-victims-mother.html.

20 Lee Mellor. *Cold North Killers*. Toronto: Dundurn Press, 2012, pp. 35–38. *And The Trial of Joseph LaPage the French Monster, for the Murder of the Beautiful School Girl Miss Josie Langmaid. Also, the Account of the Murder of Miss Marietta Ball, the School Teacher, in the Woods, in Vermont*. Philadelphia: Old Franklin Publishing House, 1876.

21 http://www.atlasobscura.com/places/josie-langmaid-monument https://www.geocaching.com/seek/gallery.aspx?guid=269a94da-8da7-4452-a2e8-ac02e28791c3.

22 Attorney General of Massachusetts. *The Official Report of the Trial of Thomas W. Piper for the Murder of Mabel H. Young in the Supreme Judicial Court of Massachusetts*. Boston: 1887, pp. 768–69.

23 Christopher Daley. *Murder & Mayhem in Boston: Historic Crimes in the Hub*. Charleston, SC: Arcadia Publishing Inc., 2015, Kindle ed. (Kindle location 881).

24 *Boston Directory*. Boston: 1873, p. 608.

25 Attorney General of Massachusetts. *The Official Report of the Trial of Thomas W. Piper*, p. 692.

26 "A Murderous Monster—Ordinary Confessions of Crime by a Sexton." *Auckland Star*, vol. VII, issue 1984, 19 June 1876, p. 2.

27 Robert D. Kepple and William J. Birnes. *The Psychology of Serial Killer Investigations*. New York: Academic Press, 2003, pp. 77–95.

28 US Marshals Office. "History of Fingerprinting," http://www.usmarshals.gov/usmsforkids/fingerprint_history.htm.

29 BBC. "DNA Pioneer's 'Eureka' Moment," http://news.bbc.co.uk/2/hi/programs/newsnight/8245312.stm.

30 Attorney General of Massachusetts, *The Official Report of the Trial of Thomas W. Piper*, p. 769.

31 "Piper, the Murderer: Another Statement from the Culprit." *New York Times*, May 27, 1876, p. 1.

32 "Telegraphic Brevities." *New York Times*, March 21, 1889, p. 2.

33 B. E. Cotting, MD. "The Belfry Murder Case: Reported to the Roxbury Society for Medical Improvement, February 17, 1876." *The Boston Medical and Surgical Journal*, vol. 94, no. 15, April 13, 1876, p. 414.

34 "A Mania for Killing, Thomas W. Piper's Confession." *New York Times*, May 13, 1876, p. 2. *And* Harvard University, Warren Anatomical Museum Catalog Number 8209: "Portion of fractured skull from victim of the 'Boston Belfry Murderer,'" http://repository.countway.harvard.edu/xmlui/handle/10473/1827.

35 Daley, *Murder & Mayhem in Boston* (Kindle locations 1051–58).

36 "A Mania for Killing, Thomas W. Piper's Confession," *New York Times*, May 13, 1876, p. 2.

37 "The Murderer Piper: Card from Sheriff Clark of Boston—He Will Not Make Public the Detailed Confession." *New York Times*, June 1, 1876, p. 5.

38 Edgar D. Peixotto. *Report of the Trial of William Henry Theodore Durrant*. Detroit: Collector Publishing, 1899, p. 60.

39 Herbert Asbury. *The Barbary Coast: An Informal History of the San Francisco Underworld*. New York: Alfred A. Knopf, 1933, p. 254.

40 http://www.annalsofcrime.com/04-05.htm. *And* http://www.historicalcrimedetective.com/killer-theodore-durrant.

41 http://www.servantgirlmurders.com (retrieved February 2, 2016).

42 Rebecca Salinas. "A Look Back at the Serial Killer That Terrorized Austin in the 1880s." *My San Antonio*, April 28, 2015, http://www.mysanantonio.com/150years/major-stories/article/A-look-back-at-the-serial-killer-that-terrorized-6222438.php (retrieved February 2, 2016).

9. SLOUCHING TOWARD WHITECHAPEL: SEX CRIMES IN BRITAIN BEFORE JACK THE RIPPER

1 http://www.pbs.org/kqed/demonbarber/penny/index.html (retrieved February 2, 2016).

2 Blaine L. Pardoe. *Sawney Bean: Dissecting the Legend of the Scottish Cannibal*. London: Fonthill, 2015.

3 Vronsky, *Female Serial Killers*, pp. 94–109.

4 Katherine Watson. *Poisoned Lives: English Poisoners and Their Victims*. London: Hambleton and London, 2004, p. 67.

5 Barbara Benedict. "Making a Monster: Socializing Sexuality and the Monster of 1790." In Helen Deutsch and Felicity Nussbaum, eds. *"Defects" Engendering the Modern Body*. Ann Arbor: University of Michigan Press, 2000, p. 128.

6 Nathan Jenkins. *The Trial of Renwick Williams (Commonly Called the Monster)*. London: 1790, p. 4.

7 *Select Criminal Trials at Justice Hall in the Old Bailey*. Edinburgh: Peter Hill and Longman & Rees, 1803, p. 413.

8 Jan Bondeson. *The London Monster: A Sanguinary Tale*. London: Free Association Books, 2000, p. 75.

9 Barbara Benedict, "Making a Monster," in *"Defects" Engendering the Modern Body*, p. 128.

10 Bondeson, *The London Monster*, p. 165.

11 *The Annual Register for the Year 1805*. London: 1807, p. 390.

12 J. L. I'on. "Postmortem Appearance of Eliza Grimwood." *The Lancet*, vol. 30, no. 772, June 16, 1938, pp. 399–400.

13 David Leafe. "Oliver's Murderous Twist: The Bloody Killing of the Real-life Nancy That So Obsessed Charles Dickens It Drove Him to an Early Grave." *Daily Mail*, April 18, 2009, http://www.dailymail.co.uk/femail/article-1171577/The-bloody-killing-real-life-Nancy-obsessed-Charles-Dickens-drove-early-grave.html. *And* John Adcock. "Who Murdered Eliza Grimwood?" *Yesterday's Papers*, October 20, 2010, http://john-adcock.blogspot.ca/2010/10/who-murdered-eliza-grimwood.html (retrieved February 2, 2016).

14 *The Alton Murder: The Police News Edition of the Trial and Condemnation of Frederick Baker*. London: 1867, p. 15.

15 "Remarks on this Dreadful Tragedy." In *The Alton Murder,* pp. 14–15.

16 Albert Barrère and Charles Godfrey Leland. *A Dictionary of Slang, Jargon & Cant.* London: The Ballantyne Press, 1889, p. 354.

17 Walter Hubert Downing. *Digger Dialects: A Collection of Slang Phrases Used by the Australian Soldiers on Active Duty.* London: Lothian Book Publishing Company, 1919, p. 22.

10. *RAPTOR:* JACK THE RIPPER AND THE WHITECHAPEL MURDERS, 1888

1 See for example: Robin Odell. *Ripperology: A Study of the World's First Serial Killer and a Literary Phenomenon.* Kent, OH: Kent State University Press, 2006.

2 https://www.goodreads.com/shelf/show/jack-the-ripper (retrieved February 3, 2016).

3 Stewart P. Evans and Keith Skinner. *Jack the Ripper: Letters from Hell.* Gloucestershire: Sutton Publishing, 2001, p. 8.

4 Dane Ladwig. *Dr. H. H. Holmes and the Whitechapel Ripper. And* http://www.dailymail .co.uk/news/article-2241334/Was-Chicago-doctor-serial-killer-Londons-Jack-Ripper -Descendant-American-murderer-investigates-links-notorious-criminals.html; *and* Donald Bell. "Jack the Ripper: The Final Solution." *The Criminologist,* Summer, 1974.

5 http://www.eastlondonadvertiser.co.uk/news/dracula_may_have_been_jack_the _ripper_whitechapel_society_is_told_1_3214396. *And* http://swallowingthecamel .me/2013/11/10/top-10-stupidestweirdest-jack-the-ripper-theories.

6 Stewart P. Evans and Keith Skinner, *Jack the Ripper,* p. ix.

7 Donald Rumbelow. *The Complete Jack the Ripper* (1988 ed.). London: Penguin Books, 1988, p. vii.

8 Peter Stubley. *1888: London Murders in the Year of the Ripper.* Stroud, Gloucestershire: The History Press, 2012, Kindle ed. (Kindle locations 2076–78).

9 https://www.google.com/maps/d/u/0/viewer?mid=znNfXxzuBPKU.k7defDElF7Ic& hl=en_US.

10 Stephen Knight. *Jack the Ripper: The Final Solution.* London: George G. Harrap, 1976.

11 Robert D. Keppel, Joseph G. Weis, Katherine M. Brown, and Kristen Welch. "The Jack the Ripper Murders: A *Modus Operandi* and Signature Analysis of the 1888–1891 White-chapel Murders." *Journal of Investigative Psychology and Offender Profiling,* no 2, 2005, pp. 1–21.

12 L. Forbes Winslow. "To the Editor." *The Times,* September 12, 1888.

13 Larry Wilson. *Criminal Major Case Management: Persons of Interest Priority Assess-ment Tool.* Boca Raton, FL: CRC Press, Taylor & Francis Group, 2012, pp. 201–2.

14 *Home Office Correspondence 1782–1979,* HO 144/221/A49301C, ff. 220-223. National Archives, UK.

15 Dr. George Bagster Phillips' testimony before a coroner's inquiry in the death of Annie Chapman and the testimony of Dr. Frederick Gordon Brown in the death of Catherine Eddowes.

16 HO 144/221/A49301C, ff. 220-223, *Home Office Correspondence 1782–1979.* National Archives, UK.

17 Robert Keppel with William Birnes. *The Riverman: Ted Bundy and I Hunt for the Green River Killer.* New York: Simon & Schuster, 1995.

18 Javier Rodrigues. "A Real-life *Silence of the Lambs." The Houstonian,* September 19, 2006, http://houstonianonline.com/2006/09/19/a-real-life-silence-of-the-lambs.

19 Robert D. Keppel, Joseph G. Weis, Katherine M. Brown, and Kristen Welch, "The Jack the Ripper Murders."

20 Supervisory Special Agent John E. Douglas. *Unsub; AKA: Jack the Ripper*, NCAVC Homicide (Criminal Investigative Analysis). Department of Justice, FBI: July 6, 1988, pp. 1–7.

21 http://www.casebook.org/suspects (www.casebook.org is one of the better resources on the Whitechapel Murders on the Internet, along with http://www.jack-the-ripper .org *and* http://content.met.police.uk/Site/jacktheripper).

22 http://www.casebook.org/dissertations/robhouse-kosminski.html.

23 http://content.met.police.uk/Article/The-Suspects/1400015320719/1400015320719 (retrieved on 6 February 2016).

24 D. Kim Rossmo, Heike Lutermann, Mark D. Stevenson, and Steven C. Le Comber. "Geographic Profiling in Nazi Berlin: Fact and Fiction (Unclassified). *Geospatial Intelligence Review*, vol. 12, no. 2, 2014, pp. 44–57.

25 Samantha Lundrigan and David Canter. "Spatial Patterns of Serial Murder: An Analysis of Disposal Site Location Choice. *Behavioral Sciences and the Law Journal*, no. 19, 2001, p. 601.

26 Kim Rossmo. Geographic Profiling, presentation at the NCIS Conference 1998, https://www.e-education.psu.edu/geog885/sites/www . . . /krossmo.pdf.

27 George Tita and Elizabeth Griffiths. "Traveling to Violence: The Case of a Mobility-Based Spatial Typology of Homicide. *Journal of Research in Crime and Delinquency*, vol. 42, no. 3, August 2005, pp. 277–78.

28 Wesley English. *Geoprofile: Jack the Ripper.* http://www.wesleyenglish.com/geoprofile /infamous-cases/jack-the-ripper.

29 S. C. Le Comber, B. Nicholls, D. K. Rossmo, and P. A. Racey. "Geographic Profiling and Animal Foraging." *Journal of Theoretical Biology*, no. 240, 2006, pp. 233–40. *And* R. A Martin, D. K. Rossmo, and N. Hammerschlag. "Hunting Patterns and Geographic Profiling of White Shark Predation." *Journal of Zoology*, no. 279, 2009, pp. 111–18. *And* S. C. Le Comber, D. K. Rossmo, A. N. Hassan, D. O. Fuller, and J. C. Beier. "Geographic Profiling as a Novel Spatial Tool for Targeting Infectious Disease Control." *International Journal of Health Geographics*, no. 10, 2011, pp. 35–42. *And* M. D. Stevenson, D. K. Rossmo, R. J. Knell, and S. C. Le Comber. "Geographic Profiling as a Novel Spatial Tool for Targeting the Control of Invasive Species." *Ecography*, no. 35, 2012, pp. 704–15. *And* C. Bennell and S. Corey. "Geographic Profiling of Terrorist Attacks." In R. N. Kocsis, ed. *Criminal Profiling: International Theory, Research, and Practice.* Totowa, NJ: Humana Press, 2007, pp. 189–203. For land border illegal migration profiling, see: http://www.txstate.edu/gii/projects/land-border-illegal -migration-profiling.html.

30 D. Kim Rossmo et al. (unclassified 2014).

31 http://www.telegraph.co.uk/news/uknews/10880601/We-know-where-Jack-the -Ripper-lived-experts.html; http://www.txstate.edu/gii/projects/jack-the-ripper.html.

32 Robert House in "Aaron Kosminski Reconsidered," http://www.casebook.org /dissertations/robhouse-kosminski.html.

33 Robert D. Keppel, Joseph G. Weis, Katherine M. Brown, and Kristen Welch, "The Jack the Ripper Murders," pp. 17–18.

34 John Travis. "Sea-bathing from 1730 to 1900." In Stephen Fisher, ed. *Recreation and the Sea.* Exeter: University of Exeter Press, 1997.

35 Colin Wilson. *A Criminal History of Mankind.* New York: Carroll & Graff, 1990.

36 Michel Foucault. *Madness and Civilization*, trans. R. Howard. New York: Pantheon, 1965, p. 210.

11. THE FRENCH RIPPER: THE FORENSICS OF SERIAL MURDER IN THE BELLE EPOCH, 1897

1 Alexandre Lacassagne. *Vacher L'Eventreur et les Crimes Sadiques.* Lyon: A. Storck, 1899, p. 47.

2 Douglas Starr. *The Killer of Little Shepherds: A True Crime Story and the Birth of Forensic Science.* New York: Knopf Doubleday Publishing Group, 2010, Kindle ed. (Kindle location 665).

3 Starr, *The Killer of Little Shepherds* (Kindle location 1013).

4 For histories of forensics, see: Starr, *The Killer of Little Shepherds.* And Colin Wilson. *Written in Blood: A History of Forensic Detection.* London: Grafton Books, 1989. And Colin Beavan. *Fingerprints: The Origins of Crime Detection and the Murder Case That Launched Forensic Science.* New York: Hyperion, 2001. And Katherine D. Watson. *Forensic Medicine in Western Society: A History.* London and New York: Routledge, 2011. And R. J. Parker. *Forensic Analysis and DNA in Criminal Investigations.* St. John's, Newfoundland: R. J. Parker Publishing, 2015.

5 Lacassagne quoted in: Marc Renneville. *"Les transformations du droit pénal et les progrès de la médecine légale, de 1810 à 1912." Archives d'anthropologie criminelle,* 1913, p. 364; quoted by Robert Kennedy in: *Statement by Attorney General Robert F. Kennedy to the Permanent Subcommittee on Investigations of the Senate Government Operations Committee.* Washington, DC: 25 September 1963.

6 Émile Fourquet. *Les vagabonds: Les vagabonds criminels. Le Problème du vagabondage.* Paris: Marchal et Billard, 1908.

7 James Ellroy. *LAPD '53.* New York: Abrams, 2015, p. 113.

8 See the brilliant book: Michael Newton. *Rope: The Twisted Life and Crimes of Harvey Glatman.* New York: Pocket Books, 1998.

9 Starr, *The Killer of Little Shepherds* (Kindle locations 2929–30).

10 http://gw.geneanet.org/antistar?lang=Fr.&pz=marcel+andre+henri+felix&nz=pet iot&ocz=0&p=pierre&n=vacher&oc=1 (retrieved February 14, 2016).

11 S. Waller, ed. *Serial Killers—Philosophy for Everyone: Being and Killing.* Hoboken, NJ: Wiley, 2010, Kindle ed., p. 69.

12 Alexandre Lacassagne. *Vade-mecum du médecin-expert.* Lyon: A. Storck, 1892.

13 Hans Gross. *Criminal Investigation: A Practical Handbook for Magistrates, Police Officers, and Lawyers.* English edition translated and adapted to Indian and Colonial practice: Madras: 1906, p. 116.

14 Dr. Hans Gross. *Handbuch für Untersuchungsrichter als System der Kriminalistik (Handbook for Examining Magistrates as a System of Criminology),* 2 vols., 1893. And US Department of Justice. "Psychopathy." *FBI Law Enforcement Bulletin,* vol. 81, no. 7, July 2012.

15 Mary Ellen O'Toole, Matt Logan, and Sharon Smith. "Looking Behind the Mask: Implications for Interviewing Psychopaths." *FBI Law Enforcement Bulletin,* vol. 81, no. 7, July 2012, pp. 14–19.

16 Quoted in: Starr, *The Killer of Little Shepherds* (Kindle locations 3067–70).

12. RED TIDE RISING: SERIAL KILLERS IN THE FIRST HALF OF THE TWENTIETH CENTURY, 1900–1950

1 https://www.nist.gov/featured-stories/who-was-detective-x.

2 *The Times and Democrat,* 28 June 1906; *St. John Daily Sun, Daily Mail,* 1 May 1906; *The Home Daily Sentinel,* 16 June 1906; *The Queanbeyan Age,* September 6, 1907.

3   Everard Meade. "From Sex Strangler to Model Citizen: Mexico's Most Famous Murderer and the Defeat of the Death Penalty." *Mexican Studies/Estudios Mexicanos*, vol. 26, issue 2, Summer 2010, pp. 323–77.

4   Mike G. Aamodt, *Serial Killer Statistics.*

5   Mike G. Aamodt, *Serial Killer Statistics.*

6   Philip Jenkins. *Using Murder: The Social Construction of Serial Homicide.* New York: Aldine de Gruyter, 1994. *And* "Serial Murder in the United States 1900–1940: A Historical Perspective." *Journal of Criminal Justice*, vol. 17, 1989, pp. 377–92.

7   Eric Godtland and Dian Hanson. *True Crime Detective Magazines 1924–1969.* Köln: Taschen, 2013, p. 65.

8   J. Paul de River. *The Sexual Criminal.* Burbank, CA: Bloat, 2000, p. 65. (Originally published by Charles C. Thomas, Springfield, IL, 1949.)

9   Mike G. Aamodt, *Serial Killer Statistics.*

13. AMERICAN GOTHIC: THE "GOLDEN AGE" OF SERIAL KILLERS, 1950–2000

1   Christopher Beam, quoting Harold Schechter. In "Blood Loss: The Decline of the Serial Killer." Slate, January 5, 2011, http://www.slate.com/articles/news_and_politics/crime/2011/01/blood_loss.html.

2   Vronsky, *Female Serial Killers*, p. 354

3   https://theodorerobertcowellnelsonbundy.wordpress.com/tag/carole-ann-boone/. *And* http://www.absolutecrime.com/married-to-murder-the-bizarre-and-true-accounts -of-people-who-married-murderers.html#.WZdvlRuWw8w.

4   http://www.spokesman.com/stories/1996/jul/14/it-was-a-match-made-in-prison -ewu-professors.

5   Amy Mackie. "Part 3: I Am the Real Veronica Compton." *Pelican Bomb*, August 23, 2016, http://pelicanbomb.com/art-review/2016/part-3-i-am-the-real-veronica-compton.

6   Don E. Jacobs. *Criminal Psychology: Sexual Predators in the Age of Neuroscience.* Dubuque, IA: Kendall Hunt Publishing Company, 2006, p. 52.

7   Mike G. Aamodt, *Serial Killer Statistics.*

8   D. Kim Rossmo. *Geographic Profiling.* Boca Raton, FL: CRC Press, 2000, p. 14.

9   Mike G. Aamodt, *Serial Killer Statistics.*

10   Hickey, *Serial Murderers and Their Victims*, seventh ed., p. 446. *And* http://skdb.fgcu .edu/info.asp.

11   Mike G. Aamodt, *Serial Killer Statistics.*

12   Kenna Quinet. "The Missing Missing: Toward a Quantification of Serial Murder Victimization in the United States." *Homicide Studies*, vol. 11, no. 4, November 2007, pp. 319–39.

13   Alec Wilkinson. "The Serial-Killer Detector." *The New Yorker*, November 27, 2017.

14   Ressler quoted in Philip Jenkins. *Using Murder: The Social Construction of Serial Homicide*, p. 67.

15   *New York Times*, February 2, 2017, https://www.nytimes.com/2017/02/14/nyregion /etan-patz-pedro-hernandez-guilty.html.

16   Philip Jenkins. *Using Murder*, pp. 58–59.

17   John Gill. "Missing Children: How Politics Helped Start the Scandal." FatherMag.com, 2000. http://www.fathermag.com/006/missing-children/abduction_2.shtml.

18   Michael Fumento, Hudson Institute. *American Outlook*, Spring 2002, http://www .fumento.com/exploit.html.

19   Gill, "Missing Children," http://www.fathermag.com/006/missing-children/abduc tion_3.shtml.

20 Gill, *Ibid.*

21 Hickey, *Serial Murderers and Their Victims*, seventh ed., pp. 336–39.

22 Joel Best. "Missing Children, Misleading Statistics." *Public Interest*, 92, 1988, p. 92.

23 Ronald M. Holmes and Stephen T. Holmes. *Profiling Violent Crimes: An Investigative Tool.* Thousand Oaks, CA: SAGE Publications, 2009. Kindle ed., pp. 116–17.

24 Kenneth Chew, Richard McCleary, Maricres Lew, and Johnson Wang. "The Epidemiology of Child Homicide in California, 1981 Through 1990." *Homicide Studies*, vol. 3, no. 2, May 1999, pp. 151–69.

25 US Department of Justice, Federal Bureau of Investigation. *VICAP Crime Analysis Report* (FD-676 (Rev. 3-11-86) OMB No. 1110-0011. Quantico, VA, 1986.

26 Peter Vronsky. "Zebra! The *Hunting Humans* 'Ninja' Truck Driver Serial Killer." In *Serial Killers True Crime Anthology 2015, Volume 2.* St. John's, Newfoundland: R. J. Parker Publishing, 2014.

27 https://www.propublica.org/article/the-fbi-built-a-database-that-can-catch-rapists-almost-nobody-uses-it.

28 Special Agent Ann Todd, FBI Office of Public Affairs, Quantico, VA, to Peter Vronsky, e-mail 8 December 2014: ". . . Given the demanding nature of their work, the FBI's National Center for the Analysis of Violent Crime (NCAVC) is unable to provide assistance with your request . . . the FBI's website provides information regarding the role of the NCAVC in serial murder investigations and may be a helpful resource . . ."

29 https://archives.fbi.gov/archives/news/stories/2008/august/vicap_080408 (retrieved March 25, 2017).

30 http://www.canada.com/news/Researchersquestioneffectivenesshightechpolicedatabaseviolence/6164630/story.html.

31 http://www.nationmaster.com/country-info/compare/Canada/United-States/Crime.

32 R. Emerson Dobash and Russell P. Dobash, *When Men Murder Women*, p. 109.

14. *DIABOLUS IN CULTURA*: SERIAL-KILLING RAPE CULTURE "SWEATS," THE "GREATEST GENERATION," AND THEIR SONS OF CAIN

1 Simon Harrison, *Dark Trophies* (Kindle locations 4297–98).

2 Iris Chang. *The Rape of Nanking.* New York: Basic Books, 1997.

3 Harry S. Stout. *Upon the Altar of the Nation: A Moral History of the Civil War.* New York: Penguin Books, 2006.

4 William McCarter. *My Life in the Irish Brigade: The Civil War Memoirs of Private William McCarter, 116th Pennsylvania Infantry.* Boston: Da Capo Press, Incorporated, 1996, p. vii. *And* Phillip Thomas Tucker and Pia Seija Seagrave, eds. *The History of the Irish Brigade: A Collection of Historical Essays.* Fredericksburg, VA: Sergeant Kirkland's Museum and Historical Society, 1995, p. 20.

5 Tom Brokow. *The Greatest Generation.* New York: Random House, 1998, p. xxxviii.

6 P. E. Dietz, B. Harry, and R. R. Hazelwood. "Detective Magazines: Pornography for the Sexual Sadist?" *Journal of Forensic Sciences*, vol. 31, issue 1, January 1986, pp. 197–211.

7 Max Allan Collins, George Hagenauer, and Steven Haller. *Men's Adventure Magazines in Postwar America.* Köln: Taschen, 2004, pp. 285–364.

8 Collins, Hagenauer, and Haller, *Men's Adventure Magazines in Postwar America*, p. 470.

9 See for example: Collins, Hagenauer, and Haller, *Men's Adventure Magazines in Postwar America. And* Adam Parfrey. *It's A Man's World: Men's Adventure Magazines, the Postwar Pulps.* Los Angeles: Feral House, 2003. *And* Tom Brinkman. *Bad Mags 2.* Lon-

don: Headpress, 2009. *And* David Saunders. *Norman Saunders.* St. Louis, MO: The Illustrated Press, 2008. *And* Eric Godtland and Dian Hanson, *True Crime Detective Magazines 1924–1969. And* Google Images: "pulp adventure magazines," https://www .google.ca/search?q=pulp+adventure+magazines&biw=1164&bih=569&source =lnms&tbm=isch&sa=X&ved=0ahUKEwi38-PCg8vLAhVFnoMKHYlgC88Q _AUIBigB or Google Images: "true detective magazines," https://www.google.ca /search?q=true+detective+magazines&biw=1164&bih=569&source=lnms&tbm =isch&sa=X&ved=0ahUKEwiXh9vXg8vLAhXrkYMKHV9JBx8Q_AUIBigB.

10   Collins, Hagenauer, and Haller, *Men's Adventure Magazines in Postwar America,* p. 470.

11   Collins, Hagenauer and Haller, *Men's Adventure Magazines in Postwar America,* p. 9; Godtland and Hanson, *True Crime Detective Magazines 1924–1969,* p. 234.

12   Dave Grossman. *On Killing: The Psychological Cost of Learning to Kill in War and Society.* New York: Open Road Media. Kindle ed., pp. 135–36.

13   Marlise Simons. "UN Court, for First Time, Defines Rape as War Crime." *And* United Nations, Security Council Resolution 1820, Adopted by the Security Council at its 5916th meeting, on 19 June 2008.

14   J. Robert Lilly. *Taken by Force: Rape and American GIs in Europe During World War II.*

15   Michael Snape. *God and Uncle Sam: Religion and America's Armed Forces in World War II.* Woodbridge, UK: Boydell Press, 2015, p. 513. *And Harper's Index World War II,* http://harpers.org/sponsor/thewar/harpers-index-wwii-edition/index.html [retrieved March 10, 2016].

16   US Department of Justice. *Uniform Crime Reports [United States], 1930–1959.* Republished by Inter-University Consortium for Political and Social Research, http://www .icpsr.umich.edu/icpsrweb/NACJD/studies/3666.

17   http://www.statista.com/statistics/191137/reported-forcible-rape-cases-in-the-usa -since-1990.

18   http://www.visualnews.com/2015/07/28/the-rape-statistics-you-need-to-know.

19   David Wilson. "The Secret War." *The Guardian,* March 27, 2007, http://www.theguard ian.com/commentisfree/2007/mar/27/thesecretwar [retrieved March 17, 2016].

20   Home Office. Freedom of Information Records Release, April 2006: HO 45/25603. *WAR: Offenses Committed by US Forces Personnel in the UK; Liaison Between the Police and the US Military.* National Archives, UK.

21   Ben Fenton "Wartime GIs Went on Rampage of Rape and Murder." *The Telegraph,* April 25 2006, http://www.telegraph.co.uk/news/uknews/1516599/Wartime-GIs -went-on-rampage-of-rape-and-murder.html [retrieved March 17, 2016].

22   Mary Louise Roberts, *What Soldiers Do: Sex and the American GI in World War II.*

23   Harvey Levenstein. *We'll Always Have Paris: American Tourists in France Since 1930.* Chicago: University of Chicago Press, 2010, p. 92. *And Life Magazine,* December 10, 1945, p. 20.

24   Jennifer Schuessler. "The Dark Side of Liberation." *New York Times,* May 20, 2013, http://www.nytimes.com/2013/05/21/books/rape-by-american-soldiers-in-world -war-ii-france.html?_r=0.

25   Jennifer Schuessler, *Ibid.*

26   Alice Kaplan. "A Hidden Memorial to the Worst Aspects of Our Jim Crow Army." *Chicago Tribune,* September 25, 2005. *And* James McAuley, "A Tsunami of Lust: American's Liberation of France Was Not Innocent." *Prospect,* May 31, 2013, http://www .prospectmagazine.co.uk/arts-and-books/what-soldiers-do-review-france-second -world-war [retrieved 17 March 2016].

27   Kaplan, "A Hidden Memorial to the Worst Aspects of Our Jim Crow Army."

28 Guy Walters. "Did Allied Troops Rape 285,000 German Women?" *Daily Mail*, March 25, 2015, http://www.dailymail.co.uk/news/article-3011930/Did-Allied-troops-rape -285-000-German-women-s-shocking-claim-new-book-German-feminist-exposing -war-crime-slandering-heroes.html; *and* http://www.spiegel.de/international/germany/ book-claims-us-soldiers-raped-190-000-german-women-post-wwii-a-1021298.html; *and* http://www.dailymail.co.uk/news/article-2975016/New-book-alleges-Allied-sol- diers-raped-one-million-Germans-end-Second-World-War.html [retrieved March 17, 2016].

29 Miriam Gebhardt. *Als die Soldaten kamen* (*When the Soldiers Came*). Munich: DVA/ Random House, 2015; *and Crimes Unspoken: The Rape of German Women at the End of the Second World War*, Malden, MA: Polity Press, 2017.

30 http://adb.anu.edu.au/biography/leonski-edward-joseph-10814.

31 Quoted in Schuessler, "The Dark Side of Liberation."

32 Mark Kurlansky. "Days of Infamy 'Smoke' and Mirrors." *Los Angeles Times*, March 9, 2008. http://articles.latimes.com/2008/mar/09/books/bk-kurlansky9.

33 Anil Aggrawal. "A New Classification of Necrophilia." *Journal of Forensic and Legal Medicine*, no. 16, 2009, pp. 316–20.

34 John W. Dower. *War Without Mercy: Race & Power in the Pacific War*. New York: Ran- dom House, 1989.

35 Richard James Aldrich. *The Faraway War: Personal Diaries of the Second World War in Asia and the Pacific*. New York: Doubleday, 2005.

36 *Life* magazine, May 22, 1944, p. 35, http://time.com/3880997/young-woman-with-jap -skull-portrait-of-a-grisly-wwii-memento/ [retrieved March 30, 2016].

37 Simon Harrison. "Skull Trophies of the Pacific War: Transgressive Objects of Remembrance." *Journal of the Royal Anthropological Institute*, vol. 12, issue 4, 2006, pp. 817–36.

38 E. B. Sledge. *With the Old Breed: At Peleliu and Okinawa*. Random House Publishing Group. Kindle ed., p. 119.

39 James J. Weingartner. "Trophies of War: U.S. Troops and the Mutilation of Japanese War Dead, 1941–1945." *The Pacific Historical Review*, vol. 61, no. 1, February 1992, pp. 53–67. citing: Dispatch No. 191225 Attached to Memorandum for Commander in Chief, US Fleet, August 5, 1944. Chief of Naval Operations, Record Group 38, Wash- ington, DC: National Archives and Record Administration (NARA).

40 See the poem on http://www.ppu.org.uk/learn/poetry/poetry_otherwars1.html. *And* Laurence Goldstein. "'The Imagination Problem': Winfield Townley Scott and the American Wars." *WTA* (*War Literature and the Arts*) *Journal*, vol. 14, nos. 1 and 2, 2002, pp. 59–77

41 P. Willey and Paulette Leach. "The Skull on the Lawn: Trophies, Taphonomy, and Fo- rensic Anthropology," in Dawnie Wolfe Steadman (ed.), *Hard Evidence: Case Studies in Forensic Anthropology*. New York: Routledge, 2009, citing William M. Bass, "The Occurrence of Japanese Trophy Skulls in the United States." *Journal of Forensic Sci- ences*, vol. 28, no. 23, 1983, pp. 800–3.

42 Josephine M. Yucha, James T. Pokines, and Eric J. Bartelink. "A Comparative Tapho- nomic Analysis of 24 Trophy Skulls from Modern Forensic Cases." *Journal of Forensic Sciences*, vol. 62, no. 5, September 2017.

43 https://bangordailynews.com/2010/08/26/news/bangor/japanese-trophy-skull-finally -returning-home/.

44 P. Malone. "Macabre Mystery: Coroner Tries to Find Origin of Skull Found During Raid by Deputies." *Pueblo Chieftain*, August 25, 2003, p. A5. *And Pueblo Chieftain*, November 2003, p. B1. *And Pueblo Chieftain*, May 17, 2004, p. A10.

45 https://www.duffelblog.com/2012/06/man-unsure-grandfathers-wwii-japanese-skull
    -collection/.

46 Simon Harrison, *Dark Trophies* (Kindle location 3374).

47 P. S. Sledzik and S. Ousley. "Analysis of Six Vietnamese Trophy Skulls." *Journal of Fo-
    rensic Sciences*, vol. 36, no. 2, 1991, pp. 520–30.

48 http://www.slate.com/articles/briefing/articles/1997/05/skull_session.html.

49 Laurence Miller. "Serial Killers: I. Subtypes, Patterns, and Motives." *Journal of Aggres-
    sion and Violent Behavior*, no. 19, 2014, pp. 1–11.

50 Jack Olsen. *The Misbegotten Son: The True Story of Arthur J. Shawcross.* New York: Is-
    land Books, 1993, p. 179.

51 Margaret Cheney. *Why: The Serial Killer in America.* Lincoln, NE: Back Imprint
    Books, 2000, pp. 7–8.

52 Katherine Ramsland, *Confession of a Serial Killer* (Kindle locations 710–11).

53 https://www.duffelblog.com/2012/06/man-unsure-grandfathers-wwii-japanese-skull
    -collection/.

54 Robert K. Ressler, Ann W. Burgess, and John E. Douglas, *Sexual Homicide*, pp. 16–19.

55 R. P. Brittain. "The Sadistic Murderer." *Medicine, Science and the Law*, vol. 10, 1970, pp.
    198–207. *And* R. Langevin, M. H. Ben-Aron, P. Wright, V. Marchese, and L. Handy.
    "The Sex Killer." *Annals of Sex Research*, Clark Institute of Psychiatry, Toronto, vol. 1,
    issue 21988, pp. 263–301.

56 See: http://www.gettyimages.ca/detail/news-photo/filthy-cluttered-kitchen-of-alleged
    -mass-murderer-ed-gein-news-photo/50425931.

57 The photographs can be seen at: http://www.murderpedia.org/male.G/g/glatman
    -harvey-photos-2.htm.

58 http://www.silviapettem.com/books.html.

59 Katherine Ramsland. *The Sex Beast* (Crimescape). New York: RosettaBooks, 2013,
    Kindle ed.

60 Mark Pettit. *A Need to Kill.* New York: Ballantine Books, 1990. *And* Robert K. Ressler
    and Tom Shachtman. *Whoever Fights Monsters: My Twenty Years Hunting Serial Kill-
    ers for the FBI.* New York: St. Martin's Press, 1992.

61 Katherine Ramsland. *Confession of a Serial Killer* (Kindle locations 1292–93, 1458–59,
    and 3289–91).

62 Harold Schechter. *The Serial Killer Files.* New York: Ballantine Books, 2003, p. 265.

CONCLUSION: POGO SYNDROME: THINKING HERDS OF CRAZIES IN THE TWILIGHT OF THE GOLDEN AGE OF SERIAL KILLERS

1 http://www.slate.com/articles/news_and_politics/crime/2011/01/blood_loss.html.

2 Hickey, *Serial Murderers and Their Victims*, seventh ed., p. 239.

3 FBI Uniform Crime Reports, 2014, https://www.fbi.gov/about-us/cjis/ucr/crime
   -in-the-u.s/2014/crime-in-the-u.s.-2014/tables/table-12 [retrieved 10 February 2016].

4 https://www.fbi.gov/news/stories/latest-crime-statistics-released.

5 https://ucr.fbi.gov/crime-in-the-u.s/2016/crime-in-the-u.s.-2016/tables/table-10

6 Janet McClellan, *Erotophonophilia* (Kindle location 85).

7 For claims serial murder is declining, see for example: James Alan Fox and Jack Levin,
   Extreme Killing: Understanding Serial and Mass Murder. Thousand Oaks, CA: Sage
   Publications, 2011. *And* Enzo Yaksic at http://serialhomicidecollaborative.blogspot.ca
   /2013/08/an-attempt-to-explain-decline-in.html.

8 Hickey, *Serial Murderers and Their Victims*, seventh ed., p. 239.

9   Hickey, *Ibid.*, p. 239.

10 Hickey, *Ibid.*, p. 241.

11 Office of Justice Programs, Bureau of Justice Statistics. *Violent Victimization Committed by Strangers, 1993–2010*, NCJ 239424. Washington, DC: U.S. Department of Justice, December 2012, p. 18. *And* FBI Uniform Crime Reports. Expanded Homicide Data 2013. US Department of Justice, 2013, https://www.fbi.gov/about-us/cjis/ucr/crime-in-the-u.s/2013/crime-in-the-u.s.-2013/offenses-known-to-law-enforcement/expanded-homicide; https://ucr.fbi.gov/crime-in-the-u.s/2015/crime-in-the-u.s.-2015/offenses-known-to-law-enforcement/expanded-homicide.

12 Mark Riedel. "Counting Stranger Homicides." *Homicide Studies*, vol. 2, no. 2, May 1998, pp. 206–19.

13 Katherine McCarthy. *Invisible Victims: Missing and Murdered Indigenous Women*. St. John's, Newfoundland: VP Publications, 2017.

14 Uniform Crime Reports (UCR), FBI, http://www.fbi.gov/about-us/cjis/ucr/; *and* https://www.fbi.gov/news/stories/2009/april/highwayserial_040609 [retrieved March 28, 2016].

15 http://serialhomicidecollaborative.blogspot.ca/2013/08/an-attempt-to-explain-decline-in.html.

16 https://www.longislandpress.com/2016/12/30/how-websleuths-sparked-revelation-in-long-island-serial-killer-case.

17 US Department of Justice, FBI Behavioral Analysis Unit, National Center for the Analysis of Violent Crime. *Serial Murder: Pathways for Investigations*. Washington, DC: 2014, p. 47.

18 Enzo Yaksic, Lindsey DeSpirito, and Sasha Reid. "Detecting an Observable Decline in Serial Homicide: Have We Banished the Devil from the Details?" Unpublished paper in progress, 2017, courtesy of Enzo Yaksic, Northeastern University.

19 http://www.newsweek.com/campus-rapists-and-semantics-297463; *and* http://jezebel.com/1-in-3-college-men-admit-they-would-rape-if-we-dont-ca-1678601600; *and* http://online.liebertpub.com/doi/pdf/10.1089/vio.2014.0022.

20 R. J. Parker. *Social Media Monster: Internet Killers*. St. John's, Newfoundland: R. J. Parker Publishing, 2015.

21 Institute of Criminal Science, University of Copenhagen, Denmark. "Pornography and Rape: Theory and Practice? Evidence from Crime Data in Four Countries Where Pornography Is Easily Available." *International Journal of Law Psychiatry*, vol. 13, nos. 1–2, 1991, pp. 47–64.

22 Christopher J. Ferguson and Richard D. Hartley. "The Pleasure Is Momentary . . . The Expense Damnable?: The Influence of Pornography on Rape and Sexual Assault." *Aggression and Violent Behavior*, vol. 14, no. 5, 2009, pp. 323–29.

23 Michael Flood. "The Harms of Pornography Exposure Among Children and Young People." *Child Abuse Review*, vol. 18, no. 6, 2009, pp. 384–400.

24 Stephen Singular, *Unholy Messenger*, pp. 101–2.

25 Vernon J. Geberth. *Sex-Related Homicide and Death Investigation: Practical and Clinical Perspectives*. New York: CRC Press, 2003, p. 506.

26 Akop Nazaretyan. "Fear of the Dead as a Factor in Social Self-Organization." *Journal for the Theory of Social Behavior*, vol. 35, no. 2, 2005, p. 164.

27 *Weekly World News*, April 6, 1999, p. 46.

28 Karl Vick. "Violence at Work Tied to Loss of Esteem." *St. Petersburg Times*, December 17, 1993.

29 Samuel P. Huntington. "The Clash of Civilizations?" *Foreign Affairs*, Summer 1993, https://www.hks.harvard.edu/fs/pnorris/Acrobat/Huntington_Clash.pdf.

AFTERWORD: "SERIAL KILLERS NEED HUGS TOO"

1 John Lennon popularized the phrase in his song "Beautiful Boy (Darling Boy)" on the 1980 *Double Fantasy* album by Lennon and Yoko Ono, his last before his murder. The line can originally be traced back to a 1957 *Reader's Digest* article that attributes it to John Allen Saunders, one of the writers behind the Publishers Syndicate comic strips *Steve Roper and Mike Nomad*, *Mary Worth*, and *Kerry Drake*. Its original context and appearance have never been successfully identified. *And* http://quoteinvestigator.com /2012/05/06/other-plans.

2 http://news.nationalgeographic.com/2017/07/forensic-dogs-amelia-earhart-spot -where-died.

INDEX

ABOUT THE AUTHOR

Peter Vronsky, PhD, is an investigative historian and a former film and television documentary producer. He is the author of *Serial Killers: The Method and Madness of Monsters* and *Female Serial Killers: How and Why Women Become Monsters* and a contributor to R. J. Parker's annual *Serial Killers: True Crime Anthology* series, currently in its fifth year of publication. He is an authority on Canada's first modern battle, which he has written about in his definitive book, *Ridgeway: The American Fenian Invasion and the 1866 Battle That Made Canada*.

Peter Vronsky holds a PhD from the University of Toronto in the fields of criminal justice history and the history of espionage in international relations. He teaches history at Ryerson University in Toronto. He divides his time between Toronto, Canada, and Venice, Italy.

Visit his website at www.petervronsky.org.